PRAISE FOR *THE SECRET TEXTS OF*

"John Opsopaus has reached into the fire and retrieved Plethon's work for us to study. Moreover, he does so with a deep knowledge of the Pagan philosophy of the Hellenistic world, explaining Plethon's ideas and framing them understandably for us to use. Plethon is a vital link in the Golden Chain of philosophers who preserved the knowledge of the gods. John Opsopaus has spent many years bringing theurgy back into living practice. This book is a collaboration between them, bringing Plethon's wisdom alive and returning to us one of the great teachers in our Pagan heritage."

—**Brandy Williams, author of *Practical Magic for Beginners***

"*The Secret Texts of Hellenic Polytheism* sheds much needed light on the life and works of an enigmatic figure who, almost single-handedly, sought to stem the tide of cultural change and preserve a spiritual tradition that was in danger of disappearing forever. Dr. Opsopaus skillfully connects the fragments that survived into a living tapestry and a workable system that allows us to better understand, apply, and benefit from Plethon's noble life-work."

—**Hercules Invictus, host of *Mount Olympus* podcast**

"Unlike the Florentine Neoplatonists Ficino and Pico, who remained Catholic no matter how wide they cast their syncretistic net, Plethon, who influenced them, was a Neoplatonic pagan. John Opsopaus does him justice by presenting him as such. Opsopaus's book is also perhaps the clearest and most lucid guide to Plethon's vision of reality: from the ineffable One (Zeus) down to 'matter.' As a work of solid historical scholarship and as a guide to contemporary Pagan practice, I recommend it most warmly."

—**Jay Bregman, emeritus professor of history/ religious studies at the University of Maine**

The Secret Texts of

HELLENIC
POLYTHEISM

About the Author

John Opsopaus, PhD, (Tennessee) has practiced magic and divination since the 1960s and his fiction and nonfiction have been published in various magical and Neopagan magazines (over thirty publications). He designed the Pythagorean Tarot and wrote the comprehensive *Guide to the Pythagorean Tarot* (Llewellyn, 2001) and *The Oracles of Apollo* (Llewellyn, 2017). He frequently presents workshops on Hellenic magic and Neopaganism, Pythagorean theurgy and spiritual practices, divination, and related topics. Opsopaus was a Third Circle member of the Church of All Worlds, past coordinator of the Scholars Guild for CAW, and past Arkhon of the Hellenic Kin of ADF (A Druid Fellowship). He is also a university professor with more than twenty-five years of experience reading ancient Greek and Latin.

To Write to the Author

If you wish to contact the author or would like more information about this book, please write to the author in care of Llewellyn Worldwide Ltd. and we will forward your request. Both the author and publisher appreciate hearing from you and learning of your enjoyment of this book and how it has helped you. Llewellyn Worldwide Ltd. cannot guarantee that every letter written to the author can be answered, but all will be forwarded. Please write to:

John Opsopaus PhD
℅ Llewellyn Worldwide
2143 Wooddale Drive
Woodbury, MN 55125-2989
Please enclose a self-addressed stamped envelope for reply,
or $1.00 to cover costs. If outside the U.S.A., enclose
an international postal reply coupon.

Many of Llewellyn's authors have websites with additional information and resources. For more information, please visit our website at
http://www.llewellyn.com.

JOHN OPSOPAUS PHD

The Secret Texts of

HELLENIC POLYTHEISM

A Practical Guide *to*
the Restored Pagan Religion *of*
George Gemistos Plethon

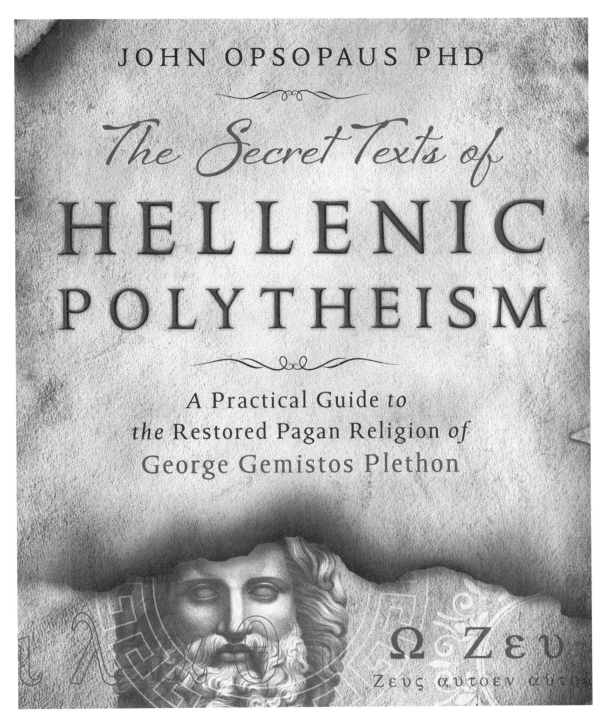

Ω Ζευ
Ζευς αυτοεν αυτο*

Llewellyn Publications | Woodbury, Minnesota

FIRST EDITION
First Printing, 2022

Book design by Christine Ha
Cover design by Kevin R. Brown
Interior art on pages 49, 62, 63, 66, and 70 by the Llewellyn Art Department

Library of Congress Cataloging-in-Publication Data
Names: Opsopaus, John, author.
Title: The secret texts of Hellenic polytheism : a practical guide to the
   restored pagan religion of George Gemistos Plethon / John Opsopaus.
Description: First edition. | Woodbury, Minnesota : Llewellyn Publications,
   2022. | Includes bibliographical references and index. | Summary:
   "Translations and commentary on Plethon's complete system of Neopagan
   theology and religious practice focused on the Hellenic pantheon and
   deeply rooted in ancient Greek paganism. Includes rituals, prayers,
   invocations, and hymns for holiday and daily use along with Plethon's
   complete sacred calendar"— Provided by publisher.
Identifiers: LCCN 2022001913 (print) | LCCN 2022001914 (ebook) | ISBN
   9780738770932 (paperback) | ISBN 9780738771069 (ebook)
Subjects: LCSH: Gemistus Plethon, George, active 15th century. |
   Paganism—Byzantine Empire—Early works to 1800. | Philosophy—Byzantine
   Empire—Early works to 1800.
Classification: LCC B785.P564 O67 2022 (print) | LCC B785.P564 (ebook) |
   DDC 186/.4—dc23/eng/20220216
LC record available at https://lccn.loc.gov/2022001913
LC ebook record available at https://lccn.loc.gov/2022001914

Llewellyn Publications
A Division of Llewellyn Worldwide Ltd.
2143 Wooddale Drive
Woodbury, MN 55125-2989
www.llewellyn.com

Printed in the United States of America

CONTENTS

ACKNOWLEDGMENTS

A published book is a team effort, and it is my pleasure to thank the team of Llewellyn professionals who have manifested this book. First, I am delighted to thank Elysia Gallo, Senior Acquisitions Editor, who supported this project and made many valuable suggestions on an early draft. I am also grateful to the production editor, Lauryn Heineman, for her many suggestions and meticulous editing, which have improved this book in numerous ways. Thanks are due also to Christine Ha for interior design and to Kevin Brown for the attractive cover. I'm also indebted to Aundrea Foster, marketing copywriter, and to Kat Neff, publicist extraordinaire, for telling the world about this book. I thank them and the rest of the Llewellyn team who have helped me bring you the words and ideas of George Gemistos Plethon.

Introduction

The Christian church had been divided against itself for four hundred years when in 1439 theologians from the two sides gathered in Italy to see if they could heal the doctrinal schism. Among them was a layperson, a philosopher, who was not so much interested in the Christian schism as in defending the superiority of Platonism, favored in the East, over Aristotelianism, favored in the West. And he succeeded, revitalizing interest in Platonism in Western Europe. Among his listeners was Cosimo de' Medici, who was so inspired that he vowed to create a Platonic Academy and did so in Florence twenty years later. It became the fountainhead for an infusion into European philosophy, art, literature, and spirituality of Platonic ideas and, more generally, of the philosophy, values, and literature of the Pagan classical world.

This philosopher was George Gemistos—later called "Plethon"—and he came from Mistra, near the site of ancient Sparta. What was not known then, and was only suspected until after his death, was that he was a practicing Neopagan and had developed a Neopagan religion based on ancient Platonism. This was confirmed when his *Book of Laws* was discovered after his death, and his enemies used it to condemn his Paganism.

Plethon's book was a complete theology but also provided rituals and practices, even a sacred calendar. It also taught ethics and outlined a system of laws, for, like ancient philosophers, he was a lawgiver and social organizer. (Indeed, his work has similarities to Plato's *Republic* and *Laws*.)

1

Plethon's book came into the hands of his longtime enemy, a churchman named Scholarios, who by then was Patriarch of the Eastern Orthodox Church. It confirmed his long-standing suspicion of Plethon's heretical beliefs. Therefore, he burned the manuscript, an act of intellectual and spiritual vandalism that took four hours, as he himself reported. He preserved only enough of the book, he bragged, to prove Plethon's "crime."

The only silver lining to this tragedy is that the parts Scholarios preserved are the ones that are most useful for those of us who want to practice Plethon's worship of the Greek gods, for they are the parts that best proved his Neopaganism. Scholarios also preserved the table of contents, and so we know the titles of the chapters he destroyed. Surely it would be better if we had them, but they are less relevant for Neopagan practice in our time, and some of them can be reconstructed from Plethon's other writings and those of other Platonists. After Scholarios's act of wanton destruction, Plethon's admirers and students gathered the remnants of his book (about two-fifths of the original) and copied it, which is why we still have it today. My translation of the surviving parts is in appendix B.

Why, you might ask, should we care about this fragmented work, except as a historical relic and evidence of religious intolerance? Because it is a complete system of Neopagan theology and religious practice focused on the Hellenic pantheon, with roots deep in ancient Paganism but in many ways adapted to modern times (although written more than five hundred years ago). We may not agree with all Plethon's conclusions, but I think we should consider them, since his is the most modern well-developed Pagan theology to come down to us.

Those of us who worship the gods of ancient Greece have had an advantage over many other Neopagan traditions due to the abundance of archaeological and literary evidence from the ancient Greek world and more than five hundred years of scholarship in the classics. Thus, we know a great deal about the religious and spiritual beliefs and practices of our Pagan ancestors, and we can use this as a basis for our Neopagan worship. On the other hand, although we know a little about household worship, which can inform our practice today, much of what we know concerns the civic cult of the gods, which was conducted at the temples and sanctuaries during major festivals. Unfortunately, we do not have the large temples, the multitudes of worshippers, or access to the sacred sites in order to celebrate the ancient rites, at least to that scale. Therefore, we have to adapt ancient practices for individual or small group practice.

When I began practicing Hellenic Neopaganism in the 1980s, there was little information. Most groups who had a Hellenic focus were doing "Wicca with Greek god names"; others had practices with roots in the Hermetic Order of the Golden Dawn. I eagerly read Woodhouse's *George Gemistos Plethon: The Last of the Hellenes* when it was published in 1986, but I was disappointed that he did not translate the invocations or hymns. Therefore, I decided to go back to my ancient Pagan predecessors—all the way back to the Homeric gods and the religious practices of ancient Greece. Thus, I hit the books and learned as much as I could of what is known about ancient Hellenic religious practice. I adapted what I learned to our world today (for religion evolves, like everything else) and worked with others to develop practices and rituals grounded in our Pagan heritage.

In 1995 I founded the Omphalos, a networking organization for Neopagans following Graeco-Roman traditions. We were a minority among Neopagans, and the Omphalos was a means for contacting others who worshipped the same gods and for organizing group activities. Initially, the Omphalos operated through postal mail, but in the late 1990s it moved onto the (then new) internet and established a web presence called "The Stele." (It is still there as a sort of historical artifact!) Along with other Omphalos members, I developed rituals and theological explorations, which we put on the web to help others establish a Hellenic practice.

Over time I learned that the most sophisticated and well-developed Pagan theology was that formulated by the Neoplatonists, including Plotinus, Porphyry, Iamblichus, Damascius, and Proclus. These included some of the last teachers of Pagan theology in the Platonic Academy before the Christian emperor Justinian I ordered the Pagan schools to be closed in 529 CE. This is the theology on which Plethon founded his Neopagan Hellenistic religion, essentially picking up where those brilliant philosophers left off.

Not only did Plethon present a Neopagan theology, but he gave detailed instructions for practicing it, which you will learn in this book (along with the theology). This includes a complete sacred calendar, with rituals and prayers for the holy days, as well as invocations, prayers, hymns, and rituals to be performed on a daily basis.

So far as I know, there is no complete English translation of Plethon's *Book of Laws* (although at least one is in progress). Therefore, I have prepared my own working translation, included as appendix B, which I have checked against the partial English translations, summaries, and paraphrases in Woodhouse's *George Gemistos Plethon*, Hladký's

Philosophy of Gemistos Plethon, and Anastos's "Plethon's Calendar and Liturgy," and against the French translation by Pellissier in Alexandre's *Pléthon: Traité des Lois*. Translations from Plethon in this book are my own, unless otherwise stated. Appendix A contains my translation of Plethon's *Summary of the Doctrines of Zoroaster and Plato*, and appendix C is his *Commentary on the Magical Oracles*, both of which are useful for understanding his philosophy.

This book will be useful to anyone who feels drawn to worship the Greek gods but might be having trouble establishing a practice that is both in the ancient Greek tradition and suited to modern Neopaganism. Even if you have an established Hellenistic practice, this book will teach you more about your gods from the Platonic perspective and may suggest ways your rituals and ceremonies can be improved. Plethon's religious ceremonies are straightforward but effective in connecting us with our gods.

Although Plethon wrote his *Book of Laws* in the fifteenth century, he traced his ideas back through Greek religious thinkers to the most ancient sages of the Western world.[1] Indeed, he traced it back to Plato, but before Plato to Pythagoras, to the Seven Sages of ancient Greece, and even to Cheiron the centaur and Teiresias the blind seer, to King Minos and the Brahmans of India, and to the Persian Magi and their leader Zoroaster, who, by his reckoning, lived five thousand years before the Trojan War! Moreover, this "ancient theology," as it came to be called, predates even Zoroaster, according to Plethon, for the gods gave it to sages in the early dawn of humankind.[2]

You will find that Plethon's philosophy is quite modern, in spite of being written more than five hundred years ago. Therefore, you will have little trouble integrating it with the modern scientific understanding of the world. This is because contemporary science is essentially Platonic—even Pythagorean—and so its worldview is very similar to Plethon's (although of course there have been many specific discoveries over the intervening centuries).

Indeed, if one were to sit down now to design a Neopagan religion devoted to the Greek gods and based in ancient Platonic philosophy, it would not be much different from what Plethon gave us over a half millennium ago. Plethon had an advantage over

---

1. George Gemistos Plethon, *Book of Laws*, translated by John Opsopaus, I.2.2–5. See appendix B of this book.

2. Plethon, *Laws* III.43.7.

most of us, however, because he was deeply immersed in the Greek philosophical and cultural traditions.

During his lifetime, George Gemistos was known as "the second Plato" due to his deep understanding of Platonic philosophy. Late in his life (but perhaps earlier in private), he began calling himself "Plethon" (Πλήθων, pronounced PLEE-thone); this was in effect his Neopagan name. It puts him in the lineage of great Platonic philosophers, which one of his admirers expressed: Plato—Plotinus—Plethon. Since this was his Neopagan name and we are concerned here with his Neopagan religion, I refer to him usually as "Plethon."

INFORMATION ABOUT SPELLING AND CITATIONS

Explaining a centuries-old Pagan religion for modern worshippers requires balancing readability and familiarity against historical and linguistic accuracy. Here I explain my strategy, but feel free to skip it, since it is not essential to understanding what follows.

For the most part I have used the familiar anglicized names of the Greek gods and philosophers; thus I write Apollo, Plato, and Aristotle rather than Apollôn, Platôn, and Aristotelês. However, I spell Plethon's name with the "n" retained, since that is the common scholarly convention, although the spelling "Pletho" is also used. However, I have preferred the Greek ending -os over the Latinized -us (thus, Dionysos, Hephaistos, and Kronos), but this shouldn't cause any confusion. I make some ad hoc exceptions for the sake of familiarity, thus Plotinus and Proclus in preference to Plotinos and Proklos.

In particular, I have used the spelling "Pluto" for Plethon's Πλούτων (Ploutôn) because this god is connected with Persephone and the souls of mortals, like Hades, equivalent to Roman Pluto, but less like Ploutôn, the ancient Greek god of wealth (πλοῦτος, *ploutos*). Suit yourself.

Plethon's religion can be practiced in English or any other language, and no knowledge of Greek is necessary. Nevertheless, many Neopagans prefer to recite certain phrases in the old language; moreover, it is often informative to know the Greek word that I have translated into English. Therefore, when I mention a Greek word I show it both in the Greek alphabet and also in Roman transcription.[3]

---

3. For the most part I have used the transliteration system of the American Library Association and the Library of Congress. In brief: ʽ = "h," η = "ê," υ = "u" or "y," φ = "ph," χ = "ch," ψ = "ps," and ω = "ô;" other letters are transcribed by their cognate Roman letters (e.g., β = "b," γ = "g").

Many of us who practice Hellenismos (Hellenic Paganism) prefer to use the age-old pronunciation of our Pagan predecessors, but Plethon was a Byzantine Greek and pronounced the language in the modern way. I happen to use the reconstructed ancient pronunciation in my own practice, because that has been my habit for decades, but there is certainly nothing wrong with pronouncing Greek in the modern way, as Plethon would have done. Or do everything in English. Plethon's invocations and hymns are not magic spells; the exact words and sounds are not critical.

As is conventional when writing about Platonic philosophy, I will capitalize the names of Platonic Forms or Ideas: for example, Being, Identity, Fire. In many cases they are in fact names of deities. I capitalize the words "Form" and "Idea" when they are technical terms for the transcendental Platonic Forms or Ideas, as opposed to ordinary uses of the words "form" and "idea." I use both "Form" and "Idea" to translate the Greek εἶδος (eidos), sometimes choosing one or the other to reinforce an association, sometimes using them both together, as in the preceding sentences.

A few words about citations. References to Plethon's *Book of Laws* are to the book, chapter, and paragraph number in my translation of the surviving parts in appendix B. For example, "*Laws* III.34.3" means book III, chapter 34, paragraph 3. References to my translation of his *Summary of the Doctrines of Zoroaster and Plato* in appendix A are by paragraph number (e.g., *Summary* 3). Plethon's *Commentary on the Magical Oracles of the Magi of Zoroaster*, translated in appendix C, is cited by Plethon's oracle number (e.g. "*Magical Oracles* 3" for the oracle itself, "*Commentary* 3" for his commentary on it). My translations from Plethon's *On Virtue* are from Tambrun-Krasker's edition of the Greek text and cite her section and page number (e.g., "*Virtues* A.1.1" for section A.1, page 1). Classical works are cited in the standard way. For example, Plato's dialogues are cited by Stephanus page numbers (e.g., "Plato, *Republic* 2.377e–378d"), which have been used for five hundred years and allow the passage to be found in the Greek text or in any translation of the dialogue (so long has the publisher has included them!). Modern works, which can be found in the bibliography, are cited by author or editor, shortened title, and page.

I

The Ancient Wisdom

————⟨∞⟩————

In his *Book of Laws* Plethon writes that his philosophy and theology have been handed down through a long lineage of the wise and that he is not inventing anything new, for the gods have given this knowledge to all people in common. It is what will be called in the Renaissance "the ancient theology" (Lat., *prisca theologia*) and "the perennial philosophy" (Lat., *philosophia perennis*). However, it is not merely traditional or inspired ("revealed"), according to Plethon, but has been preserved because it is based on notions common to humankind and supported by reason.[4]

Therefore, Plethon outlines a lineage comprising six lawgivers, seven legendary sages, seven sages of ancient Greece, and eight Platonic philosophers.[5] This is the *Golden Chain* of Pagan sages, philosophers, and spiritual teachers whom Plethon credits with his philosophy and religion. This lineage is mostly legendary up to the Seven Sages of ancient Greece, but many ancient Platonists accepted some version of the Golden Chain as their philosophical heritage. I will say a little about each link in Plethon's chain, for I think it is interesting and worthwhile to know the lineage of your spiritual path, but if you are anxious to get to the core of the teachings, feel free to skim the following or to skip it entirely; once you are practicing the religion, you will probably

---

4. Plethon, *Laws* III.43.7.

5. Plethon, *Laws* I.2.2–5.

want to come back and learn about its roots. The legends are curious and fun, but don't take them too seriously!

The Six Lawgivers

You may be surprised to see that the Golden Chain begins with six lawgivers (Grk., νομοθέται, *nomothetai*), but in the ancient world it was common for religious leaders and philosophers to found and to reform social institutions based on divine law, which is also Plethon's intention with his *Book of Laws*.[6] What better authority on how to live and organize society than those who are inspired by the gods?

The first of the six lawgivers, and the most ancient sage in Plethon's lineage whose name is known, is **Zoroaster**. Plethon observes, however, that because this ancient theology is timeless, it predates even Zoroaster, arising in the depths of the past, and has been known in other times and places.[7]

Zoroaster was the ancient religious reformer of the Medes and Persians, who, according to Plethon, lived five thousand years before either the Trojan War or the Return of the Heracleidae (descendants of Heracles).[8] According to his chronology, the Return was in 1103 BCE, and the end of the Trojan War was traditionally dated to 1184 BCE, which puts Zoroaster in the seventh millennium BCE.[9] Based on linguistic and other evidence, many modern scholars date him to the second millennium BCE, but others as late as the seventh or sixth centuries BCE.[10] Even in the ancient world there were widely divergent opinions on when he lived. Indeed, long ago Pliny the Elder (23–79 CE)

---

6. Plethon, *Laws*, preface.

7. Plethon, *Laws* III.43.7.

8. Plethon, *Laws* III.43.7.

9. This chronology is presented in Plethon's "A Method of Fixing the Sun, Moon, Conjunctions, Full Moons and Period of the Planets with Tables Established by Himself" in Tihon and Mercier, *George Gemistus Plethon: Manuel d'astronomie*. See also Tihon, "*Astronomy of George Gemistos Plethon*," 113; Hladký, *Philosophy of Gemistos Plethon*, 249, n. 42.

10. *Oxford Classical Dictionary*, 4th ed. (2012), s.v. "Zoroaster."

thought there might be two Zoroasters![11] Plethon, however, thought he was the most ancient sage whose name is known.[12]

"Zoroaster" (Ζωροάστρης, *Zôroastrês*) is the Greek name for the ancient Iranian religious reformer Zarathustra, who founded the Zoroastrian religion, which is still practiced in India, Iran, and other places. He is also an important figure in several other religions, including Manichaeism and the Bahá'í faith. He developed an ethical system called *Mazdayana*, which is Avestan (early Iranian) for "love of wisdom (*mazda*)." According to Pliny, the Greeks studied Zoroastrian philosophy, and when Pythagoras later coined the word *philosophia* (φιλοσοφία) from *philo-*, love, and *sophia*, wisdom, he was imitating the Zoroastrian term.[13] Plethon saw Zoroaster as the founder of the line of Magi (Μάγοι, *Magoi*), the Persian priest-philosophers to whom the Platonists traced their philosophy.[14]

The second lawgiver listed by Plethon is **Eumolpos**, whom he credits with founding the Eleusinian Mysteries, and who thereby convinced people of the immortality of the soul.[15] His name means "good singer," and he is a legendary bard and priest of Demeter and Dionysos.[16] The families of priests who oversaw and managed the Mysteries, the Eumolpides and Kêrykes, were descended from Eumolpos and his youngest son Kêryx (whose name means "herald").

The third lawgiver is **Minos**, the first king of Crete and the son of Zeus and Europa.[17] (You might recall the myth that tells how Zeus, in the form of a beautiful white bull, spirited Europa away to Crete.) He is supposed to have lived three generations before the Trojan War (traditionally 1194–1184 BCE). Every ninth year he retired to a cave, where he communed with his father Zeus, receiving divine inspiration in legislation.[18] He was so respected for his governance by the Olympian gods that after his death

---

11. Pliny, *Natural History* 8:30.2.

12. Plethon, *Laws* III.43.7.

13. Pliny, *Natural History* 8:30.2.

14. Plethon, *Commentary* 1.

15. Plethon, *Laws* I.2.2.

16. *Oxford Classical Dictionary*, 4th ed. (2012), s.v. "Eumolpus."

17. Plethon, *Laws* I.2.2.

18. Plato, *Laws* 624b.

he was made one of the three underworld judges of the dead (with his brother Rhada-manthys and half-brother Aeacus).[19] He was known as a wise and generous ruler, and the constitution he wrote for Crete was the basis of Lycurgus's constitution for Sparta.

In fact **Lycurgus** is the fourth lawgiver listed by Plethon.[20] His dates are also uncertain, but he might have lived around 820 BCE. He traveled to Crete, where he studied the laws of King Minos. Returning to Greece, he consulted the Delphic Oracle, and on the basis of what he had learned and the Oracle, he reformed the government of Sparta. To ensure his reforms would endure, he told the Spartans he was going to Delphi to offer thanks to Apollo, and he made them swear not to change anything until he returned. But he never returned from Delphi, and so the Spartans never abandoned his laws.

The fifth lawgiver was **Iphitos**, King of Elis, who restored the Olympic Games after the Dorian "invasion," namely the return of the Heracleidae (the descendants of Heracles).[21] He did this on the advice of the Delphic Oracle. He had asked how the Greeks could avoid civil war and pestilence, and the Oracle ordered that he celebrate the Olympic Games in honor of Zeus and that there be a truce during the time of the games. This "Olympic Truce" was established by Iphitos, Lycurgus, and Cleosthenes of Pisa in the ninth century BCE.

Numa Pompilius (753–673 BCE), the second king of Rome, is the sixth lawgiver in Plethon's list.[22] He is supposed to have studied with Pythagoras, the first to claim the title "philosopher," but their dates make this unlikely; more realistically, he might have studied with the Pythagoreans in Italy.

Numa was credited with various magical acts to protect Rome, to obtain prophecies, and for other purposes.[23] He is supposed to have had nightly discussions with the gods, especially a nymph named Egeria and Jupiter Elicius, an aspect of the god associated with religious knowledge. From these conversations, he learned how to legislate for the

---

19. *Oxford Classical Dictionary*, 4th ed. (2012), s.v. "Minos."

20. Plethon, *Laws* I.2.2.

21. Plethon, *Laws* I.2.2.

22. Plethon, *Laws* I.2.2.

23. *Oxford Classical Dictionary*, 4th ed. (2012), s.v. "Pompilius, Numa."

Romans, and he established the fundamental religious rites and institutions of Rome. In this way he encouraged the Romans to be less warlike and to live in peace. Numa also reformed the calendar, fixing the beginning of the year by the winter solstice, as did Plethon (see chapter 4).[24]

Numa recorded his divine conversations in two bundles of sacred books: seven in Latin on religious law and seven in Greek on ancient philosophy.[25] He ordered them to be buried with him when he died, for he thought it better that the Romans follow the living religious traditions rather than be bound by static books. When his tomb was accidentally opened some five centuries later (181 BCE), the books were found, but the Roman Senate ordered them to be burned, for they considered them too dangerous to read or even to possess. Some scholars think they contained Pythagorean doctrines, which the Senate considered subversive.[26]

THE SEVEN LEGENDARY SAGES

Next Plethon lists seven legendary sages, either groups or individuals, who contributed to the ancient theology.[27] Among the "barbarians" (non-Greek speakers), Plethon mentions the ancient **Brahmans** of India, whom he writes are almost as early as Zoroaster.[28] Their lawgiver was Dionysos or Bacchus, who came to the Indians from some other land. He writes that this is the same soul who, many centuries later, was reborn as the Dionysos of the Greeks, the son of Semele.[29] The Brahmans, of course, were the priestly caste of ancient India, and several Greek sages were said to have studied with them, including Pythagoras, Lycurgus, and Apollonius of Tyana. Plethon also mentions incidentally the

---

24. Anastos, "Plethon's Calendar and Liturgy," 206.

25. Livy, *History of Rome*, 1.

26. A. Delatte, "Les doctrines pythagoriciennes des livres de Numa," *Académie royale de Belgique, Bulletin de la classe des lettres et des sciences morales et politiques* 22 (1936): 19–40.

27. Plethon, *Laws* I.2.3.

28. Plethon, *Laws* III.43.9. The fundamental meaning of *barbaros* (βάρβαρος) in ancient Greek is "non-Greek speaker" ("babblers"). It was not always a derogatory term, and ancient Greek philosophers admired the more ancient wisdom of "barbarian" peoples such as the Egyptians, Persians, and Indians.

29. Plethon, *Laws* III.43.9.

ancient sages of the Western Iberians, by which he might mean the Celts of the Iberian Peninsula (Spain and Portugal), but he writes that none of their laws nor the names of their lawgivers have come down to us.[30]

Perhaps surprisingly, Plethon does not include the Egyptians among the non-Greek contributors to the ancient theology. He does mention their ancient lawgiver Mênês (the Greek form of Egyptian *Min*), the first king of Egypt and founder of the first dynasty. He "established a religion ... with useless and bad rites," according to Plethon, although the foundation of the religion was sound.[31] Unfortunately he also set down laws that prevented later reformers from eliminating these defects, and so he is not in the Golden Chain.

Second among the ancient "barbarian" sages, Plethon names the **Magi** (Μάγοι, *Magoi*) of Media (a region of ancient Iran).[32] According to Herodotus, the Medes take their name from the witch Medea, who fled to that country after she escaped King Aegeus of Athens.[33] (Modern Kurds consider themselves descendants of the Medes, but scholars differ on the matter.)

The ancient Greeks and Romans believed that the Magi were followers of Zoroaster and that they were the priestly caste serving the Medes and Persians. Plethon believed that the Chaldean Oracles, which were treated almost like sacred scripture among Neoplatonists, were handed down from Zoroaster and the Magi, and so he called them the Magical Oracles (Grk., Μαγικὰ Λόγια, *Magika Logia*; Lat., *Oracula Magica*), and that is what I will call them in this book.[34] (See appendix C for Plethon's *Commentary on the Magical Oracles*.)

Next Plethon turns to colleges of ancient sages among the Greeks, the first of whom are the **Kouretes** of Crete, whom he credits with defeating the false religious doctrines of the Giants (Γίγαντες, *Gigantes*), whom he calls "godless beings who fought against

---

30. Plethon, *Laws* III.43.9.

31. Plethon, *Laws* III.43.8.

32. Plethon, *Laws* I.2.3.

33. Herodotus, *The Persian Wars (Histories)* 7.62.

34. Plethon, *Commentary* 1, 14, epilogue. The name "Chaldean Oracles" is equally inaccurate; it was applied first in the Renaissance and was not used by ancient Neoplatonists, who had no specific name for these oracles.

the gods."[35] He writes that these impious men claimed that everything in the universe is mortal except for one creator god; in other words, they taught monotheism.[36] The Giants were described as earth-born, and in fact Plato writes that materialist philosophers are like the Giants who tried to toss the gods out of heaven and drag them down to earth.[37] With the force of irrefutable logic, Plethon writes, the Kouretes proved the existence of the supercelestial and celestial gods (described in chapter 3) and the eternity of the works of Zeus, of his children the gods, and of the whole cosmos.[38] Thus, they defeated the false theology of the monotheist Giants.

Under this interpretation, the myths about the attack of the Giants on the gods (the Gigantomachy) are metaphors for the Giants' false teachings about the gods. The ancient Greeks generally understood the defeat of the Giants to represent the triumph of Olympian religion—with its principles of cosmic harmony and rational intelligibility—over an earlier religion focused on violence and disorder. The materialist Roman philosopher Lucretius (c. 99–c. 44 BCE) thought it represented the victory of reason over superstition.[39] According to ancient sources, the Kouretes were religious, scientific, and magical specialists, and also lawgivers in ancient Crete, which is why Minos called them down from their mountain to purify his palace after the birth of the monstrous Minotaur.[40] Numa Pompilius was supposed to have learned magic from the Kouretes or a similar fraternity.

Next among the ancient sages of Greece come the **priests of Zeus at Dodona**, who interpreted the oracles of the god.[41] Dodona was the oldest Greek oracle—predating even Delphi—founded in the second millennium BCE, according to Herodotus.[42] The sanctuary was shared by Dione, who also delivered oracles there. An oak sacred to Zeus grew in the sanctuary of the temple, and the priests and the priestesses (called πελειάδες,

---

35. Plethon, *Laws* I.2.3.

36. Plethon, *Laws* I.2.3.

37. Plato, *Sophist* 246a–c.

38. Plethon, *Laws* I.2.3.

39. Lucretius, *On the Nature of Things* 5.110–125.

40. Harrison, *Epilegomena*, 19–26, 50–52, 107–8, 184, 194, 246.

41. Plethon, *Laws* I.2.3.

42. Herodotus, *The Persian Wars* 2.54–57.

peleiades, "doves") listened to the oracular rustling of the wind in its leaves. It stood there until cut down by the Christian emperor Theodosius, who forbade all Pagan worship in 391–92 CE.

Next among Plethon's ancient sages is **Polyidus**, whose name means "seeing many things."[43] He was known for his prophetic abilities, his skill in divination, and his knowledge of life and death. Minos consulted him for his wisdom. For example, after Minos's son Glaucus disappeared, the king visited the Kouretes, who told him to consult the person who could solve a certain riddle.[44] Polyidus succeeded and therefore Minos ordered him to find Glaucus, and Polyidus discovered that he had fallen into a cask of honey in a wine cellar and drowned. Minos ordered Polyidus to bring the child back to life and he succeeded through his observation and herbal magic.

The sixth of the ancient sages is **Teiresias**, whom Plethon credits with much wisdom, including the knowledge of the soul's ascent to heaven and its recurring return to earth: the doctrine of reincarnation.[45] In mythology, Teiresias is a blind seer who practiced several forms of divination, such as interpreting the songs and flight of birds, seeing visions in the smoke and flames of altar fires, and reading the entrails of sacrificed animals. He lived as a woman for seven years (the result of a magical transformation). As a consequence, he was able to testify that women enjoy sex more than men, and according to some stories, Hera struck him blind for revealing this secret. In recompense, Zeus gave him the gift of prophecy, thus replacing his outer vision with inner vision.

The last of these ancient sages was **Cheiron** the centaur, "tutor to many heroes of his time, to whom we owe much knowledge and important discoveries," according to Plethon.[46] In the *Iliad* he is called "the wisest and most just of the centaurs."[47] He was a foster son of Apollo, who taught him music, healing, prophecy, and many other arts, including astrology and other forms of divination. These he passed on to his protégés, who included Achilles, Aeneas, Jason, Theseus, and many others. Among them was

---

43. Plethon, *Laws* I.2.3.

44. Apollodorus, *Library* 3.3.1–2, 310–13; Hyginus, *Fabulae* 136, 115–16.

45. Plethon, *Laws* I.2.3.

46. Plethon, *Laws* I.2.3.

47. Homer, *Iliad* 11.831.

Medus, the son of Medea by Jason, who fled with her to the land later known as Media, homeland of the Magi. The *Precepts of Cheiron* is an ancient poem, possibly by Hesiod, that is supposed to contain Cheiron's teachings to Achilles; only a few fragments of it survive. One of the precepts is "First, whenever you come to your house, offer good sacrifices to the eternal gods."[48]

THE SEVEN SAGES OF ANCIENT GREECE

Next in Plethon's Golden Chain are the Seven Sages of ancient Greece, whose names and dates are summarized in this table:[49]

The Seven Sages of Ancient Greece	
Chilon of Sparta	fl. 6th cent. BCE
Solon of Athens	c. 630 – c. 560 BCE
Bias of Priene	fl. 6th cent. BCE
Thales of Miletus	624/623 – c. 548/545 BCE
Cleoboulus of Lindos	fl. 6th cent. BCE
Pittacus of Mitylene	c. 640 – 568 BCE
Myson of Chenai	fl. 6th cent. BCE

The story is that when Helen was being brought back to Greece from Troy, she threw her golden tripod overboard, because she thought (correctly) that people would fight over it.[50] Many centuries later it was found, and indeed disagreements broke out over who should keep it. Therefore they sent it to the wisest person they knew, the philosopher Thales of Miletus, to decide. He didn't consider himself to be the wisest, so he sent it to Bias of Priene, who felt the same way, and sent it on again. And so it

---

48. Evelyn-White, *Hesiod, Homeric Hymns, and Homerica*, 73.

49. Plethon, *Laws* I.2.4. Some ancient sources give slightly different lists.

50. Diogenes Laertius, *Lives* 1.28–33.

continued until it passed through the hands of seven sages when it came back to Thales. Therefore these seven sages decided together that the tripod should be offered to Apollo at Delphi, for he is the source of all wisdom. They also erected three tablets containing 147 wise sayings, known as "the Precepts of the Seven Sages" or "the Delphic Maxims." (You can read more about the Precepts of the Seven Sages and learn how to cast the Oracle of the Seven Sages in my book *The Oracles of Apollo*.)

THE EIGHT PHILOSOPHERS

The final part of Plethon's Golden Chain comprises eight important philosophers of the Pythagorean-Platonic tradition, who established the foundations of Plethon's religion.[51] The first of these is **Pythagoras** himself, who lived from approximately 570 to 495 BCE.[52] He was born to an amulet maker and his wife on Samos, a large island off the coast of Asia Minor, and lived there until he was about forty. Many people remember Pythagoras only for the Pythagorean theorem (about the sides of a right triangle), which they learned in school, but he was much more influential as the founder of a spiritual tradition that pervades science as well as Western religion and esotericism.

Pythagoras is supposed to have learned the wisdom of many lands around the Mediterranean, including the Egyptians, Phoenicians, Babylonians, Persians (i.e., the Magi), and, according to some, the Hindu sages.[53] Some authors list Thales of Miletus and Bias of Priene (two of the Seven Sages) among his teachers. Eventually (c. 530 BCE), Pythagoras came to Croton in Italy, where he founded an initiatory secret society in which his wisdom was taught and preserved.

Pythagoras was not only a philosopher and mage; he was also a lawgiver. He provided moral instruction to the Greek colonists in Italy and helped them organize their states more effectively. In later years suspicion and political opposition to the Pythagoreans grew, and they were ultimately driven out (c. 510 BCE). It is unclear whether Pythagoras was killed in this uprising or escaped.

---

51. Plethon, *Laws* I.2.5.

52. Plethon, *Laws* I.2.5.

53. See for example Diogenes Laertius, *Lives* 8, and Iamblichus, *On the Pythagorean Way of Life*, chs. 2–5.

Second among the philosophers after Pythagoras is **Plato** (c. 428–348/347 BCE).[54] He is supposed to have learned much of his wisdom from the Pythagoreans but also from Socrates (c. 470–399 BCE). He is the first sage in the Golden Chain whose writings have survived to our time reasonably intact and the first about whom we have reasonably factual biographical information.

He lived most of his life in Athens. His name "Platôn" (Πλάτων) is probably a nickname referring to his broad shoulders (he was a wrestler) or perhaps to the breadth of his learning (πλάτος, *platos*, means breadth); his legal name was Aristocles.

Plato's most important contribution was his description of the Platonic Ideas or Forms: ideal models or essences of the things in material reality, but existing in another, immaterial reality, outside of time and space. Plethon's *Book of Laws* and its appendix called *Epinomis* were probably inspired by the Platonic dialogues called *The Laws* and *Epinomis*.

The third in Plethon's (non-chronological) list of philosophers is **Parmenides**, who lived from the late sixth to early fifth century BCE in Elea, a Greek colony in southern Italy.[55] Like others in the Golden Chain, he was a lawgiver, legislating for his native city.

Parmenides wrote a long poem *On Nature*, which survives only in fragments. It seems to describe a sort of shamanic journey or theurgic descent to Kore (the Maiden, Persephone), the queen of the underworld, who taught him about the nature of reality. According to Plethon, Kore is especially responsible for our mortal nature, which is symbolized by the underworld (see chapter 3).

Parmenides was known especially for his knowledge of the nature of reality. Plato's theory of Forms was significantly influenced by him, and his dialogue *Parmenides* is concerned with Being. Later Platonists interpreted it to define the nature of the One and the structure of the Platonic realm of Forms.

Next in the Golden Chain is **Timaeus** from Locri in southern Italy, a fifth-century BCE Pythagorean philosopher.[56] Plato studied with him, according to Cicero, and later wrote a dialogue called *Timaeus*, which presented Pythagorean-Platonic theories of the

54. Plethon, *Laws* I.2.5.

55. Plethon, *Laws* I.2.5.

56. Plethon, *Laws* I.2.5.

origin and structure of the cosmos.[57] This work was very important for later Platonists, one of whom wrote that he would be content if all books were lost except the *Chaldean Oracles* and the *Timaeus*!

There is a surviving book, *On the Nature of the World and the Soul*, attributed to Timaeus, but scholars doubt that he wrote it. (Indeed, a few scholars doubt the existence of Timaeus!) Nevertheless, generations of Platonists (including Plethon) thought that it contained genuine Pythagorean philosophy.

Fifth in Plethon's list of philosophers is **Plutarch** of Chaeronea (c. 46–c. 140 CE), which is a small town about fifty miles from Delphi.[58] He is best known for his *Parallel Lives of the Eminent Greeks and Romans*, but also wrote the *Moralia*, a collection of seventy-eight philosophical and esoteric essays (not necessarily about morality) usually organized into fourteen books. For the last thirty years of his life, he was a priest of Apollo at Delphi, and his essays on ancient religion and esoteric lore were an important source for Plethon (as they still are for us today).

The sixth philosopher is **Plotinus** (204–270 CE), who was born in Roman Egypt and studied philosophy in Alexandria.[59] Later he joined a military expedition into Persia with the hope of learning from the Magi and the Brahmans, but the expedition was unsuccessful and his plans were thwarted. At the age of forty he moved to Rome, where he set up his school, which admitted women as well as men, including Amphiclea, the daughter-in-law of Iamblichus, the last philosopher in Plethon's Golden Chain.

Plotinus developed Platonic philosophy in a new, more spiritual direction, which historians of philosophy call Neoplatonism or Late Platonism. In particular, Plotinus stressed the ineffability of the transcendent One, the most fundamental principle of unity in all things. Plotinus's most famous student was Porphyry, who wrote a biography of his master and gathered his writings into a collection called the *Enneads* (six groups of nine essays each), which is a valuable source of Neoplatonic philosophy.

---

57. Cicero, *Librorum de re publica* 1.16.

58. Plethon, *Laws* I.2.5.

59. Plethon, *Laws* I.2.5.

Porphyry (c. 234 – c. 305 CE) is also the seventh philosopher in Plethon's list.[60] He was born in Tyre, an ancient Phoenician city, now a part of Lebanon. He wrote many important works, but most have been lost or destroyed, such as his *Against the Christians*, of which some fragments remain. Unfortunately his *Philosophy from Oracles*, which analyzed the Magical Oracles and other divine oracles, also survives only in fragments.

The last philosopher in Plethon's list, and therefore the last in his Golden Chain, is **Iamblichus** of Chalcis (c. 245 – c. 325 CE), a city in modern Syria.[61] Iamblichus was probably a student of Porphyry, but eventually returned to Syria to found his own school in Apamea (near Antioch). A number of Iamblichus's works survive in whole or in part, including *On the Pythagorean Way of Life*. One of the most important is commonly known as *On the Mysteries of the Egyptians*; it explains the theory and practice of "theurgy," the Neoplatonic ritual practices for congress with the gods (to be explained in chapter 11).

From *On the Mysteries*, it appears that Iamblichus disagreed with his teacher Porphyry about the importance of theurgy: Iamblichus thought it was essential, Porphyry less so. More recently, some scholars have argued that the difference is more a matter of emphasis than a fundamental disagreement, essentially an illusion resulting from the fragmentary nature of the evidence.[62] This is a relevant question for Plethon's religion, for he seems to have favored the more contemplative practices of Plotinus and Porphyry over the more ritualistic and "magical" spiritual practices of Iamblichus and Proclus, who is not on his list.

Indeed, the absence of Proclus (412–485 CE) is surprising, for he was the most famous Platonist in late antiquity and one of the last heads of the Platonic Academy in Athens. Moreover, Plethon's worst enemy, Scholarios, accused him of plagiarizing his ideas from Proclus and of trying to hide the fact by not naming him in his Golden Chain.[63] In fact, most of Plethon's ideas can be traced to the philosophers whom he does list, but it is still surprising that he omitted Proclus, whose works were very influential

---

60. Plethon, *Laws* I.2.5.

61. Plethon, *Laws* I.2.5.

62. E.g., Addey, *Divination and Theurgy in Neoplatonism*, ch. 4.

63. Hladký, *Plethon*, 168.

in Plethon's time. Perhaps it was because Proclus was so closely associated with theurgy, which was not so important for Plethon.

This brings us to the end of the Golden Chain along which Plethon traced his philosophical lineage. It is his version of the ancient theology or perennial philosophy.

THE MAGICAL ORACLES

Another important source for Plethon's theology—and also for other Neoplatonists—was the Magical Oracles, which were inspired (or channeled) verses treated almost as sacred scripture; it has been called the "Bible of the Neoplatonists."[64] Nowadays they are most commonly known as the Chaldean Oracles, but Plethon attributed them to the Zoroastrian Magi and therefore called them the Magical Oracles (Μαγικὰ Λόγια, *Magika Logia*).[65] There is nothing particularly "Chaldean" (Babylonian) about them, except that Neoplatonists attributed them to Julian the Chaldean and his son Julian the Theurgist (second century CE). They were not called "Chaldean Oracles" before Ficino did so in his fifteen-century Latin translation, but that name spread in Christian circles; the Pagan Neoplatonists usually called them simply "the oracles" (τὰ λόγια, *ta logia*).

Today the oracles survive only in fragments; the biggest is a dozen lines long, but many are only a word or two. Plethon's text includes thirty-six distinct oracles comprising a total of sixty lines. Most of these had been collected already in the eleventh century CE by Michael Psellos, a Byzantine scholar, who was Christian but accused of Paganism for his interest in Platonism. Plethon did not include six of the oracles that Psellos listed, perhaps because they were too magical for his taste, and he corrected the text of several others.

The Magical Oracles are quite obscure and they must be interpreted allegorically and symbolically to discern their meaning, which is why most of the Neoplatonists wrote commentaries on them; Plethon wrote two. The longer *Commentary on the Magical Oracles of the Magi of Zoroaster* presents the text of the oracles and discusses them line by line (see appendix C). Since the oracles have been recovered from many different sources, their original order is unknown, but Plethon arranges them systematically, beginning with those dealing with the human soul and ascending the scale of being

---

64. Majercik, *Chaldean Oracles*, 2.

65. Plethon, *Commentary*, epilogue.

up to the first principle. The shorter *Brief Explanation of the More Obscure Passages in the Oracles* provides an abbreviated summary of their meaning, but proceeding in the opposite order.[66]

The Magical Oracles influenced Plethon's philosophy and theology, and so I will quote them and discuss his interpretation at the appropriate places in later chapters. Although not named in his Golden Chain, they are implicit in two essential links: Zoroaster and his Magi.

---

66. An English translation of Plethon's oracle text and the *Brief Explanation* can be found in Woodhouse, *Plethon*, 51–54. I have provided a translation of the *Commentary*, including my translations of the oracles in appendix C.

II

Plethon and His Book of Laws

Around 1355 to 1360, George Gemistos, who later called himself "Plethon," was born in a well-educated and affluent family in Constantinople, the capital of the Eastern Roman Empire.[67] His family seems to have been influential in religious institutions, and his father was probably Protonotarios (First Secretary) at Hagia Sophia Cathedral. George does not seem to have been interested in the church—he later expressed his opposition to monks and their lifestyle—but is assumed to have received a good education from private tutors (as opposed to church schools or secular universities). Not much is known about his education, and what we have comes from a very hostile source: Scholarios, who burned his book and exposed his Paganism.[68] He wrote that George studied classical Greek literature, but not just to improve his language and writing (as Orthodox Christians were permitted to do)—he loved the ancient Pagan poets and philosophers.[69] Scholarios also wrote that he was possessed by the same "demons" as Julian, the Roman emperor who restored Paganism for a short time in the fourth century CE.[70]

---

67. A detailed discussion of Plethon's life and times can be found in Woodhouse, *George Gemistos Plethon*, and Siniossoglou, *Radical Platonism in Byzantium*, which also discusses the tradition of Pagan philosophy in Byzantium. Factual information in this chapter is primarily from these sources.

68. Scholarios, *Œuvres complètes* 4:151–5, relevant parts translated in Woodhouse, *George Gemistos Plethon*, 24.

69. Scholarios, *Œuvres complètes* 4:152.

70. Scholarios, *Œuvres complètes* 4:152.

Scholarios claimed that George studied under a certain Elissaios (the Greek form of Elisha), a Jew who was also a polytheist.[71] Unfortunately, nothing is known of this Elissaios, but it seems unlikely Scholarios made him up entirely; nevertheless, we have to be skeptical about the other details he provides. He related that under Elissaios George studied Aristotle and the Persian and Arab commentators on Aristotle.[72] In particular, Scholarios writes that George was converted to "polytheistic Hellenism" (Paganism) by him.[73] On the other hand, in the Middle Ages Jews were frequently accused of "corrupting" Christians, and George could have learned all his philosophy from Greek sources.[74] According to Scholarios's account, George worked for Elissaios and was supported by him for a number of years.[75] At some point they moved from Constantinople into the territory of the Ottoman Turks, where George continued in his service and as a student. Eventually, they returned to Constantinople. In the course of his rant, Scholarios implies that George should be burned like his teacher, but it is unlikely Elissaios was actually burned.[76] Although it was a capital crime for a Christian to "Hellenize" (convert to Paganism) or sacrifice to Pagan gods, execution by burning was not practiced at that particular time and place.

In any case, George Gemistos left Constantinople in about 1405, when he would have been around fifty years old. Scholarios implies that he was exiled by the emperor Manuel for teaching his students Paganism, but he complains that there was no public condemnation of Gemistos, and so it might be that Gemistos left voluntarily.[77] Thereafter, Gemistos settled in the Greek city of Mistra near the site of ancient Sparta. Apparently, Mistra was a city in which free thought was tolerated and in which the old traditions lived on. Whatever may have been the circumstances of his departure from Constantinople, Gemistos was a highly respected philosopher, teacher, and counselor to the Despot of Mistra, for whom he was Protonotarios (First Secretary). Gemistos

---

71. Scholarios, *Œuvres complètes* 4:152–53.

72. Scholarios, *Œuvres complètes* 4:152–53.

73. Scholarios, *Œuvres complètes* 4:153, 162.

74. Hladký, *Plethon*, 195–97.

75. Scholarios, *Œuvres complètes* 4:153.

76. Scholarios, *Œuvres complètes* 4:162; Woodhouse, *George Gemistos Plethon*, 27.

77. Scholarios, *Œuvres complètes* 4:153; Woodhouse, *George Gemistos Plethon*, 24. Hladký, *Plethon*, 193–94, argues that he was more likely sent on a diplomatic mission.

married and we know that he had at least two sons. Except for his trip to Italy to attend the Council of Union (to be discussed shortly), he seems to have lived out his life peacefully in this way until his death in 1452 or 1454.

To situate Gemistos in his time, it is worth noting that Gutenberg, an approximate contemporary of Gemistos, published his Bible, the first printed book in the West, in 1439, and therefore Gemistos is unlikely to have seen a printed book. Copernicus and his heliocentric theory of the solar system would not come for another century. Gemistos lived on the cusp of what was to become the Renaissance.

THE COUNCIL OF UNION

The Council of Union, which was convened in 1438 and lasted until 1439, was intended to repair the schism between the Roman Catholic and Greek Orthodox (that is, Western and Eastern) branches of the Christian church, which had been drifting apart since about 1000 CE. The representatives of the two factions met first in Ferrara, Italy, but moved the council to Florence early in 1439 (due to the plague, among other reasons).

Gemistos, who by then was about eighty years old, accompanied the Orthodox delegation as a lay philosopher. One of his students, Mark Eugenikos, the Metropolitan (bishop of a large city) of Ephesus, led the faction opposed to union, but another of his students, Bessarion, Metropolitan of Nicaea and later a Roman Catholic Cardinal, was in favor of it.

Gemistos himself was opposed but doesn't seem to have cared too much one way or the other, presumably because he was at heart a Hellenic Pagan. In the end, the Council achieved a partial union by 1445, but it didn't last long; the schisms of Christianity, however, were not especially relevant to Gemistos's Paganism. He writes that he was bored during the Council and spent his time discussing ancient Greek philosophy with the Italian humanist scholars, who were rediscovering ancient Greek literature.[78] In particular, he thought that the scholars of the Western church, who constructed their Christian theology around Aristotelian philosophy, had an imperfect understanding of both it and Platonic philosophy. In fact, both in the West and East, Platonic philosophy was suspect, and too much interest in it could get you accused of heresy or even "Hellenism" (Paganism).

---

78. Plethon in Migne, *Patrologiae Graeca* 160:1017C–D, translated in Woodhouse, *George Gemistos Plethon*, 156.

According to the Christian philosopher George Trebizond, who fancied himself an apocalyptic prophet and expressed a lifelong hatred of Plato, while in Florence Gemistos told him that in a few years the whole world would have a single religion. Trebizond asked whether it would be Christ's or Mohammad's, and Gemistos replied, "Neither, but one not differing from Paganism."[79] Trebizond became a fanatical enemy of Gemistos, second only to Scholarios, and so he is not a reliable witness, and his account was written after the *Book of Laws* was revealed, so we must take his story with a grain of salt. He later prayed that God would "repress the Platonists who are rising in Italy."[80]

To pass the time and enlighten the Italian philosophers, Gemistos gave a series of lectures on Platonism and wrote an essay, "On the Differences of Aristotle from Plato," which survives and is an important explanation of Platonism.[81] These were the lectures that the young Cosimo de' Medici (1389–1464) heard, which fired his imagination and inspired him to found a Platonic Academy in Florence twenty years later. It became a fountainhead for the spread of Platonic philosophy in the Italian Renaissance, revitalizing its art, literature, philosophy, spiritual practices, and magic.

PLETHON

About this time, Gemistos began to call himself Plethon, but probably not publicly and only as the author of the *Book of Laws* (and perhaps to his Pagan students).[82] This is a kind of pun, for in Greek *gemistos* (γεμιστός) means "full" and *plêthôn* (πλήθων) means "abundant." There is also the obvious similarity to the names Plato (Πλατῶν, *Platôn* in Greek) and Plotinus (Πλωτῖνος, *Plôtinos*), which puts him in good company. One of his followers and admirers, Demetrios Kabakes, agreed, writing simply:

Plato—Plotinus—Plethon[83]

---

79. Woodhouse, *George Gemistos Plethon*, 168; see also Hladký, 226–30, and Siniossoglou, *Radical Platonism*, 128.

80. Woodhouse, *George Gemistos Plethon*, 366.

81. Plethon's "Differences" is translated in Woodhouse, *George Gemistos Plethon*, 192–214.

82. Hladký, *Plethon*, 235–36.

83. He wrote this in the margin of his notes on a conversation (Masai, *Pléthon*, 386).

Later, Marsilio Ficino, the head of Cosimo's Florentine Academy, praised "the Greek philosopher Gemistos (with the cognomen Plethon, as though a second Plato)."[84]

Gemistos's enemies criticized his adoption of the name "Plethon," suggesting that he was implying that he was Plato reincarnated.[85] (Platonists were known for believing in reincarnation, which was rejected by Christians.) They claimed Plethon was trying to convince people to follow his doctrines by implying he had come down from heaven. In fact, Plethon seems to have had no such intention. He did not seek to convert others, and he thought that he had provided sufficient philosophical proof of his doctrines and that he had no need to imply they were divinely inspired.[86]

Moreover, there was nothing unusual about adopting an additional name, either during that era or earlier. Monks did it routinely, as did others, who added a name alluding to their occupation or other distinctive features. Even Plato's birth name wasn't Plato; it was Aristocles. Indeed, when Scholarios retired to a monastery in 1450, he took the ecclesiastical name "Gennadios," thereby adding hypocrisy to insult!

A SECRET PAGAN ORDER?

After the Council of Union, Plethon (as I will call him from now on) returned to Mistra, where he remained for the rest of his life. There he continued his philosophical activities and provided services for the rulers, with whom he was on reasonably good terms. Presumably he was practicing his Neopagan Hellenism with a small group of followers. Scholarios makes a case for a Pagan order, a secret brotherhood or *phratry* (φρατρία, *phratria*), in Mistra, which he considered a hotbed of Hellenism and heresy. In fact, Plethon was not trying to convert his students to Hellenism; he initiated into his mysteries only "those who chose" Platonism on their own.[87] There cannot have been

---

84. Ficino, *Opera Omnia* (= *Marsilii Ficini … opera*) 2:1537; Plotinus, Porphyry, and Ficino, *Plotini* […] *Operum*, Prooemium, translated in Woodhouse, *George Gemistos Plethon*, 156.

85. Woodhouse, *George Gemistos Plethon*, 187, 366.

86. Plethon, *Laws* III.43.7.

87. Migne, *Patrologiae Cursus Completus, Series Graeca* 160:814C (Alexandre, *Pléthon*, 390–91). This is the funeral oration on Plethon by a certain monk Gregorios, who was a student of the master. He added that Plethon "was very busy with secret and divine matters, and an initiator in the highest heavenly doctrines" (*Patrologiae Cursus Completus, Series Graeca* 160:813BC; Alexandre, *Pléthon*, 388).

many, or his activities would have been exposed in such a small town as Mistra and the authorities would have been obliged to respond.

Nevertheless, Scholarios's suspicions were not unfounded.[88] There are hints of a long-standing tradition of Pagans concealing their true beliefs under a veil of orthodox Christianity. The emperor Julian (331–63 CE) hid his Paganism until he took office in 361 CE. Eunapius (b. 346 CE), who composed biographies of the Pagan Neoplatonists of the third and fourth centuries and was hostile to Christianity, wrote that it was easy for Pagans to pretend to be Christians.[89] The most famous disciple of the Pagan philosopher Hypatia, who was murdered by Christians in 415 CE, was Synesius (c. 373–c. 414 CE); he became a Christian bishop but wrote to his brother that he could keep his previous (Pagan) beliefs in private.[90] Another strategy, common from the fifth century, was to write commentaries on Pagan texts, claiming to explain them while denying belief in them. Pagan traditions were often passed down in the secular schools, where the church had less authority and where "those who chose" could learn the secret teachings. Already in the eighth century Christian priests and monks warned of covert Pagan groups pretending to be pious Christians but teaching myths, rituals, divination, and Hellenic ceremonies. Platonism in particular was seen as a threat, which is one reason Aristotle was favored in the West, as his doctrines were considered less dangerous to Christian theology. The monks of Mount Athos in Greece, in contrast, called Plato "the Greek Satan" and spit whenever his name was mentioned.[91]

The development of Byzantine humanism in the ninth century reawakened interest in Pagan philosophy, and especially Platonism, and brought new accusations of "Hellenism" (i.e., Paganism). For example, Leon Choirosphaktes (c. 840–919), known as Leon the Philosopher or Mathematician, taught at the secular School of Philosophy of Magnaura. He was accused of venerating Zeus and the other gods and was exiled, probably escaping execution only because he was related to the emperor. The School of

------

88. The existence of an underground Platonist tradition in Byzantium is argued at length in Siniossoglou, *Radical Platonism*, 1–124.

89. Eunapius, Universal History fragment 48.2 in Blockley, *Fragmentary Classicising Historians of the Later Roman Empire*, vol. 2, 74–77.

90. Synesius, *Epistles* 105, in Hercher, *Epistolographi graeci*, 703–6.

91. Siniossoglou, *Radical Platonism*, 3.

Philosophy prepared the ground for later cultivation of Pagan Platonism. Because of this rebirth of interest in classical antiquity, many Pagan texts were copied and therefore survive to our time.

I have already mentioned Michael Psellos (c. 1017–c. 1078), from whom Plethon copied his text for the Magical Oracles. He wrote of discovering the streams of gold and silver from the past and allowing them to flow again.[92] Although he argued that Platonism was useful for the church and took many opportunities to propose Christian interpretations of Pagan texts and to defend his orthodoxy, he was accused of being a secret Pagan, of being seduced by Plato, and of destroying Orthodoxy from the inside. His student and successor, John Italos was another influential philosopher who promoted Platonism; although he scrupulously added "of course we don't believe this" when he wrote about it, he nevertheless was condemned and some of his teachings were declared heretical.[93]

By the fourteenth century, Pythagoras, Plato, and Platonic philosophers were being referred to as the "enlightened ones" (πεφωτισμένοι, *pephôtismenoi*; Lat. *illuminati*).[94] Discussion groups devoted to philosophy and related topics began to form; they were called "theaters of the wise" (θέατρα σοφῶν, *theatra sophôn*), but members had to be discreet. The philosopher Theodore Metochites (1270–1332) said there were informers—he calls them "leeches"—eager to report suspicious ideas: "if you fail and commit a tiny error, even in one word or one notion, you will be immediately destroyed."[95] One of these groups was established by Demetrios Kydones (1324–1398), an ardent proponent of Platonism and likely one of Plethon's teachers. A number of these Platonists eventually migrated from Constantinople to Mistra, where ancient traditions were honored and thought was freer, and Plethon might have learned of this from Kydones, influencing him to go there too. In summary, you can see that there was a long tradition of studying Platonism in Byzantium, with hints and suspicions of outright Paganism. Plethon's project was far from unprecedented.

---

92. Psellos, *Chronographia* 6.43, translated in Psellus, *Fourteen Byzantine Rulers*, 177.

93. Siniossoglou, *Radical Platonism*, 81.

94. Siniossoglou, *Radical Platonism*, 27, 30, 96. Siniossoglou argues that the Byzantine Illuminati had similar goals to eighteenth-century European Illuminati: a rational religion and a secular state.

95. Siniossoglou, *Radical Platonism*, 90.

THE CASE OF JUVENAL

Scholarios claimed to have discovered Plethon's Paganism when he visited Mistra in 1427, but if that is so, he kept quiet about it until the 1440s; more likely it is a case of 20/20 hindsight.[96] The danger to Plethon was real, as illustrated by the fate of an unfortunate Pagan named Juvenal (Iouvenalios), who was open about his religion.[97] Scholarios had hounded him across Europe, both denouncing him to his face and lobbying with religious and civil leaders to get Juvenal expelled from one city after another. He bragged that his spies had intercepted letters between Juvenal and other Pagans.

Finally, around 1450 Juvenal was cruelly tortured and executed by Manuel Raoul Oises, a government official in the Peloponnese. His ears were cut off, his right hand was chopped off, and his tongue was cut out; then he was drowned in the ocean (a mercy by that point). In 1451 Scholarios wrote a letter to Oises congratulating him on the execution.[98] He wrote that he had been aware of Juvenal's Paganism from before the Council of Union and that Juvenal, an ex-monk, had learned it in a secret Pagan phratry in Mistra. He encouraged further persecutions and executions of "those impious and accursed Hellenists, or rather shameless apostates from true piety, by fire and sword and water and every means."[99]

While there is no evidence that Juvenal and Plethon knew each other or that they belonged to a secret phratry, Scholarios clearly believed that Plethon was the source of the heresy. Although he did not mention the names "Gemistos" or "Plethon," he blamed Juvenal's teachers, who "champion Hellenism in talking and writing, trying to revive genealogies of the gods and their names undefiled by the poets and their simple rituals, as they put it themselves, and constitutions and all those decadent and extinct ideas."[100] Phrases such as these, which are quotations or close paraphrases of Plethon's

---

96. Woodhouse, *George Gemistos Plethon*, 39.

97. The case of Juvenal is described in Siniossoglou, *Radical Platonism*, 134–48, and Woodhouse, *George Gemistos Plethon*, 315–17.

98. Scholarios, *Œuvres complètes* 4:476–89. Discussed and partly translated in Woodhouse, *George Gemistos Plethon*, 315–18.

99. Scholarios, *Œuvres complètes* 4:476, translated in Woodhouse, *George Gemistos Plethon*, 315.

100. Scholarios, *Œuvres complètes* 4:479, translation modified from Woodhouse, *George Gemistos Plethon*, 316. See Plethon, *Laws*, preface for parallels. The relevant texts are extracted and compared in Hladký, *Plethon*, 305–6.

Laws, show that Scholarios had access to at least some parts of Plethon's book. Therefore, Scholarios's letter is a thinly veiled accusation of Plethon and a recommendation that he be punished at least as severely as Juvenal.

Nevertheless, Plethon does not seem to have been concerned; apparently his position was secure, perhaps because he was not publicly professing Paganism or seeking converts. In their public exchanges of letters, Plethon and Scholarios remained cordial, though differing sharply on matters of Platonic and Aristotelian philosophy. Scholarios's vitriol erupted after the philosopher's demise.

THE FATE OF THE *BOOK OF LAWS*

Plethon died on Monday, June 26, 1452 (although some scholars argue for 1454); he would have been nearly one hundred years old. (Interestingly, this is the same day on which the Pagan emperor Julian died in 363 CE.) We know nothing about his death—presumably it was peaceful—and he was survived by his sons, Demetrios and Andronikos. Cardinal Bessarion, one of Plethon's students, wrote them a touching consolation laced with Pagan allusions. Plethon apparently did not live to see or hear of the fall of Constantinople to the Turks in 1453. Gennadios (that is, Scholarios) was captured and sold as a slave, but the Sultan Mehmed II ordered that he be released and made him Patriarch of the Orthodox Church, a post that he accepted reluctantly and resigned several times.

At the time of Plethon's death, Mistra was ruled by a certain Demetrios and his wife Theodora. Theodora, in particular, seems to have been hostile to Plethon's suspected Paganism, and they confiscated Plethon's *Book of Laws* after his death. The philosopher's followers were eager to get access to the book and to study it, but Theodora was reluctant to permit it, and so she sent the book to Gennadios to get his opinion. He wrote back that he was horrified at the Pagan heresy and told his tale of Plethon's "corruption" by the Jew Elissaios.[101] He sent the book back to Theodora so she could earn the "divine reward" for burning it, but she shrank back from destroying the work of so famous a philosopher.

Although the exact chronology of events is unclear, it seems that when Mistra fell to the Turks (1460), Demetrios and Theodora fled to Constantinople, where Gennadios

---

101. Scholarios, *Œuvres complètes* 4:151–55.

was Patriarch, and brought the book with them.[102] There she insisted that Gennadios destroy the book; "and so we committed it to the flames," he writes.[103] As previously mentioned, it took him about four hours to rip out more than half of the pages and to burn them. He preserved the parts that he thought were most damning, which would prove Plethon's heresy and justify his own vandalism. Moreover, Gennadios ordered that if anyone else had a copy, they must burn it or suffer excommunication.[104] There is evidence that he also burned Plethon's *Summary* and at least some of his *Commentary on the Magical Oracles of the Magi of Zoroaster*, but there were multiple copies of these works and so they survive intact.[105]

AFTERMATH

After this catastrophe, Plethon's students and other followers were anxious to preserve what remained of the *Book of Laws*. A few small parts (such as the chapter on Fate) had already been circulated and existed in multiple copies, but for the majority of it, there was only Plethon's own copy, which Gennadios had mostly destroyed.

One of those who preserved the remains was Michael Apostoles (1422–c. 1480), who was a fierce defender of Plato over Aristotle. He wanted to become a disciple of Plethon late in the philosopher's life (1450–51) and sent letters to him through a mutual friend. The letters were filled with praise for "the divine Plato" and overtly Pagan mentions of Zeus, Apollo, Hermes, Demeter, and other gods. It is not known whether his overtures were successful (and perhaps Plethon was not accepting new students at his advanced age), but after Plethon's death and the destruction of his book, Apostoles was diligent in preserving the remnants and in promoting Plethon and Platonism.

Another devoted follower of Plethon (although probably not a formal student) was Demetrios Raoul Kabakes (1397–1487), who came from an aristocratic family in Mistra. He was a committed Pagan for most of his life. At the age of seventy-four he noted that

---

102. Siniossoglou, *Radical Platonism*, 139.

103. Scholarios, *Œuvres complètes* 4:171, translated in Woodhouse, *George Gemistos Plethon*, 360.

104. Scholarios, *Œuvres complètes* 4:171–72; see also Woodhouse, *George Gemistos Plethon*, 360; Hladký, *Plethon*, 224.

105. Siniossoglou, *Radical Platonism*, 140. Plethon's *Summary*, *Laws*, and *Commentary* are translated here in appendices A, B, and C, respectively.

he dedicated himself to Helios the Sun at age seventeen and never wavered thereafter.[106] Kabakes was an admirer of the emperor Julian, who had briefly restored Paganism in the Roman empire a thousand years before, and praised Julian's "Hymn to King Helios" (which still survives).[107] In fact, on a manuscript of the hymn, Kabakes scribbled a note expressing disappointment that Plethon had not made greater use of Julian's writings.[108]

Like Apostoles, Kabakes gathered the fragments of the *Laws* and copied them—one of the most important surviving manuscripts is his—so that we have them today. His spelling was notoriously bad—further evidence that he was not a student of Plethon, who was meticulous in his language—but we owe to him the preservation of many texts. (His manuscript containing the *Laws* also contains the hymns of Synesius, a student of the Pagan martyr and Platonist Hypatia of Alexandria.) Kabakes concealed his Paganism throughout much of his life and in fact had cordial correspondence with Scholarios during that period when Scholarios suspected Plethon of Paganism but didn't have the evidence of the book. As I mentioned before, it was Kabakes who wrote "Plato—Plotinus—Plethon" in the margin of his notes of a conversation with Bessarion, in which the latter said that after Plotinus, there had been no wiser man in Greece than Plethon.[109]

Although Basilios Bessarion (1403–72) was a student of Plethon, he apparently never saw the *Book of Laws*, nor was he initiated into Plethon's Paganism. Nevertheless, although he later became a cardinal (and was twice a candidate for the papacy), he remained devoted to Plethon's philosophy and had one of the largest collections of Gemistos Plethon's manuscripts in the author's hand (not including the *Laws*). Despite his orthodoxy, Bessarion wrote a letter of condolence to Plethon's sons in which he spoke of their father "joining the mystical chorus of Iacchos with the Olympian gods."[110] He praised their father as the

---

106. Woodhouse, *George Gemistos Plethon*, 35.

107. Julian, "Oration IV: Hymn to King Helios" 130B–158C, in *Works of Emperor Julian*, 1:352–435.

108. Woodhouse, *George Gemistos Plethon*, 34–35.

109. Masai, *Pléthon*, 386.

110. Bessarion in Alexandre, *Pléthon*, 404, translated in Woodhouse, *George Gemistos Plethon*, 13.

wisest man in Greece since Plato and wrote that, if the doctrine of reincarnation were true, then one would suppose that Plethon had Plato's soul.[111]

Plethon was buried in Mistra, but his bones were moved to Rimini in 1464 by Sigismondo Malatesta, the hereditary lord of Rimini. He was a successful military leader and a patron of philosophy and the arts, but with a dubious reputation and Pagan sympathies (he was twice burned in effigy at Rome by Pope Pius II). He had admired Plethon from afar and invited him to his court at Rimini, but Plethon was very old by then, and it is unknown whether he even received the invitation. Malatesta led a campaign into the Peloponnese with the aim of freeing it from the Ottoman Turks. It was unsuccessful, but while he was at Mistra he decided to rescue his hero's remains from the Turks and give them a final resting place in friendly lands. He placed the philosopher's bones in a sarcophagus in the outer wall of the Tempio Malatestiano, a Neopagan temple, designed by the famous Leon Battista Alberti as the final resting place for Malatesta's mistress and later wife, Isotta. A plaque labels the tomb of "Gemistos the Byzantine, Prince of philosophers."[112] The pope condemned this temple for being "full of pagan works."[113] The fanatical Christian George Trebizond blamed Malatesta's bad health (and eventual death) on the presence of Plethon's remains and repeatedly urged Malatesta and his relatives to toss the bones into the sea, but no one would desecrate the tomb, still there, of the greatest Greek philosopher since Plotinus.[114]

THE BOOK OF LAWS AND ITS REMAINS

At the beginning of his *Book of Laws* (Νόμων Συγγραφή, *Nomôn Syngraphê*), Plethon tells us briefly that it presents "theology after Zoroaster and Plato," in which "the traditional names of the gods of our Hellenic ancestors have been preserved for the gods recognized by philosophy."[115] The book includes "ritual reduced to simple practices, without superfluity, and yet sufficient." In addition, it teaches ethics according to Zoroaster and Plato

---

111. Bessarion in Alexandre, *Pléthon*, 404–5.

112. Masai, *Pléthon*, 365, translated in Woodhouse, *George Gemistos Plethon*, 374.

113. Woodhouse, *George Gemistos Plethon*, 160.

114. Hladký, *Plethon*, 230.

115. Plethon, *Laws*, preface.

but also the Stoics, politics adapted from Sparta's with Platonic modifications, and natural science based primarily on Aristotle; it also touches on other topics, including logic, Greek antiquities, and health.

The *Laws* was divided into three books (parts) comprising 105 chapters, of which sixteen survive in whole or in part. We know this because each of the books had a table of contents, and they have survived (because they were attached to the book's covers), and so we can see what Scholarios's destructive hand has taken from us.[116] Of the thirty-five chapters of book I, the first five survive, including a description of the Golden Chain, some general principles of theology, and a prayer to the gods of learning (see page 36). All of book II (twenty-seven chapters) is lost, except for the chapter on Fate, which had circulated separately before Plethon's death, and a short chapter on the rational behavior of some animals. Book III had forty-three chapters, of which nine survive in whole or in part. These include valuable chapters on the emanation of the gods, the sacred calendar, ritual structure, ritual invocations, ritual hymns, and an appendix (*Epinomis*), which summarizes Plethon's theology.[117] Some of surviving chapters are quite short, but others are very long, and it is estimated that two-fifths of the book has survived the wanton destruction of Scholarios.[118] What we have is very valuable, but the list of destroyed chapters makes us grieve all the more for what we have lost.[119]

In addition to the *Laws*, we have Plethon's "Summary of the Doctrines of Zoroaster and Plato," which lays out his theology in twelve principles, "the most necessary principles to know for whoever wants to think wisely."[120] Plethon seems to have given copies to his followers, and Bessarion had one in Plethon's handwriting (which survives). His work *On the Differences of Aristotle from Plato* fills in many details of his philosophy.[121]

---

116. See Plethon, *Laws*, table of contents, in appendix B.

117. The invocations and hymns are presented with instructions and explanations in our chapters 6, 7, and 8; my translation of Plethon's original text is in appendix B (Plethon, *Laws* III.34–5).

118. Hladký, *Plethon*, 252.

119. See Plethon, *Laws*, table of contents, in appendix B.

120. Ζωροαστρείων τε καὶ Πλατωνικῶν Δογμάτων Συγκεφαλαίωσις. My translation is included as appendix A.

121. Περὶ ὧν Ἀριστοτέλης πρὸς Πλάτωνα Διαφέρεται, translated in Woodhouse, *George Gemistos Plethon*, 192–214.

Concerning ethics, we also have his *On Virtues* (or *Excellences*), which I explain in chapter 9.[122] We also have his *Commentary on the Magical Oracles of the Magi of Zoroaster*, which I have already mentioned.[123] These all help us understand Plethon's religion and put it into practice.

No doubt much was unwritten and conveyed orally; he wrote, "Plato, like the Pythagoreans before him, preferred not to write on such subjects but to communicate them orally to his students, because they would be wiser if they had the knowledge in their souls rather than in books."[124] In some cases we can infer some of these oral teachings from the writings of other Neoplatonists, especially those in the Golden Chain, and I have used that information in this book (see chapter 10 for reconstructed doctrines).

PRAYER TO THE GODS OF LEARNING

As did Plethon in his *Book of Laws*, I think it is appropriate to begin with his "Prayer to the Gods of Learning":

> Come to us, O gods of learning, whoever you may be, in whatever number you may be, you who preside over knowledge and the truth, who distribute them to whomever you please, according to the decrees of the almighty father of all things, King Zeus. Without you we would be unable to accomplish such a great work. Come guide our reasoning, and grant this work to obtain the best possible success, and to be like a treasure always open to those people who want to lead the most beautiful and best conduct in public or private life.[125]

---

122. Περὶ Ἀρετῶν.

123. Μαγικὰ λόγια τῶν ἀπὸ Ζωροάστρου μάγων, translated in appendix C.

124. Plethon in Migne, *Patrologiae Cursus Completus, Series Graeca* 160:983D, translated in Woodhouse, *George Gemistos Plethon*, 43.

125. Plethon, *Laws* I.4.

III

The Gods

⌐⌐⌐

Murder, rape, incest, vengeance, torture, cannibalism, thievery, deceit, rage: the Greek gods committed them all, according to the myths handed down through the ages in ancient Greece. Indeed, ancient philosophers and other ancient thinkers observed that people attributed to the gods all the personality traits and behaviors that were reprehensible among mortals. How could such gods be worthy of our worship?

Some Platonist philosophers, among others, argued that we needed to interpret the myths allegorically or metaphorically, that the crimes they recounted were veiled descriptions of spiritual and occult relationships and processes. Nevertheless, myths might be misinterpreted by the uneducated—by those who didn't know the allegorical code—and the uninformed might feel free to behave like the gods in the myths. For this reason, Plato recommended banishing poets from his ideal republic because they mislead the public about the gods and might lead people astray, and he was against trying to find hidden meanings in them. Nevertheless, Plato understood that some things can only be expressed through myths, and he authored nearly a dozen of his own.[126]

Plethon agreed with Plato, and so his theology contains very little traditional Greek mythology, which you may know and love.[127] Indeed, some of the things he writes about the relations among the gods directly contradicts what one finds in Homer and

---

126. For Plato's criticism of poets and their myths, see his *Republic* 2.377e–378d and 10.596–608b.

127. Plethon, *Laws*, preface.

37

Hesiod (who also, it must be mentioned, often contradict each other and other poets). But if Plethon doesn't get his knowledge of the gods from traditional sources, such as Homer and Hesiod, then where does he get it?

From Platonic theology. For the Platonists have analyzed and explained the necessary structure of the divine worlds: which gods must exist and what must be their functions. Thus he can use philosophical principles to map out and explain the genealogies of the gods and their offices and to determine their attributes. But he realizes that this is too abstract for most people, and so he gives these gods their traditional names from the Greek pantheon, which is deeply embedded in the Western tradition. For example, the chief divine principle is named Zeus, for that is the name for the chief god familiar from ancient Greek religion and mythology. Once we understand who and what the gods are and what are their functions and relationships, we may call them by any names we like, even by the names of the gods of another pantheon, but Plethon's background was Hellenic. He writes that even if the names of the gods have been sullied by the poets, the stain is not permanent and can be eliminated if we use the names in a way that is pure and healthy, not fraudulent or evil.[128] (Before he can tell us more on this topic, however, the chapter breaks off, thanks to Scholarios's destruction.)

PERSONIFICATION

I think that Plethon was wise and psychologically astute in retaining the traditional names of the gods and, as we will see, personifying them in his invocations and hymns (see chapters 6, 7, and 8). For although the gods are defined philosophically, it is natural and psychologically helpful to personify them—to imagine them and to relate to them in human form (or occasionally animal or plant form, but still with humanlike minds). Since many of the gods guide and govern human affairs, it is natural for them to relate to us in a humanlike way. Moreover, we have evolved to engage with other humans better than with any other sort of thing, and therefore, personifying the gods in our imagination is a natural way to experience them. In this way it is psychologically easier to feel devotion and respect for them.

---

128. Plethon, *Laws* III.32.2.

Although the gods are Platonic Ideas, existing independently of us, they also have archetypal images (reflections, instantiations) in our collective unconscious. Because this is the *human* collective unconscious (the unconscious mind characteristic of *Homo sapiens* as a species), these archetypes are usually anthropomorphic, but sometimes theriomorphic (having animal form) combined with some human characteristics (e.g., speech). (As Xenophanes wrote 2500 years ago, if horses and cattle had gods, they would look like horses and cattle.[129] Although he intended this as a criticism of anthropomorphic deities, in fact it is just as it should be!) Therefore, the gods most often manifest themselves to us in ways that are relevant to human life. Moreover, they also appear in these forms in our dreams.

We can understand the gods abstractly and intellectually in the ways Plethon describes them, but that is not the best way to understand them concretely and personally, in the much richer way we understand one another, especially our family, friends, and close associates. For that, we need the gods to be represented concretely in a form that we have evolved to understand: in human form. This is more important for the practical and spiritual matters of our lives than is the more theoretical understanding that comes from philosophy and theology. However, we should never forget that gods are not people; they assume a human form for our benefit, but they are gods, not humans.

Personification is especially important in *theurgy* (direct interaction with gods: see chapter 11), for we invoke gods (and their daimons) through the use of symbolic images, which are rooted in the human psyche and tune the theurgist's soul to the characteristic energy of the god. Personification also aids theurgic communication, for it is much easier to talk to an anthropomorphic god or daimon, which has understandable expressions and body language, than to an abstract shape or vague cloud (or to an abstract idea!). One of the Chaldean Oracles (not in Plethon's collection) informs theurgists, "For you these bodies have been bound / upon the self-revealing apparitions."[130] Although very experienced

---

129. Xenophanes, frag. LM 8D14 (DK 21B15) in Laks and Most, *Early Greek Philosophy III*, 30–31. The LM number refers to a fragment's location in Laks and Most's recent collection of fragments from the pre-Socratic philosophers. I also provide the equivalent DK (Diels-Krantz) number, which is used in many older collections.

130. My translation of oracle 142 in Majercik, *Chaldean Oracles*, 102–103, or des Places, *Oracula Chaldaica*, 101.

theurgists may be able to engage the divine more directly as these "self-revealing appari-tions," most of us will depend on anthropomorphic manifestations.

Therefore, just as Plethon retains the traditional names for the gods, we can use the familiar images of them, which we know from art and literature, because they arose in the authentic tradition and reflect the unconscious archetypes. We can also retain many of the traditional attributes of the gods, which strengthens our symbolic connection to them; some traditional epithets of the gods can also be used. In all these cases we must ensure that the image is consistent with our philosophical understanding of the god, or at least not contradictory to it. As in the poets' myths, some of what has been handed down is not appropriate and should be abandoned, but we should not ignore the value of allegorical interpretations and of deep, though perhaps not rationally expli-cable, symbolic associations. There is of course much classical art, easily available on the internet and in books, that you can use in your religious practice.

THE ORDERS OF REALITY

As other Platonic philosophers in the Golden Chain had done, Plethon analyzed reality into a hierarchy of three orders.[131] The lowest order is our physical world, where things exist in time and space, in which everything is mortal, coming to be at one time and pass-ing away at a later time. Beings interact in this world by means of their physical bodies (and, in more modern terms, by physical forces). This is where we live our mortal lives.

The highest order is the realm of **Platonic Forms** or **Ideas**, which are objective abstrac-tions or essences (οὐσίαι, *ousiai*) that exist independently of individual human minds. They are non-physical and do not exist in space or time. The best and most familiar examples are mathematical abstractions, such as geometrical shapes and numbers. Think of a geometrical form such as an equilateral triangle. While your thought of it can come or go, the abstract Idea "equilateral triangle" is independent of time; it is eternal, outside of time altogether. Or think of the natural numbers 1, 2, 3, and so on. Relationships among them, such as $1 + 2 + 3 + 4 = 10$, are also eternal; this relationship did not begin at some point in time—it was true before the big bang—nor will it ever change or cease to exist.

---

131. Plethon, *Laws* III.43.3; Plethon, *Commentary*, epilogue.

According to Plethon and other Platonists, this highest realm is where the **supercelestial gods** reside.[132] (Zeus has a unique position, described later.) These gods therefore are eternal in the strict sense of being atemporal or outside of time; they are also outside of space. They are nowhere and "nowhen." They are called "supercelestial" (ὑπερουράνιος, *hyperouranios*) because they are outside the universe, outside the world contained in the heavens (Lat., *caelum*; Grk., οὐρανός, *ouranos*). They are non-physical, and so they are invisible; they cannot be perceived by our senses. Like eternal relationships among numbers or geometrical forms, the supercelestial gods exist in an eternal order or harmony, which Plethon describes.[133]

There is an ancient principle of Pythagorean philosophy that if any unified system has parts, then those parts must be connected in order for it to be unified whole. The parts must have some common boundary, or there must be a meditating element connecting them; otherwise, they would be just a bunch of parts, not a connected unity. In particular, if the parts are opposed in some sense, then they cannot share a common boundary in that respect, and thus there must be a meditating element, which shares a boundary with each of the opposites.

This situation holds between the highest realm of eternal, immutable, non-physical beings and the lowest realm of mortal, changeable, physical beings. Therefore, for the cosmos to be a unified whole, there must be a meditating realm that connects the highest and lowest together. This is the realm of the **celestial gods** (the stars and planets), which are visible and exist in time and space, within the heavens. They are not eternal (αἰώνιον, *aiônion*), but neither are they mortal; they are everlasting (ἀΐδιον, *aidion*). In other words, they have no beginning and no end in time. Nevertheless, they are ever-moving, ever-changing in time. The nature of the celestial gods is described in more detail later in this chapter.

---

132. Plethon, *Summary* 2; Plethon, *Laws* I.5.3.

133. Plethon, *Laws* I.5.7.

In his *Summary of the Doctrines of Zoroaster and Plato* Plethon reduces his philosophy to twelve principles or key ideas, which, he writes, any wise person must accept.[134] There are four principles each on the gods, the cosmos, and humankind:[135]

Concerning the Gods

1. The gods exist, the chief of whom is Zeus.

2. The gods look after us, either directly or through their subordinates.

3. The gods are causes of the good, not of evil, for humans and other beings.

4. The gods act according to an immutable fate emanated from Zeus.[136]

Concerning "the All" (the Cosmos)

5. The All, including gods of the second and third orders, was created by Zeus and is everlasting.

6. The All is a unity assembled from many things.

7. The All was created perfectly.

8. The All is preserved immutably.[137]

Concerning Humankind

9. The human soul, being akin to the gods, is immortal and everlasting.

10. The human soul is always attached to one or another mortal body and, by joining the immortal to the mortal, contributes to the unity of the All.

11. Because of human kinship with the gods, the good is the goal that suits our life.

---

134. Plethon, *Summary*, preface.

135. You might wonder if these three groups of principles correspond to the three levels of reality, but they do not. The explanation, rather, is that Platonists like to organize things by threes.

136. Plethon, *Summary* 2–3.

137. Plethon, *Summary* 4.

12. The gods, by fixing the laws of humankind, place our happiness in the immortal part of our being.[138]

All the foregoing is rather abstract, I'm afraid, but it will give you some orientation in the Platonic cosmos as explained in more detail in the remainder of this chapter. Understanding the nature of the gods is important for understanding our relationship to them. However we should not forget that Plethon's philosophy and theology are a means to an end; they are tools to help us live meaningful lives in harmony with the gods. They are a map, but they are useless unless we follow the path.

ZEUS: THE ONE ITSELF

It is a principle of Platonic philosophy that all existing things depend for their being on other things higher in the scale of being. Thus, the being of the celestial gods depends on the being of the supercelestial gods, and the existence of mortal things on earth, such as us, depends on higher beings, including the celestial and supercelestial gods. But where do the supercelestial gods, the highest beings, get their being? To avoid an infinite regress of higher and higher beings—which would explain nothing—Platonists found it necessary to postulate a first and highest principle, sometimes called the Ineffable One (τὸ ἄρρητον ἕν, *to arrhêton hen*). It is the ultimate principle by which anything is something, and Plethon calls it **Zeus**.[139]

The supercelestial beings or essences (οὐσίαι, *ousiai*) must get their being from something that transcends being, from something *super-essential* (ὑπερούσιος, *hyperousios*). Since it is beyond being, it is beyond distinctions of *what is* and *what is not*; it is beyond differences and duality. Therefore, it is the ultimate principle of unity, but it is even beyond the distinctions of unity and multiplicity, or of identity and difference.

You will think that I have been reduced to babbling, and that is, in an important sense, true. Because this first principle, which for lack of a better name we call "the Ineffable One" or Zeus, is beyond being, we really cannot talk about it comprehensibly. This is why it is called "ineffable." This translates the Greek word *arrhêton* (ἄρρητον), which means "unsayable, inexpressible, unspeakable"—that is, what is inexpressible in words or incomprehensible—but it also refers to the secrets taught in the Mysteries,

---

138. Plethon, *Summary* 5.

139. Plethon, *Summary* 2; Plethon, *Laws* I.5.10–11.

which must be experienced and are unlawful to speak about. How then can we know or say anything about the Ineffable One? Fundamentally, we cannot. But we can come to grasp it nonverbally by contemplative practices (discussed in chapter 11) and then use words to circumnavigate and point toward it, as I am doing here. Platonism presents one of the earliest examples of an **apophatic** or **negative theology**, in which we approach deity not by saying what it is, but rather by saying what it is not. This ultimate unsayability must be kept in mind as I proceed to say more about Zeus!

In fact, Plethon does not stress the ineffability of the first principle to the same degree as other Platonists; it is not completely beyond our intellectual understanding. Nevertheless, because of his unique nature, Plethon calls Zeus exceptional (ἐξαίρετος, *exairetos*) and refers to him by a number of special names, including the One-Itself (αὐτοέν, *autoen*), the Supremely One (ἄκρως ἕν, *akrôs hen*), the Pure One (εἰλικρινῶς ἕν, *eilikrinôs hen*), and Being-Itself (αὐτοών, *autoôn*), because he is the source of being.[140]

Since the being of the other gods depends on Zeus, the exceptional first principle, Plethon writes that Zeus *creates* them, but this is a metaphor.[141] He also calls Zeus their *cause*, but this does not imply he made them at some point in time; Zeus is an ontological cause, a higher form of being on which a lower form depends. If we don't keep this in mind, we may fall into the trap of thinking of Zeus as a superhuman craftsman with a dark curly beard and wearing a toga.

Nevertheless, Plethon follows convention in calling Zeus "Father" (πατήρ, *patêr*), for traditionally Zeus was called "father of gods and mortals." To emphasize his special nature, he also calls him Self-Father (αὐτοπάτωρ, *autopatôr*) and Progenitor (προπάτωρ, *propatôr*); Paternal Principle and Father are also names for the supreme god in the Magical Oracles.[142]

In their enigmatic way, the Oracles proclaim, "The Father snatched Himself away, / and didn't close His Fire in Noeric Power."[143] Plethon explains that this means he is uncreated and exists separate from the other gods.[144] His divinity (his fire) transcends

---

140. Plethon, *Laws* III.34.2, 37.

141. Plethon, *Summary* 2, 4; Plethon, *Laws* I.5.2–4.

142. Plethon, *Laws* III.34.19, 37, 67, 82; Plethon, *Laws* III.35.1, 3; Plethon, *Commentary* 30, 32, 35.

143. Plethon, *Magical Oracles* 35.

144. Plethon, *Commentary* 35.

even the second god, Poseidon, here called the Noeric (Mental) Power (δύναμις νοερά, *dynamis noera*), because he is the Idea of the Platonic Ideas. He adds that it is not because of envy that the Father's unique form of divinity is not bestowed on others, but because it is impossible.[145]

Plethon also calls Zeus "eldest demiurge" after the creator-craftsman god (δημιουργός, *dêmiourgos*) in Plato's *Timaeus*.[146] All these names are just metaphorical expressions to give us a way of referring to an idea that is, in the end, beyond description. Since the supercelestial gods are eternal—outside of time—Zeus does not create them at some point in time. In fact, since Zeus is the cause of the eternal realm of gods and Platonic Forms, he transcends eternity itself and is called **pre-eternal** (προαιώνιος, *proaiônios*).[147] Because he emanates the essences—in other words, because he is the cause of their being—he is called **super-essential** (ὑπερούσιος, *hyperousios*): beyond the essences (οὐσίαι, *ousiai*).[148]

Therefore, Plethon tells us, there are actually three ranks of gods: Zeus is alone in the first rank, and he emanates the second rank, the supercelestial gods, who in turn emanate the third rank, the celestial gods.[149] The Platonic **Second Letter** refers enigmatically to "three kings": the first is the principle of everything and the cause of all goodness, the second governs secondary things, and the third governs the tertiary.[150] Likewise in Plethon's pantheon each of the ranks of gods has a king: Zeus for the first, Poseidon for the second, and Helios for the third. He writes that this agrees with Plutarch's explanation of the Zoroastrian system, in which all beings are divided into classes governed by Horomazês (Ahura Mazda), Mithras (Mithra), and Arimazês (Ahriman, Angra Mainyu), each of whom produced six other gods.[151]

Plethon summarizes his theology in three principal axioms, which concern respectively Zeus, the nature of the gods, and human nature; they will be discussed in the

---

145. Plethon, *Commentary* 35.

146. Plethon, *Laws* III.35.1, 15.

147. Plethon, *Laws* III.15.5.

148. Plethon, *On the Differences of Aristotle from Plato*, translated in Woodhouse, *George Gemistos Plethon*, 207.

149. Plethon, *Summary* 2, 4; *Laws* I.5.2, III.43.1.

150. Plato, *Epist.* 2, 312e1–e4.

151. Plethon, *Commentary*, epilogue.

appropriate places.[152] His first axiom is that "the principle of all things, that supreme god who, in the language of our fathers, is called Zeus, is supremely good, lacking no perfection to be the best possible."[153] Plato already called the highest principle "the Good" (τὸ ἀγαθόν, *to agathon*), and Plethon also calls Zeus the Good-Itself (αὐτοαγαθός, *autoagathos*), the Excess of the Good (ἀγαθοῦ ὑπερβολή, *agathou hyperbolê*), and the Supremely Good (ἄκρως ἀγαθόν, *akrôs agathon*).[154] Therefore, Zeus is the source of all the good in the cosmos by way of the gods and daimons, all of whom are also entirely good, according to Plethon.[155] This is because what is necessary is better than what is contingent, and therefore the greatest necessity is the greatest good, but this is Zeus, who by definition is the principle of everything and does not depend on anything else: "this first necessity, which alone exists absolutely and by itself while all things exist through it, this necessity which we call the absolute Good, Zeus."[156]

This interpretation is supported by Plethon's commentary on a Magical Oracle: "Nought incomplete rolls from Paternal Principle."[157] "Paternal Principle" (πατρικὴ ἀρχή, *patrikê archê*) is one of the names used by the Oracles for First-Father, namely Zeus. Therefore, everything proceeding from this first principle is complete and in this sense perfect. This is a rather abstract notion of the good, however, which we cannot simply equate with the moral goodness in social terms (see chapter 9 on ethics). The Oracles also assure us that the first god is neither terrible nor frightening: "The Father makes not fear, but pours persuasion on."[158] This means, according to Plethon, that the Father is a source not of terror but of love, "for he, being extremely good, is not the cause of harm, and therefore frightening, but is the cause of all good to all; whence he is loved by all."[159]

Plethon's description of Zeus might sound suspiciously like the God of monotheistic religions, but there are important differences. First, as we will explore in detail, Plethon's

---

152. Plethon, *Laws* III.43.1.

153. Plethon, *Laws* III.43.1.

154. Plethon, *Laws* III.34.2, 16, 37, 52, 69; III.35.1, 3.

155. Plethon, *Summary* 3; Plethon, *Laws* I.5.1, III.43.1–2.

156. Plethon, *Laws* II.6.2, 6.

157. Plethon, *Magical Oracles* 5.

158. Plethon, *Magical Oracles* 36.

159. Plethon, *Commentary* 36.

theology is polytheistic: there are many gods; more precisely, it is a **henotheistic** religion, which means a polytheistic religion with one chief god. Moreover, the other gods play a critical role in our universe, and in fact are often more relevant to us than Zeus, because they are nearer and not so ineffable.

You might also wonder why this ineffable principle of unity, which is beyond all distinctions, is assigned a male gender. Why is this highest god not hermaphroditic or androgynous or entirely genderless? Is this evidence of an age-old patriarchal bias in theology? Probably. Plethon was in many respects a man of his time, as were the other Platonists. However, aside from the fact that Plethon wanted to use the traditional Greek names for the gods, and the highest god was traditionally named Zeus, he has an additional, philosophical reason. As was common in ancient Greek thought (and will be discussed next), Form was associated with the masculine and Matter with the feminine. Therefore, he thought that this entirely immaterial pre-essential essence, this Form above all Forms, needed to be male.

DIVINE GENDER

Plethon's theology might strike the modern Neopagan as patriarchal, for the chief deity, who might be mistaken for a monotheistic God, is Zeus, and the second deity is Poseidon. Only thereafter do we encounter a goddess, Hera. In the lower ranks we have a more balanced pantheon: in total, eleven gods (including Zeus) and twelve goddesses. Clearly, incorporeal gods and goddesses do not have penises or vaginas (or X and Y chromosomes), so what does it mean for a deity to be male or female?

In the context of Plethon's theology, a deity is considered male if it is more active and more associated with Form, and a deity is considered female if it is more passive and more associated with Matter.[160] The traditional gender associations of these philosophical and metaphysical attributes come from the ancient Greek prescientific understanding of sexual reproduction. Because the volume of semen is relatively small, because the child is nourished by the mother both before and after birth, and because menstrual fluid resembles flesh and blood, it was natural to think that the father contributed the form and the mother contributed the matter to the child. (Even in ancient times, however, it was recognized that the mother also contributes to the form of the child, often more so than the father.)

Instead of being given traditional names and genders, Plethon's deities could be denoted by abstract descriptions. Instead of Apollo, we could have "Idea of Identity," and instead of Artemis, "Idea of Difference." Plethon thought this approach would be confusing to anyone but philosophers (and probably to them as well); it certainly does not inspire devotion! Therefore, Plethon decided to rehabilitate the traditional gods' names from the poet's scandalous stories. Moreover, I would add, we experience the gods as gendered personalities, so it is useful to consider them male and female, even though it may tend to perpetuate gender stereotypes. (Recall "Personification" on page 38.)

THE SUPERCELESTIAL GODS

Zeus directly produces the supercelestial gods, divided into Olympians and Titans. Although Plethon uses the metaphors of "father" and "child" to describe this relationship, Zeus produces these other gods only in the sense similar to the number 1 producing 2, 3, and the rest.[161] This is not a process that took place in time; it is an abstract relationship. It is more accurate to say that the other gods are eternal emanations of Zeus; their existence depends on him. Moreover, unlike the numbers 1, 2, 3, and so on, which go on forever, Plethon tells us that the emanation of the gods is like a process of logical division, which has to stop when the indivisible is reached.[162] Therefore, there is a particular fixed number of supercelestial gods, 22 in Plethon's analysis (see figure 1). Because Zeus is the ultimate principle of unity, each god represents a particular aspect of this unity. The first division is between Form and Matter, which is the emanation of the first gods after Zeus, Poseidon and Hera, the king and queen of the supercelestial gods. Plethon calls them children of Zeus, but of course in traditional mythology they are his brother and sister.[163] We must remember that Plethon's theology is based on a philosophical analysis of the gods and their nature and is not bound by traditional sources.

---

161. Plethon, *Laws* III.15.3.

162. Plethon, *Laws* III.15.3.

163. Plethon, *Summary* 2; Plethon, *Laws* I.5.2, III.15.12–13.

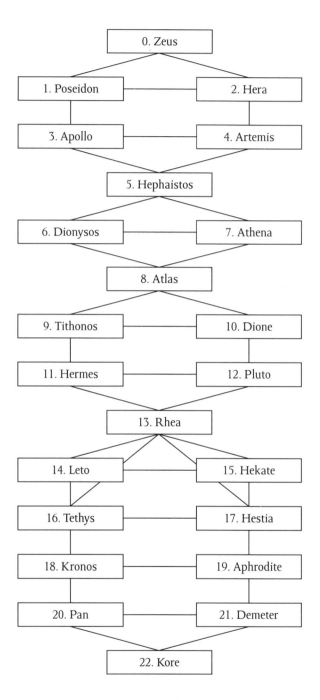

Figure 1. Supercelestial Gods

The supercelestial gods occupy the realm of the eternal, immaterial Platonic Forms or Ideas. The timeless interrelationships among them are purely intellectual—logical, we might say—so that they form an integrated whole, a harmonious community. The gods receive their attributes from each other, for Zeus, "their king and father … established among his children a community and a reciprocity of benefits, the most beautiful gift that he granted them after participation in his essence."[164]

By making distinctions (dividing the opposites he contains), Zeus unfolds being and emanates the gods in a specific logical order in which superior gods are models for inferior gods, which are like images of the former. In accord with a common Neoplatonic **Triadic Principle**, each of these gods has three timeless "movements": it *remains* in itself, it *proceeds* outward to produce its lower images, and these lower images *turn back* to their origins and seek to imitate them. Plethon writes that the relation of model to image is the closest possible, and so the gods are tightly bound together.

Plethon's second axiom asserts "there must be a reciprocal relationship between essences and their mode of generation."[165] This implies a relation between the three orders of reality and the gods that produce them. Thus, Zeus creates all the supercelestial gods, for only he has the power to directly emanate eternal beings. There are two classes of supercelestials, the gods of Olympus and the gods of Tartarus, also called Titans. The Olympians are superior in that they can produce (emanate) immortal beings, namely the celestial gods, who are immortal (everlasting) but not eternal (atemporal) because they exist in time. Finally, the Tartareans have the least power, and produce only mortal or perishable beings in the physical world. I think of the Olympians as the gods of logic, mathematics, and physics, since the laws and truths in these disciplines are eternal (although our limited knowledge of them changes in time). The Titans then are the gods of nature, for living things are born and die and evolve through time.

Plethon calls the Olympians the "legitimate" children of Zeus, and the Titans his "illegitimate" children.[166] He doesn't explain this peculiar terminology, but perhaps he is alluding to classical Greek mythology in which many of the gods were born of illicit

---

164. Plethon, *Laws* I.5.3.

165. Plethon, *Laws* III.43.1.

166. Plethon, *Laws* I.5.4, 6.

relationships. Looking at the Greek words doesn't help much. On one hand, γνήσιος (*gnêsios*) refers to something belonging to the race (from *genos* = race, stock, tribe, family, genus, class) and therefore lawfully begotten or legitimate, and by extension genuine, true, or qualified. On the other hand, its regular opposite, νόθος (*nothos*), refers to a bastard and more generally to something illegitimate, spurious, counterfeit, false, or not genuine, but Plethon makes abundantly clear that the Titans are good and worthy of our worship; they are inferior only in being responsible for the perishable aspects of reality, which are not in any sense evil and in fact are necessary for the perfection of the cosmos. Therefore, I will translate these terms as *high-born* and *low-born*, which seems to capture better their meaning in Plethon's theology.

Poseidon: Form

Poseidon is the first emanation of Zeus, and therefore Plethon calls him the eldest and most venerable (πρεσβύτατος, *presbytatos*) of the children of Zeus, a metaphor, of course, to express the fact that he is the first emanation and therefore nearest to Zeus in his essential nature.[167] Because he is generated by Zeus alone, he is called "motherless" (ἀμήτωρ, *amêtôr*).[168] Plethon also calls him, more philosophically, "Form-Itself" or "Idea-Itself" (αὐτοεῖδος, *autoeidos*).[169] He is the first and supreme god in the realm of Forms, and hence he contains in himself all the Forms. He is not any particular Form or Idea, but the Form of all Forms, the Idea of all Ideas (εἶδος εἶδῶν, *eidos eidôn*).[170] One possible reason why Plethon called this god "Poseidôn" is that his name can be explained as "Master of Forms" (πόσις εἶδῶν, *posis eidôn*).[171]

Plethon also calls Poseidon "Limit-Itself" (αὐτοπέρας, *autoperas*) because a thing is delimited, made definite and determinate, by its Form, which gives it its essential properties.[172] The Greek word translated "limit" (πέρας, *peras*) refers to boundaries that separate

---

167. Plethon, *Summary* 2; *Laws* I.5.2, 14; III.15.12; II.34.3, 21, 24, 73; III.35.4, 17.

168. Plethon, *Summary* 2; *Laws* III.34.3.

169. Plethon, *Laws* III.34.24.

170. Plethon, *Laws* III.15.12.

171. Masai, *Pléthon et le Platonisme de Mistra*, 279–80.

172. Plethon, *Laws* III.34.24.

one thing from another, including one Idea from another, but also to limits that prevent something from being unlimited, unbounded, or indefinite. Poseidon is also "Beauty-Itself" (αὐτοκαλόν, *autokalon*) for a thing's beauty is determined by its form, by the relation of its parts or, more generally, by a harmonious relation of its properties.[173]

In his *Commentary on the Magical Oracles*, Plethon writes, "The Second God, who first before all other things proceeded from the Father and supreme god, these oracles call all along the Father's Power, his Intellectual Power, and the Paternal Mind."[174] He is called the Intellectual (or Noeric) Power, because he is the power of the cosmic *Nous* (Mind), which contains all the Ideas.[175] Plethon writes that he is the chorus leader (κορυφαῖος, *koryphaios*) of the gods, who are our intellectual guides.[176]

The Oracles also call Poseidon the Second Nous because he comes after the Father, Zeus. Plethon observes that because Zeus is ineffable and beyond comprehension, most people mistake Poseidon for the creator of the cosmos, which is the meaning of the Magical Oracle: "The Father finished everything and handed them / to Second Nous, whom you, the human tribe, call First."[177] In other words, Second Nous (Poseidon) gets credit for what First Nous (Zeus) has ultimately caused.

Hera: Matter

Just as Poseidon is the Platonic Idea or Form of Forms, so **Hera** is the Idea or Form of Matter, where *matter* (Grk., ὕλη, *hulê*; Lat., *materia*) refers to whatever receives form or definition, not just physical matter. It is this abstract idea of matter that causes the diversity of things, that allows one instance of a Form to be different from another instance of a Form. For example, Poseidon contains the Form Triangle, but it is Hera who creates the potentially infinite multitude of possible triangles in the physical world and in our individual minds. Metaphorically, we might say that Hera gives birth to all particular triangles. Thus, like Poseidon, Hera contains all the Forms in herself, but whereas he

---

173. Plethon, *Laws* III.34.24.

174. Plethon, *Commentary* 12.

175. Plethon, *Magical Oracles* 34.

176. Plethon, *Commentary* 33. See also *Laws* III.34.28, 30, 70.

177. Plethon, *Magical Oracles* 32.

contains them as determinate Ideas or Forms, she contains them in all their potentially infinite diversity and abundance.

Interestingly, this also makes Hera the goddess who contains all numbers and magnitudes, because the Forms in Poseidon differ in type or quality, but their unlimited instances in Hera differ in quantity; the infinity of numbers exist as a unity in her. The numbers that we humans comprehend are just images or shadows of those that exist in Hera. By contemplating them, we are led to grasp the Forms, to know the gods, as Plato taught. Matter and space, in a broad abstract sense, are required for endless reproduction and diversity among things. Plethon calls Hera "the seat here for the forms" within our material world.[178]

Poseidon and Hera are the Ideas of Form and Matter, respectively. In accord with the sexual metaphor, Plethon tells us that the contributions of Poseidon and Hera to creation are analogous to semen and menstrual fluid (traditionally—but inaccurately—associated with the form and matter, respectively, of a fetus).[179] Both gods contain all their offspring in potential form, but in different ways. We will see that this sexual metaphor is applied also at the lower levels of creation. Poseidon and Hera are king and queen of the Olympians, but father and mother of the celestial gods. Plethon calls Hera "Motherless Mother" (ἀμήτωρ μήτηρ, *amêtôr mêtêr*) because she, like all the supercelestial gods, emanates from Zeus without the benefit of the female element.[180] This is because the supercelestial gods are immaterial Forms or Ideas; she, in fact, as the Form of Matter, creates the possibility of multiplicity and material existence.

For the reasons we have seen—that Poseidon and Hera are the father and mother of the celestial gods, who are their "high-born" offspring—Plethon calls them husband and wife, and this will seem very strange to anyone familiar with Greek mythology, in which Hera is always the wife of Zeus.[181] Indeed, they are the archetypal married couple. Plethon's relationships are dictated by the logic of his theology. The first principle, whom he has decided to call Zeus, is above and beyond distinctions. Therefore, in

---

178. Plethon, *Laws* III.35.5.

179. Plethon, *Laws* III.15.13.

180. Plethon, *Laws* III.34.21.

181. Plethon, *Laws* III.34.3, 21, 42; III.35.5, 6.

particular, the distinction of Form and Matter, and by extension of god and goddess, must come after him. To the primary Ideas of Form and Matter he gives the names Poseidon and Hera.[182] Below them are four pentads of supercelestial gods, as we will see.

Apollo and Artemis: Identity and Difference

Plato's dialogue *The Sophist* (254b–c) discusses five "greatest kinds" (μέγιστα γένη, *megista genê*) or highest categories, which are closely connected with the highest pentad of gods below Poseidon and Hera. These greatest kinds are Being, Identity, Difference, Rest, and Motion. After Poseidon and Hera, the next gods in the order of emanation are Apollo and Artemis, twin children of Zeus in Greek mythology.

Plethon tells us that **Apollo** rules and governs Identity (τὸ ταὐτόν, ταὐτότης, *to tauton, tautotês*); he gives each thing its identity—that is, he makes it what it is—by uniting its various properties into one thing. For example, the identity of the number three is grounded in a synthesis of its properties: it is odd, it is prime, it follows two, it is the square root of nine, and so on. So each thing is a unique combination of its characteristics. In this way Apollo creates harmony in the cosmos, just as in music harmony is a combination of differing tones into a coherent whole.[183] He also maintains concord among souls, and so he is responsible for justice and wisdom. He is the god of unity, as shown by his name, *Apollôn* (Ἀπόλλων), which philosophers explained as meaning "not many" (ἀ + πολλοί, *a + polloi*) and "simple" (ἁπλοῦν, *haploun*).[184] He establishes the unity of the individual Forms. Another reason to call the Idea of Identity "Apollo" is that he is traditionally the leader of the Muses, who are the patrons of the arts and sciences, and he is often shown holding a lyre to symbolize that he is the source of harmony. As he bestows beauty in the arts, so he bestows grace on our bodies, and as a traditional god of healing, he grants us health (the harmony of the body). We invoke him to inspire our love in divine beauty. He purifies and restores integrity.

Complementary to Apollo is his twin sister **Artemis**, who is the Idea of Difference or Otherness (τὸ θάτερον, *to thateron*; ἑτερότης, *heterotês*); she causes the differentiation

---

182. A possible explanation of Plethon's names comes from Proclus, who notes that both Poseidon and Hera address Zeus as "Father," but that could be simply a term of respect (Hladký, *Plethon*, 115).

183. Plethon, *Laws* III.34.27, III.35.7.

184. E.g., Plato, *Cratylus* 405c.

of wholes into their separate parts.[185] Therefore, she divides Forms, separating the differing species within a genus, according to the specific identities given them by Apollo. For example, she separates the class of number into odd and even, and further into the individual numbers; she divides a triangle into its three constituent line segments. She multiplies the unity of the Ideas into the particular and individual things belonging to them, and in addition she divides these physical things into their parts, each part with its own identity. She analyzes and articulates the constituents of any whole.

Artemis is also, according to Plethon, responsible for giving our bodies moderation, power, strength, and soundness (ἀρτεμής, *artemês*).[186] But she is especially responsible for giving our immortal souls courage and self-control by separating them from our inferior parts (our mortal bodies), which is a kind of purification.

By the way, Plethon did not consider the body and its pleasures to be evil, and he was opposed to monkish asceticism. But we each are the union of a higher soul, which is immortal and created by the Olympian gods, and a body, which is mortal and created by the Titans. We humans are thus essential to the perfection of the cosmos, for we are the boundary that joins the immortal and mortal realms of being. Nevertheless, just as the gods govern us, it is appropriate that the higher parts of our souls govern and regulate the lower parts. We invoke Artemis for aid in avoiding error and for guidance in living rightly.

The complementarity of Apollo and Artemis is consistent with Plethon's association of male gods with unity and female goddesses with diversity and multiplicity.[187] Things are similar to each other in some respects and differ in others, and so Apollo and Artemis together establish the structure of the realm of Forms or Ideas by unifying them within themselves and differentiating them from one another.

Hephaistos, Dionysos, and Athena: Stability and Change

The five "greatest kinds" defined by Plato do not correspond directly to the five gods after Poseidon and Hera. As you've seen, the Ideas of Identity and Difference correspond to Apollo and Artemis. The remaining three Ideas are Being, Rest, and Motion, but, as will

---

185. Plethon, *Laws* III.34.27.

186. Plethon, *Laws* III.35.8. Plato suggests this etymology for her name in his *Cratylus* 406b.

187. Plethon, *Laws* III.34.25.

be explained, the next three gods correspond to Rest and two different kinds of Motion. Therefore, Plethon is dividing the Idea of Motion, and Being seems to correspond to Zeus as Being-Itself.[188] Let us consider the three gods who govern Rest and Motion.

Hephaistos is the Idea of Rest (στάσις, *stasis*); he governs stability and permanence in temporal reality. He is also the source of changelessness and immutability, and thus he establishes all the gods in their eternal relationships; he grants them their domains of responsibility. Therefore Plethon calls him the leader of the supercelestial gods after Poseidon.[189] As the source of stability in our world, he provides everything its permanent and proper location or seat in space. We invoke Hephaistos to keep us steadfast in the path of virtue and excellence or whenever we need to be firm.

It is unclear why Plethon names the Idea of Rest "Hephaistos," but it may be an esoteric interpretation of two traditional myths concerning him.[190] In "The Return of Hephaistos," he was angry at his mother, Hera, because she had rejected him due to his lameness, and so he made a magical golden throne for her. When she sat in it, she could not get out (thus the idea of permanence and place). The other gods could not convince him to return to Olympus to free her, until Dionysos got him drunk and led him back. (We will see that Dionysos governs self-caused motion, especially leading upward to the gods.) In the "The Net of Hephaistos," Hephaistos lays a trap for his wife Aphrodite and her lover Ares (they represent love and strife, the two fundamental forces in the cosmos, according to Empedocles).[191] When they are in bed making love, he traps them with an unbreakable net, thus immobilizing them. He invites all the other gods to have a laugh at the pair until Poseidon convinces him to release the lovers.

Another of Plato's greatest kinds, and complementary to Rest, is Motion or Change (κίνησις, *kinêsis*), which Plethon divides into Active Motion and Passive Motion, as Plato also does in the *Phaedrus* and *Laws*.[192]

---

188. Plethon, *Laws* III.34.27. These correspondences are discussed by Hladký, *Plethon*, 105.

189. Plethon, *Laws* III.35.13.

190. Hladký, *Plethon*, 116–17.

191. Empedocles, LM 22D73 (DK 31B17) in Laks and Most, *Early Greek Philosophy V: Western Greek Thinkers*, Part 2, 410–23.

192. Plethon, *Laws* III.34.27, III.35.10–11; Plato, *Phaedrus* 245c–246a; Plato, *Laws* 10.893b–896.

The Idea of Active Change or Self-Motion (αὐτοκινησία, *autokinêsia*) is named **Dionysos**, also called **Bacchus**. This is the motion characteristic of souls, which have their own ends and purposes, which they seek to fulfill. Therefore, he is the creator of all immortal souls, including those of celestial gods, daimons, and humans. Such self-directed movement, seeking its own end, its own entelechy, is organized by looking toward what is best for itself (and others of its kind), its own perfection, seeking its own "good," and so this motion looks up to the cause of its being. Thus, Dionysos lifts us up, leading up toward what is more perfect, toward the gods. Such motion is motivated by desire for the good.

If you think of Dionysos as the god of drunkenness and wild revelry, then you may be surprised at his role in Plethon's system, but it is consistent with the understanding of Dionysos in the Platonic tradition. To make this clear, I need to review some Dionysian mythology and how it was interpreted by Platonists to teach an important spiritual lesson. For the most part I will be following Damascius, who led the Platonic Academy in Athens until all the Pagan schools were closed by the Christian emperor Justinian I in 529 CE.[193]

In an Orphic poem Dionysos was the son of Zeus and Persephone and was destined to succeed him.[194] Hera, however, was jealous because she was not the mother, and so she sent the Titans to seduce the child with toys. While he was distracted, especially by his own face in a mirror, they carved him into seven pieces and cooked and ate six. Therefore, Zeus blasted the Titans with his thunderbolt, burning them to ash, which therefore combined Dionysos's divine essence with the Titan's material substance.[195] Humans were made from this ash, so we are both divine and mortal. Athena retrieved the seventh part, his heart, and took it to Zeus, who made a potion that he gave to Semele, a mortal woman, which made her pregnant with Dionysos. Zeus had promised to grant her every wish, but she was tricked by Hera into demanding to see the god as he really is. He showed himself and she was destroyed by the divine fire. Zeus rescued the fetus from her womb and sewed it into his "thigh" (a euphemism for his testicles),

---

193. Westerink, *Damascius: Commentary on Plato's* Phaedo §§165–72, 98–105.

194. Kerényi, *Gods of the Greeks*, 252–9.

195. In Orphic mythology (but not Plethon) the Titans are born of Earth.

from which Dionysos was eventually reborn, whole again and divine. Thus, he was called the twice-born god and the first Bacchus.

What an odd story! Let's see what the Platonists make of it. Damascius writes, as do Plato and Plethon, that Dionysos is the cause of all motion and change in the cosmos because, as Plato shows in the *Phaedrus*, only an immortal soul can be the originating cause of change (for soulless things are moved by other things) and Dionysos is the creator of immortal souls.[196] As he was dismembered by the Titans, so the prime mover is fragmented and dispersed in the material world. As a consequence, the world soul is spread throughout the cosmos and fractures into individual souls in individual bodies. These fragments are disordered and chaotic and lack unity. Because of his double birth, Dionysos has a double nature: indivisible as a god in Olympus (the realm of Ideas) and divided and fragmented in the material world. Humans are similarly twofold: fragmented when sunk in our Titanic material nature, distracted by all amusements around us and by our egos, but unified and whole when we ascend toward the gods.

As dismembered Dionysos was reborn through Semele and Zeus, becoming reunified and ascending to divinity, so also the philosopher, seeking to reunify their fragmented soul, strives to become a Bacchus by dedication to the god and by becoming like him. This is accomplished by freeing the soul from the body, so far as possible while still alive, and reuniting the fragments of its essential nature. This is literal ecstasy because the soul stands outside (Grk., *ek* + *stasis*) the body. By giving our heart to Zeus, who is the unitary source of all the eternal Ideas, we dwell among the gods, and the disconnected pieces of our psyche are reunited; we are reborn whole. Thus, Dionysos is both the liberator and unifier of the soul, and to become a Bacchus is to be freed from the bonds of the material world and to possess a soul that is whole and complete.

Plato famously wrote, "The narthex-bearers are many but the Bacchi are few."[197] In other words, many people carry the Dionysian narthex staff in the religious processions, but very few have been initiated into the Dionysian mysteries and have experienced the liberation granted by the god. The philosopher, however, who becomes a Bacchus

---

196. Westerink, *Damascius: Commentary on Plato's* Phaedo §171, 104–5; Plato, *Laws* 672a5–d4; Plato, *Phaedrus* 245c–246a; Plethon, *Laws* III.34.27.

197. Plato, *Phaedo* 69c, my translation.

rises above the chaos of Becoming and becomes aware of the confused lives of the mere narthex-bearers.

Ancient Platonists taught that initiation into philosophy progresses through the same three degrees as initiation into the Mysteries: purification, illumination, and union.[198] In philosophical initiation each stage reinterprets the four cardinal virtues or excellences (prudence, justice, fortitude, self-control) at successively higher levels (see chapter 9 on the excellences).[199] In the first degree of initiation, purification, they are interpreted as cathartic or purificatory virtues. In a philosophical context purification means separating the soul from the distractions of embodiment and concentrating one's attention into the immortal part of the soul (see chapter 10 on philosophical purification).

We invoke Dionysos to strengthen our aspiration for the best and to live a life worthy of the gods. And when we fail to act reasonably, we ask Dionysos to bring us back quickly to reason and virtue. As philosophers (lovers of wisdom), we call on him to help us live the Dionysian life, by detaching from the confusion of our embodied lives and by striving to unify our minds and to raise them to the divine, to help us to become Bacchi.

The goddess **Athena** is the Idea of Passive or Other-Caused Motion—of change that is not self-generated but is caused by something outside of itself. These are physical changes, impulses and reactions, caused by one thing responding to another. They include internal bodily changes that are passive processes and not motivated by desire for the good; they are reactive and "mechanical." Because such changes must be transmitted by some physical medium, Athena regulates forms and processes that are inseparable from matter. In contrast, Dionysos oversees processes that are self-caused and therefore are independent of matter and separable from it. This is why the immortal higher soul is separable from the body but physiological processes are not. Dionysos and Athena are the Ideas of goal-directed and reactive change, respectively.

I have mentioned the Neoplatonic Triadic Principle by which Ideas have three "movements": remaining in themselves, proceeding downward into greater manifestation, and turning back toward their causes (see page 50). This principle is embodied in

---

198. Westerink, *Damascius: Commentary on Plato's* Phaedo §168, 100–1.

199. Westerink, *Damascius: Commentary on Plato's* Phaedo §149, 90–91.

these three gods. Plethon associates Hephaistos with a staying or abiding (μονή, *monê*), by which the Idea remains itself, its changeless permanence.[200] Athena is associated with procession (πρόοδος, *proödos*) and thrusting outward (ὦσις, *ôsis*), by which the Idea emanates and manifests. Dionysos is associated with the return (ἐπιστροφή, *epistrophê*) and a pulling or attraction (ὁλκή, *holkê*) toward the higher Idea that draws the manifested form toward its perfection.

If you are familiar with Athena as a goddess of wisdom, Plethon's use of her name for the Idea of Other-Caused Change may be surprising, but Neoplatonic discussions of her can help us understand.[201] First, Athena is traditionally a goddess of craft: she invented weaving and other technologies. In other words, she takes Ideas and manifests them in the material world; thus, "Worker" (Ἐργάνη, *Erganê*) is one of her ancient names. In some ways she is similar to Hephaistos, another craftsperson; in mythology they were both born from a single parent: Athena from Zeus, Hephaistos from Hera. In other ways they are complementary: Hephaistos is the craftsman for the gods, so his workmanship remains on Olympus, but Athena is the patron of human crafts that benefit us on earth. He remains, she manifests.

Next, Athena is traditionally a goddess of warcraft and defense, which is how she is treated in most of the ancient hymns.[202] As such, she uses physical force wisely, especially for repelling attack. In a well-known myth she pushed Hephaistos away to keep him from raping her: getting rid of something unwanted. She is also named "Pallas," which Plato derives from armed dances and the verb *pallein* (πάλλειν), which means to shake something or to be shaken (πάλλεσθαι, *pallesthai*): other-caused motion.[203]

Athena's spear and shield symbolize her functions. Her spear represents the power by which Ideas govern change in the material world, *proceeding* into manifestation (as opposed to the Ideas of Hephaistos, which *remain* above in Olympus). Athena stands aloof and untouched above the physical changes that she causes, governing them from on high. Therefore, she is called "lover of wisdom" because her Ideas govern change in

---

200. Plethon, *Laws* III.34.27; III.35.10, 11, 13.

201. Van den Berg, *Proclus' Hymns*, 281–96.

202. Van den Berg, *Proclus' Hymns*, 275.

203. Plato, *Cratylus* 406d–407a. See also Hladký, *Plethon*, 117.

the world, but she is called also "lover of war" because she protects the realm of Ideas from contamination by materiality, preserving the metaphysical priority of the Ideas, as symbolized by her shield.

The inside of the shield in Phidias's statue of Athena that stood in the Parthenon depicted the Gigantomachy, in which Athena used her shield to protect the gods from the earthly Giants, whom Plethon interprets as materialist philosophers and monotheists who deny the divinity of our world (discussed in chapter 1). Proclus teaches that the Gigantomachy also takes place in each of our souls, for we side with the Giants or gods depending on whether we are governed by the parts of our souls born of Earth or the parts born of Olympus.[204] In this war, Athena protects us from the emotional excesses and irrational behaviors that keep us mired in the fragmented and chaotic material world and alienated from spiritual unity; she slays the beasts of our emotions and calms the waves of Becoming.

Therefore, it is Athena's courageous and relentless defense that allows Dionysos to return to Zeus; she provides the cover that allows him to seek the Good and to *return* to his source. Even though Dionysos's body—which is our embodied soul—is dismembered, Athena rescues his heart—which symbolizes the *nous*—and brings it to Zeus intact, whence it may be reborn unified and complete. Our fragmented souls think disjointed ideas one after another, but our Bacchic *nous* grasps Ideas immediately and holistically. As Bacchi, our individual, personal *nous* returns to the universal *Nous* of Zeus.

Summing up, we can see that Dionysos and Athena are a complementary pair analogous to the twins Apollo and Artemis. They are alike in being born from Zeus without benefit of a mother and are both traditionally androgynous, as befits deities of transformation. As a pair, they are complementary to Hephaistos, the Idea of changelessness, also born from a single parent, Hera. These three gods represent Ideas that *remain* immutable above (Hephaistos), *proceed* into the material world, governing change (Athena), and serve as a goal for sentient souls seeking to *return* above (Dionysos).

Now that we understand Athena better, we can see that we can call on her for aid in the crafts and for her protection. Hers is the power to effect change, especially in the material world. Whenever, through lack of wisdom or prudence, we have committed some fault,

---

204. Van den Berg, *Proclus' Hymns*, 285.

we invoke her to inspire us with intelligence and to bring us back to correct behavior. She can separate us from all that is superfluous, useless, distracting, dangerous, or obstructive. Thus, Plotinus taught that we should think of our soul like a statue.[205] We chisel away a little that's superfluous here, smooth and polish a little there, and work at it until we have shaped it and made it as beautiful as we are able: an image of a god. Athena can protect us and help us in this project, to reach our spiritual goal: to make ourselves Bacchi.

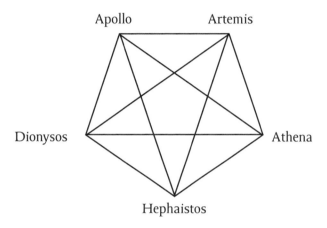

Figure 2. First Pentad

After Poseidon and Hera, the remaining twenty supercelestial gods are grouped naturally in four pentads, or groups of five. If they have a triad over dyad (3 + 2) or monad over tetrad (1 + 4) structure, then their relationships are represented by an upright pentagram. If they have a dyad over triad (2 + 3) structure, as does this pentad (Apollo, Artemis, Hephaistos, Dionysos, Athena), then it is represented by an inverted pentagram (which, needless to say, does not imply anything nefarious).[206] You will gain many

---

205. Plotinus, *Enneads* 1.6.9.

206. Plethon does not arrange the gods in a pentagram (although it was an ancient Pythagorean sign) nor mention their pentadic structure, which might have been discovered by Schultze, *Geschichte der Philosophie der Renaissance, Erste Band: Georgios Gemistos Plethon und seine reformatorischen Bestrebungen,* 170. Nevertheless, this pentadic structure helps us understand the relations among the gods.

deep insights by contemplating the connections in these pentagrams. Plethon calls the group of Poseidon, Hera, and this first pentad the **seven elder** or **superior deities**.[207]

Atlas, Tithonos, and Dione: Gods of Heavenly Souls

The second pentad of Olympian gods produce immortal beings in the heavens and on earth; they produce the souls of beings who exist in time but are everlasting and in that sense immortal. The higher three, Atlas, Tithonos, and Dione, are the gods who emanate the celestial gods, the gods who reside in the heavens (described under "The Celestial Gods" on page 74). Since Plethon lived more than a century before Copernicus, he thought that Earth was at the center of the universe and that Earth was surrounded by seven revolving planetary spheres, all surrounded by the sphere of fixed stars, including the zodiac.[208] In this view the stars and planets are visible gods, the **celestial gods**. Although we now know that Earth and other planets revolve around the sun, we will see that the ancient perspective has psychological validity in Plethon's theology. Plethon's chapters on the celestial gods were burned by Scholarios, but in chapter 10 I provide a possible reconstruction of his doctrines.

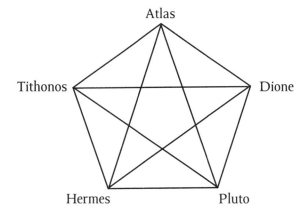

Figure 3. Second Pentad

---

207. Plethon, *Laws*, table of contents, III.35.6.

208. Plethon uses the Greek word *astra* (ἄστρα) for the fixed stars and the word *asteres* (ἀστέρες) for the planets, sometimes qualified as "wandering" (πλάνητες ἀστέρες, *planêtes asteres*); both *astron* (ἄστρον) and *astêr* (ἀστήρ) are ordinary Greek words for "star."

Atlas is the Idea of the Celestial Gods as a whole. Presumably, Plethon names this god "Atlas" because in traditional mythology Atlas supports the heavens.

Below Atlas is **Tithonos**, the god who is the Idea of the Planetary Gods, which correspond to the sun and moon and the five lesser planets (Mercury, Venus, Mars, Jupiter, Saturn). Although we now know there are other planets orbiting the sun, they were unknown in Plethon's time and not part of his system. Since these modern planets are not visible to the naked eye, they do not have the same psychological and spiritual importance as the ancient seven.

Even if you know your Greek myths, you might be unfamiliar with Tithonos; in fact he is not exactly a god in traditional mythology. According to one story, he was a mortal astronomer who stayed up every night studying the stars and planets. Therefore, Eos, the goddess of the dawn, saw him every morning and fell in love with the handsome young man. They married and she begged Zeus to grant him immortality, but she made the tragic mistake of failing to request eternal youth to go along with it. So Tithonos, though immortal, grew ancient and finally shriveled into no more than a voice, although some sources say that Eos restored him to health and vigor with "oriental drugs."[209] Tithonos seems an odd choice of name for the god of the planets, and Plethon does not explain his reasons. Perhaps he chose this name because Tithonos is an immortal astronomer and so associated with the planets. Since he lives in the House of Dawn, he can observe all the traditional planets, including the sun. It is also possible that Plethon used divination or theurgical techniques to discover the name of this god.

After Tithonos comes **Dione**, the goddess who is the Idea of the Fixed Stars, which include the zodiac and other stars that appear to revolve in lockstep around Earth. In myth, Dione is often associated with water, and so this seems an odd name for the goddess of the fixed stars. Some Orphic sources, however, make her the daughter of Ouranos (Heaven). The name "Dione" is a feminine form of "Zeus" (root *Di-*) and may be interpreted "goddess of the bright sky."[210]

---

209. Bell, *Bell's New Pantheon* (1790), s.v. "Tithonous."

210. Kerényi, *Gods of the Greeks*, 68.

Hermes and Pluto: Gods of Earthly Souls

Not only are there immortal beings in the heavens, but there are also earthly beings with immortal souls: daimons and people. **Hermes** is the Idea of Earthly Daimons (χθόνιοι δαίμονες, *chthonioi daimones*) and is the god who emanates and rules them. They have aethereal bodies that are pure, unageing, and immortal. As Hermes is the divine messenger, so daimons are the emissaries between gods and humans and the closest divine beings to us; Plethon stresses that they are entirely good.[211] They are discussed in greater detail later in this chapter (see "The Earthly Daimons" on page 77) and in chapter 10.

We come now to **Pluto**, who emanates the immortal human mind (νοῦς, *nous*), the lowest immortal being.[212] In other words, Pluto is the Idea of the Immortal Human Soul. Plethon names the god *Ploutôn* (Πλούτων), a Greek god of the underworld equated with the god Hades and Roman Pluto (which is why I use the spelling "Pluto" for this god). Plato derives the name from *Ploutos* (πλοῦτος, wealth), also considered a god, because in the end everything returns to the lord of the underworld, who is also the source of the riches and bounty found in the earth. It might seem odd to name the god of immortal human souls after the god of the dead, but Pluto cares for our souls between incarnations. We invoke him to protect us here on earth and to lift us eventually to the higher regions. Also, as we will see later, Kore, or Persephone, is the goddess responsible for our mortal bodies and therefore Pluto and Kore, as king and queen of the underworld, create us as embodied immortal souls; they provide our immortal and mortal parts. Plato also discussed the old Orphic idea that the body is a tomb (σῶμα σῆμα, *sôma sêma*) and, therefore, that when we are incarnated on earth we are actually living in the lower world ruled by Pluto and Kore.[213]

Pluto is the Idea of the Immortal Human Soul, which confers consciousness on our mortal bodies. Plethon tells us that Pluto contains in a state of unity the fate and destiny of every individual human soul.[214] Therefore, the heroes are gathered around Pluto, for he is their patron and they are our paragons. As the god of the human

---

211. Plethon, *Laws* III.34.6.

212. You might wonder whether Plethon thinks animals have immortal souls; I will discuss this later (under "Animal Souls" on page 81).

213. Plato, *Gorgias* 492e–493a; Plato, *Cratylus* 400b–d.

214. Plethon, *Laws* III.15.20, III.35.20.

conscious mind, Pluto is also the source of all human creativity, for he contains in a state of unity every work of art or craft that a human might produce. (Plethon writes that this is analogous to the way Hera contains all numbers in herself in a state of unity.[215]) Whenever someone creates something, it comes as inspiration from Pluto—Plato calls him "the wealth-giver"—but each person receives their own unique inspiration.

Goddesses of the Elements

The third pentad of Olympians comprises five goddesses who emanate the elements (στοιχεῖα, *stoicheia*): Rhea, Leto, Hekate, Tethys, and Hestia. They are all goddesses because the elements are Ideas of matter; they are the substance of the material world. The pentagram represents many important relationships among the Ideas of the elements, which I'll discuss later.

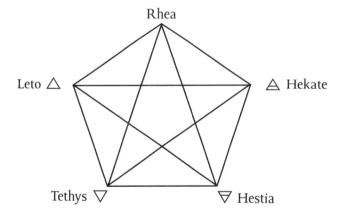

Figure 4. Third Pentad

Rhea is the Idea of the Elements in general, but, as you probably know, we are not talking about elements in the same sense as in modern physics and chemistry, which came centuries after Plethon lived. Rather, these are the four ancient elements Fire, Air, Water, and Earth (symbolized by △, △, ▽, and ▽, respectively), but in Plethon's philosophy

---

215. Plethon, *Laws* III.15.20.

the elements represent general states and processes in the material world.[216] As such, they are eternal (timeless) Platonic Ideas existing outside of our world, but they are produced by the lowest rank of Olympians, who are nearest to the world enclosed in the heavens, which exists in time and space. They are the direct governors of natural processes. Plethon calls the goddess of all the elements "Rhea" (Ῥέα), presumably because Platonists connected her name with the ever-changing flux or flow of things in the material world (ῥοή, *rhoê*, flux, flow; from ῥέω, *rheô*, to flow or be in an ever-changing state).[217]

Leto is the Idea of the highest element, Fire (πῦρ, *pyr*), which Plethon also calls *Aether*.[218] In ancient Greek, *aithêr* (αἰθήρ) refers to the bright, pure air of the heavens, which is above the ordinary lower air (ἀήρ, *aêr*) that surrounds us, but philosophers also connected the word *aithêr* to *aithô* (αἴθω), which means to burn or blaze. Each of the four elements has an associated power or quality, and for Fire it is warmth (θερμόν, *thermon*), which gives Fire the secondary power of separation or discrimination (διακριτικόν, *diakritikon*); it loosens structures and relationships; it unbinds things. We can think of the way things melt or evaporate when they are heated. As a consequence, heat causes mixed things to disassociate into their separate parts, as in distillation. Fire also has a natural upward movement, as we see in a flame, which is why Aether is the outermost elemental sphere, above air, water, and earth; it is ever-moving, but because it cannot rise above the heavens, it moves in endless cycles there. The celestial gods (planets and stars), which rotate around the earth, have bodies made of the purest and brightest Fire, which is why they are visible to us. This is because they are nearly immaterial, and Aether is the least dense, most subtle element. The souls of daimons and humans also have aethereal vehicles, which are warm, but not so fiery as those of the celestials gods, and so they are invisible. Humans of course also have material bodies composed of all the elements (see "Visible Beings" on page 73).

Why did Plethon call the Idea of Fire "Leto"? One probable reason is that in Greek mythology Leto is the mother (by Zeus) of the twins Apollo and Artemis, from whom

216. I capitalize the names of the philosophical elements to distinguish them from the ordinary use of the terms fire, air, water, and earth.

217. E.g., Plato, *Cratylus* 402b.

218. Plethon, *Laws* III.34.27, 44.

emanate the "greater lights" of the heavens, the Sun and Moon; they are the most visible manifestations of the aethereal Fire.

Hekate is the Idea of Air, the complementary element to Fire, for its quality is cool (ψυχρόν, *psychron*) and it has the power of connection (συνεκτικόν, *synektikon*).[219] Whereas Fire fuels change and drives things apart, Air allows them to settle into a stable state; it allows their internal connections to solidify into strong bonds. Like Fire but to a lesser degree, Air has a natural tendency to rise, but it is also expansive; it tends to spread in space.

It is not obvious why Plethon called the goddess of Air "Hekate." One possibility is that he saw her power of connection in the common *Hekate Triformis* depiction of the goddess, in which she has three heads or three complete bodies joined together. She is also the goddess of the crossroads (τρίοδος, *triodos*) where three roads converge. He might also have been thinking of Proclus's citation of an Orphic text in which Hekate is the daughter of Leto.[220]

Fire and Air are complementary elements—warm and cool, separating and connecting—as shown by the horizontal line between them in the third pentagram (see figure 4 on page 66). As opposed to Water and Earth, they are the two active elements, for by their separating and connecting power they are the primary causes of change in the material world. They combine in the warm, breath-like animating spirit (πνεῦμα, *pneuma*) found in all living things. Proclus writes that Fire and Air are both subtle and mobile.

The Idea of Water (ὕδωρ, *hydôr*) is **Tethys**, who in traditional mythology is the goddess of fresh water and the mother of the river gods.[221] The principal quality of Water is wetness (ὑγρόν, *hygron*), which gives it the power of dissolution (διάρρυτον, *diarryton*). This is another sort of separation, which relates Water to Fire, as shown by the leftmost line of the pentagram (connecting $\triangle$ and ∇). Conversely, the warmth of Fire melts things, which is a process of dissolution producing a watery fluid. So Fire creates Water. Dissolution involves a loosening and breaking of relationships, so that they have the potential of reforming in different ways; it loosens things up. Water is denser than Fire

---

219. Plethon, *Laws* III.34.27.

220. Hladký, *Plethon*, 120.

221. Plethon, *Laws* III.34.27.

and Air, and its natural motion is to descend. It is, however, like Air in being expansive and conforming to the shape of its container.

The last and lowest element is Earth (γῆ, *gê*), which is complementary to Water, as indicated by the horizontal line joining them in the pentagram. Its quality is dryness (ξηρόν, *xêron*), which gives it the power of compaction, fixation, or solidification (πηκτόν, *pêkton*). In contrast to dissolution, dryness establishes, stabilizes, and fixes the relationships among a thing's parts, like a metal solidifying, a crystal forming, or clay drying. This is aided by the cool connecting power of Air, and this relationship is shown in the right-hand edge of the pentagram (connecting △ and ▽).

The Idea of Earth is called **Hestia** by Plethon, which is a surprising choice, since she is the goddess of the hearth fire, and so might seem a natural choice for the goddess of Fire.[222] According to Plato, however, whereas traditionally the other Olympian gods travel about, Hestia, as the hearth goddess, remains behind, in the center like the earth, an anchor of permanence and stability for the household, the temple, and the city.[223] Moreover, the philosopher Anaxagoras and the playwrights Sophocles and Euripides apparently associated the Earth with Hestia because they both remain in the center.[224]

Water and Earth are more passive than Fire and Air and are responsive to the forces of Fire and Air. Both are heavy, and their natural motion is downward. Proclus writes that they are relatively dense and immobile. The crossed edges on the third pentagram (△▽ and △▽) indicate how the warmth of Fire can melt the structure of Earth, changing it to its opposite Water, and the coolness of Air can freeze the chaotic flux of Water, changing it to stable Earth. More generally, the separation of Fire and the fixation of Earth are in opposition to each other, as are the connection of Air and the dissolution of Water.

With the goddesses of the elements we come to the end of the Olympians, the "high-born" children of Zeus, who are capable of generating immortal beings; the remainder of the supercelestial gods dwell in Tartarus.

---

222. Plethon, *Laws* III.34.27.

223. Hladký, *Plethon*, 120.

224. Plato, *Phaedrus*, ed. Yunis, 140; Iamblichus, *The Theology of Arithmetic*, 40.

The Titans: The Gods of Tartarus

With the Titans, the gods who dwell in Tartarus, we come to the fourth pentad. Plethon calls them the illegitimate (νόθος, *nothos*) children of Zeus, but since all the supercelestial gods are produced by Zeus alone without benefit of sex, "illegitimate" here seems to mean only that the Titan have less power than the Olympian gods, and as explained previously, I call them "low-born."[225] Specifically, the "low-born" gods of Tartarus generate perishable things, whereas the "high-born" Olympians generate things that are imperishable and eternal. Certainly, the Titans are as worthy of worship as the Olympians, as Plethon makes clear.[226]

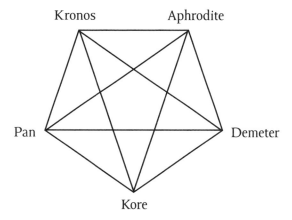

Figure 5. Fourth Pentad

Kronos and **Aphrodite** are the king and queen of the gods of Tartarus, an image of Poseidon and Hera, the king and queen of the gods of Olympus. As such, Kronos is the Idea of Perishable Form, the cause of the forms of the things in the physical world, all of which are perishable. Likewise, Aphrodite is the Idea of Perishable Matter, the matter of things in the physical world, temporarily organized by the forms (recall "Divine Gender" on page 47). Although the elements themselves are eternal, their combinations

225. Plethon, *Laws* I.5.4, 6; III.34.2, 40; III.35.12.

226. Plethon, *Laws* III.34.4; III.35.12, 19.

in particular forms are impermanent; all living beings on earth are mortal. As Hera contains in herself the unending series of numbers, Aphrodite contains the unending generations of mortal things, which are endless, not by individually lasting forever, but through reproduction.

Since Kronos is the leader of the Titans in traditional mythology, his name is a reasonable choice for the chief of the Tartarean gods. Another possible reason is the similarity between the Greek words *Kronos* (Κρόνος) and *khronos* (χρόνος), which means a period of time, a season, an age, or a lifetime. This connection was noticed in ancient times and is discussed by Plutarch, who is in the Golden Chain.[227] Therefore "Kronos" is a good name for the Idea of things that come to be and pass away in time. As we will see, Kronos has the aid of Helios in generating perishable nature (see "The Celestial Gods" on page 74).

Aphrodite is a more confusing choice, since in mythology she is not the wife of Kronos (usually Rhea) or even a Titan. However, as a goddess of sex and reproduction, it is reasonable that Aphrodite presides over the transmission of eternity into the mortal world by the succession of beings. Proclus writes that she manages all conjunctions in heaven and on earth, and that she perfects their "generative processions."[228] Plutarch remarks that some dwellers in the west call the winter Kronos, the summer Aphrodite, and the spring Persephone; he writes that they "believe that from Kronos and Aphrodite all things have their origin."[229] Perhaps these considerations motivated Plethon to call this goddess "Aphrodite."

Next among the Titans we come to **Pan** and **Demeter**, who are the Ideas of Animals and Plants, respectively. These names make sense, for traditionally Pan is the god of wild animals, and Demeter is the goddess who brought agriculture to Greece and who rejuvenates plant life each spring when her daughter Kore returns to her from the underworld. Plethon did not know about microorganisms—they had not been discovered yet—and we may wonder what god generates them. Some of them are animal-like, others plant-like, and so they might come from Pan and Demeter, respectively. Or perhaps they come from Kronos and Aphrodite, who generate mortal things in general. A third possibility

227. Plutarch, *Isis and Osiris* 32.363D, in Plutarch, *Moralia: Vol. V*, 76–77.

228. Hladký, *Plethon*, 121.

229. Plutarch, *Isis and Osiris* 69.378E, in Plutarch, *Moralia: Vol. V*, 160–61; see also Hladký, *Plethon*, 120–21.

is that they are generated by other, unnamed Titans, for after Pan and Demeter, Plethon mentions "all the other [Titans] have received different parts, some greater some lesser, of mortal things."[230]

Finally, we come to the last of the named Titans, **Kore** (the Maiden), also known as Persephone, who is the Idea of the Mortal Human Body, which includes its physiological processes. As previously mentioned, she joins with her husband Pluto in creating humans: he provides our immortal soul and she provides the rest. By thus connecting the immortal with the mortal, human beings have the unique position of straddling on the immortal-mortal boundary; we are in effect the linchpins joining these two parts of the cosmos into a unity. This is how Plethon interprets the traditional myth in which, under orders of Zeus, Pluto abducts Kore to be his wife.[231] They reign as king and queen of the underworld, and thus there is an alliance by marriage between the gods of Olympus and Tartarus.

The Generations of the Gods

Plethon explains how Zeus generates first the Olympian gods, then the Titans, and from them the celestial gods.[232] This will seem backward if you are familiar with traditional Greek genealogies of the gods, such as Hesiod's *Theogony*, in which there are three generations of gods: first the primordial gods ruled by Ouranos (Heaven) and Gaia (Earth), next the Titans ruled by Kronos and Rhea, and finally the Olympians ruled by Zeus and Hera. The two orders can be reconciled as follows. Plethon describes the generation of the gods in their order of ontological causation or emanation, in the priority of their being. Traditional mythology describes the gods in the order in which they were discovered. People first became aware of the gods of nature, of earth and heaven, of the sun and moon, of the planets and stars: the celestial gods of the third order. Later they discovered the higher gods of the second order, who are the eternal Ideas. First they discovered the Titans, who govern perishable nature, and later the Olympians who organize the eternal Ideas. (This might have been the discovery of the Pythagorean-Platonist schools, at least

---

230. Plethon, *Laws* III.34.33.

231. Plethon, *Laws* III.34.33.

232. Plethon, *Summary* 2; Plethon, *Laws* III.34.40–43.

in the Western Tradition.) Finally, especially with the middle and later Platonists, we have a recognition of the highest order of reality, the Ineffable One, whom Plethon calls Zeus.

VISIBLE BEINGS

The supercelestial gods are outside the heavens; indeed, they exist outside of time and space and do not have physical bodies. Within the heavens—which is to say, within the physical universe—are those embodied beings that exist in time and space. These include the celestial gods in the sky above and the daimons and human beings here on earth. As the supercelestial gods are created by Zeus, so the celestial gods and daimons—the third order of gods—are created by Poseidon with the assistance of the other Olympians. Plethon calls them "the children of the children of Zeus" and "the creations of the creations."[233] As the supercelestial gods are organized in a Cosmic Nous or Mind, so the celestial gods are governed by a Cosmic Psyche or Soul, which Plethon calls "the Mistress of All Life."; she is the animating soul of our world.[234]

The celestial gods of the third order differ from those of the second (the supercelestials) in that they have a body. Their body (σῶμα, *sôma*) is governed by their soul (ψυχή, *psychê*), which is governed by their mind (νοῦς, *nous*), which comes from Zeus. This establishes a bond or communion between the supercelestial and celestial orders, for each being within the sphere of heaven has an image of Zeus inside. Poseidon uses the matter provided by Olympian Hera to create the bodies of immortal beings (celestial gods, daimons, and humans) and matter provided by Titan Aphrodite to create the bodies of mortal beings (non-rational animals). For immortal beings, the body is dependent on the soul for its existence; for mortals, the soul is dependent on the body, and therefore ceases to exist when the body dies. The souls of the immortal beings must be embodied in order to live in time and space, and so they are carried by "vehicles" (ὀχήματα, *ochêmata*), which are composed of the aethereal element (Fire). It is very hot and fiery in the vehicles of the celestial gods, and so they are visible in the sky. In the vehicles of daimons and humans it is only warm like the breath, and so invisible. Since celestial gods, daimons, and humans have aethereal vehicles, our proper home is the

---

233. Plethon, *Laws* I.5.2.

234. Plethon, *Commentary* 12.

aethereal sphere—namely the heavens, to which humans return between incarnations. We human beings have, in addition to the vehicles of our souls, a mortal physical body, which is created by Kore and of course visible because made of denser elements (Air, Water, and Earth).

All the immortal beings are also the rational beings—with minds or intellects—but their natures differ. The celestial gods have perfect understanding of everything; the daimons have correct opinions but lack perfect understanding (they know what is true, but not why); and we humans are fallible, with both imperfect understanding and opinions that are sometimes false. Fortunately, we can seek the truth from the gods and daimons.

Let's consider the celestial gods, daimons, and human beings in order.

The Celestial Gods

The celestial gods are perceptible to us as the seven visible planets and the fixed stars. They are the "high-born" children of Poseidon, analogous to the Olympian gods, who are the "high-born" children of Zeus. Before describing them, however, we need to consider them from a modern perspective.

Plethon lived a century before Copernicus showed that the planets revolve around the sun and not around Earth. (Interestingly, in ancient times Pythagoras had already stated that Earth and other planets revolved around a central fire, and so Copernicus called his "new" idea the "Pythagorean theory.") Plethon died 150 years before Galileo aimed his telescope at the sky and saw that the moon has mountains and craters and that Jupiter has its own moons. Although he made accurate astronomical measurements, Plethon thought Earth was the center of the universe around which seven visible planets (including the sun and moon) moved in their individual spheres, surrounded by a sphere of very slowly moving fixed stars. Now we know better; the planets revolve around the sun. Moreover, we know that the stars are like our sun and that the planets are worlds in some ways like our own. Humans have walked on the moon and soon will visit Mars. How do we reconcile Plethon's celestial gods with modern astronomy?

Plethon's theology describes gods, who are Ideas in a Platonic sense. Some of these Ideas exist outside of time and space, and they are the supercelestial gods, to whom Plethon gives familiar names, such as Apollo and Artemis, so that we can understand

and relate to them better. We know that Apollo—the Idea of Identity—is not a young man with a lyre, but we can relate to the Idea more easily in this form; the image is a symbol of the Idea. Moreover, symbols are not unimportant; true symbols are psychologically potent and can tune our souls to the energies of specific gods.

The third order of gods, the celestial gods, exist in time and space, but are everlasting and interact with us from afar. They are well symbolized by the visible planets and stars, which we observe in the heavens above us. Of course, they are not literally everlasting—they have been around for "only" a few billion years and will eventually come to an end—but for all practical purposes, they are everlasting and unchanging. They are beautiful and perfect, shining in the sky. They move in orderly patterns, reflecting the celestial gods' orderly administration of the world in which we live. Therefore, the stars and planets are good symbols of the celestial gods of the third order. Proclus calls the study of these spiritual stars and planets, which transcend the physical bodies, "hyperastronomy" (from ὑπεραστρονομέω, *hyperastronomeô*) to distinguish it from the mundane science. With this in mind, let's get back to Plethon.

Poseidon creates the first of the celestial gods, **Helios** the Sun, as an image of himself. He is the leader of the rest, and therefore he is the boundary between the supercelestial and celestial realms but also the bond that unites them into one cosmos. The second celestial god is, naturally, **Selene** the Moon, who is the wife of Helios. The "greater lights" Helios and Selene are the king and queen of the celestial gods, an image of Poseidon and Hera, the king and queen of the Olympians. Following them are the other five visible planets (so the seven planets are an image of seven superior Olympian gods). Each planet is the visible image of an eternal Idea. Plethon uses the following "Chaldean" names (so called, but actually Greek):[235]

Helios	Sun
Selene	Moon
Stilbôn	Mercury
Eôsphoros or Phôsphoros	Venus

---

235. Plethon, *Laws* III.34.34, III.35.9.

Pyroeis	Mars
Phaëthôn	Jupiter
Phainôn	Saturn

As we have seen (see "The Titans" on page 70), the gods of Tartarus are the Ideas of perishable things, and Helios uses these to create the perishable things of the material world. He provides the form and joins it with the matter provided by Selene. Together they draw down the Ideas into the material world: Helios those that are more active and formal, Selene those that are more passive and material. The Titans complete and perfect the process of creation, as appropriate to their particular functions. In this, the five lesser planets assist and also participate in governing the daimons and humans. Plethon calls the planets our "splendid guardians."[236]

The planets have their traditional astrological effects on our souls. This is supported by Plethon's interpretation of the following Magical Oracle:

> Incline not down. Beneath the Earth there lies a cliff,
>   which draws one down the seven steps…
>   beneath her is the throne of dire Necessity.[237]

Just as in the Oracles fire often symbolizes the divine, here Earth symbolizes mortal nature, and the seven steps are the Fate that is dependent on the planets. The oracle warns against being too attached to the mortal body, according to Plethon, which is bound by Fate and Necessity (Ἀνάγκη, *Anangkê*), for then our desires will be unsatisfied and we will be unhappy.[238]

Plethon does not tell us much about the fixed stars as celestial gods. Their function seems to be perpetual contemplation of "what really exists," the Ideas and their cause, Zeus.[239] We would know more if we had the five chapters on the celestial gods that

---

236. Plethon, *Laws* III.35.9.

237. Plethon, *Magical Oracles* 2. Contemporary scholars do not consider the last line to be part of the oracle, but Plethon did.

238. Plethon, *Commentary* 2.

239. Plethon, *Laws* III.34.6, 45.

Scholarios burned, but see "Powers of the Seven Planets" in chapter 10 (page 207) for what we may reconstruct.

The Earthly Daimons

The earthly daimons are the "low-born" children of Poseidon and are the nearest deities to humankind. As explained earlier in the "Visible Beings" section, their souls have aethereal vehicles, which are not fiery like the celestial gods, but warm like breath and invisible. These are subtler and nobler than our mortal bodies; theirs are unadulterated by mortal nature, and therefore, daimons are immortal, though existing in time and space.

As images of the gods, daimons know what is true, but they are incapable of understanding the reasons their opinions are true, which the celestial gods do understand. Because they are infallible in their opinions, daimons do not experience evil, and Plethon insists that all daimons are good, which is the opinion of Pythagoras and Plato as well.[240] (The notion of evil daimons was refuted in two of the destroyed chapters of the *Book of Laws*, as we know from their titles.[241]) Daimons, as the divine beings nearest to us, who serve the higher gods, are the direct source of all goodness for us, which ultimately comes from the gods.

The goodness of daimons is also supported by Plethon's interpretation of a Magical Oracle: "And Nature prompts belief that daimons all are pure, / and evil matter's offspring are both kind and good."[242] He explains that "Nature" here refers to natural reason, by which we understand that all things that proceed from Zeus, who is good, must themselves be fundamentally good. This applies even to things that arise from matter, which is "evil" only insofar as it is the substance farthest removed from Zeus, the source of goodness. If even base matter is fundamentally good, yet even more so are the daimons.

Plethon lists a number of ways that daimons assist us.[243] They protect us and preserve us. They purify us, making us good and noble, and they aid our ascent to divinity.

---

240. Plethon, *Laws* I.5.9, III.34.6, III.35.14.

241. Plethon, *Laws*, table of contents.

242. Plethon, *Commentary* 20.

243. Plethon, *Laws* III.35.14.

They cure our bodies and minds, for they easily correct our thinking. Sometimes, indeed, daimons punish us, but this is either for the greater good as determined by the gods and Fate, or it is for our personal improvement. Magical Oracle 21 reads, "Avengers, the restraints of people," and Plethon comments, "vindictive daimons clasp people close or restrain and drive them from vice and excite them to virtue."[244] See chapter 10 for a reconstruction of Plethon's doctrines on daimons.

Human Beings

I think it will be helpful to say a little about Plethon's ideas on the human soul (ψυχή, *psyché*), which he attributes to the followers of Pythagoras and Plato, and probably much earlier to the Magi, the followers of Zoroaster.[245] They are relevant both to our relationship with the gods and to Plethon's ethical teachings (explained in chapter 9).

As explained earlier in the section "The Orders of Reality," there are three orders of reality. Highest is the realm of Ideas, the eternal Forms that are independent of matter; these are the supercelestial gods, each an eternal mind (νοῦς, *nous*) existing outside of time and space. The lowest order is the physical world, in which the forms are embodied in matter and therefore depend on it. These forms exist in space and time, and when their material embodiments cease to exist, so do they, as physically existing forms. In this realm are mortal animals, whose non-rational souls cease to exist when the animal dies. Between these two orders is the realm of rational souls, which are possessed by celestial gods, daimons, and humans. A rational soul (λογικὴ ψυχή, *logikê psyché*) is a *nous*, like that of the supercelestial gods, but projected into time and space.

Rational souls must be embodied in order to have effects in the physical world, but the celestial gods and daimons have immortal bodies. Although the human rational soul is also immortal, and its existence does not depend on matter, it is nevertheless bound to matter, its mortal body, which it organizes and controls. This is in fact the purpose of humankind in the cosmos: in order that the hierarchical emanation of the cosmos be complete and harmonious, the immortal realm of the gods must be united

---

244. Plethon, *Commentary* 21.

245. Plethon, *Commentary* 14. Although Platonists disagreed on many specific issues, Plethon's theory is, in general terms, Platonic. Although, like many Platonists, he believed these ideas came from Pythagoras, the Magi, and Zoroaster, there is not much evidence of it.

with the mortal realm of the physical world. Humans, by combining immortal souls with mortal bodies, provide the link. A Magical Oracle states,

> Since Psychê, by the Father's Power a radiant fire,
> remains immortal, she is Mistress of all Life,
> and holds full measures of the Cosmos's many clefts.[246]

As Plethon explains, this means that the soul is a divine and mental (noetic) power that comes from "the Father's Power"—namely the Second God—and is therefore immortal. She has unending life, although she will occupy many different "clefts" or places—physical bodies—in the world, in accord with the lives she has lived.

Plethon gives two arguments for the immortality of the human soul.[247] First, because the rational soul knows the immortal gods, which are eternal Ideas, it must be eternal itself. Second, according to Plethon, no being willingly destroys itself, but since some people commit suicide, they must believe at some level that they have immortal souls and the gods would not maliciously instill such a false belief.[248] (This is not a very convincing argument, in my opinion.)

Plethon also explains why humans are endlessly reincarnated into mortal bodies.[249] It is a consequence of the perpetuity of the universe and Plethon's belief that there is a finite, fixed number of immortal human souls. Therefore, on the one hand, if each of the finite number of human souls were incarnated only once, then an *everlasting* bond between the immortal and mortal realms would not be maintained. On the other hand, if we were permanently embodied, then our immortal souls would immortalize our physical bodies (which the soul sustains), and humankind would not be fulfilling its function of uniting the immortal and mortal parts of the cosmos. Therefore, according to Plethon, there is no escape from the cycle of reincarnation, but other Platonists disagreed. In any case, you must decide for yourself whether you believe in reincarnation

---

246. Plethon, *Commentary* 12. The Second God is Poseidon, or more generally all the supercelestial gods, but the soul comes more directly from Pluto.

247. Plethon, *Laws* III.43.4.

248. Plethon, *Laws* III.43.5.

249. Plethon, *Laws* III.43.6.

and the immortality of the human soul. It was an almost universally accepted belief throughout the entire Pythagorean-Platonic tradition.

Let's look a little more closely at the human soul. According to Plethon's third axiom, substances or essences (οὐσίαι, *ousiai*) are always correlated with their actions. In other words, the same essences produce the same actions, and the same actions must result from the same essences.[250] Therefore, we can see that humans are a composite of two essences. The reason is that, on one hand, because humans have animal bodies, they must have non-rational souls (ἄλογοι ψυχαί, *alogoi psychai*) like other animals. On the other, because humans can contemplate and know the gods, and even approach knowledge of the supreme god Zeus, humans must have a rational soul, like the celestial gods and daimons. These two activities require two corresponding essences.

The term "rational" (λογικός, *logikos*) in this context can be misleading, since it does not refer exclusively to step-by-step logical reasoning (sometimes called "discursive reason": διάνοια, *dianoia*), but also to the ability to grasp the eternal Ideas, often by a sort of immediate intuition. This intuitive vision is the faculty that Platonic philosophy aims to develop by strengthening the introspective eyes of the soul.

The human non-rational soul includes the faculties of imagination and sense perception, as well as other faculties. Plethon describes it as an image of the rational soul, and the two are connected through the imagination (φαντασία, *phantasia*), which is the highest faculty of the non-rational soul.[251] He writes that the imagination is the faculty in us that is nearest to the divine (represented by the rational soul), and he explains that the purpose of sacred rites is to act on our imagination.[252] By evoking symbolically potent images in the imagination, our rational souls are inspired by the divine Ideas and elevated to the gods. These images may result from sense perceptions—especially the sights, sounds, smells, and movements of ritual—and so our non-rational soul needs embodiment.

The human soul is connected to the physical body by a subtle body called the *aethereal vehicle*, which is animated by the non-rational soul. This aethereal body is a subtle spirit (πνεῦμα, *pneuma*), which intermingles with the vital spirit of the physical body,

---

250. Plethon, *Laws* III.43.4.

251. Plethon, *Laws* III.34.54.

252. Plethon, *Laws* III.34.17.

thus integrating body and soul into one. As explained on page 73, humans, daimons, and celestial gods all have these aethereal bodies, which are immortal. In the case of the daimons and celestial gods, these are their only bodies, but humans have in addition a (mortal) physical body. During each of our incarnations, the aethereal vehicle provides the "glue" between our immortal soul and our mortal physical body.

Although our physical body is mortal and should be subject to our higher soul (*nous*), it fills an essential role in the unity and harmony of the cosmos, and so we should care for it. This is the meaning of the Magical Oracle that reads "Leave not the dross of matter on a precipice."[253] As Plethon explains, we should not neglect our physical body ("the dross of matter"), which is subject to various misfortunes, "but take care of it while in this life, to preserve it in health as much as possible, so that it may be pure and in all other respects correspond with the soul."[254] This physical care is reinforced by spiritual practice: "If thou extend the fiery mind to piety's work, the flowing body thou shalt save."[255] As Plethon explains, if we devote our divine mind to prayer and religious ritual, then we will preserve better our mortal body (though ever-changing in the flux of the material world) and make it sounder.

Animal Souls

Aristotle's three-part model of the human soul will help us understand Plethon's ideas on the animal soul.[256] The lowest part of the human soul is the **vegetative soul**, which is responsible for fundamental vital processes, such as nutrition and growth. All animals, and even plants, have vegetative souls. Humans and other animals also have a **sentient** or **animate soul**, which includes the faculties of perception and movement. Together, the vegetative and animate souls constitute the **non-rational** or **lower human soul**. Throughout the 1800 years from Plato to Plethon, most Greek philosophers believed that only humans and higher beings (daimons, gods) have the third, higher part, **a rational soul**, which is capable of conceptual thought, of knowing the eternal Ideas, of comprehending

---

253. Plethon, *Magical Oracles* 16.

254. Plethon, *Commentary* 16.

255. Plethon, *Commentary* 18.

256. Aristotle, *On the Soul*, books 2–3.

the gods. Moreover, Plethon argued that since things that can know each other must be to some degree alike, and since we can understand eternity and contemplate the immortal gods, our rational souls must be immortal.[257]

Through the centuries, many people have perceived a gulf between the cognitive abilities of humans and other animals, mainly because only humans seem to speak complex languages, which is evidence of conceptual thought.[258] There have been exceptions, however, to this general belief that animals are entirely non-rational; for example, Porphyry thought animals are capable of rational thought (*logos*) because of their complex communication and ability to learn, plan, and exhibit other intelligent behaviors.[259] Furthermore, especially over the last century, science has discovered sophisticated thinking, learning, culture, and communication in many animal species, and so there is less of a gap than traditionally assumed.[260] Therefore, it is reasonable to conclude that some animals, at least, have rational souls akin to ours.

If animals have rational souls, are they immortal, for Plethon claimed that it is our rational souls that are immortal? Some ancient Platonists argued that immortality extends to the non-rational soul, but others claimed that it is limited to beings with a *nous* in their rational soul (presumably just humans and higher beings), for the *nous* allows us to know the gods and other eternal Ideas; yet others argued that no earthly beings are immortal.[261] Plethon clearly did not think animals have immortal souls, but you will have to make up your own mind or choose to remain at peace in your uncertainty.

---

257. Plethon, *On Cleope* 172–73, summarized in Woodhouse, *George Gemistos Plethon*, 114–15. See also Hladký, *Plethon*, 22–23.

258. *Oxford Classical Dictionary*, 4th ed. (2012), s.v. "animals, attitude to." This is a brief survey of attitudes toward animals in the classical world.

259. Porphyry, *Abstinence* 3.1–23 (80–95).

260. In fact, Plethon's *Laws* II.26, "Reasonable action of some animals," discusses the intelligent behavior of animals, such as bees, ants, and spiders, and even some plants and nonliving things, but he attributes it to the world soul rather than to individual rational souls.

261. Westerink, *Damascius: Commentary on Plato's* Phaedo §177, 106–9.

IV

The Sacred Calendar

Plethon writes that the sacred calendar should be determined by nature and be governed by the two chief celestial gods: Helios and Selene, the Sun and Moon, who together define earthly time.[262] Therefore, he defines the year by the motion of the sun and the month by the motion of the moon, both as measured by the best scientific means available. Despite this modern orientation, his calendar is based on ancient practices handed down in the Golden Chain.[263] Plethon uses his calendar to organize the weekly holy day rituals within each lunar month and the more extensive annual holy day celebrations at the quarters of the year. (The particular holy days are discussed in detail later in this chapter.) Most of these holy days have precedents in the ancient Greek world, but Plethon updates them for his time and ours. Each of us has to decide how closely we can follow his sacred calendar, but I think it is important to be conscious of where we are in the year and month; it is one form of devotion to Helios and Selene.

THE DAY

Plethon's day begins at midnight, just like our modern secular day, and so it is familiar and easy to use. In this he was following the recommendation of Plutarch, one of the sages in

---

262. Plethon, *Laws* III.36.19.

263. Possible sources of Plethon's calendar and rituals are explored by Anastos, "Pletho's Calendar and Liturgy."

his Golden Chain, a Platonic philosopher and high priest at Delphi. In ancient Greece, in contrast, the day began at sundown. Therefore, for his holy days Plethon makes an exception to his ordinary rule and follows the ancient tradition, beginning the celebration at sundown the day before (the holy day eve) and concluding at sundown on the holy day, thus following Helios. In chapter 5 I will explain this in more detail.

THE MONTH

In many cultures, the month is measured by the moon, as it was in ancient Greece, a connection indicated by the words *mên* (μήν), month, and *mênê* (μήνη), moon. Therefore, Plethon's sacred month is governed by Selene, the Moon goddess, and it is born from the embrace of Selene and Helios, the day during which the conjunction of the moon and sun occurs, as determined by astronomy (as opposed to naked-eye observation, as in some cultures).[264] (In fact, Plethon had considerable skill in astronomy, and wrote a paper providing more accurate techniques for determining the positions of the planets.[265]) The day during which conjunction occurs is called Old-and-New (Ἕνη καὶ Νέα, *Henê kai Nea*) because it is actually part of both months, according to the Athenian lawgiver Solon, one of the Seven Sages: the old month before the moment of conjunction and the new month after it.[266] The first full day of the new month is the day after Old-and-New and is called New Moon (Νουμηνία, *Noumênia*).

The month is divided into four weeks of seven days (ἑβδομάδες, *hebdomades*), with several extra days to complete the month.[267] Seven, of course, is a sacred number, especially among the Pythagoreans, and connected with both the moon and Apollo at Delphi. The days are not named after the planetary gods, as they are in most European languages, including English, for that was not the ancient Greek practice. Rather, they are numbered relative to the "quarters" of the month, counting both up and down. (Plethon numbers the days relative to each quarter of the month, but in ancient Greece they were numbered relative to each third.)

---

264. Plethon, *Laws* III.36.19.

265. Tihon and Mercier, *George Gemistus Plethon: Manuel d'astronomie.*

266. Plutarch, *Solon* 25.3, in Plutarch, *Lives: Vol. I*, 474–75.

267. Plethon, *Laws* III.36.20.

After New Moon (the first day of the month), which is a holy day, the days count up, from Second Waxing (ἰσταμένου, *histamenou*) to Eighth Waxing, which is a holy day. Then the days count down, from Seventh Middle (μεσοῦντος, *mesountos*) to Second Middle, which is followed by the holy day Midmonth (Διχομηνία, *Dichomênia*), which is approximately when the moon is full. After Midmonth we count up again from Second Waning (φθίνοντος, *phthinontos*) to Eighth Waning, which is a holy day. The last week counts down from Seventh Departing (ἀπιόντος, *apiontos*) to Second Departing. This brings us to the last days of the month, which are holy days.

It is approximately 29½ days from one conjunction to the next, and so lunar months are either 29 days long (called **hollow months**) or 30 days long (called **full months**). Therefore, after four seven-day weeks, we have one or two days left at the end of the month. In full months, Second Departing is followed by Old Moon (Ἕνη, *Henê*) and Old-and-New; in hollow months, Old Moon is omitted, and Old-and-New immediately follows Second Departing. Both Old Moon and Old-and-New are holy days.

Therefore, an ordinary month includes five or six monthly holy days during which there are special rites (see chapter 5): New Moon, Eighth Waxing, Midmonth, Eighth Waning, Old Moon (in full months), and Old-and-New.[268] However, as previously mentioned and explained in detail in chapter 5, the ceremonies begin at sundown on the holy day eve.

The sacred month is summarized in this table:

The Sacred Month

Lunar Day	Plethon's Name
1	New Moon
2–7	2nd–7th Waxing
8	8th Waxing
9–14	7th–2nd Middle
15	Midmonth (Full Moon)
16–21	2nd–7th Waning

---

268. Plethon, *Laws* III.36.21.

Lunar Day	Plethon's Name
22	8th Waning
23–28	7th–2nd Departing
29	Old Moon (omit for hollow month)
29/30	Old-and-New

THE YEAR

As the sacred month is governed by Selene, the Moon, so the sacred year is regulated by Helios, the Sun, and Plethon agrees with Plato and other ancient Greeks on the importance of the annual ceremonies occurring in the correct seasons of the year.[269]

Plethon determines the new year by the winter solstice. Although ancient Greek cities had different calendars, and many began their year in the spring, Plethon writes that the new year should come with the return of Helios after the winter solstice (as determined by astronomers).[270] This was the practice in ancient Rome and was instituted by the lawgiver Numa, according to Plutarch (both of whom are in Plethon's Golden Chain). Plutarch writes that this is a natural beginning to the year, for with the return of the light we are brought closer to the lord who rules this changing world, Helios.

In our modern civil calendar, the winter solstice in the Northern Hemisphere occurs around December 21, but in the old Roman calendar it occurred on December 25, which was celebrated as the birthday of the Unconquered Sun (Lat., *Sol Invictus*, Grk., Ἥλιος Ἀνίκητος, *Hêlios Anikêtos*). The new year began with the first noticeable shortening of shadows eight days later, on January 1, and during this period, the Festival of the Unconquered Sun was celebrated, according to the Pagan emperor Julian.[271]

In Plethon's calendar the new year begins with the New Moon following the winter solstice, which is called First Month, since Plethon numbers his months rather than naming them. The solar year is approximately 365¼ days, which is not a whole number

---

269. E.g., Plato, *Laws* 7.809c–d. See also Anastos, "Plethon's Calendar and Liturgy," 193–95.

270. Plethon, *Laws* III.36.19–20.

271. Julian, "Oration IV: Hymn to King Helios" 156B–C, *Works of Emperor Julian*, 1:428–29.

of lunar months; twelve lunar months are about 354 days and thirteen are about 384. Therefore Plethon's sacred year is either twelve or thirteen lunar months long, depending on how soon First Month follows the winter solstice. This might all sound more complicated than it actually is, and so the next section explains how to work with Plethon's sacred calendar.

Just as there are regular monthly holy days, there are also regular annual holy days in Plethon's sacred calendar.[272] Surrounding the New Year are fourteen or fifteen days of celebration encompassing the last week of Last Month (either Twelfth or Thirteenth Month, as appropriate) and the first week of First Month. There are also annual celebrations around Eighth Waxing of Fourth Month, Midmonth of Seventh Month, and Eighth Waning of Tenth Month. These annual holy days divide the year into approximate quarters, but they do not align closely with the Neopagan/Wiccan Wheel of the Year, since the year does not begin exactly on the winter solstice and might begin up to four weeks after it. The celebration of these annual holy days is described in chapter 5.

PRACTICAL MATTERS

It is not difficult to use the sacred calendar introduced by Plethon. I suggest you do your scheduling toward the end of each lunar month. The key date is Old-and-New Moon, which Plethon defines as the conjunction of the sun and moon as determined by the best scientific means. Therefore, there is no anachronism in looking up the date and time on the internet or using an app to determine it. According to Plethon, Old-and-New is the last day of the preceding month, and the next month begins at midnight following conjunction.[273] This day is New Moon for the next month.

Therefore, determine Old-and-New for the current month and also for the next month. Number the days 1, 2, 3, and so on or with Plethon's names, and you will see whether you need a 29th day (Old Moon) before the next Old-and-New. You can do

---

272. Plethon, *Laws* III.36.12, 21.

273. Plethon, *Laws* III.36.20.

this by hand or very easily with an electronic spreadsheet (and I have one for you on my website: http://opsopaus.com/resources.html).[274]

Once you have determined the New Moon, all the other days follow in order, and you will know the days on which the monthly holy days occur, and you can plan your month. Of course, Plethon's "weeks" are not the same as our weeks, and so the holy days won't necessarily fall on weekends. I will discuss some ways to deal with this issue in chapter 5.

There remains the issue of Plethon's sacred year and the annual ceremonies. In the Northern Hemisphere, Plethon's year is not too different from our civil year, and of course there are historical reasons for this, but the New Year can come as late as January 22 if there was a conjunction just before the winter solstice. But what do we do in the southern hemisphere? Start the year after the winter solstice in June, or start it after the December solstice to agree with the Northern Hemisphere? For the reasons given by Plethon and his sources for starting at the winter solstice, namely honoring Helios at this time when the light returns, I think it is important to start at the winter solstice, in December in the north and June in the south.[275] The sacred years of northern and southern Hellenists will then be six months out of sync (as they are for many Neopagan religious calendars), but they are used primarily for determining local religious ceremonies, and for that purpose it is important that they are synchronized with the solar year. We will continue to use our ordinary civil calendars for secular purposes.

To determine your New Year, look up the date and time for the winter solstice. When you determine the calendar for Twelfth Month, you will know whether the solstice falls in that month. If it does, then it is a twelve-month year, and the First Month of the new year follows Twelfth Month. If it does not, then you will need a Thirteenth Month, and the new year's First Month will follow it.

---

274. Conveniently, Plethon's calendar is included *The Ultimate Pagan Almanac* by Jean-Louis de Biasi and Patricia Bourin (Theurgia Publications, www.theurgia.us).

275. Plethon, *Laws* III.36.19.

V

Rites and Rituals

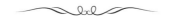

Plethon gives very precise directions for worshipping the gods on both ordinary days and holy days. In both cases there are morning, afternoon, and evening services, which have the same general ritual structure. The following section defines the order of service as defined by Plethon, and the subsequent sections explain the arrangement of the morning, afternoon, and evening rituals on both ordinary days and holy days.[276] You might be a bit overwhelmed by the detail, but don't despair! As explained later in this chapter, it is not necessary to do all of this, as even Plethon acknowledges. We are fortunate to have these ritual details, should we choose to follow them.

ORDER OF SERVICE

Plethon tells us that the religious ceremonies should be conducted in consecrated temples if available, and if not, then in places free from human bones or excrement and from containers for them.[277] This reflects ancient Pagan attitudes, for a temple was defiled if someone died in it, and it had to be purified and reconsecrated (see chapter 10). Pagans were therefore shocked at the Christian practices of keeping relics—pieces of the corpses of

---

276. Anastos, "Plethon's Calendar and Liturgy," analyzes sources and precedents for Plethon's rituals.

277. Plethon, *Laws* III.36.1.

saints and martyrs—in their churches and of conducting funerals in them. It seemed to be offensive and disrespectful to the gods. The steps in the ceremony are numbered in order.

⌁

(1) The worship service begins with a proclamation by the sacred herald (ἱεροκῆρυξ, *hierokêrux*), who may regularly fill this office or may be designated for a particular service by the priest, if there is one, or by the most venerable person present.[278] The herald proclaims:

> Hear ye, worshipers of the gods (Ἀκούετε, οἱ θεοσεβεῖς; *Akouete hoi theosebeis*). Now is the time to address our morning (or afternoon or evening) prayer to the gods. With all our reason, with all our judgment, with all our soul, let us invoke all the gods and especially Zeus who reigns over them.

The herald makes this proclamation once on ordinary days, twice on holy days, and thrice on New Moon. It is followed by three adorations of the gods, as follows.

(2) The first adoration is for the Olympian gods. All the worshippers kneel on both knees. They then look up and raise their arms and palms to the sky, while intoning, "O gods, be propitious," (Ἵλεῳ εἴητ᾽, ὦ θεοί; *Hileô eiêt᾽, ô theoi*) in the Hypophrygian mode (see chapter 8 on the musical modes, page 166). They then lift their left knees so they are kneeling on their right knees and momentarily place their right hands on the ground to call the Olympian gods as a group.

(3) The second adoration is for all the other gods (i.e., the Titans, the celestial gods, and the daimons). The worshippers again kneel on both knees, look up, raise their hands, and intone, "O gods, be propitious," but in the Phrygian mode. They then kneel on their left knees and momentarily touch the ground with their left hands to call these gods.

(4) The third adoration is for Zeus. The worshippers kneel on both knees, raise their faces and hands, and intone, "King Zeus, be propitious" (Ζεῦ βασιλεῦ, ἵλαθι; *Zeu basileu, hilathi*), in the Hypodorian mode. Everyone then bends forward to touch their

---

278. The order of service is presented in *Laws* III.36.1–18, as are the various prayers and invocations (my translations). Plethon's chapter on the priesthood (*Laws* I.22) was destroyed, so we don't know anything about the priests in Plethon's religion, neither how they were trained or what were their functions. Clearly, however, they were not required for worship.

hands and foreheads to the earth momentarily. This invocation and gesture is repeated three times.

You will have to decide if you are going to try to chant the short invocations ("O gods, be propitious"; "King Zeus, be propitious") in the correct musical modes; see chapter 8. You also might choose to invoke them in Greek, but that is not in the slightest necessary.

After this **threefold adoration of the gods**, the main body of the service follows, which involves (5) the recitation of one or more invocations or prayers and (6) the chanting or singing of hymns. Before an invocation, the sacred herald says, "Let us listen to the invocation," and before the hymns, "Let us listen to the hymns to the gods." Worshippers kneel during the invocations.

(7) The service comes to a close with a concluding proclamation. For the ordinary service the herald pronounces,

> Since we have addressed the gods and have been our best according to law, and since we have kneeled on both knees and offered this final prayer, let us be liberated.

On holy days the herald proclaims this longer concluding proclamation:

> Because we have addressed the gods and performed the sacred rites according to law, we are indeed liberated, each of us having become better by our association with them. In everything we do, let us be mindful of Zeus and the gods, so far as our nature may follow. Let us strive, so far as we are able, first for freedom from the worst part of ourselves and from suffering, and thereafter for power over ourselves, for independence, and for decency according to nature. Let us take care for the preservation of the natural qualities of each of us by the restitution of what has been established, especially so that we might be perfected. In all these things and in every way, insofar as we are such people, let us follow the gods, and thereby in this way alone let us prepare, as is the ability of each of us, for blessedness to come. But also, since we have reclined on both knees and offered this final prayer, let us be liberated.

(8) In either case there is a concluding prayer. The priest, if present, prays three times with upraised hands:

> May King Zeus and all the gods, who as overseers under Zeus have settled our matters, be kind to all of you.

The other participants respond, singing in the Dorian mode, after the three repetitions: "Be it so! (εἶεν, *eien*)"—"Be it so!"—"Be it so also for you, O holy one!"

If the priest is absent, then the herald makes this proclamation (which substitutes "us" for "you") three times, but without upraised hands:

> May King Zeus and all the gods, who as overseers under Zeus have settled our matters, be kind to all of us.

The other participants respond "Be it so!" each time (in the Dorian). This concludes the service.

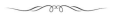

The specific ceremonies are described in detail later in this chapter, the invocations are collected in chapters 6 and 7, and the hymns can be found in chapter 8. Here is a summary outline of the regular service:

Order of Service

Proclamation (1, 2, or 3 times)	
Threefold Adoration	Adoration of Olympian gods
	Adoration of non-Olympian gods
	Adoration of Zeus (3 times)
Invocation(s)	
Hymns	
Conclusion	

A few words about direction (which Plethon doesn't mention). If you have an altar, it is appropriate to face it during the service. Alternately, you might face the east, which was a frequent ancient Greek practice; another possibility is to face east for the morning service, south for the afternoon service, and west for the evening service. These all work well.

Timing of Services

Plethon calls for morning, afternoon, and evening worship services.[279] He specifies that the morning service should be after rising from bed and before breakfast if one eats breakfast or before the work of the day if one doesn't. The afternoon services are between the middle of the day and the evening meal. The evening service occurs between the evening meal and bedtime, except that the evening service at the end of a holy day fast must be held after sunset and before the evening meal (which, of course, breaks the fast).

Kneeling and Bowing

It will be worthwhile to say a few words about the kneeling and bowing prescribed by Plethon since, at least in my experience, these ritual actions are not common in contemporary Neopagan practice. I suppose our democratic and antiauthoritarian ideals make us reluctant to bow down before anyone, even a god! However, there are important spiritual benefits from these practices, known in esoteric traditions, and this may be why Plethon prescribes them in such detail. (They also have ancient precedents, as explained later.)

In the ancient world the knees were considered to have concentrations of vital power (πνεῦμα, *pneuma*). (This is why one might clasp the knees of a superior in supplication.) Therefore bending the knee represents submission of one's vital force to the higher power from which it comes. Here, kneeling and bowing are gestures of submission to the gods, which acknowledge their greater power, and that the gods are the ultimate source of all that is good. Although we are ultimately subject to the gods and dependent on them, we can act intentionally, opening ourselves to receive these blessings. Thus, gods and mortals come together for the greater good, establishing a harmony of above and below. By bowing and prostrating before the gods, we present ourselves as their children and students, eager to receive their guidance and instruction. We remind

---

279. Plethon, *Laws* III.36.1.

ourselves that although we are in the noble lineage of the gods, we are nevertheless mere humans. Acknowledging our dependence on the gods encourages an attitude of humility, which guards against ego inflation, spiritual pride, and arrogance, which are traps for those on the contemplative path and an impediment to progress. Dwelling too much in the mind and spirit can fool you into thinking you are above the merely human. "Know thyself," as Apollo advised, one meaning of which is "Know that you are human."

Plethon does not explain the reasons for these particular gestures, but I think we can get some insights from Tantric Buddhism. Sinking to the hands and knees and touching the forehead to the ground is a way of purifying yourself of the Five Delusions, which are pride, anger, ignorance, jealousy, and attachment. These are destructive emotions that impede our progress, and by prostrating with these five points of contact with the earth, we can visualize them draining out of us and into Mother Earth to be purified and recycled as positive energy.

We can be too much in our heads, and these ritual actions reach into our souls deeper than conceptual thought. These ritual actions bring mind, speech, and body together, working toward their integration, their essential harmony; it is a kind of yoga. This should be our goal, for the gods have made us humans, and we should live as humans to the fullest extent possible. As Plethon writes, we are the link between the immortal and the mortal.[280]

Practical Matters

Some practical matters. Plethon's rituals are obviously designed for groups, but what if you are worshipping alone? Certainly, you could omit the opening proclamation, which is unnecessary, but you might find it worthwhile to repeat it, even if you are alone, since it sets your intention for the following ritual.

As you will see, each of the secular day services will take the better part of an hour, and so you are looking at nearly three hours of religious practice on ordinary days and substantially more on holy days (as explained later in this chapter). I don't know what the pace of life was like in Mistra five hundred years ago, but I think many of us

---

280. Plethon, *Laws* III.31.3; III.34.7, 46, 49, 53.

today will have trouble following this schedule. Therefore, since the majority of the time is consumed by the invocations, in chapter 7 I have provided an abbreviated version for each of them, which you might find more practical. I will mention also some of Plethon's own suggestions for shortening the services. Nevertheless, you should try to incorporate the full versions in your practice, perhaps on holy days or when you are first learning Plethon's religion, because the longer invocations will deepen your understanding and connection to the gods.

Plethon apparently recognized the demands of performing the full services, for in the *Laws* he suggests some practical adaptations.[281] He writes that if "some laziness afflicts" us, especially on secular days, we can leave out the invocations altogether, and recite the hymns immediately after the threefold adoration. Indeed, writes Plethon, if we are even lazier, the hymns can be omitted, so we have only the threefold adoration.

It might be difficult or dangerous for some people to kneel or bow down, but there are many alternatives. During the (relatively lengthy) invocations in chapter 6, one may stand or sit. Instead of kneeling and touching the right or left hand to the earth, you can stoop down and touch the earth. If that is too difficult, bow at the waist and stretch the hand down without attempting to reach the ground. Instead of prostration, stoop to touch the ground with both hands while bowing the head, or just bow the head while stretching your arms downward. You get the idea. Approximate the gesture in a way that is safe and comfortable for you. Indeed, Plethon writes that those with infirmities can omit prostration altogether and just sing or recite the adorations.

Finally, Plethon notes that some people may be obliged to live a pious (Neopagan) life among those who are ignorant and indifferent (presumably he has intolerant Christians in mind).[282] Such people are advised to adapt the rituals in any way they find appropriate. They can finish their worship by kissing their upturned right hand (blowing a kiss, in effect). He adds that if the *Book of Laws* rests upon a table in the temple or someplace else, then they might touch it first and then kiss their hand. Given Plethon's situation living among intolerant Christians, perhaps this was his practice.

---

281. Plethon, *Laws* III.36.15.

282. Plethon, *Laws* III.36.15.

In all these cases you can see that Plethon is not adamant that these rituals be followed to the letter. They are not magic spells. Rather, they are effective practices intended to symbolize our relation to the gods and to bring us closer to them. Find a practice that works for you.

Sources

You may wonder where these rituals came from, whether they were made up by Plethon.[283] In fact, for the most part they come from our Pagan predecessors. For example, the practice of performing three daily prayers was common among Pagans in late antiquity, and we read that Proclus worshipped the Sun at sunrise, noon, and sunset. The Pagan emperor Julian recommended it as well.[284] Pagan prayers and libations often included a request (in just such words as Plethon uses) for the gods to "be propitious" ("kind," "gracious" are other good translations). The threefold adoration may be inspired by the ancient practice of making three libations: the first to the Olympian gods, the second to the heroes and daimons, and the third to Zeus the Savior. The triple adoration of Zeus is consistent with the triple repetition common in ancient Greek ritual and magic.

The upraised face and hands, touching the ground, the triple prostration or bow, and kneeling on both knees are all known from ancient Pagan ritual. Kneeling on one knee is also ancient. While Plethon specifies using the right and left hand for the Olympian and non-Olympian gods, respectively, he does not say on which knee to kneel.[285] I have decided to kneel on the same side as the hand, since kneeling on the right knee is generally seen as a greater honor than kneeling on the left. Honoring the Olympian gods with the right hand and the other gods with the left has precedents in both Plato and Plutarch, both of whom are in Plethon's Golden Chain. Blowing a kiss to the gods was also an ancient practice.

Although Plethon might have borrowed some ritual details from the Orthodox Christian practice of his time, most of his ritual seems to be securely rooted in ancient Pagan practice.

---

283. Additional information on Plethon's sources can be found in Anastos, "Plethon's Calendar and Liturgy."

284. Julian, "Letter to a Priest" 302A–B, *Works of Emperor Julian*, 2:328–29.

285. Plethon, *Laws* III.36.4.

ORDINARY WORSHIP SERVICES

In this section I will describe the worship services for an ordinary day, a day that is not a monthly or annual holy day. The basic order is (1) proclamation, (2) threefold adoration, (3) invocations (see chapters 6 and 7) and hymns (chapter 8), and (4) conclusion. This has slightly different forms for the morning, afternoon, and evening services, each of which is just the order of service described previously (see page 92), with the proclamation repeated once, the appropriate hymn for the month and day, and the shorter conclusion.

For an **ordinary morning service**, the order is:

- Proclamation

- Threefold adoration

- Morning Invocation to the Gods

- Monthly hymn for current month (Hymns 3–15)

- Daily hymn for current day (Hymns 22–27)

- First Perennial Hymn to Zeus (Hymn 1)

- Conclusion

There are thirteen monthly hymns (Hymns 3–15), one for each of the twelve or thirteen sacred months of the year, and there are six daily hymns (Hymns 22–27), one for each ordinary day of the sacred week. There is an exception in Twelfth Month if it is the last month of the year: the morning service uses the hymn for Thirteenth Month (Hymn 15); therefore, this hymn, and the gods it honors, are not neglected, even if there is no Thirteenth Month.

The **ordinary afternoon service** follows this order:

- Proclamation

- Threefold adoration

- First Afternoon Invocation to the Gods

- First part of Second Perennial Hymn (Hymn 2)

- Second Afternoon Invocation to the Gods

- Second part of Second Perennial Hymn (Hymn 2)

- Third Afternoon Invocation to Zeus

- Monthly hymn for current month (Hymns 3–15)

- Daily hymn for current day (Hymns 22–27)

- First Perennial Hymn to Zeus (Hymn 1)

- Conclusion

The first part of the Second Perennial Hymn comprises its first five verses, and the second part comprises the remaining four verses.[286] There is an exception in Twelfth Month if it is the last month, in which case the afternoon service uses the hymn for Thirteenth Month (Hymn 15).

The **ordinary evening service** follows this order:

- Proclamation

- Threefold adoration

- Evening Invocation to the Gods

- Monthly hymn for current month (Hymns 3–15)

- Daily hymn for current day (Hymns 22–27)

- First Perennial Hymn to Zeus (Hymn 1)

- Conclusion

The evening service is modified when the following day is a holy day, as I will explain in the next section ("Holy Day Worship Services"). In Twelfth Month, regardless of whether it is the last month, the evening service uses the monthly hymn for Twelfth Month (Hymn 14).

The daily hymns are determined by the numbers assigned to the days. For example, the first daily hymn (Hymn 22) is for the days called "second" in every week, the second daily (Hymn 23) is for the days called "third," and so on, up to the sixth daily (Hymn 27), for days called "seventh." Thus, the first daily hymn is used for Second Waxing, Second Middle, Second Waning, and Second Departing. Therefore, in the Waxing and Waning weeks, in which the numbers increase, the hymns will be sung in order (22, 23, ..., 27),

---

286. Plethon, *Laws* III.36.7.

but in the Middle and Departing weeks they will be sung in reverse order (27, 26, ... , 22). The daily hymns are prayers for the gods' support in acquiring the specific excellences (virtues) under the general virtues of self-control, fortitude, and justice (explained in chapter 9).

Holy Day Worship Services

The services for holy days are longer and include musical accompaniment, if it is available, which is not used on ordinary days; the holy day services still follow the order of service described previously (see page 92).[287] Since holy days begin at sunset on the preceding day, the first service is the **holy day eve service** following the evening meal on the holy day eve:[288]

- Proclamation twice (thrice for New Moon)
- Threefold adoration (three times)
- Evening Invocation to the Gods
- Sacred hymn for the holy day (Hymns 16–21) twice, with music
- Monthly hymn for current month (Hymns 3–15) twice, with music
- First Perennial Hymn to Zeus (Hymn 1) thrice, with music
- Conclusion (holy day)

The holy day conclusion, which closes the service, has the longer final proclamation from the herald (see page 91). As I will explain later in connection with the monthly schedule, there is an exception for the celebration of the Old-and-New Moon in that the monthly hymn is for the new month, not the old one. In Twelfth Month, regardless of whether it is the last month, the holy day eve service uses the monthly hymn for Twelfth Month (Hymn 14). The holy day eve service begins the fast, which continues until the evening service on the holy day (see "Fasting" on page 101).

---

287. Plethon, *Laws* III.36.7, 14.

288. Although days normally begin at midnight in Plethon's calendar, for holy days he makes an exception and returns to the ancient Greek practice in which the new day, and therefore the holy day fast, begins at sundown and continues to the following sundown.

The order for the **holy day morning service** is:

- Proclamation twice (thrice for New Moon)
- Threefold adoration (three times)
- Morning Invocation to the Gods
- Sacred hymn for the holy day (Hymns 16–21) twice, with music
- Monthly hymn for current month (Hymns 3–15) twice, with music
- First Perennial Hymn to Zeus (Hymn 1) thrice, with music
- Conclusion (holy day)

There is an exception in Twelfth Month if it is the last month in that the holy day morning service uses the hymn for Thirteenth Month (Hymn 15).

The **holy day afternoon service** is as follows:

- Proclamation twice (thrice for New Moon)
- Threefold adoration (three times)
- First Afternoon Invocation to the Gods
- Second Perennial Hymn (Hymn 2), with music
- Second Afternoon Invocation to the Gods
- Second Perennial Hymn (Hymn 2), with music
- Third Afternoon Invocation to Zeus
- Sacred hymn for the holy day (Hymns 16–21) twice, with music
- Monthly hymn for current month (Hymns 3–15) twice, with music
- First Perennial Hymn to Zeus (Hymn 1) thrice, with music
- Conclusion (holy day)

Notice that on holy days the second perennial hymn is performed complete each time, not divided as in the ordinary service.[289] There is an exception in Twelfth Month if it is

---

289. Plethon, *Laws* III.36.7.

the last month in that the holy day afternoon service uses the hymn for Thirteenth Month (Hymn 15).

The **holy day evening service after the fast** is celebrated between sunset and the evening meal and thus ends the fast. This is the order of service:

- Proclamation twice (thrice for New Moon)
- Threefold adoration (three times)
- Evening Invocation to Zeus after the Fast
- Sacred hymn for the holy day (Hymns 16–21) twice, with music
- Monthly hymn for current month (Hymns 3–15) twice, with music
- First Perennial Hymn to Zeus (Hymn 1) thrice, with music
- Conclusion (holy day)

There are slight changes in the text of the Evening Invocation to Zeus after the Fast depending on the specific holy day (detailed with the invocation in chapter 6). In Twelfth Month, regardless of whether it is the last month, the holy day evening service uses the monthly hymn for Twelfth Month (Hymn 14).

FASTING

For Plethon a holy day is a fast (νηστεία, *nêsteia*), but fasting is perhaps not a common practice in contemporary Neopaganism. Although Plethon refers to fasts several times in the *Book of Laws*, he does not describe them in the surviving parts, and they are not mentioned in the titles of the chapters that were destroyed. Therefore, we must look at common Greek practices to infer what fasts were for him.

In the Greek tradition, the purpose of fasting is not deprivation or sacrifice; it is about control, in particular, control of the desires that can dominate our lives. Thus, it is a spiritual discipline that we practice in order to become better (more excellent) and in particular to live with greater freedom. By fasting, we acquire greater control over our desires. Fasting relates especially to control of the lowest part of the soul, called the **appetitive soul**, which is conventionally associated with the belly, the bodily seat of our desires. Therefore, fasting is especially related to the excellence or virtue of self-control (σωφροσύνη, *sôphrosunê*), also translated as self-mastery, moderation, temperance, and mental health (see chapter 9). The goal of self-control is to become more godlike by needing as little as possible, for the gods need nothing at all. Under self-control, fasting pertains to a specific virtue (κοσμιότης, *kosmiotês*) that may be translated as orderliness, moderation, propriety, decorum, or dignity, which are all somewhat misleading translations. It is the first specific virtue that Plethon teaches us to cultivate.[290] Orderliness relates especially to controlling the need for pleasure, and fasting teaches us to practice this self-sufficiency by abstaining from unnecessary desires and by limiting those that are necessary, such as food and drink.

Therefore, the most common form of fasting is to restrict our food and drink: limiting ourselves to simple food and drink that are sufficient for our bodily needs but not superfluous. Abstaining from meat and fish is typical. Light and dry foods energize the aethereal vehicle and facilitate a spiritual state. It is not necessary to abstain from food entirely, although that is one option. From the perspective of effective spiritual practice, it is wise to begin with modest fasting before attempting more extreme forms, which are not necessary. The goal is better self-control, not self-denial or self-abuse.

Control of desire is not limited to food. Traditional fasts have also included sexual abstinence. In the modern world, fasting might also include abstinence from television, from social media, video games, and anything else for which you might have a strong desire. If there is something you feel that you absolutely must have, then consider abstaining from it, or at least restricting it, during your fast. It will improve your self-control and increase your freedom.

For Plethon, a holy day begins at sundown on the holy day eve and continues until sundown on the holy day. Therefore, the fast begins the preceding day after supper and before the evening holy day eve service, and it ends on next day with the holy day evening service after the fast (which uses the Evening Address to Zeus after the Fast: chapters 6 and 7). Supper is taken after this service, breaking the fast.

---

290. Plethon, *On Virtues*, B.14.15.

MONTHLY HOLY DAYS

Plethon defines six monthly holy days: New Moon, Eighth Waxing, Midmonth, Eighth Waning, Old Moon (in full months), and Old-and-New Moon.[291] They divide the lunar month into four natural quarters, as anciently recommended by Aristotle and Theophrastus.[292]

The **New Moon** holy day celebrates the birth of the month, for all beginnings are divine, according to Plato; Plutarch writes that it is the holiest day of all, and Proclus especially honored it (two of whom are in the Golden Chain).[293] According to Hesiod, the first day is sacred to Zeus, the first principle and father of everything, and Plethon's New Moon holy day is dedicated to Zeus.[294] It is an auspicious day.

Eighth Waxing is a week later, at the moon's first quarter, and celebrates all the Olympians, the second order of gods, but especially Poseidon and Hera, who immediately follow Zeus in rank. The eighth day is sacred to Poseidon, according to Plutarch and Proclus, and good for religious observations.[295]

The **Midmonth** holy day is for all the gods and occurs near the full moon, which was the best of days, according to Hesiod.[296] It completes the favorable waxing half of the month, but the days around Midmonth are all auspicious.

Eighth Waning is a week later, at the moon's third quarter, and honors the non-Olympian gods (the third order), including Kronos and the Titans, Helios and the planetary gods, the fixed stars, and the beneficial daimons. There seems to be no ancient precedent for this holy day, but it complements Eighth Waxing for the Olympian gods. This part of the month was considered inauspicious, because the Moon's illumination was noticeably diminishing (ἀποφράς, *apophras*, unlucky, unmentionable,

---

291. Plethon, *Laws* III.36.10, 21.

292. Anastos, "Plethon's Calendar and Liturgy," discusses the ancient precedents for the monthly holy days.

293. Plato, *Republic* 2.377a; Plutarch, *That we ought not to borrow* 2.828A, in Plutarch, *Moralia: Vol. X*, 318–19; Marinos, *Life of Proclus* 19, in *Extant Works*, 62–63.

294. Hesiod, *Works and Days*, in *Hesiod: Vol. 1*, 765–70.

295. Plutarch, *Theseus* 36.3–4, in Plutarch, *Lives: Vol. I*, 84–87; Proclus, "On *Works and Days*" 788, in Gaisford, ed., *Poetae minores Graeci* 2.433.

296. Hesiod, *Works and Days*, in *Hesiod: Vol. 1*, 819–20.

from ἀποφράττω, *apophrattô*, to be stopped up or diminished).[297] On these "forbidden days" (ἀποφράδες, *apophrades*) business was avoided, the sanctuaries were closed, and oracles were unavailable. This might not be practical today, but it is advisable to be careful at this time of declining lunar energy; it is certainly not a good time for starting something new.

On **Old Moon** we worship Pluto, the leader and protector of human nature, and also his wife Kore, Queen of the Underworld; together they preside over our immortal souls and mortal bodies, respectively. We also celebrate the departed heroes, who care for us. In ancient times it was customary to pour libations for the dead.

On **Old-and-New**, as we pass from the old month to the new, a time of rebirth, we worship Zeus and call on him and his children to release us from the bondage of our faults and to help us recover from them. Plethon, following Hesiod and Proclus, recommends it as a day for relaxing, examining oneself, assessing the past month, and forming intentions for the coming month.[298] We spend time on introspection and self-criticism, reviewing our shortcomings and mistakes, but also celebrating and praising ourselves when we have done what is right.

Here is an outline of the entire month:

The Sacred Month

Day	Morning	Afternoon	Evening
New Moon	Holy day services with first sacred hymn (Hymn 16)		
2–6 Waxing	Ordinary services		
7 Waxing	Ordinary	Ordinary	Holy day eve with second sacred hymn (Hymn 17)
8 Waxing	Holy day services with second sacred hymn (Hymn 17)		
7–3 Middle	Ordinary services*		

---

297. Anastos, "Plethon's Calendar and Liturgy," 247.

298. *Laws* III.36.21.

Day	Morning	Afternoon	Evening
2 Middle	Ordinary*	Ordinary*	Holy day eve with third sacred hymn (Hymn 18)
Midmonth	Holy day services with third sacred hymn (Hymn 18)		
2–6 Waning	Ordinary services		
7 Waning	Ordinary	Ordinary	Holy day eve with fourth sacred hymn (Hymn 19)
8 Waning	Holy day services with fourth sacred hymn (Hymn 19)		
7–3 Departing	Ordinary services*		
2 Departing	Ordinary*	Ordinary*	Holy day eve with fifth sacred hymn (Hymn 20)
Old Moon (omitted if hollow)	Holy day morning with fifth sacred hymn (Hymn 20)	Holy day afternoon with fifth sacred hymn (Hymn 20)	Holy day eve with sixth sacred hymn (Hymn 21)
Old-and-New	Holy day morning with sixth sacred hymn (Hymn 21)	Holy day afternoon with sixth sacred hymn (Hymn 21)	Holy day eve with first sacred hymn (Hymn 16) and monthly hymn for new month

*Recall that in the (reverse numbered) Middle and Departing weeks, the daily hymns are sung in their decreasing order (Hymns 27, 26, . . . , 22).

As previously noted, there is an exception to this schedule in Twelfth Month when the year is only twelve months long. During this month, the thirteenth monthly hymn (Hymn 15) is used for the morning and afternoon services, and the twelfth monthly hymn (Hymn 14) is used for the evening services.

ANNUAL HOLY DAYS

In addition to the regular monthly holy days, there are five annual celebrations, each lasting several days.[299] The New Year celebration is devoted to Zeus, Eighth Waxing of Fourth Month honors the Olympians, Midmonth of Seventh Month celebrates all the gods, Eighth Waning of Tenth Month is for the non-Olympian gods (Titans, celestial gods, daimons), and Old Year celebrates Pluto, Kore, the heroes, and mortals. These are described in detail in the following sections.

Old Year and New Year Holy Days

The Old Year and New Year holy days are explained together because they are connected, as death and rebirth. The season lasts fourteen or fifteen days, extending over the last week of Last Month (which is Thirteenth Month if the year has it, or Twelfth Month otherwise) and continuing through the first week of First Month. Because the year begins with the New Moon following the winter solstice, New Year may occur from December 21 to January 21 in the Northern Hemisphere and from June 21 to July 21 in the Southern Hemisphere (see chapter 4 on the sacred calendar).

The Old Year celebrations are focused first on Pluto and Kore, who are directly responsible for our souls and bodies, and on the heroes who lived in the past. We thus contemplate our mortality and how all mortal things come to an end. The focus then shifts to Zeus the creator and to the support we receive from the gods in our lives.

The last four days of Last Month (Twelfth or Thirteenth Month) and the first three days of First Month are holy days (beginning as usual on the preceding evening), but the arrangements are a little complicated because Last Month may be either hollow or full. This is because the services that normally occur on Old Moon (omitted in a hollow month) are moved back to Third Departing. The following outline will make this clear.

> ***Seventh and Sixth Departing of Last Month:*** The ordinary services are performed, except that they are accompanied with music, if possible, whereas ordinary services do not typically have music.

---

299. Plethon, *Laws* III.36.11–13.

Fifth Departing of Last Month: The ordinary morning and afternoon services are performed, except that they are accompanied with music, if possible. If Last Month is full, then there are ordinary evening services with music, but if it is hollow, then we begin the holy day fast with the ordinary evening service for Fourth Departing (third daily hymn, Hymn 24), but perform the monthly and daily hymns twice and with music. This first day of the fast is devoted to introspection and correction of ourselves.

Fourth Departing of Last Month: In a full Last Month, the morning and afternoon services are the ordinary ones for Fourth Departing. In a hollow month, we perform the morning and afternoon holy day services for Old-and-New with the sixth sacred hymn (Hymn 21), continuing the fast and devoting ourselves to introspection and self-correction. In the evening we perform the ordinary service for Third Departing (second daily hymn, Hymn 23), but we sing the monthly and daily hymns twice with musical accompaniment.

Third Departing of Last Month: In the morning and afternoon we celebrate the holy day services for Old Moon (the fifth sacred hymn, Hymn 20). This holy day is devoted to Pluto and to the departed, especially those who died in the past year. In the evening we perform the ordinary service for Second Departing, but the monthly and daily hymns are sung twice with music.

Second Departing of Last Month: In the morning and afternoon we perform the holy day service for Old-and-New Moon with the sixth sacred hymn (Hymn 21). This holy day is devoted to introspection and self-correction. In the evening is the holy day eve service for the following day (Old Moon if full, Old-and-New if hollow).

Old Moon: If Last Month is full, then the next day is Old Moon. In the morning and afternoon we perform the holy day service for Old-and-New Moon with the sixth sacred hymn (Hymn 21). In the evening we perform the holy day eve service for Old Moon with the fifth sacred hymn (Hymn 20). The Old Moon holy day is for Pluto, the heroes, and departed family and friends.

Old-and-New Moon of Last Month: The morning and afternoon holy day services use the sixth sacred hymn (Hymn 21). This holy day is devoted to introspection and self-correction. The evening commences the New Year with the holy day eve service for the New Moon with the first sacred hymn (Hymn 16) preceded by monthly hymn for First Month (Hymn 3). The New Moon is devoted to Zeus.

This begins the new year, and in First Month the ordinary and holy day services are altered slightly in that whenever the first monthly hymn (Hymn 3) is sung, it precedes the other hymns (rather than coming second, as is usual for holy day services). The focus is on Zeus as creator and preserver, and as the guide in our lives.

New Moon of First Month: In the morning and afternoon we perform the holy day services for New Moon with the first sacred hymn (Hymn 16). This holy day is devoted to Zeus. In the evening we perform the ordinary service for Second Waxing (first daily hymn, Hymn 22), but sing the monthly and daily hymns twice and with music. In all these services, the first monthly hymn (Hymn 3) precedes the other hymns.

Second Waxing of First Month: In the morning and afternoon we continue the holy day services for New Moon with the first sacred hymn (Hymn 16). This holy day is devoted to Hera. In the evening we perform the ordinary service for Third Waxing (second daily hymn, Hymn 23), but sing the monthly and daily hymns twice and with music. In all these services, the first monthly hymn (Hymn 3) precedes the other hymns.

Third Waxing of First Month: In the morning and afternoon we continue the holy day services for New Moon with the first sacred hymn (Hymn 16). In the evening we perform holy day evening service to finish the new year fast. This holy day is devoted to Poseidon.

Fourth Waxing to Seventh Waxing of First Month: We perform the ordinary services for these days (as given previously) but with musical accompaniment, which is normally omitted for the ordinary services.

Eighth Waxing of Fourth Month

This springtime holy day honors all the Olympian gods, especially Zeus, Poseidon, and Hera. It is celebrated as follows:

Seventh Waxing of Fourth Month: In the morning and afternoon, perform the ordinary service for the seventh day, but with music. In the evening we have the holy day eve service with the second sacred hymn (Hymn 17), which begins the fast.

Eighth Waxing of Fourth Month: Celebrate the usual holy day services with the second sacred hymn (Hymn 17). The fast is done after the evening service.

Seventh Middle of Fourth Month: Ordinary services for the seventh day, but with musical accompaniment.

Midmonth of Seventh Month

This is a summer holy day for all the gods; it is celebrated in this way:

> ***Second Middle of Seventh Month:*** In the morning and afternoon, perform the ordinary services for the second day, but with musical accompaniment. In the evening, perform the holy day service with the third sacred hymn (Hymn 18), which begins the fast.

> ***Midmonth of Seventh Month:*** Perform the holy day services with the third sacred hymn (Hymn 18). The fast is done after the evening service.

> ***Second Waning of Seventh Month:*** Perform the ordinary services for the second day, but with musical accompaniment.

Eighth Waning of Tenth Month

This is an autumn festival for the non-Olympian gods, including Kronos and the Titans, Helios and the celestial gods, and the daimons: all those responsible for mortal nature. It is celebrated according to this schedule:

> ***Seventh Waning of Tenth Month:*** In the morning and evening, perform the ordinary services for the seventh day, but with musical accompaniment. In the evening perform the holy day eve service with the fourth sacred hymn (Hymn 19), which begins the fast.

> ***Eighth Waning of Tenth Month:*** Celebrate the holy day services with the fourth sacred hymn (Hymn 19). The fast is done after the evening service.

> ***Seventh Departing of Tenth Month:*** We perform the ordinary service for the seventh day, but with musical accompaniment.

VI

Invocations

—◦◦◦—

Plethon composed invocations (or "addresses": προσρήσεις, *prosrêseis*), which are to be recited, in whole or in part, in the morning, afternoon, and evening services.[300] The directions for their rituals are in chapter 5; the texts of the invocations are collected here for convenience. Since the invocations are quite long, I have provided abbreviated versions in chapter 7. Depending on the time you have available, you may prefer the abbreviated versions, but it is worthwhile to go through the complete versions from time to time, say, on holy days. (See also "Practical Matters" in chapter 5.)

In addition you will see that each of these invocations contains a "holy day supplement," which is a middle part that should be included on holy days, but skipped on ordinary days.

MORNING INVOCATION OF THE GODS

This invocation has a holy day supplement beginning with "Above all, grant us, O gods, both now and always" and ending "where envy can find no place" (indicated in the following text). Reciting the invocation requires about 20 minutes on holy days and 10 minutes when shortened on ordinary days.

---

300. Plethon, *Laws* III.34. Plethon's text is in appendix B; the text in this chapter is edited lightly for recitation.

111

INVOCATION

O King Zeus, Being-Itself, One-Itself, Good-Itself, you are great, great in reality, and supremely great! You have not been produced by anything, you do not proceed from any cause, nothing is or has been before you. For you alone are pre-eternal. Alone of all things, you are entirely uncreated, while you are the first cause and founder of all that exists. Through you and from you everything comes, everything is born, everything is established and maintained in the best possible order, both those beings that are eternal and supercelestial, and those who live in our heaven and exist in time, some immortal, others mortal and so placed in the last rank of beings. The eternal and supercelestial you yourself create and provide with all their benefits, but to temporal beings you give other benefits by means of the various beings born directly from you. You ensure that they are as perfect as possible, not only in themselves, but the most useful for the order of the All, which is your supreme goal.

After Zeus, you too are great, O Lord Poseidon, the greatest and firstborn child of the greatest and first father, though motherless, the most powerful and most perfect work of your father. You are the leader of all the others after your father, the second father and second creator of this universe.

After him and with him are you, O Queen Hera, first daughter of Zeus, wife of Poseidon, mother of the gods within the heavens,[301] leader of the procession into multiplicity of inferior beings. And all you in turn, O Olympian gods, motherless and high-born children of great Zeus, you together create all the immortal beings within the heavens, in common with Poseidon, your leader and eldest brother. Your place is with them, O Lord Pluto, protector of our immortal principle.

You too are blessed, O Lord Kronos. Among the low-born children of Zeus, motherless like all those born of Zeus himself, you are the eldest and preside over all of mortal nature. After him and with him are all the rest of you, O Titans, O Tartareans, cocreators, together with Kronos, your leader and eldest brother, of your portions of this mortal nature, though your own essence is eternal.

---

301. The celestial gods.

You too are blessed, O Lord Helios, the eldest and most powerful of the high-born children of Poseidon and Hera. For Poseidon received from his father Zeus this brother mind younger than himself, and with this brother mind he created a soul, but he created a body with Hera, since this goddess produces matter.[302] They are the most beautiful, good, and perfect soul and body of all souls and bodies, and of his works. Then by uniting them to this mind, and submitting the body to the soul and the soul to the mind, Poseidon made Helios a sort of boundary and bond between the supercelestial and celestial realms. You, Helios, are leader of all the heavens and creator, in common with Kronos, of the entire mortal nature within it.

After Helios and with him, we greet you, O wandering Planets, you whose origin and composition are similar to those of your leader, your eldest brother. You share with him sovereignty over affairs of mortal nature and also over the race of earthly daimons, according to the division assigned to each of you, as well as sovereignty over our souls. After them, we address you, O highest Stars, you who were created to contemplate beings with an exact understanding of all things, and especially to sing the great hymn to Zeus. Last, you too are blessed, O terrestrial daimons, gods of the last degree, who, serving the other gods, immediately touch our life and nature, but who are, like all gods, infallible and immune to evil.

May all the blessed gods favorably and kindly accept this morning prayer. It is you, O gods, who, under the direction of Zeus, administer and watch over human affairs. It is you who, among other benefits devised for us, have separated our life into sleep and wakefulness, which is necessary for the preservation of this mortal body for the duration assigned to it. So from that moment when we wake and leave our bed, grant us to live rightly and well—in the way that suits you best—as we pass this day, this month, this year, and the rest of our lives. You have the right to communicate, without envy, a part of what is yours

---

302. That is, Zeus created the eternal mind (*nous*) of Helios, whose everlasting soul was created by Poseidon and whose everlasting celestial body was created by Hera. Poseidon assembles Helios, the Sun, as a celestial god, from this mind, soul, and body.

to whomever it is possible. So grant it to us, who have a nature that is immortal but mixed. And because you have attached us to this mortal part for the fullness and harmony of the All, so that there is a boundary and bond between the two parts, yours immortal and completely pure, the other mortal and perishable, at least grant that we are not completely dominated by the mortal element.[303] May the ruling and excellent part of our nature, which is akin to yours, follow you as much as possible in everything and everywhere; may it dominate and govern our inferior part, and to this end, O gods, support us as far as possible. Assist us in all the actions, all the works that we undertake, to be directed according to your reason and your wisdom, that the mortal and non-rational principle not dominate us, and that we not be distanced from you by being carried away by the erring part of our nature. On the contrary, let us exercise the most authoritative part of our being, the immortal essence akin to yours, to follow you unceasingly, as much as possible, and to draw closer to you, who are always good and happy, to maintain with you, as much as possible, an intimate alliance, a familiar communion, adapting each of our actions to be especially fitting to this kinship, so that, as far as possible, we might regulate our mortal nature and, to the extent of our strength and by this communion, fare most happily.

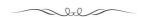

BEGINNING OF HOLY DAY SUPPLEMENT

Above all, grant us, O gods, both now and always, as a first favor, to have an understanding of you, which is the source of all goodness for us. For there can be in us nothing more beautiful nor more divine than thought in general, which is the most divine act of our most divine part, and no use of thought could be more beautiful nor more blessed than that which relates to you and to the great Zeus, since it is impossible, without our knowing Zeus, to get a correct idea of you gods, nor without our knowing you, to get a correct idea of Zeus. Indeed,

---

303. By combining in ourselves both immortal and mortal substances, humans are the linchpins that join the immortal and mortal parts of the universe into a harmonious whole.

one does not comprehend his supreme goodness if one does not consider him as the creator of you, as good and blessed ones produced from him. For this king of everything, who is supreme goodness itself, wanted to be the principle and the cause of powerful and excellent ones similar to himself, and so he engendered you as the second rank of the gods. Then he gave the highest among you, the Olympians, the power to produce a third order of divinities, the celestial gods and daimons, in order to make you, as much as possible, yet more like him in this respect.

Thus, divinity is composed of three divisions of which the first, the greatest, and the most august is that of Zeus; the other two emanate from him, one immediately, the other by the intermediary of the second; thus, he made all that is good. But it is King Zeus, completing this admirable whole, who has made it perfect and one. He composed it of both immortal and mortal beings, the generation of whom he shared with you gods. Moreover, he crafted a bond in it between the two parts, your divine race and the human race.

O gods, executors of the purpose of Zeus, you have given us a place among beings, you have united an immortal form akin to yours, namely our soul, with a mortal nature, and you have fixed our happiness first in our immortal principle, then in the good and in the sharing of the good, which you have allowed to come to us—in other words, in the imitation of yourselves, in which absolute goodness resides. But the contemplation of beings is for you one of the greatest goods, so it must also be for us the best of actions and the height of happiness, especially when we raise our thought toward what is greatest and most noble among all beings—that is to say, toward you, and toward Zeus, who commands you and all things, then toward the whole universe, and finally to the knowledge of ourselves who are in it. To obtain each of these benefits and all others to which we can aspire, help us, O gods, without whom no good is possible.

But, as the first of all benefits, establish in us the preceding doctrines and others like them. And since you have deigned to instruct us about our origin and the place we occupy in the All, keep us free so far as possible, safe from the misfortune and humiliation due to our lower part, and prevent us from being disturbed by whatever happens contrary to our purpose. For in the first place these things must be nothing to us, since they reach only our mortal nature and not the upper part of our being, which is immortal and in which you have fixed our happiness. And secondly, it is not possible that things are always given to us as we would like them to be, for there would be nothing mortal in us if we did not suffer such misfortunes, and we would no longer be a compound of two parts, one immortal, the other mortal. And finally, you wanted us to be in the middle of the All.

Moreover, to the extent of our condition and what you have given us, we must use what you have given, so grant us to use it with constancy and freedom, for you have provided us with a superior reason as a weapon against misfortune, a weapon which we are fortunate to have. For we would be foolish to rebel against those more powerful than us, and it would be unjust to seek what our masters have not given us, instead of being grateful for what is already granted, which certainly is not to be despised. May we never blame you for any of these things, nor desire other than what you have given, but yielding gently to Fate, and knowing that you treat us always as favorably as possible, and sharing, among other things, our intelligence with yours, let us share also in all your will.

Let us never have any resentment against people, who after all are born to act as they themselves think, and who cannot affect us if we know how to turn our attention to ourselves and to desire what is best. Let us not recoil before a task that is good and dear to you, coming down from you, being hindered by fear either of the labor, or of losing some of what is not really our own, or of disapproval from ignorant people.

Strengthen our thinking and most divine part to be powerful and the master of all our other faculties, as much as it can, regulating the others according to nature, the superior over the inferior, so that it imposes limits on each of them. As for the pleasures of the body, let us cling to them as moderately as possible, insofar as they do not seem to be able to harm the good state of our body and soul, even if they do not contribute to making it the best possible.[304] Let not a dishonest and extraordinary pleasure harm our soul and perhaps our body too.[305] Let us consider riches, instruments of pleasure, only as a means of satisfying the reasonable needs of life, and take care not to allow our desire to grow without bound, for it is an inexhaustible source of ills.

Let us take into account the opinions only of noble, good people, sure of finding in them witnesses and supporters of good actions. Let us pay no attention to those people who, on the contrary, have only false ideas about the noble and good, and let us seek their esteem only so long as it never distracts from virtue wherever duty is involved. Thus may we never be conquered by a vain opinion harmful to virtue.

Of the bonds and relations which you have established between us and those with whom we interact, grant that we preserve them inviolate by rendering to each what is due them by virtue of these relations, and especially to those of our community, beginning with our ancestors, who are for us your own images and whom indeed you have established as the cause of our mortal part. Let us be trusty in procuring for each person all the good proper to our relations with them, and let us never be voluntary causes of evil, and never be destructive, awful, or unsociable. May we, devoted to the common good of the community and the family of which we are a part, always hold this good before our own, thus following you, O gods born of the great Zeus, the great Good-Itself, entirely One-Itself, who has created and produced the All in its totality and in its parts: in its parts, each of which is the best and most beautiful possible; in its totality, one and multiple at the same time, itself a consonance with itself, of what has proceeded and perfected itself, to be even better and more beautiful.

---

304. In other words, there is nothing wrong with satisfying physical desires, even those that are unnecessary and do not contribute to our higher aspirations, but the gods are asked for aid in exercising rational self-control so they are satisfied moderately. See chapter 9 on the excellences, especially self-control and "orderliness."

305. "Extraordinary" here is translated from ἄτοπος (atopos), which has a range of meanings, including extraordinary (especially of pleasures), out of place, strange, exotic, unsuitable, outrageous, shocking, perverse, unnatural, and foul. I think we should interpret this as pleasures that are inappropriate in their character or degree.

And you gods are always the causes of good, both among yourselves and for the other beings that you preside over and govern, for the parts as for the whole, always and everywhere preferring the common good of the whole to the share of each individual.

Let us fulfill your sacred rites as best as possible and especially as is appropriate to you, who lack nothing, for these rites are a means of molding and impressing our imagination, the faculty closest to the divine part of our being, to bring it up to what is good and divine, and at the same time to make it more submissive and obedient to our most divine part.[306] Let us make holiness and piety consist in not neglecting anything in the rites consecrated to you, but without exceeding the measure sufficient to mold our imagination. Make us in all things as perfect as possible, and in our actions keep us safe from mistakes by these laws and other similar rules useful for life. If we fall into some fault, swiftly bring us a sufficient correction by setting before our minds a healthier reason, an exact discernment of good and bad, the surest way to cure our soul of mistakes and vice.

In this way, allied with you to the extent of our strength, we will enjoy, as much as we are allowed, the greatest goods that exist in you, where envy can find no place.

END OF HOLY DAY SUPPLEMENT

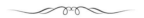

Following you as much as possible in all our conduct, we will be associated with you by the identity of our actions. In our hymns in your honor, we will borrow the holiest images of you from the highest part of our being, and with you, and above you, we will celebrate great Zeus, in the contemplation of whom all who can share in it find the most perfect and most blessed state.

---

306. That is, the purpose of these rituals and prayers is not to change the gods, but to change us. See chapter 10 for the reconstructed doctrine on prayer and sacrifice.

O Zeus, the greatest and most eminent of the gods, O Self-Father Father, O Eldest Creator of Everything, All-Powerful and Absolute King, by whom all dominion and all power over all other beings is established, directed, and governed, under you and under your supreme authority, O Master most sovereign and at the same time most gentle, to whom all things are subject in all righteousness and for their own good, if these things are born and if they exist, it is by you, it is also for you, who lack nothing, but who, being supremely good, wanted to make all things as good as possible.

Of all good things, you are the first and the last, so that you do not seek good elsewhere than in yourself, for you are the Good. You are for the blessed the unsparing sponsor of their blessedness. You are the benefactor who lavishes on all beings the greatest goods and those most consistent with the good of the Whole.

Everything is full of your glory. To thee sing all the classes of gods, who regard this worship as the most excellent and most blessed of their acts. To thee also sings Poseidon, your first and most powerful child, who presides over other beings for all good things and above all others. To thee sings Hera his wife, Motherless Mother of all the gods within the heavens. Likewise to thee sing all other Olympian gods. To thee sing Kronos and the Titans, who rule mortals. To thee sing Helios, leader of heaven, and his siblings and subordinates, the Planets, and the entire choir of the higher Stars. To thee sings the entire earthly race of daimons, who are nearest to us, and finally to thee sing we in the last rank, the human species. Each of these beings sings according to their power.

We too sing to you, and we beseech you to distribute to us the greatest goods possible. Be propitious and preserve us. Govern us in the midst of the All and grant us finally what you have judged is best for us and is, at the same time, fixed from all eternity.

AFTERNOON INVOCATIONS OF THE GODS

First Afternoon Invocation of the Gods

The holy day supplement in this invocation begins with "Apollo has under his law iden-tity" and ends with "ever changing, although uncreated in time." Reciting the invocation requires about 6 minutes on holy days and 5 minutes when shortened on ordinary days.

INVOCATION

O Lord Poseidon, of all the children of most great Zeus, you are the oldest and the most powerful. You were born of the absolutely uncreated self-father, and you yourself are not entirely uncreated, since you proceed from a cause, but you surpass all created beings by the greatness and the dignity of your power. Thus, your father has entrusted you with authority over all things, you who are essentially Form-Itself, Limit-Itself, Beauty-Itself, from whom all beings receive form and limit with the share of beauty that suits them. You are, after the great Zeus, the father and the oldest creator of the gods of the third class, of those enclosed within the heavens.

After you comes Queen Hera, born of the same father as you, but inferior to you in dignity as in nature, for it is necessary that in the supercelestial regions where you reign there not be several equal divinities; each one must be of its kind, so you each might have similarities par excellence with the One-Itself, who has engendered you. It is Hera's origin and nature to be responsible for presiding over the procession, the increase, and the infinite multiplication of things of a lower order. This is because, proceeding originally from you, the most perfect of things created, she created in herself the plurality of beings, and cohabiting with you in a chaste and divine manner, she became the mother of your divine children.

Then, in their order come all the other Olympian gods, your brothers and sisters, the high-born children of King Zeus. Their nature varies, superior in some, inferior in others, but all have received appropriate portions, which they rule under your authority.

Apollo has under his law identity; Artemis, diversity; Hephaistos, immutability and stability; Dionysos, voluntary movement and attraction leading upward towards perfection; Athena, movement and impulse caused by something else and the repulsion of the superfluous; Atlas, the stars in general, his high-born children; Tithonos, the planets, and Dione, the fixed stars. Hermes has authority over terrestrial daimons, the last class of subordinate deities; Pluto, over the most elevated part of our being which constitutes our immortal nature; Rhea, over the elements in general; but in particular, Leto presides over the aether and the heat, which separates the elements; Hekate, over the air and the cold, which brings them together; Tethys, the water and moisture, which makes them fluid; Hestia, the earth and the dryness, which makes them compact. All these gods, high-born and most powerful children of King Zeus, occupy Olympus, which is to say, the summit of the supercelestial region, the holiest of all. It is from there that, according to their attributes, they govern under your direction the mutable universe, which can be called created because it is the product of a cause and is the object of a creation, ever changing, although uncreated in time.

You, Poseidon, subject to King Zeus alone, are the guide and chorus leader of all others; it is you who marks the limit of their action and who orders the All. Thus, it is you that we first address, since you attend to our most authoritative and immortal part, the creation under your direction.

We honor you and thank you for the goods you have given us and that you give us. We sing hymns to you, and after you and with you we celebrate your brothers and sisters, the Olympian gods. O you divinities eternal and superior to time, for whom there is neither past nor future, but for whom everything is present and actual, receive favorably and kindly our afternoon address, which we offer from the lowest degree where we are placed, in time and withdrawn from eternity, at this hour when already the greater part of the day has passed, so that our good disposition is strengthened by remembrance of you, and that we do not let perish, by the succession of days, months, and years, what is divine in us, but on the contrary, thanks to you, we preserve it imperishable and uncontaminated.

O Lord Poseidon, and you, O Pluto, who watch over us, and all of you Olympians, without you we are not permitted to enjoy any good. Help us make virtue easy for ourselves, and help us in good deeds, which assure us a share of happiness. All are worthy of your assistance, but above all, those who contemplate and celebrate great Zeus, to whom we turn last, the one who is for us, for you, and for all beings the dispenser of all graces, and the very first chorus leader for us as rational beings, and who grants, as far as attainable by each of us, the contemplation of his essence, and thus puts the finishing touch on all his benefits.[307]

Second Afternoon Invocation to the Gods

The holy day supplement is in two parts in this invocation. On ordinary days, skip the second paragraph, then recite up to "You and your six siblings and attendants," take out the underlined names of the six planets, and resume with "travel around, and you all, together with Kronos and the other Titans." Continue to the end of the invocation. On fasting days nothing is omitted except the passage relating to the meal, the underlined portion beginning "Grant, O gods, now that we have spent," since it takes place later. Reciting this invocation with the supplement requires about 4 minutes on holy days and 3 minutes when shortened on ordinary days.

INVOCATION

O Lord Kronos, you are the first of the Titans, the low-born children of supreme Zeus, which is why you have received authority over them. With Helios, leader of our heavens, you are responsible for the creation of mortal nature.

---

307. That is, everything in the universe benefits from the goodness of Zeus, but especially we who contemplate and celebrate him.

Aphrodite, your companion, presides over the transmission of perpetuity into mortal things by succession. Under you are all those appointed to govern this nature according to the various portions they have received.

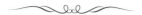

BEGINNING OF HOLY DAY SUPPLEMENT

Pan reigns over the non-rational animals, Demeter reigns over plants, and all the others have received different parts, some greater some lesser, of mortal things. Among them is Kore, the god who directs our mortal part. Pluto, who presides over our immortal soul, has carried off this goddess as his wife; thus an Olympian god, in love with a Titan goddess, establishes a link between Tartarus and Olympus by the decrees of Father Zeus.

END OF HOLY DAY SUPPLEMENT

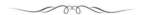

And you, O Lord Helios, born both of great Zeus by the divine mind that is in you, and also of Poseidon by the nature of your soul and body, his oldest and most powerful son, you are the common boundary between the supercelestial gods and those within the heavens, and you have been established by your father Poseidon as leader of the heavens. You and your six siblings and attendants—Selene [Moon], Eôsphoros [Venus], Stilbôn [Mercury], Phainôn [Saturn], Phaëthôn [Jupiter], and Pyroeis [Mars][308]—travel around, and you all, together with Kronos and the other Titans, perfect the whole of mortal nature. It is you, Helios, who, in the highest regions of our heavens, conduct this magnificent and numerous choir of celestial bodies. Under you also comes the earthly race of daimons appointed to serve the other gods. Finally, you preside over our immortal part, and with the help of Kronos and the Titans under him, you form our mortal part, and you preserve us, as

---

308. Omit the underlined names of the planets except on holy days. You can use their ancient names (Selene, Eôsphoros, etc.) or the modern names (Moon, Mercury, etc.) or both.

much as fated each of us. This is why, after Poseidon and the other Olympian gods, we also worship you and thank you for the goods we have from you.

We pray to those of you who lead us to guide our immortal nature toward the good and beautiful, and so far as possible to render our mortal nature tractable and useful. <u>Grant, O gods, now that we have spent most of the day fulfilling our duties, to take the nourishment necessary for our mortal body with virtue—that is, having obtained it rightly—and with good will for those preparing it and equally for our dinner companions, and with moderation and beneficial for our health, and further, with purity and vigor.</u>[309] Grant us to use the rest of this day and our life in the best and noblest way in our power. Help us at last to contemplate and to sing hymns to King Zeus whenever necessary, but especially at this moment, so that we celebrate him as worthily as possible.

Third Afternoon Invocation: The Most Important of All, Addressed to King Zeus

In this invocation the holy day supplement begins "That is why we celebrate and praise you" and ends with "presides over this act and all that is beautiful." Reciting this invocation requires about 14 minutes with the supplement on holy days and 6 minutes when shortened on ordinary days.

INVOCATION

Being-Itself, One-Itself, Good-Itself, O Zeus, you alone owe existence to no other cause than yourself, you alone are a really essential essence and an absolute unity, not a multiple unity.[310] For neither could several similarly uncreated beings come together in one whole, since they would need another being more powerful to assemble them, nor could one uncreated being merge with others proceeding from himself, because there would be no common nature between this self-existent principle and the beings who, having proceeded from him,

---

309. Omit underlined part on days of fasting.

310. That is, the first principle, as absolute unity, cannot have any parts, nor could there be several first principles that join together.

would be distinguished from him by this difference. But only you are the unity; you are always and in all ways identical to yourself. You are the Good, you are supremely good in yourself, and you have an immeasurable superiority over all other beings, which are descended from you and perfected by you. O Father of Fathers, Self-Father, Demiurge of Demiurges, Uncreated Creator, King of Kings, who rules over all rulers, you alone are absolute master and independent, nothing can be against you, but, commanding all of the gods great or small, you fix each in their state and dispense their laws; you direct and set them straight by your most upright and unchanging will. O Master, greatest and highest Master, at the same time most gentle of all masters and lords, to you everything, from the first to the last of beings, is connected as to its original principle to serve in a just servitude, which is the supreme good for them, for it is through you that they were created and exist, by you and for you who had no need of them, but who wanted to satisfy your supreme goodness by producing all the benefits possible to the most perfect degree possible.

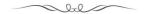

BEGINNING OF HOLY DAY SUPPLEMENT

That is why we celebrate and praise you, all of us, though our lot is the last degree of rational nature. We honor you and offer you the most pious homage in our power, for our every religious exercise concerning you is the most blessed of acts. The intelligent and reasonable nature of the gods celebrates you much better than we do.

For indeed, O God pre-eternal and in all ways uncreated, in the supreme goodness of your judgment, you have not disdained to be both father and creator of generated gods, some by yourself without a mother, the others through the oldest of those same gods produced from you. For you are the author of the class of beings closest to your nature, both immutable and eternal, and, without the concurrence of infinitely divisible matter, by yourself you are the creator who produced beings existing in themselves, gods more than others like you, the supercelestial gods. None of them is equal to the other, but some are relatively inferior to others, so that each of them, being one in individuality, is thus like you as much as possible, but collectively they form a sufficient number and a great and perfect system, the entire supercelestial order, so that each in their individuality might altogether be a common unity.

You divided these gods into two families; one is made up of your high-born children, the Olympian race of gods; the other is the race of Titans, your low-born children, who share an origin from you, but are limited to a lesser power and dignity. Kronos is the oldest of the Titans and their leader.

The oldest and most powerful of the Olympians, and at the same time of all the gods, is the great Poseidon, whom you made the most perfect image of yourself possible, the limit of perfection in the entire generation of beings. To make him even more like yourself, you gave him sovereignty and leadership over everything, and moreover the faculty of producing and creating all beings enclosed in the heavens, but by summoning some of his siblings for each of these creations. Then, organizing the heavens for you and by your example, and contriving to perfect it to contain the most beautiful things, he begets a third order of gods composed of body and soul in order to more closely preserve and order things.[311]

Now, as Poseidon begets them, taking as his model his own essence and the essences around him, entirely separate from matter, he also creates forms for our heavens and makes it out of them, but forms in no way separated from matter. On the contrary, he unites them to the matter provided by Hera, his sister and his wife, so that they are images and modeled on those higher forms. He forms a double class.[312] One is entirely inseparable from matter, depending on it; they are all the non-rational species. The other one is in no way not dependent on matter, but on the contrary keeps matter dependent on it. Although not actually

---

311. The third order are the celestial gods.

312. In the first class the form (including the soul) depends on the body, so when the body ceases to exist, so does the soul; thus non-rational souls are necessarily embodied and mortal. In the other class (rational souls), the form is potentially separable from a body even if it is never actually separated from a body.

separated, it is potentially separated and thereby more akin to your supercelestial nature; it is the rational soul.[313]

Rational soul is divided into three species. The first, which Poseidon made with scientific understanding of everything, are his high-born offspring, the race of celestial gods, the stars. The second, which does not have scientific understanding of everything, but has right opinion of everything, are his low-born children, the terrestrial race of daimons, the last race of gods, who assist the higher gods. The third does not have a correct opinion of all things, but is fallible and is not the most perfect of his productions; it is our human soul, which comes immediately after the race of daimons.

As for the other, non-rational substance, Poseidon made four principal species of body: fire, air, water, and earth. Choosing the most beautiful of these, the one which contains the least matter with the greatest volume, namely fire, he made vehicles for souls: of its bright and fiery part he made the vehicle of the souls of stars, and of the invisible and aethereal part, the vehicles of the souls of daimons and humans. Thus, always uniting a soul to a body, he has composed the three lower classes of immortal and rational living beings. However, he employed his siblings, the other Olympian gods, as assistants, each taking their part in the generation and creation of the immortals here within our heavens, namely of the three living species and of the four principal species of bodies.[314]

Of the stars, Poseidon made one class numerous, motionless, busy contemplating beings and glorifying you. But he also perfected seven planets, each corresponding to its particular eternal Idea. First he united each of them to its own Idea or Intelligence, and then he combined the eternal intelligence, a soul, and a body into a certain triple nature, which serves as an association and a bond between the supercelestial order and the heavens, an admirable relation

---

313. Some forms exist only if they are embodied in matter, and if the bodies are destroyed, they cease to exist (because the matter no longer has that form); such are non-rational souls, which depend on a body for their existence. Rational souls exist independently of bodies, although in fact they are always existing in one body or another (they are potentially, but not actually, separated).

314. The four principal species of bodies are immortal because the elements may change their form but never cease to exist.

established by his all-powerful laws.[315] He made the most beautiful and the best of them, Helios, the supreme limit of the perfection of the powers in the heavens. He united him to the most powerful of the embodied intelligences, and charged him with the government of the whole heaven, because the All must also have its share of mortal nature, so that it is in fact entirely complete.[316]

You entrust the creation of mortal things to Helios and also to Kronos, the eldest of your low-born children. Both, charged with this mission, produce animals and plants of all kinds, and everything akin to them, each helped in this creation by his siblings, Kronos by the Titans, Helios by the planets. These latter, in their movement and revolution, now approaching, now withdrawing, rearranging themselves, thereby make mortal creatures, for the other creators of these mortal creatures, the Titans, abide and are incapable of accomplishing their creation without the partnership of the planets. They receive our souls, which Poseidon has made immortal but not quite pure, and they attach our souls to a mortal nature, during the time prescribed for each of us, and later free them from this place. In this way they construct from these substances, according to your laws and under the orders of their leader Poseidon, a bond between the two parts of the universe, the immortal and the mortal.

Thus, all of the beings created by you are divided into three natural orders: the first, immutable and eternal, of which you yourself are the creator; the second, everlasting, but mutable and temporal, over the generation of which presides Poseidon, the most powerful of your children; the last finally, inferior and entirely mortal, whose creation Helios and Kronos together administer.[317] You have united these three classes, the first to the middle by the system formed by Helios and the other planets, and the middle to the last through the establishment

---

315. That is, each planetary god has its individual eternal intelligence, which is akin to the supercelestial gods, combined with an everlasting soul and fiery aethereal body.

316. The celestial gods and the Titans collaborate to create mortal nature, and in this sense the celestials serve to unite immortal and mortal realms.

317. The three orders are supercelestial gods, celestial gods and daimons, and mortal beings. The celestial gods stand at the junction of the eternal and temporal realms; humans stand at the juncture of the immortal and mortal.

of us and our affairs. You have made a unified and perfect whole containing the fairest things, an immortal generation, neither earlier nonexistent and later suddenly returning whence it came, nor sometime to be destroyed again.[318] At the same time, you perpetually preserve an immutable form, for neither could you fail to do what is most righteous, nor again fail to remove what is worse than the fairest possible.

In this All, you have given to all rational nature a sublime privilege: the faculty of knowing you and contemplating you, which you have granted to us in the last rank of nature. So, in concert with all the races of gods, we celebrate you as we are able and under the direction of great Poseidon, who also presides over this act and all that is beautiful.

END OF HOLY DAY SUPPLEMENT

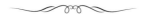

You are truly great and immensely great, you who, being the extreme and supreme limit of all dignity, dispense to each of the other gods and of all kinds, the share of dignity that is rightly theirs and best befits the whole. Thus you made us a boundary and bond between the ordained parts, the immortal and the mortal.

This is the place you have chosen to assign to us in the All, and for us, as for the gods, you made happiness consist in the good, giving more to some, less to others, always in view of the general harmony. At the same time, you have made it possible for wrongdoers to correct themselves, though easier for some, more painful for others. Thus, you have disposed all for the greater good of each being and for the greater benefit of the entire Whole, delivering all things to an eternal, inevitable fate, and fulfilling all this by the gods to whom you have entrusted this care. So be propitious, save us, and lead us with this All, in the manner you have judged is best concerning us and fixed from all eternity.

---

318. That is, the universe it eternal, neither created in time nor coming to an end.

EVENING INVOCATION OF THE GODS

In this invocation the holy day supplement extends from "but especially for the following, the greatest and the most perfect of those we enjoy or can enjoy" (below) through "Thanks be to you for all your benefactions in general" (page 133). This invocation requires about 17 minutes on holy days with the supplement and 10 minutes when shortened on ordinary days.

INVOCATION

O King Zeus, we thank you, first and especially you, for all the benefits we ever have possessed, that we now possess, or that we ever will possess. Being the Good yourself, there is no other good beside you, for you are at once the first and the last for all beings, in a word, the supreme principle of all good things. After Zeus, it is you, O Poseidon, and all of you gods, who transmit to us the benefits from Zeus. It is you that we thank always and on every occasion for all your gifts...

BEGIN HOLY DAY SUPPLEMENT

...but especially for the following gifts, the greatest and the most perfect of those we enjoy or can enjoy.

First, you gods placed us in the middle, between your immortal nature and mortal nature, and you honored us as the common boundary and bond of these two parts. You raised us above all that is mortal by our kinship with you, by participating in your immortality and by this glorious blessedness, which resembles yours, but in a much lesser degree. Moreover, you grant us to be involved with you in other ways, first of all by our knowledge of you, then by grasping the remaining beings with our reason, sharing this ability especially characteristic of you, which you deigned to share with us, and finally, by our knowledge of ourselves, for by this faculty, which you gave us, we are close to you, who especially know yourselves. That is how you arranged that the best part in us be appointed to command all the rest of us.

Besides, you gods granted that the faculty that comes first after the superior part in us and dominates all the rest—the imagination—be useful to us for rituals, and that it form and model itself as much as possible on what is best in our superior part, to be more obedient to reason and enjoy the good and divine nature.

You gods also granted us, through our goodness toward our family and toward the whole human race, to imitate you, who are always the cause of good and never of evil. You granted that we associate with one another in this civic community, which brings us closer to you, making us as similar as possible to you, who are children of the same father, King Zeus, who is Unity-Itself, and you united in the closest possible community. In addition, you grant that the part of our soul that leans on opinion be ruled by the best part of us, treating as unworthy what it judges to be useless, but greatly esteeming what alone is useful to it and in some way advantageous for virtue.

Thus, you gods did not allow us to be entirely subject to our mortal part, but granted us, if we understand what is better, the power to govern ourselves by our superior part, enjoying pleasures when it permits, without enjoying them to the point of license, but by imposing upon them order and a proper bound, taking as a measure of the enjoyment of these strong needs the reasonable needs of the mortal part, so as to be free, even while remaining here on earth. You also granted that we not regard as terrible what can happen to this mortal part against our will, when it is your decision to remove us from participation in your happiness, either through the daimons, the subordinate class to you, their masters, or through the fault of our family and this human race, either for our purification and care in the first case, or in the other by those exhibiting reckless ignorance about the soul.[319] Often you even grant that we choose, indeed, to seek what must hurt our lower part, to the point of sacrificing it sometimes entirely for the sake of the good and for the utility of our superior part, so much

---

319. That is, when bad things happen to us, we may regard them either as the gods' way of improving us or as a consequence of the ignorance of other people.

did you grant our immortal part to govern the mortal. Such are the great and good gifts with which you favored us, raising and embellishing our stronger and sovereign part by the understanding with which you often inspire us.

You gave faculties to our mortal part in order to serve our immortal part, to profit from its assistance, and to taste certain pleasures that are proper to us, blameless and without danger for our superior part. Among not a few others, eyes endowed with sight are the most useful of our senses for the observation of many other things and principally for inspection of those celestial bodies by which we learn so many beautiful things, especially the numbering of the days, months, and years, by which we can measure our life so we conduct our affairs with regularity and good order. Likewise, the ears were furnished for hearing, and the mouth for the voice; they are indispensable organs for associating with others through what we each think in our soul, so that our bodies do not completely prevent a commonality of thought. You also gave us the sense of smell in our nose to enjoy the innocent pleasure of fragrances and to distinguish healthy food from harmful, often from afar even before tasting it, according to whether it is pleasant or unpleasant. You placed the sense of taste in our mouth to judge the flavors that are healthy for our nourishment, often with pleasure, as soon as we touch them. All in all, you granted these faculties by which we are able to choose the nourishment of our life, a necessary offering to our mortal part, indispensable food for replenishing the matter that, ever changing, comes and goes so long as it is granted us to be preserved by you.

It is in view of this mortal and perishable part that you gods granted intercourse of men and women, which is so persuasive due to its pleasure. By this institution our whole species is maintained in the same state forever by an uninterrupted succession of births, each filling the place of one leaving since a fixed number of souls is allowed, and at the prescribed periods of time you assign them a succession of bodies, so you do not lack their service.

In addition, you gods granted us to compensate for the insufficiency and weakness of our physical bodies by the techniques of the arts, varied according to their object, and for that you have given us hands, instruments suitable for preparing so many works of all kinds. You granted us to use the strength and the special aptitudes of non-rational animals for our purposes, and to appropriate to ourselves the advantages of their nature.

For all these goods, it is to you, O King Zeus, first and foremost, that we must give thanks, as to the first and most powerful of our benefactors. After him, it is you, O gods, through whom these goods come from Zeus, and we have the most proper and deepest gratitude toward you, by whom, without any obligation and without any hope of return, we have been granted and we are still granted so many benefits, and to you who, good in yourselves, so want to spread the greatest abundance of goods, to share them as much as possible. Thanks be to you for all your benefactions in general ...

END OF HOLY DAY SUPPLEMENT

... but especially first and foremost for those by which you bring our soul to the rationality of virtue and goodness. For these are the most excellent of all goods, and you bestow them on the sovereign part of our being; there are none of them that do not come to us from you or through you. For it is you, the first and second ranks of gods, who receive the goods emanating from Zeus, some of them eternal in duration, the others not eternal but everlasting, and all alike unmixed with evil.[320]

After you gods and by you, we in our turn receive the benefits, but they are intermittent and no longer perfectly continuous. Yet they are still everlasting because of their perpetual renewal and the immortality of our soul. For you give all your solicitude to this intelligence, our most divine attribute, which binds us to you by a kind of kinship. You are constantly pushing us toward goodness and

---

320. These ranks are the first and second below Zeus: (1) the eternal supercelestial gods and (2) the immortal celestial gods and daimons.

we are heading in the right way, knowing that we too will fare especially happily and blessedly as long as we are able to follow you and reach your goodness.

But when, yielding to the association with our mortal part, we move away from you gods, when we depart from you and don't think what we should, we fall, as a result of this abandonment, into faults, into error, and into a state both wicked and worthless. You, then, raise us up and straighten us, either immediately by the inspiration of better thinking, or by imposing various judgments if our bad dispositions prevent us from yielding at once to the wisdom that inspires us. In every way you bring us back again to goodness, either while we remain here or depart thither.[321] When you happen to punish us, it is to correct our mistakes and to heal vices, of which it is impossible for us not to have a share because of our mortal part, which you have associated with the other, immortal part. You mixed in us these disparate parts, mortal and immortal, first of all because it seemed necessary to you for the universal harmony, then because in this general society of beings you destined us to roles that are certainly not useless or despicable. We give thanks to you, who punish only for the sake of kindness and our good, and who created us immortal in our stronger and most sovereign part and provided us everlasting blessings by your perpetual renewal.

Hear, O gods, our nightly evening prayer, which we send you. If in this day we have failed and transgressed your laws, or in our past life if we have failed and have not yet corrected our mistakes, grant us deliverance and uprightness again. Prepare us with better judgment for good deeds, and give us reason to distinguish good from bad decisions, and cleanse us of the evils attached to us. Grant the growth of the good on each occasion, but with both prompt deliverance and correction of past and present mistakes until one day, after having fulfilled the time that you have assigned to this life, we may come to that other, happier, and more divine life, in which we shall be delivered from the troubles of our mortal body. For if you have bound us to mortality for the sake of the community of the Whole, you have also assigned us a time after which our divine part returns, and each time its turn comes, it will enter into a life more divine and more in

---

321. That is, either here on earth or in the heavens between incarnations.

conformity with its nature. It will go to celebrate with those who have departed before, will engage more intimately with those of you whose nature is closer to ours, will learn from them what it is necessary to know, and will enjoy in all ways a better and more beautiful lot, so that it is not always filled with the miseries of this mortal body, but that it also might have a much better and more divine life, surpassing this life in all respects and especially by its much longer duration.

Since you produce the better from the worse, so far as possible, you are inclined to grant longer-lasting goods, and what is good much more than what is not, especially when you grant that we understand much clearer and better whatever concerns us. So grant us to remember to the greatest extent each past life, either here or there, and to connect together in our memory those memories seized now by a profound forgetting[322] because we have, during the first age of this life, crossed the River Lethe, and during the rest of the time we remain in the gloom of our mortal nature.[323] Moreover, we will then have a clearer fore-knowledge of the future, of which now we have but a scant image, which comes to us from the daimons, the race closest to ours, while sleep rids us of the tumult of sensations, or which is revealed sometimes to those receiving a vision by a more divine extension of their thinking.[324]

And you, O blessed heroes, whose nature surpassing ours is closest to divinity, you who, during your life among us here, are for us in common the sources of the great benefits that Zeus sends us through the gods, hail to you! And you, our ancestors, our parents, who are images of divinity for us and the immediate origins of our mortal nature, and you also, housemates and comrades, clansmen[325] and kin, you who, older or younger, have arrived first in that more divine and blessed life, and you too, companions and friends, and you, our fellow citizens, especially you who have presided over our common good, and especially

---

322. λήθη, *lêthê*.

323. That is, when we are reborn, we cross the River of Forgetfulness and forget our previous incarnations.

324. The daimons bring us inklings of the future through dreams and waking visions.

325. These are the *phratores*, including also the brothers (and sisters) belonging to a phratry (clan).

you who have lost your life for the freedom of the community with the same belief, either for the preservation of their existence and well-being, or for the righting of disturbances that are not right: hail to all of you! And when the fate from the gods calls us, as they have called you, give us a gracious and kind welcome when we come as friends among our friends.

And all of you daimons, especially those of you who are nearest us, and above you, Pluto, our protector, be kind to us, attend us here below so that we become good and honest, and when we go thither at the appointed time, welcome us kindly. All of you, O gods who watch over us, care for us now and always, so we might fare well and honorably, and this night grant us the rest necessary for our mortal body in a pure bed, free from any wrongdoing.[326] Inspire us kindly while we sleep, guide our soul in a dream to your company, and awaken us whole and free of evil, willing to walk in the straight way that will lead us to the good and to all that pleases you. Grant us to do all that is good, and to sing your praises properly, and with you and in addition to you to celebrate great Zeus.

O Self-Father Zeus, father and immediate origin of all motherless gods, the supercelestial gods, O eldest demiurge of all that exists, even through intermediaries, O truly supreme and sovereign King, you who alone and independently hold all the powers under your control, O absolute master of all things, you are truly great and immensely great, all things are full of your power and magnificence. Be propitious, preserve us, govern us with the All according to what you have judged is best for us and what is also fated from all eternity.

INVOCATION OF ZEUS AFTER THE FAST

Recite this invocation on all Old-and-New Moons and fasts. In First Month include the part about the beginning and end of the year and in addition this part: "this month and year at which we have arrived and," which is about the new year (both indicated in the

---

326. Based on his remarks elsewhere (e.g., *Laws* III.31.5), I think we can safely assume that Plethon approves of only monogamous heterosexual relations. In this regard his opinions are typically medieval. We, however, can interpret "wrongdoing" as just those behaviors that are dishonest, abusive, degrading, or nonconsensual.

text on page 142), but omit them in other months. On the two fasts of Last Month that are before Old-and-New, remove the whole part concerning the boundary day of the two months (indicated in the text on page 140), which applies only to Old-and-New. Reading this invocation requires about 14 minutes with the supplement on holy days and 13 minutes when shortened on ordinary days.

INVOCATION

O King Zeus, you are the One-Itself and entirely uncreated, supremely One and in no way different from yourself. You are the first and last of good things, and in no way different from the Good, but you yourself create the Good and the All, which is produced from yourself, and is always whole and neither comes to be in time, nor ever will end. You organized a unity out of the many with agreements among them. Furnishing yourself with the best of beings, you made them one in the best way, preserved by you through all eternity. You are perfect in your highest singularity and possess nothing in yourself better or worse than anything else, indeed nothing entirely different, but you yourself completed and perfected this All by filling it with all kinds of Ideas, some higher, some lower, and entirely whole.

You begat great Poseidon in the All, the most perfect of your creations and the most similar to you, and you entrusted him with leadership of everything, nor will he abandon providence for the very uttermost of beings. You bestowed power on him and a similar nature on the others, and granted him to guide this power and to produce whatever you might need from them; in all respects, he manages their tasks well. You set up the entire intellectual and supercelestial order by yourself and filled it with all kinds of Ideas indivisible in their essence, all of them immutable minds, all these beings together and actually in one mental act of mutual contemplation, in a second divine order of gods.[327] You united them under their chorus leader Poseidon into one, most beautiful cosmos, and gave it eternity as its measure of life. You put in it nothing passing, but all things existing forever and remaining as they are.

---

327. That is, the supercelestial gods.

Also by your arrangement these heavens are organized under great Poseidon and your other creations, the gods, as an image of your intellectual and eternal order, and these heavens are composed now of mortal and immortal things, so that the All might be completed perfectly for you, containing all things that it was possible to have in creation.[328] Moreover the entire, endless time conferred a measure of life on it and became your image of eternity.[329] It is already past or yet about to be; it does not exist and exists not yet; it is always in a present moment, which is always becoming one thing after another; the present divides past and future time.

In it great Poseidon, obeying you, placed the divine race of stars, combining the best form of soul with befitting bodies. Among them he placed great Helios, joining him with the divine mind of those produced in your eternal order, in order to bind in it two substances, eternal and temporal.[330] And he appointed Helios, the strongest of the gods in the heavens, to be their leader and the creator of all mortal nature with Kronos, its especial archon and ruler. He also gave Helios six other helpers for these tasks and provided them a similar constitution, but in no way his equal.

Moreover Helios does not cease, through day and night, from measuring time for us by his unending cycles, completing each of them together with the revolutions of the entire aether. During the day, light is provided fully and beautifully for the eyes of those above the earth, and during the night for those below the earth, each making way for the other, and by these increases and decreases there is equity in the cosmos, the two taking and giving in turn. The creator of these things organized the month by each meeting of Helios and Selene, who is second to Helios in power. She takes her borrowed light from him, and she appears to us each night, at the times when she comes. Helios kindly provides

---

328. The third order of creation, which exists in time and space, includes both immortal beings (the celestial gods, daimons, and human souls) and mortal beings (human bodies, other animals, plants, etc.).

329. Plato calls time the moving image of eternity at *Timaeus* 37d.

330. Helios has an eternal mind, like the other gods, and an everlasting soul and body; thus, he unites the timeless eternal realm to the temporal heavens.

the year by his cycles around the zodiac and the ecliptic and provides the hours by his coming and going.

Your eldest child, Poseidon, guiding the creation of these heavens by your laws, placed in it the race of daimons, the last race of gods, standing midway between the stars and us. For after these races of gods, by your providence Poseidon himself placed our souls within the vault of heaven as a necessary boundary between, on one hand, everlasting things and the perpetual goods of the races of gods and, on the other, those beings subject to death. Our souls are also everlasting and enjoy goods resembling those of the gods, not perpetually, but intermittently, as they are lost and restored again, for you needed such a species in the All so that it might be sufficiently complete and perfect.[331] Moreover, it is unified, each part joined to another, not full of various separated kinds, but gradually changing little by little, each part sharing with those in between. Such are our souls, assembled by you, which became entangled with these mortal bodies. The separated mortal and immortal natures were brought together in us and bound together into one, so that these two natures would not be separated, but there would be some mixture of the mortal with the immortal things nearest them, through a discontinuous participation in good things, at some times clothed in a body and at other times set free and living by itself, and thus always withdrawing by turns through the whole of unlimited time, so that there is only such a conjunction as this.

By means of Poseidon and your blessed children, the gods, you have placed us here in the All, wherefore let us be pleased with our position, and let us be completely grateful to you for such as we are and for every other benefit of any kind that you have given us or might give us from time to time, and most especially for the share of divinity that you have given us. Since we make mistakes because of this position, in each instance you have assigned a correction and actions to raise us up and bring us close to divinity.

---

331. Humans are twofold, with a mortal physical body and an immortal soul, which always resides in its aethereal vehicle, which is bound to the physical body during incarnation. Thus, we are the link between the mortal and immortal realms of the All.

BEGINNING OF OLD-AND-NEW MOON HOLY DAY SUPPLEMENT

And now, on this day when we celebrate again the boundary between the departing month and the new one arising, when the two gods draw together, <u>and in addition the boundary between the completed year and that beginning, precisely when Helios turns during the winter</u>[332] and during this day of Selene's conjunction, when she grows again from her smallest, on this very day they have examined us and our lives and judged the mistakes we have made, how we have fallen short, and the wrongs we have committed. From these we beg our deliverance and correction.

END OF OLD-AND-NEW MOON HOLY DAY SUPPLEMENT

Having accepted our evening prayer, our kneeling, and our all-day fast, which we have established for ourselves as symbols of our love for you and as a service that is especially proper, but also most useful for we who serve, release us from the evils that come to us through thoughtlessness, and in their place grant us what is good, making present goods better and granting those that we lack but are proper.

You have offered us correct thought and judgment about what is good and bad according to the gods, to whom such things have been entrusted. You are indeed the mightiest purifier of faults and bad souls and the mightiest provider and guardian of what is good. So grant us, with the circuit of days, months, and years, the growth of the good each time, but also prompt deliverance from past and present wrongs, and our restoration to what is proper.

---

332. Underlined text is included only during Last Month (for the old and new year holy days). "When Helios turns during the winter" is the winter solstice.

We know happiness and blessedness are granted us through virtue and good-ness, until one day, after having fulfilled the time that you have assigned to this life, we may come to that other, happier, and more divine life, in which we shall be delivered from the troubles of our mortal body. For if you have bound us to mortality for the sake of the community of the Whole, you have also assigned us a time after which our divine part returns, and each time its turn comes, it will enter into a life more divine and more in conformity with its nature.[333] Our superior part will celebrate with those of its kind who have already departed, whom we ourselves remember now and hereafter, and will engage more inti-mately with the gods closer to us, will learn from them what it is necessary to know, and will enjoy an entirely better and more beautiful lot, so that it is not always filled with the miseries of this mortal body, but also that it might have a much better and more divine life, surpassing the other in all respects and especially by its much longer duration; seeing that because you produce the bet-ter from the worse, so far as possible, you are inclined to impart longer-lasting goods, and goods much more than evils.

But, O Master, grant us when we arrive there, O Master of Everything, to mingle with the gracious and kindly heroes there, whose nature above ours is clos-est to divinity, those who, during their lives among us here, were for all of us in common the sources of the great goods you sent to our ancestors and parents, who are images of you and the gods, and also to our housemates, comrades, kin whom-soever, who happen to have arrived in that more divine and blessed life, and also to companions, all fellow citizens, and others presiding over our common good, and especially to those who lost their life for the freedom of the community with the same belief, either for the preservation of their existence and well-being, or for the righting of disturbances that are not right. You have united us with the good and honest among them, and granted us to celebrate and to encompass everything under our protector, Pluto, and the other gods in charge of us. The most beautiful and most divine of all feasts and festivals is the manifest contemplation of you, the first cause of everything.

---

333. Our souls spend some time in the celestial realms between incarnations.

In the present, may you grant that we be released from erring, first purified of guilt and acceptable to you and your gods, which is a sacred service you perform, and afterward may you bring about that we eat our modest meal and go to sleep in a clean bed, which is indispensable for the preservation of our mortal body for the duration you have assigned it.[334] And may you send us dreams so the gods can meet with us, guiding our souls, and raising us out of evils without suffering, to celebrate your holy festivals in a holy way, and to pass through <u>this month and year at which we have arrived and</u>[335] our remaining life as blamelessly as possible and thereby especially dear to you, and also to accomplish other good things, both honoring the gods, your children, as is fitting, through whom, so far as it concerns you, human affairs are arranged, and then celebrating you as first principle of everything.

O Self-Father Zeus, father and immediate origin of all motherless, supercelestial gods, O eldest demiurge of all things, both directly and by means of those born of you, O truly supreme and sovereign king, who alone and independently hold all the powers under your control, O absolute master of all things, you are great, truly great, and immensely great. Everything is full of your power and magnificence. Be propitious, preserve us, govern us with the All according to what you have judged is best for us and what is also fated from all eternity.

---

334. The meaning here is not that the bed is recently laundered, but that it is "undefiled" (ἀμόλυντον, *amoluton*) by unacceptable sex (which we can interpret according to contemporary mores).

335. Underlined text to be included only during Last Month.

VII

Abbreviated Invocations

———⌇———

As you have seen, the morning, afternoon, and evening invocations will require something like 15 to 20 minutes to read, and this is in addition to the hymns and adorations, so the services can be quite lengthy, especially on holy days, consuming the better part of an hour. This sort of schedule is infeasible for many of us today, who have other obligations and demands on our time, so I've made these abbreviated invocations, which require only 2 or 3 minutes each.

Morning Invocation of the Gods

O King Zeus, Being-Itself, One-Itself, Good-Itself, you are great, great in reality, and supremely great! Nothing is or has been before you, for you alone are pre-eternal.

You are also great, O Lord Poseidon, the greatest and firstborn child of the greatest and first father! You are the second father and second creator of this universe. You are with him, O Queen Hera, first daughter of Zeus, wife of Poseidon, mother of the gods within the heavens, leader of the procession into multiplicity of inferior beings.

And you other Olympian gods, children of great Zeus, together with Poseidon you create all the immortal beings within the heavens. You are with them, O Lord Pluto, protector of our immortal principle.

You too are blessed, O Lord Kronos, eldest of the Tartarean children of Zeus, and the other Titans, who preside over all of mortal nature.

And you are blessed, O Lord Helios, the eldest and most powerful of the children of Poseidon and Hera. After him, we greet you, O wandering Planets and highest Stars. Lastly, you too are blessed, O terrestrial daimons, gods of the last degree, but still infallible and good.

May all the blessed gods favorably and kindly accept this morning prayer! We will follow you in our conduct and actions. In our hymns we will borrow the holiest images of you from our highest soul. With you we will celebrate great Zeus, in which all will find the most perfect and most blessed state.

We beseech you to grant the greatest goods possible. Be propitious and preserve us. Govern us in the midst of the All, and grant what you have judged is best for us and also fixed from all eternity.

AFTERNOON INVOCATIONS OF THE GODS
FIRST AFTERNOON INVOCATION OF THE GODS

O Lord Poseidon, of all the children of most great Zeus, you are the oldest and most powerful. You are Form-Itself, Limit-Itself, Beauty-Itself, from whom all beings receive the form, the limit, and the share of beauty that suits them.

After you comes Queen Hera, born of the same father as you. She presides over the procession, the increase, and the infinite multiplication of things of a lower order. For she has created in herself the plurality of beings, and by dwelling with you in a chaste and divine manner, she became the mother of your divine children. After her come all the other Olympian gods, your brothers and sisters.

You, Poseidon, subject to King Zeus alone, are the guide and chorus leader of all the others; it is you who marks the limit of their action and who orders the

All. Thus, it is you that we first address. We honor you and thank you for your gifts, both past and future. We sing hymns to you, and after you and with you we celebrate your brothers and sisters, the Olympian gods.

O you divinities eternal and superior to time, for whom there is neither past nor future, but for whom everything is present and actual, receive favorably and kindly our afternoon address, which we offer from the lowest degree where we are placed, in time and withdrawn from eternity, at this hour when already the greater part of the day has passed, so that our good disposition is strengthened by remembrance of you, and that we do not let perish, by the succession of days, months, and years, what is divine in us, but on the contrary, thanks to you, we preserve it imperishable and uncontaminated.

O Lord Poseidon, and you, O Pluto, who watch over us, and all of you Olympians, without you we are not permitted to enjoy any good. Help us to make virtue easy for ourselves, and help us in good deeds, which assure us a share of happiness.

All are worthy of your assistance, but above all, those who contemplate and celebrate great Zeus, to whom we turn last, the one who is for us, for you, and for all beings the dispenser of all graces, and the very first chorus leader for us as rational beings, and who grants, as far as attainable by each of us, the contemplation of his essence, and thus puts the finishing touch on all his benefits.

SECOND AFTERNOON INVOCATION TO THE GODS

O Lord Kronos, you are the first of the Titans, lesser children of supreme Zeus. With Helios, leader of our heavens, you are responsible for the creation of mortal nature. Aphrodite, your companion, presides over the transmission of perpetuity into mortal things by succession. Under you are all those appointed to govern this nature according to the various portions they have received.

And you, O Lord Helios, are the child both of great Zeus by your divine mind and of Poseidon by your soul and body. You are the common boundary between the supercelestial gods and those within the heavens, and have been established by your father Poseidon as leader of the heavens. You and your six siblings and attendants—the Moon, Venus, Mercury, Saturn, Jupiter, and Mars—travel around, and you all, together with Kronos and the other Titans, perfect the whole of mortal nature.

It is you, Helios, who, in the highest regions of our heavens, conduct this magnificent and numerous choir of celestial bodies. Under you also comes the earthly race of daimons appointed to serve the other gods.

Finally you preside over our immortal part, and with the help of Kronos and the Titans under him, you form our mortal part, and you preserve us, as much as fated each of us. We pray to you to guide our immortal nature toward the good and beautiful, and so far as possible to render our mortal nature tractable and useful.

Grant us, O gods, now that we have spent most of the day fulfilling our duties, to use the rest of this day and our life in the best and most beautiful way in our power. Help us at last to contemplate and to sing hymns to King Zeus whenever necessary, but especially at this moment, so that we celebrate him as worthily as possible.

THIRD AFTERNOON INVOCATION OF KING ZEUS

O Zeus, Being-Itself, One-Itself, Good-Itself, you alone owe existence to no other cause than yourself, you alone are a really essential essence and an absolute unity. O Father of Fathers, Self-Father, Creator of Creators, Uncreated Creator, King of Kings, you rule over all rulers. O Master, greatest and highest Master, at the same time most gentle of all masters and lords, all the gods serve you, which is the supreme good for them.

You are truly great and immensely great, you who, being the extreme and supreme limit of all dignity, dispense to the other gods and to everything else the share of dignity that is rightly theirs and best befits the whole. Thus, you made us a boundary and bond between the ordained parts, the immortal and the mortal. This is the place you have chosen for us in the All, and for us, as for the gods, you made happiness consist in the good, giving more to some, less to others, always in view of the general harmony. At the same time, you made it possible for wrongdoers to correct themselves, though easier for some, more painful for others.

Thus, you have disposed all for the greater good of each being and for the greater benefit of the entire whole, delivering all things to an eternal, inevitable fate, and fulfilling all this by the gods to whom you have entrusted this care. So be propitious, save us, and lead us with this All, in the manner you have judged is best for us and fixed from all eternity.

EVENING INVOCATION OF THE GODS

O King Zeus, we thank you for all the goods that we ever have possessed, that we now possess, or that we ever will possess. Being the Good yourself, there is no other good beside you, for you are at once the first and the last for all beings, the supreme principle of all good things.

Next it is you, O Poseidon, and all of you gods, who transmit to us the benefits from Zeus. It is you whom we thank always and on every occasion for all your gifts, but especially for those that bring our soul the rationality of virtue and goodness, the most excellent of goods bestowed on our sovereign part. For you give all your care to this intelligence, our most divine attribute, which binds us to you by a kind of kinship.

Hear, O gods, our evening prayer. If we have failed today or in our past life, grant us deliverance and uprightness again. Give us reason to distinguish good from bad, and grant us prompt deliverance and correction of our mistakes. And you, O blessed heroes, whose nature over ours is closest to divinity, you who are the sources of the great goods that Zeus sends us through the gods, hail to you! And you, our parents and ancestors, and you also, housemates and comrades, clansmen and kin, all you who, older or younger, have arrived first in that more divine and blessed life, hail to all of you! And when divine fate calls us, give us a gracious and kind welcome when we come as friends among our friends. And all of you daimons, and above you, Pluto, our protector, be kind to us. Attend us here below so that we become good and honest.

All of you, O gods, care for us now and always, so we might fare well and honorably, and grant us the rest necessary for our body in a pure bed, free from any wrongdoing. Inspire us kindly while we sleep, guide our soul to you in a dream, and awaken us whole and free of evil, willing to walk in the straight way that will lead us to the good and to all that pleases you.

O Self-Father Zeus, father and immediate origin of all supercelestial gods, O eldest demiurge, O truly supreme and sovereign King, be kind, preserve us, govern us with the All according to what you have judged is best for us and what is also fated from all eternity.

Invocation of Zeus after the Fast

The short paragraph beginning "Now, on this day when we celebrate again the Old-and-New Moon" is the holy day supplement used just on Old-and-New Moon holy days.

Invocation

O King Zeus, you are One-Itself and entirely uncreated, supremely One and in no way different from yourself. You are the first and last of everything good, in no way different from the Good, but you create the Good and the All, which is always whole, and neither comes to be in time, nor will ever end. You yourself completed and perfected this All, setting up the entire intellectual and supercelestial order, filled with all kinds of Ideas, indivisible in their essence, some higher and some lower, all in one mental act of mutual contemplation. You united them under Poseidon into a most beautiful cosmos and gave it eternal life.

Also by your arrangement these heavens were organized under great Poseidon and the other gods, an image of your intellectual and eternal order, and the heavens were assembled from mortal and immortal things, so the All would be perfect. Endless time is its measure of life. Great Poseidon placed in it the divine race of stars, including great Helios, to bind in it two substances, the eternal and the temporal. He made Helios the strongest of the celestial gods and their leader. With Kronos he is the creator of all mortal nature, for which he has six other helpers.

Poseidon also placed in this world the race of daimons, the last race of gods, between the celestial gods and us. And he placed our souls in the world as a necessary boundary between the everlasting gods and mortal things, though our souls are also everlasting. Thus the All was finished complete and perfect. Let us be pleased with our position and grateful for every benefit you have given us, but especially for our share of divinity.

BEGINNING OF SUPPLEMENT FOR NEW-AND-OLD MOON HOLY DAYS

Now, on this day when we celebrate again the Old-and-New Moon <u>and in addition the old and new year, when Helios makes his winter turn,</u>[336] and during this day of Selene's conjunction, these gods have examined our lives and judged our mistakes, for which we beg deliverance and correction.

END OF SUPPLEMENT FOR NEW-AND-OLD MOON HOLY DAYS

Having accepted our evening prayer, our kneeling, and our all-day fast, which are symbols of our love for you, release us from the evils that come to us through thoughtlessness, and in their place grant us what is good. You have offered us correct judgment about what is good and bad according to the gods. You are the mightiest purifier of faults and the mightiest provider and guardian of what is good. So grant us, with the circuit of days, months, and years, the growth of the good each time, but also prompt deliverance from past and present wrongs, and our restoration to what is proper.

When we have fulfilled the time assigned to this life and come to that other, happier, and more divine life, grant us, O Master of Everything, to mingle with the gracious and kindly heroes, who, during their lives here, were the sources of

---

336. Underlined text is included only during Last Month.

the great goods you sent to our ancestors. Grant us to celebrate and to encompass everything under our protector, Pluto, and the other gods in charge of us.

Grant now that we be purified of guilt and afterward that we eat our modest meal and sleep as needed by our mortal body. Send us dreams, leading our souls to meet with you, to pass through our remaining life as blameless as possible, and to accomplish other good things.

O Self-Father Zeus, father and immediate origin of all supercelestial gods, O eldest demiurge of all things, both directly and by means of those born of you, O truly supreme and sovereign king, you who hold all the powers, O absolute master of all things, you are great, truly great, and immensely great. Everything is full of your power and magnificence. Be propitious, preserve us, govern us with the All according to what you have judged is best for us and what is also fated from all eternity.

VIII

Hymns

───◦⦵◦───

Plethon composed hymns to accompany all his rituals, and we are fortunate that they survived Scholarios's destruction.[337] The places where the hymns are used in the rituals are described in chapter 5, but the texts of the hymns are gathered here for ready reference. Altogether there are 27 hymns: two perennial hymns (Hymns 1–2), which are used in all the worship services; thirteen monthly hymns (Hymns 3–15), which are sung during the worship services in the corresponding lunar months; six sacred hymns (Hymns 16–21) sung in the six corresponding monthly holy day worship services; and six daily hymns (Hymns 22–27) for the ordinary worship services on the corresponding ordinary days of each week.

Plethon's hymns have been called didactic because they describe the gods to whom they are addressed; they might not seem very poetic. But this is the way Platonic prayers work (see chapter 10). By calling to our mind the attributes of a god, which are Platonic Ideas connected to the Idea of the god, the prayer connects the idea of the god in your individual *nous* to its archetype in the cosmic *Nous*. In this way Plethon's prayers and hymns elevate our minds to the gods. Therefore, I've also added a few notes after each hymn to help you understand any points that might be obscure.

───────────

337. Plethon, *Laws* III.35.

Plethon composed his hymns in the dactylic hexameters of the Greek epics, which he called "the most beautiful of all rhythms" with a "majesty to which no other approaches." However, dactylic verse does not work so well in English, and so I've followed a common practice of translating into iambic hexameter, which follows the natural rhythms of English. The number three is sacred in Platonic philosophy, and Plethon's hymns are built on threes. There are 27 ($3 \times 3 \times 3 = 3^3$) hymns, each nine ($3 \times 3$) lines long, each line having exactly six (3×2) feet, which is considered a perfect number.[338]

Plethon's hymns are intended to be sung or chanted, sometimes with instrumental accompaniment, but if he composed music for them, it has not survived. He did however prescribe for each hymn a musical mode (scale) that was symbolically appropriate to the subject of the hymn, and these are indicated with the texts of the hymns. I am not competent to compose music for the hymns, but if you are, I encourage you to compose or improvise music. In case you want to work in the ancient Greek modes, I have included some information in the last section of this chapter. Plethon presumably composed in the musical style of his time (c. 1400), and we are free to compose in our own.

TEXT OF HYMNS

Hymn 1: First Perennial Hymn, to Zeus
Mode: Hypodorian (A)

> Zeus, Father, thou Self-Father, eldest demiurge,
> All-Father, King, the highest and most great of all,
> all-powerful, the One-Itself, the Good-Itself,
> and Being-Itself, who made all things since endless time,
> the greatest by thyself, the rest by lesser gods,
> all with perfection, to the uttermost degree.
> Be kind, protect us, lead us, as in everything,

---

338. It is perfect because it is the sum of its divisors, $1 + 2 + 3 = 1 \times 2 \times 3$. Six is also the third triangular number ($6 = 1 + 2 + 3$).

by thine illustrious children. You entrust them with
our destinies, fulfilled as just they ought to be.

The Demiurge (δημιουργός, *dêmiourgos*) is the Craftsman or creator god in Plato's
Timaeus.

Hymn 2: Second Perennial Hymn, to the Gods

Mode: Hypodorian (A)

O noble children of All-Father, Being, Zên,
you govern us with justice under his command;
so let us never fail to have you as our guides,
obeying laws that are both right and dear to you,
as best we can, the only laws to rule us well.
And you, O gods, direct us, straightening our minds,
which you have made with nature similar to yours.
And grant to us, O gods, good order in our lives,
but most of all, with you to celebrate great Zeus.

"Zên" is an old poetic form of "Zeus"; the word *zên* (ζῆν) also means to live or be
alive. Feel free to sing "Zeus" if you prefer.

Hymn 3: First Monthly Hymn, to Zeus

Mode: Hypodorian (A)

Great Zeus, Self-Father, Ianos, the Progenitor
of everything with being and receiving birth,
in truth created none of these things thoughtlessly,
but just as he exists, so do the other gods,
whom, never idle, he made mirrors of himself;
and never less than is his pow'r, he does it well
and properly, because his nature is the Good.
O Zeus, we hail thee, guarding all and reigning; hail,
most blessed; hail thee, gracious giver of all goods.

The Roman god Ianus (anglicized as Janus) is the two-faced god of beginnings and endings, of entries and exits. According to Plutarch, Numa Pompilius added the month January, named for Janus, to the Roman calendar and made it the beginning of the year.[339] (Recall that both Numa and Plutarch are in the Golden Chain.) It is surprising to find a distinctly Roman god in Plethon's hymns, but we see here that he is an aspect of Zeus.

Hymn 4: Second Monthly Hymn, to Poseidon

Mode: Hypophrygian (G)

> O Lord Poseidon, thou art firstborn son of Zeus,
> in splendor and in strength surpassing everything,
> for everything received its origin from Zeus.
> With might you make and master, second to your sire,
> preeminent, as great as is infinity,
> because of all that is, alone is he unborn.
> And by thy sire's command was granted thee to make
> the widespread heavens where we have been placed by thee.
> O Father, always kind and gentle be to us.

Poseidon, as leader of the supercelestial gods under Zeus, organizes the creation of the heavens, including the celestial gods, and everything below the heavens.

Hymn 5: Third Monthly Hymn, to Hera

Mode: Hypophrygian (G)

> August One, goddess Hera, daughter of great Zeus,
> O thou whose husband is Poseidon, thou who art
> most fair, the mother of the gods within the sky,
> the cause of matter, and the seat here for the forms,
> dispenser of all powers, and among the rest,
> what leads us into excellence and all that's fair.

---

339. Plutarch, *Numa* 19, in Plutarch, *Lives I*, 368–73.

You bring together laws for everything from which
the multitude eternally comes forth; you grant
us to live well; to virtue bring us graciously.

Hymn 6: Fourth Monthly Hymn, to the Olympian Gods
Mode: Hypophrygian (G)

Poseidon, King, the best and greatest child of Zeus,
who also governs all things from thy father born,
and Hera, holy wife of him and noble queen,
Apollo, Artemis, Hephaistos, Bacchus, and
Athena too, you seven gods are mightier
than all the rest save him, the mightiest on high.
You other gods who dwell upon Olympus peak,
ancestors of immortal souls, including us,
be ye propitious and be gracious unto us.

The Olympian gods have the power to create immortal beings who exist in space and time, including the souls of celestial gods and daimons and the immortal souls of humans.

Hymn 7: Fifth Monthly Hymn, to Apollo
Mode: Hypophrygian (G)

O Lord Apollo, chief and leader of each kind's
identity, who guides all things to unity,
who doth subject the One itself, a multitude
and a polyphony, beneath one harmony,
with concord you impart both prudence to our souls,
and justice, qualities most beautiful to have,
combined with beauty in our bodies, joined with health.
Moreover always give our souls, O Lord, desire
for things divine and beautiful. O hail, Paeán!

Apollo unites various characteristics into a harmonious whole, giving each thing its unique identity. "Paeán" (Παιάν, *Paian*) is an epithet of Apollo as healer and also refers to the ritual chants of healing and thanksgiving.

Hymn 8: Sixth Monthly Hymn, to Artemis
Mode: Hypophrygian (G)

> O Lady Artemis, who rules and who protects
> the form of difference, you receive as one the Whole
> and then up to the limit you divide each form
> in many forms, from forms to individuals,
> and from the whole to limbs and joints, and separate
> our souls from what is worse in us, and give them strength
> and self-control, and to our bodies might and health.
> But grant to us, O Queen, to flee from shameful things
> and straighten up our lives in every circumstance.

Artemis distinguishes the various, differing parts within a whole: the species within a genus, the individuals belonging to an Idea, and the distinct parts of an individual. She draws distinctions, especially between what is good and what is not.

Hymn 9: Seventh Monthly Hymn, to the Celestial Gods
Mode: Phrygian (D)

> O lord of heaven, Helios, be kind to us,
> and you, Seléne, holy mistress, be thou kind,
> and Phôsphoros and Stílbôn, of the shining Sun
> attendants always, Phaínôn and Phaéthôn too,
> and you Pyróeis; all are subject to the Sun,
> your lord, whom you assist in his concern for us
> that we not suffer need, and so we sing to you
> this hymn, to you who are our splendid guardians,
> and to the stars sent forth by providence divine.

I've added accents to aid pronunciation of the "Chaldean" planet names. If you prefer to use modern names for the five lesser planets, then replace lines three through five with: "and Mercury and Venus, of the shining Sun / attendants always, fiery Mars and Jupiter, / and Saturn; all of you are subject to the Sun."

Hymn 10: Eighth Monthly Hymn, to Athena

Mode: Hypophrygian (G)

> Athena, Lady, you who rule and govern form,
> the form that is to matter always bound, and you
> who are creator after the wide-ruling one,
> Poseidon, who before you holds all form, and you
> who are the source of ev'ry motion caused by force.
> When anything superfluous becomes attached,
> you drive off each and ev'ry one; whenever we
> act foolishly in error, then draw near to us,
> O goddess, rouse our hearts to duty with good sense.

Athena governs the manifestation of Ideas or Forms in material reality, and so these embodied forms exist only so long as their bodies retain their form. She governs physical interactions according to her eternal laws, which she preserves from material influences. Therefore, she protects our immortal souls from undesirable influences from our embodiment.

Hymn 11: Ninth Monthly Hymn, to Dionysos

Mode: Hypophrygian (G)

> O Bacchus, Father, maker of all rational souls,
> of the celestials, and of daimons, and of us,
> you follow after great Poseidon next in this
> and cause the changes drawing us by love to good,
> ascending thereby to a more desired state.
> Grant thou whenever we depart each time the good,

from action that is holier, by our mindless thought,
to lead us quickly, wisely to the good again,
nor let us be so mindless of the good too long.

Dionysos creates the rational souls of beings in space and time, which is the immortal *nous* that is capable of grasping the eternal Ideas, in the celestial gods, earthly daimons, and human beings. Such souls are properly motivated by desire for the Good, and Dionysos leads us upward to the Good, which is Zeus.

Hymn 12: Tenth Monthly Hymn, to the Titans
Mode: Phrygian (D)

> Come, let us sing to mortal nature's demiurge,
> to Kronos, Lord, the son of Zeus, and eldest of
> the low-born progeny of Zeus, Tartarean
> and Titan gods; we sing to them along with him,
> who are in all ways good, from evil far apart,
> although creating what is mortal and short-lived.
> We sing of Aphrodite, Kronos's sacred wife,
> and Pan the lord of beasts, Deméter of the plants,
> and Kore of our mortal nature, and the rest.

The Titans are "low-born" (literally "illegitimate") only in the sense that they have less power than the Olympians, for the Olympians create immortal beings but the Titans create only mortal beings. In addition to the named Titans, "the rest" create other mortal things besides animals, plants, and human bodies. On the demiurge, see the note to Hymn 1.

Hymn 13: Eleventh Monthly Hymn, to Hephaistos
Mode: Hypophrygian (G)

> Hephaistos, Lord, you rule the supercelestial gods,
> together the Olympians and Tartáreans.
> You govern with Poseidon, the wide-ruling one,

and also give to each their station and their seat;
and you're the cause of rest in this and everything,
and also you provide them everlastingness,
yourself, or with Poseidon, by his father's will.
Watch over us, and grant especially to us,
who're born, to firmly stand in noble deeds each time.

Hephaistos rules the supercelestial gods (the Olympians and Titans) in the sense that he establishes their eternal relations and offices. In general, he is the cause of stability and permanence.

Hymn 14: Twelfth Monthly Hymn, to the Daimons

Mode: Phrygian (D)

We sing of holy daimons, who are near to us,
to them and also to the other deathless ones,
for daimons serve quite well the gods who're more divine,
bestow the many benefits on our behalf,
disperse them all, which they receive from Zeus himself,
and which descend to us through all the other gods.
And thus they save us, with some purifying us,
and others elevating or protecting us,
and easily straightening our minds. And so, be kind.

Plethon stresses that all daimons are good, and we have here an enumeration of at least some of their beneficial functions: saving, purifying, elevating, protecting, and straightening our minds, as well as transmitting the benefits from the gods. See chapter 10 for more on daimons.

Hymn 15: Thirteenth Monthly Hymn, to All Gods

Mode: Hypodorian (A)

> O Zeus, supreme, who art the greatest of all gods,
> the eldest demiurge, and the All-Father too,
> and all you other gods, who are Olympians,
> or are Tartáreans, or Celestials, or of Earth,
> if we commit some bad mistake or reckless deed,
> allow us, purified, to near your blameless state,
> and let our lives be blessed; especially you, O Zeus,
> thou art, above all, the most powerful of all,
> and art together both the first and final Good.

On the demiurge, see the note to Hymn 1.

Hymn 16: First Sacred Hymn, To Zeus

Mode: Hypodorian (A)

> King Zeus, entirely unborn and Being-Itself,
> All-Father, All-Preserver, who all things conceals
> within himself, in unity and not apart,
> distributes each of them, completely one and whole,
> accomplishing the task as fully beautiful
> as can be, all in one, from envy wholly free.
> But you, O Zeus, and your illustrious children, lead
> us with the Whole, as you have judged, aligning all,
> and grant beginnings well begun and tasks well done.

Hymn 17: Second Sacred Hymn, to the Olympian Gods

Mode: Hypophrygian (G)

> Oh come and let us celebrate Poseidon, Lord,
> who is the eldest of all children born of Zeus,
> the strongest, who is second from the father, chief
> of all the progeny, of all that's near to us
> the demiurge; with him is also Hera, Queen,
> who is the eldest goddess born of Father Zeus.
> But also let us celebrate the other gods,
> who're in Olympus, and all cocreators and
> protectors of immortal things. Be kind to us.

Poseidon is the creator of everything "near to us": within the heavens, including on earth. On the demiurge, see the note to Hymn 1.

Hymn 18: Third Sacred Hymn, to All the Gods

Mode: Hypodorian (A)

> O gods who're after Zên, who is supremely good,
> you're all completely blameless and exempt from death;
> Poseidon is your chief and leader after Zeus.
> O ye above the heavens or within the sky,
> illustrious are ye all, and you we celebrate,
> because we have a nature that's akin to yours.
> O blessed ones, hail to you, the givers of all goods;
> but give to us, with lives not always free of care,
> whatever is both fair and good, and set us straight.

The gods "above the heavens" are the supercelestials and those "within the sky" are the celestial gods. For "Zên" as an alternative to "Zeus," see note to Hymn 2.

Hymn 19: Fourth Sacred Hymn, to All Those Below the Olympian Gods

Mode: Phrygian (D)

> O Kronos, of the supercelestial Titans Lord,
> who governs them, and you who all the heavens rule,
> O Helios, and the other planets following you,
> by you two the whole race of mortals is produced,
> from both of you, from Kronos and from Helios.
> Ye Titans and ye planets, subject to these two,
> are one way or another helpers; hence to you
> sing we who have these many benefits from you,
> and with you to the holy daimons and fixed stars.

Mortal nature is created by a collaboration of the supercelestial Titans, under Kronos, and the planetary gods, under Helios.

Hymn 20: Fifth Sacred Hymn, to Pluto

Mode: Dorian (E)

> Lord Pluto, thou who art of human nature chief
> and guardian, allotted thee by Zeus himself,
> and holding everything as one that separately
> occurs for us and happens; you protect us well
> in all things here and after when to thee we're raised.
> With thee are Heroes, of a kind surpassing ours,
> and also others dear to us, both fair and good,
> and Kore, thy good wife and god of Tartarus,
> who binds us, as required, to mortal life. Be kind.

Pluto is the eternal Idea of the immortal human soul, the *nous*. As such, he contains in a unified form all the ideas that arise in individual humans at various times and define the fate and destiny of every human soul. Associated with him are the heroes, who are beneficent ancestors who have been liberated from the cycle of rebirth. Pluto's wife and queen Kore creates our mortal body, which we use during incarnation.

Hymn 21: Sixth Sacred Hymn, to Zeus
Mode: Hypodorian (A)

> Zeus, Father, powerful, strong acting, cause of good,
> All-Parent, and by thine own mind transcendent good,
> we too are born with shares of goodness from the gods.
> By force of our mortality we're fallible
> but ever subject to correction once again.
> Bestow on us release from misery of mistakes
> by means of thine own children to whom it's assigned,
> approaching near the guiltless having a right mind,
> so we may follow thee, who art both gentle, kind.

Hymn 22: First Daily Hymn, Sung on the Second Day
Mode: Dorian (E)

> Let me not cease from thanking you, O blessed gods,
> for all the benefits I have because of you
> or yet will have; the highest source of them is Zeus.
> And may I not neglect the welfare of my kind,
> whatever's in my power, working willingly
> for common good, and knowing well it aids me too.
> May I not be the cause of evils such as come
> to people, but so far as I am able, good,
> so that, becoming more like you, I may be blessed.

This hymn is a threefold prayer that we not forget to thank the gods for their benefits, nor in turn neglect helping other people, nor refrain from harming them. These correspond to the three specific virtues under justice, called piety, citizenship, and goodness (see chapter 9).

Hymn 23: Second Daily Hymn, Sung on the Third Day
Mode: Dorian (E)

> O gods, don't let me savor pleasures to excess,
> but put a limit onto them, in case there comes
> from them some evil to my body or my soul.
> Don't let me be insatiable for resources,
> but measured, and in those things that the body needs
> be moderate, so independence I enjoy.
> Don't let me be enslaved to false and empty words,
> but let me judge as useful only those of them
> that bring to me divine and genuine excellence.

This hymn is a threefold prayer for liberation through moderation of desire for pleasure, wealth, and fame, which correspond to the specific virtues under self-control called orderliness, liberality, and humility (see chapter 9).

Hymn 24: Third Daily Hymn, Sung on the Fourth Day
Mode: Dorian (E)

> O gods, don't let those accidents that sometimes strike
> my mortal part destroy me, knowing that my soul's
> immortal, separate from the mortal, and divine.
> And do not let the troubles that to people come
> disturb me while I exercise my liberty,
> nor for some evil notion be in thrall to need.
> And when it comes to me to bring about some good,
> don't let me spare my mortal part, but let me care
> for my immortal soul to always be the best.

This hymn is a threefold prayer for fortitude in the face of accidents, trouble from other people, and our mortality, which correspond to the specific virtues called "high spirit," "gentleness," and "valor" (see chapter 9 for an explanation of these terms).

Hymn 25: Fourth Daily Hymn, Sung on the Fifth Day
Mode: Dorian (E)

> Blest they who always care for their immortal soul
> so that it be the best, and for their mortal part
> are not concerned, not sparing it if it's required.
> Blest they who when some mortals, acting thoughtlessly,
> attack, will never be enslaved to them, but hold
> their soul with firmness, rising o'er that wickedness.
> Blest they who do not grieve with bitter heart the luck
> that's heaven-sent, but bear it easily and mark
> alone as good what lies in their immortal part.

This hymn asserts the blessedness of those with the virtue of fortitude: namely those who focus on their immortal soul ("valor"), resist reacting to others' bad action ("gentleness"), and accept divine fate ("high spirit"); see chapter 9.

Hymn 26: Fifth Daily Hymn, Sung on the Sixth Day
Mode: Dorian (E)

> Blest they who don't unwisely cling to speakers' vain
> opinions, but by thinking for themselves pursue
> with straight intelligence the virtue that's ordained.
> Blest they who do not to an infinite degree
> pursue possessions foolishly, but ascertain
> a limit by the body's well-determined needs.
> Blest they who keep a godly bound to pleasure that
> does not invite some evil for the soul or for
> the body, but accords with virtue that's ordained.

This hymn asserts the blessedness of those with the virtue of self-control in the form of the three specific virtues called humility, liberality, and orderliness (see chapter 9).

Hymn 27: Sixth Daily Hymn, Sung on the Seventh Day
Mode: Dorian (E)

> Blest they who are not greedy for themselves, nor by
> a fearful folly cause for people evil things,
> but always good things, like the blessed gods themselves.
> Blest they who do not slight the people's common good,
> especially knowing that the common is the gods'
> concern, and therefore they do not abandon it.
> Blest they who give the gods their thanks for benefits,
> whatever they might have, before all Zên himself,
> from whom came first the fair and good in everything.

This hymn asserts the blessedness of those with the virtue of justice in the form of the three specific virtues called goodness, citizenship, and piety (see chapter 9). For "Zên" as an alternative to "Zeus," see note to Hymn 2.

MUSICAL ACCOMPANIMENT

As you have seen, Plethon prescribes a musical mode for each of the hymns and also for each of the adorations in the worship service ("Order of Service" in chapter 5). Unfortunately, none of Plethon's music survives, and so, if you want to use musical accompaniment, you will have to improvise or compose your own, at least until someone (not me!) composes music we all can use. If you're not interested in these musical matters, please feel free to skip the rest of this chapter.

The Harmoniai, or Modes

The *Book of Laws* does not prescribe particular melodies for the hymns and adorations or specify the use of specific pitches, but it does prescribe the modes (ἁρμονίαι, *harmoniai*), which are somewhat analogous to modern major and minor scales. This is because the different modes have different effects on our souls and therefore can enhance the effect of ritual. The ethical effect of music was widely understood in ancient Greece, an idea that goes back to Pythagoras, who used music to "tune" the soul so that it was "harmonious."

He is supposed to have used specific modes to heal mental and physical disorders, for the modes are based on numerological relationships that govern the microcosm (soul) and macrocosm (universe). Plato likewise, in his *Republic*, discusses the modes allowed in his ideal state.[340] He mentions only two acceptable *harmoniai*, the Dorian and Phrygian, and does not comment on the acceptability of the related Hypodorian and Hypophrygian (the four Plethon uses). In his *Laws*, Plethon gives specific reasons for his choice of modes, which will be discussed later.[341] Clearly, in accord with ancient philosophy, he thinks the correct mode is more important than the absolute pitch or particular melody of the musical accompaniment.

A **mode** (which Plethon calls a *harmonia*) is a particular arrangement in an octave of the intervals, our modern approximations being the tones (e.g., the A–B interval) and the semitones (e.g., B–C). Modern Western music commonly uses the major and minor scales, but in other times and places, many other arrangements have been used. Plethon uses four modes: Dorian, Phrygian, Hypodorian, Hypophrygian. If you are familiar with Western early music, then these names may be familiar to you, but they do not have the same meanings, for long after Plethon's time the names of the modes were rearranged, probably in 1547 by a monk, Henricus Glareanus, but he got them mixed up. For example, the modern Dorian mode is not the same as the ancient Dorian *harmonia*, which is now called Phrygian. Unfortunately, Plethon does not describe the arrangement of his *harmoniai*, but the meanings presented later are the most likely ones based on the ancient Greek and Byzantine tradition, including Aristoxenus and Aristides Quintilianus, whom Plethon studied and wrote about.[342]

Each of Plethon's four modes refers to a particular arrangement of the intervals in an octave, not to absolute pitches. We can write them in ordinary musical notation, but we have to remember that no absolute pitch is implied. For example, the Dorian mode has the ascending intervals semitone, tone, tone, tone, semitone, tone, tone. In a C-major scale this would be the ascending notes E, F, G, A, B, C, D. Since the absolute pitch doesn't matter, we could also express it A, B♭, C, D, E, F, G, but it is easier to express

---

340. Plato, *Republic* 3.398e–399c.

341. Plethon, *Laws* III.36.8.

342. Tambrun-Krasker, "Philosophie, poésie et musique chez Pléthon," 259–69.

everything in terms of a C-major scale.[343] Alternately, we can use *solfège* (specifically *movable do solfège*) in which *do re mi fa sol la ti do* is the major scale. Then the Dorian mode is *mi fa sol la ti do re mi*. Finally, we can note that the Dorian scale begins on the third degree of the major scale. The **foundation tones** (lowest note) of Plethon's four modes in a major scale are summarized in this table:

Harmonia	Foundation Tone			Focus
	Relative Degree	Solfège	C-major Degree	
Hypodorian	VI	la	A	Zeus
Hypophrygian	V	sol	G	Olympian gods
Phrygian	II	re	D	gods below Olympians
Dorian	III	mi	E	human matters

Use of the Harmoniai

Hypodorian (VI, la, A)

Plethon assigns this mode to "Zeus the King and all gods collectively, because of its grandeur and because none is better suited to the expression of proud and heroic feelings."[344] An anonymous Aristotelian philosopher describes it as "grand and steady," which is appropriate for Zeus.[345] Therefore, Plethon prescribes this mode for the third adoration, which is to Zeus, for the two perennial hymns (Hymn 1 to Zeus, Hymn 2 to all gods), for

---

343. Although these modes have a similar scale structure to various modern major and minor scales, they cannot be equated or assumed to have the same psychological effects, which have a large cultural component. Modern scales determine the harmonic structure of predominantly polyphonic music; ancient modes determine the melodic structure of Byzantine chant and ancient music, which are primarily monophonic. Furthermore, Plethon would have used *just* (or *pure*) *intonation* rather than modern *equal temperament*, which has less pure intervals. Singers and some musical instruments, including many electronic keyboards, can accommodate just intonation.

344. Plethon, *Laws* III.36.8.

345. West, *Ancient Greek Music*, 184.

monthly hymns 1 and 13 (Hymn 3 to Zeus, Hymn 15 to all gods), and for sacred hymns 1, 3, and 6 (Hymn 16 to Zeus, Hymn 18 to all gods, and Hymn 21 to Zeus).[346]

Hypophrygian (V, sol, G)

This mode is used for the Olympian gods because it "holds the second rank for grandeur and is apt to express the admiration of beautiful things."[347] That same Aristotelian philosopher wrote that Hypophrygian is appropriate for action and so for the gods who execute Zeus's plans.[348] Plethon prescribes this mode for the first adoration, which is to the Olympian gods, for monthly hymns 2 through 6, 8, 9, and 11 (Hymns 4–8, 10, 11, 13 to individual Olympians), and for the second sacred hymn (Hymn 17 to all Olympians).[349]

Phrygian (II, re, D)

Plethon uses this mode for all the other gods, including the Titans, celestial gods, and daimons because "for greatness [this *harmonia*] occupies an intermediate rank and is suitable for the expression of gentle and peaceful feelings."[350] Plato wrote that the Phrygian *harmonia* was

> to be used by him in times of peace and freedom of action, when there is no pressure of necessity, and he is seeking to persuade [a god] by prayer, or [a person] by instruction and admonition, or on the other hand, when he is expressing his willingness to yield to persuasion or entreaty or admonition, and which represents him when by prudent conduct he has attained his end, not carried away by his success, but acting moderately and wisely under the circumstances, and acquiescing in the event.[351]

---

346. Plethon, *Laws* III.36.5, 8.

347. Plethon, *Laws* III.36.8.

348. West, *Ancient Greek Music*, 184.

349. Plethon, *Laws* III.36.5, 8.

350. Plethon, *Laws* III.36.8.

351. Plato, *Republic* 398e–399c, trans. Jowett, in *Dialogues of Plato*, vol. 3.

Plethon prescribes this mode for the second adoration, which is for the gods below the Olympians, for monthly hymns 7, 10, and 12 (Hymn 9 to celestial gods, Hymn 12 to Titans, and Hymn 14 to daimons) and for the fourth sacred hymn (Hymn 19 to the gods below the Olympians).[352]

Dorian (III, mi, E)

This is the *harmonia* of the human world, for it is, according to Plethon, "reserved for people and for the gods who preside over human destinies, because of its especially agonistic character and the struggle always inherent in human affairs, due to the missteps and mistakes of our nature."[353]

Plato claims that the Dorian *harmonia* is warlike, strengthening resolve and courage in the face of danger, and endurance in misfortune and necessity.[354] Aristotle writes that Dorian induces mental mellowness and moderation and firmness in our relations with others.[355] Therefore, Plethon prescribes the Dorian mode for the fifth sacred hymn (Hymn 20 to Pluto) and for all the daily hymns (Hymn 22–27), which pray for our betterment.[356]

The use of the four modes is summarized in this table:

Harmonia	Focus	Adoration	Hymns			
			Perennial	Monthly	Sacred	Daily
Hypodorian	Zeus	3	1, 2	1, 13	1, 3, 6	
Hypophrygian	Olympian gods	1		2–6, 8, 9, 11	2	
Phrygian	gods below Olympians	2		7, 10, 12	4	
Dorian	human matters				5	1–6

---

352. Plethon, *Laws* III.36.5, 8.

353. Plethon, *Laws* III.36.8.

354. Plato, *Republic* 3.399a–c.

355. Aristotle, *Politics* 8.1340a–b.

356. Plethon, *Laws* III.36.8.

Melodic Form

Presumably, Plethon composed his hymns in the style of Byzantine chant circa 1400, but we have no way of knowing. That was the religious music of his time, but we certainly don't need to compose in this style. I do think, however, that it is worthwhile to use the modes prescribed by Plethon, since they are not arbitrary, as explained previously.

If you want to improvise or compose melodies for the hymns in these modes, the following may be helpful. The **final tone** of the melody is usually the mode's foundation tone, which functions something like the tonic in modern music. The second most important tone is the **dominant**, usually the fifth degree of the scale, which is emphasized by the melody; it may even be repeated for a sort of monotone chant. Typically each verse ends with a cadence on the dominant, except the last verse, which has a descending cadence on the final. The first verse may begin several degrees below the dominant and ascend stepwise to it. The melody is typically confined to a compass of an octave or a little more. The key pitches of each mode are summarized in this table:

Harmonia	C Major Scale	Foundation Tone			Dominant Tone		
		Relative Degree	Solfège	C Major Degree	Relative Degree	Solfège	C Major Degree
Hypodorian	A–a	VI	la	A	III	me	E
Hypophrygian	G–g	V	sol	G	II	re	D
Phrygian	D–d	II	re	D	VI	la	A
Dorian	E–e	III	me	E	VII (I)	ti (do)	B (C)

In practice, in the Dorian mode C (I, *do*) is often used as the dominant instead of B (VII, *ti*). Or ignore all of this and compose your own music in the appropriate modes!

IX

How to Be Excellent

━━━⟊⟊━━━

Plethon developed an ethical system grounded in his Neoplatonic philosophy but also drawing from Stoicism. Virtue was discussed in nine destroyed chapters of his *Laws* but also in his essay *On Virtues*, which circulated during his lifetime and was highly regarded for its style and content.[357] I have used this essay, which survives, as the basis for this chapter. It is not explicitly Pagan, but it is completely compatible with his philosophy and theology.

The Greek word *aretê* (ἀρετή), which is conventionally translated "virtue," is better translated "excellence." For example, the *aretê* of a knife is to be strong and sharp. The *aretê* of a person is to be an excellent human being, but it is necessary to determine what that means, which is the task of philosophy. Sometimes I will use the more familiar translation "virtue," but keep the meaning of *aretê* in mind.

Plethon's ethics is an example of a **virtue ethics**, which means an ethics that focuses on what it means to be a virtuous or moral person; other ethical systems focus on duties or on the consequences of actions. Plethon writes, "Virtue [*aretê*] is the disposition that makes us good," but that is not too informative.[358] His ethics is grounded in his theology, for he reminds us that "he who is truly good is God [i.e., Zeus], and we

---

357. Based on their titles (in *Laws*, table of contents), the excellences were discussed in *Laws* III.7–10, 12–13, 25–7.

358. *Virtues* A.1.1. Citations to Plethon's *On Virtues* are by section (A.1) and page (1) in the most recent edition of the Greek text (Περὶ ἀρετῶν, ed. Tambrun-Krasker). Translations are mine.

173

humans become good by following God so far as possible for humans."[359] Therefore, it is essential to understand the nature of both gods and humans so we may be more excellent. Then we may truly flourish and live meaningful lives.

THE CARDINAL VIRTUES

You will see that Plethon has a fairly detailed classification of virtues based on his philosophical analysis. It is not necessary to learn this classification, but reading through it will help you to understand better the dimensions of human excellence and to see how you can acquire the habits to live a more authentic, meaningful, and excellent human life.

Plethon's philosophical analysis of ethics begins with the observation that the excellences can be divided into those that pertain to one's mind and those that pertain to other things. The highest excellence, which is the most characteristic of humans as rational beings, is **prudence** (φρόνησις, *phronêsis*), also translatable as practical wisdom, thoughtfulness, judgment, and intention. Of the other excellences, which relate to things other than one's mind, the highest is called **justice** (δικαιοσύνη, *dikaiosunê*) or rectitude, which pertains to our relation to other people. Prudence and justice are both intellectual excellences, as are the more specific virtues derived from them and discussed later. The next two excellences relate not to other people, but to other aspects of yourself than your intellect—namely, to your lower soul and body; one virtue relates to matters under our control, the other to those that are not. The excellence pertaining to what is out of our control is called **fortitude** (ἀνδρεία, *andreia*), also translated courage. The excellence pertaining to what is under our control is called **self-control** (σωφροσύνη, *sôphrosunê*), also translated self-mastery, moderation, temperance, good sense, and soundness of mind.

You may recognize these four excellences—prudence, justice, fortitude, and self-control—as the **cardinal virtues** of ancient Pagan philosophy, but we will have to discuss what Plethon means by them and to learn how they are acquired. Plethon's analysis does not stop here, but he shows how each of the cardinal virtues implies three more specific excellences for a total of twelve. I will discuss them briefly later.

---

359. Plethon, *Virtues* A.1.1.

Self-Control

In his discussion of the excellences, Plethon starts from "the least perfect" and gradually rises to "the most perfect according to nature."[360] Therefore, he begins with self-control, which he defines as "that disposition of the soul that is sufficient for the needs of life, reduced to the minimum necessary," in terms of both quantity and intensity.[361] This excellence follows from the goal of being more godlike, for the gods need nothing at all, and so we should strive to need as little as possible for humans. He adds that these needs are relatively easy to satisfy without a great deal of effort.[362] Therefore, we should satisfy these needs with things that are inexpensive and easy to obtain, as opposed to expensive and luxurious items or services. This is an age-old Epicurean principle: if our desires are simple, then they are easier to satisfy and we will be happier. (And so the gods, having no unsatisfied needs, are therefore eternally blissful.) The Epicureans go on to say that there is no harm in enjoying better things, if you happen to have them, or in having more than the minimum necessary, so long as we don't need them to be happy and can be satisfied with the minimum.

Fortitude

The second cardinal excellence in the ascending scale is fortitude, which is "the disposition of the soul to remain firm before the violent afflictions of life."[363] The gods again are our models, for they are eternal and immutable. It is beyond the power of humans to be completely unaffected by events, but we can become more godlike by remaining firm in the face of the inevitable difficulties and painful events of life. As the gods govern lesser things and are not affected by them, so people should not give in to the inferior characteristics of themselves.

---

360. Plethon, *Virtues* A.2.1.

361. Plethon, *Virtues* A.2.2.

362. Plethon, *Virtues* A.2.2.

363. Plethon, *Virtues* A.2.2.

Justice

Plethon moves on to the virtues that pertain more to our higher, immortal souls, which are eternal parts of the cosmic hierarchy, which is a harmonious whole. As we humans belong to families, so "we are also an element of other parts greater than ourselves, which belong to a whole, that is a totality and one."[364] We should not abandon the role assigned to us by the gods, but should fulfill it as well as we are able, "for every part that is in harmony with its totality and does not disagree acts perfectly well and in accord with its nature."[365] This is justice, which is "that part of virtue that will safeguard what is appropriate for each of us with regard to our relation to others."[366] In particular, in relation to the gods we behave as appropriate "for servants and creatures facing their master and creator."[367]

Prudence

Finally, we come to the highest cardinal virtue, which is grounded in the nature of the human soul itself, as opposed to its relation to other things. And because the nature of the human soul is rational, its nature is to consider the being of each thing, how it is related to other things, and what are its causes. This excellence is **prudence**, "the last and most perfect part of virtue," the virtue that is "that speculative disposition of the soul that considers each being as it is."[368] Its concrete manifestation is philosophy, as presented in this book, and the way of life that is built on this foundation.

---

364. Plethon, *Virtues* A.2.3.

365. Plethon, *Virtues* A.2.3.

366. Plethon, *Virtues* A.2.3.

367. Plethon, *Virtues* A.2.3.

368. Plethon, *Virtues* A.2.3–4.

The Specific Virtues

Plethon explains how each of the four cardinal virtues generates three subsidiary **specific virtues** at three levels.[369] The highest rank often pertains to divine matters, the middle to public affairs, and the lowest to the individual. They are summarized in this table:

Prudence	Justice	Fortitude	Self-Control
religiousness	piety	high spirit	humility
science	citizenship	valor	liberality
good counsel	goodness	gentleness	orderliness

I will discuss the specific virtues in more detail later but here outline their relation to the cardinal virtues. We begin again with the lower order excellences and work upward.

As explained previously, the virtue of self-control is related to the needs of life, which Plethon puts in three classes: the needs for pleasure, wealth, and reputation, each of which has a corresponding excellence.[370] For pleasure the excellence is **orderliness**, modesty, propriety, decorum, seemliness, or dignity; for wealth it is **liberality** or generosity; and for reputation it is **humility**, right degree, moderation, or elegance. These translations are all somewhat misleading, but I will explain the nature of these excellences later. Hymns 23 and 26 (second and fifth daily hymns) pray to the gods for the excellences under self-control.

The next highest cardinal virtue is fortitude, which pertains to our ability to remain firm in the face of life's difficulties. Plethon observes that some of these difficulties are voluntary in that they are endured for the sake of something better, which we have chosen.[371] The rest are involuntary but may be caused by other people, who may make trouble for us, or they may be misfortunes arising in the cosmic order, acts of the gods. The excellence appropriate for these last misfortunes is **high spirit**, goodness of soul, or boldness. For those troubles undertaken voluntarily, we have the virtue of **valor** or nobility of mind, and for those troubles caused by other people, the relevant excellence

---

369. Plethon, *Virtues* A.3.4–5.

370. Plethon, *Virtues* A.3.4.

371. Plethon, *Virtues* A.3.4.

is **gentleness**, mildness, affability, or serenity. Hymns 24 and 25 (third and fourth daily hymns) pray to the gods for these excellences. (I would put gentleness on the second rank and valor on the third—and this is their order in the hymns—but Plethon has them as shown previously.)

Moving now to the higher rank of virtues, we come to justice, which pertains to our relation to other things.[372] The highest such excellence is **piety**, holiness, or reverence and respect for the gods, which pertains to our relation to divine reality. Below this is excellence in our relations with other people, called **citizenship**, civic virtue, or political conduct. Finally, we have excellence in regard to our relations to our own affairs, which is called **goodness**, uprightness, kindness, or honesty. Hymns 22 and 27 (first and sixth daily hymns) pray to the gods for these excellences.

The highest cardinal virtue is prudence, which relates to our understanding of beings, of what is.[373] The lowest specific virtue under it pertains to human affairs and is called **good counsel** or sound judgment. Next highest is excellence in understanding nature and begotten things, which is called **natural science** or knowledge of nature. Finally, the highest excellence is the understanding and contemplation of divine matters and unbegotten beings, which is called **religiousness**, holiness, or reverence and respect for the gods. (There do not appear to be any hymns that pray specifically for these virtues, but they are supported by all the hymns and invocations.)

Plethon summarizes the specific excellences as follows:

> Religiousness pertains to divine beings, science pertains to beings of nature, good counsel pertains to human affairs. Piety pertains to the divine, citizenship to public goods, and goodness to private goods. High spirit, on the other hand, refers to what is not wanted, valor relates to choices, and gentleness to what concerns people. Finally, humility has to do with reputation, liberality to wealth, and orderliness to pleasures.[374]

---

372. Plethon, *Virtues* A.3.5.

373. Plethon, *Virtues* A.3.5.

374. Plethon, *Virtues* B.14.14.

Becoming Excellent

Having classified the various excellences, Plethon suggests the order in which they should be acquired, generally from lower to higher, as described previously, but he makes some exceptions to make them easier to learn.[375] Because, in acquiring these excellences, we are changing our character, we need to practice them until they become habits, which takes time. Therefore, we do not develop these excellences one after another, but Plethon suggests the order in which we should begin working on them. It is a lifelong exercise.

The successful acquisition of the excellences depends, writes Plethon, first on "*nature and divine providence*, without which there can be nothing good, then on *reason and knowledge*, and, finally, on *practice and exercise*."[376] In other words, we need to have first a natural disposition and the ongoing aid of the gods. Second, we need to understand, through reason and knowledge, the nature of each virtue and how to develop it, as explained in the rest of this chapter. Finally, intellectual understanding is not enough; to become more excellent—to become better human beings—it is necessary to practice these excellences, to live them in our daily lives, until they become habits.

1. Orderliness

The first excellence to practice, and the basis for all the rest, is orderliness, also translated propriety, decorum, seemliness, and dignity (κοσμιότης, *kosmiotês*), the lowest specific virtue under self-control.[377] The goal of self-control is to need as little as necessary and so to become more godlike, for the gods need nothing at all. Under self-control the excellence of orderliness relates to pleasure, and to practice it we need to classify desires first as either necessary or superfluous. Necessary desires are those required for life, such as food, water, and shelter. Therefore, we should enjoy the pleasure of satisfying these necessities. (Notice, however, that excessive or gourmet food, craft beer and fine wine, and several mansions are not necessary for the needs of life!) Second, we classify the superfluous desires as either **natural desires**, those that are appropriate to humans and neither harmful nor unjust, or

---

375. Plethon, *Virtues* B.14.15.

376. Plethon, *Virtues* B.14.14, italics mine.

377. As you will see, these are not particularly good descriptions of this virtue, but they are the usual translations of the Greek word that Plethon uses. This observation applies to many of Plethon's virtues.

as **non-natural desires**, which are not. It is fine to satisfy the natural superfluous desires in moderation, but we should not be dependent on them, which decreases our freedom and ability to ensure our happiness. Fine foods, a nice car, and other luxuries (so long as they are within your financial means) would fall in this category. The remaining desires are superfluous and non-natural in that nothing about human nature demands them; they are learned needs, often absorbed from our consumer culture and from those who are trying to sell us things. Plethon writes that we will be freer and better able to ensure our happiness if we lose our desire for non-natural superfluous pleasures.[378] You can make your own list of necessary, natural superfluous, and non-natural superfluous desires (a good exercise for acquiring this excellence). By the way, in case you were wondering, Plethon has no objection to the pleasures of sex.[379]

2. Valor

The second excellence in the order of acquisition is valor or nobility of mind (γενναιότης, *gennaiotês*), which is a species of fortitude. Recall that fortitude is the excellence with which we deal with the troubles and afflictions of life. Valor deals specifically with those troubles and pains that we suffer voluntarily for the sake of some higher goal ("no pain, no gain"). This virtue helps us act effectively and acquire the other virtues, which is why Plethon puts it second in order. He observes that orderliness and valor are similar and complementary virtues, for "those who are orderly experience no less pleasure than those who are not, and those who are valorous experience no more pain than those who are not."[380] Moreover, he writes that pleasures seem to avoid those who habitually flee pain and seek pleasure, perhaps because they become satiated and less sensitive. They may become unhealthy, their body ruined. With orderliness and valor "the pleasures appear more alive and harmless."[381] Conversely, pains and trouble "seem particularly fierce against those who flee them and are lovers of pleasures, while they avoid those who are more

---

378. Plethon, *Virtues* B.1.5–6.

379. I am obliged to add, however, that he is quite intolerant of non-monogamous sex and of sexual acts that he considers "unnatural" (Plethon, *Laws* III.31); he was a man of his time and some of his social ideas are indeed medieval!

380. Plethon, *Virtues* B.3.7.

381. Plethon, *Virtues* B.3.7.

heedless of them and who bear them patiently." [382] Those who have learned to endure them are psychologically more resilient and may have more robust bodies.

3. High Spirit

The third excellence to learn, the highest species of fortitude, is *eupsychia* (εὐψυχία), a rather rare word, which may be translated as high spirit, goodness of soul, or boldness. This virtue pertains to those troubles that come to us—not from our own choice or from other people—but from the gods and from the fate ordained by them. "First, it teaches us," according to Plethon, "that we are neither a bag of flesh nor a bucket of blood and nothing else of the kind, but instead we are rational, immortal souls." [383] Therefore, we should not be overly affected by difficulties relating to our bodies or material possessions. Indeed, our bodies do not belong to us but are loaned to us by the gods for the duration of each incarnation. Therefore, we should not trouble ourselves with the difficulties arising from our material embodiment but should focus on spiritual matters.

Second, reason shows us that "things are produced according to the order ordained by divinity, and they are arranged by the Good in a good and beautiful way." [384] Certainly, it seems implausible—or even ludicrous—that "all's for the best in this best of all possible worlds," but that is often the most productive attitude to take. If we ask ourselves—or better yet, ask the gods—why we are experiencing some difficulty, and what we are supposed to learn from it, and what we are supposed to do about it, then we can reap some good out of the greatest tragedies. Plethon even admits that some of these difficulties may be punishments from the gods (generally executed by the daimons) with the intention of correcting and improving us; he compared them to medicines and to physical exercise, both of which may be painful and unpleasant. [385] Even if there is no greater plan behind our afflictions, seeking one can bring some good into the world. As Marcus Aurelius wrote, "If God, all is well, and if random, don't you be random." [386]

---

382. Plethon, *Virtues* B.3.7.

383. Plethon, *Virtues* B.4.7–8.

384. Plethon, *Virtues* B.4.8. See also Plethon's view of fate in chapter 10.

385. Plethon, *Virtues* B.4.8–9. See also Plethon, *Laws* II.6.8.

386. Marcus Aurelius, *Communings with Himself* 9.28, my translation.

4. Humility

After these, according to Plethon, we should strive to learn the excellence called humility, moderation, right degree, or elegance (μετριότης, *metriotês*), which is self-control with respect to reputation.[387] It is a characteristic of human beings, in contrast to other animals, to value the respect of other people. We can be guided by this common human desire but also led astray; indeed, we can be tyrannized by concern for reputation and fame, and so we need to keep it under careful control. First, we should rely on our own independent judgment about ourselves, our informed self-respect. Because it is also difficult to be objective about ourselves, we should pay attention to the opinions of good people and credit ourselves for the good consequences of our behavior. Conversely, we should ignore the opinions of "cowardly and foolish beings" and not strive after praise or avoid criticism for the sake of vanity.[388]

5. Liberality

Plethon tells us that those who have practiced the preceding excellences will find it easier to acquire the next, liberality or generosity (ἐλευθεριότης, *eleutheriotês*), which is self-control with respect to wealth.[389] This is because wealth can be used to obtain pleasure and, at least in part, to avoid pain and other difficulties, and wealth itself will enhance one's reputation among certain people. Therefore, if one has learned to control these desires (through the excellences of orderliness, valor, high spirit, and humility), then one will need less money. Such a person "will provide for the necessities of life by using those resources that are the easiest to gain and will delight, without labor and as far as possible, in beautiful things, taking an interest in the beauty that resides in material things."[390] Such people will not despise wealth but will value it for the good it can do.

---

387. Plethon, *Virtues* B.5.9.

388. Plethon, *Virtues* B.5.9.

389. Plethon, *Virtues* B.6.9.

390. Plethon, *Virtues* B.6.9.

6. Gentleness

The third excellence under fortitude (below high spirit and valor) is gentleness, mildness, affability, or serenity (πραότης, *praotês*), which pertains to troubles arising from other people.[391] We are the masters of ourselves, writes Plethon, but not the masters of other souls, which pursue their own purposes and happiness. Therefore, if we want them to act to our benefit, we must persuade them, and if we do not succeed, we have to take responsibility for our failure. By understanding that everyone is seeking their own good in the way that they think is best, we will be better able to bear the difficulties they might cause us and perhaps eventually to persuade them to act differently.

7. Goodness

The foregoing complete the excellences belonging to the two lower cardinal virtues, self-control and fortitude, and so we advance to those under the higher ones, justice and prudence. The first specific excellence, which pertains to justice in our own affairs, is goodness of mind and character, probity, kindness, or honesty (χρηστότης, *chrêstotês*). Plethon explains that someone who has developed the preceding virtues will be less influenced by pleasures and pains and by desire for fame and fortune; they will be better able to endure troubles, whether the causes are human or divine.[392] Therefore, they will incline to goodness, to being kind, upright, and honest with their fellow humans. They will have discovered that doing good is better than receiving good, because it is more godlike, and that suffering harm is better than causing it, for the same reason. By seeking to do good and avoid doing harm, they will be less likely to cause harm inadvertently. This excellence, therefore, disposes people to act for the benefit of the wholes of which they are parts more than for their own self-interest, just as it is best for each part of the body to submit to the whole and perform its proper function for the good of the whole. "He would not choose the place of a miserable individual but that of the savior and benefactor and, in this way, he too would become happy."[393] Thus we emulate the gods.

---

391. Plethon, *Virtues* B.7.10.

392. Plethon, *Virtues* B.8.10.

393. Plethon, *Virtues* B.8.10–11.

8. Good Counsel

The next excellence to acquire, the lowest under prudence, is good counsel or sound judgment (εὐβουλία, *euboulia*), which refers to prudence and wisdom with respect to human affairs.[394] Developing the preceding virtues prepares you to acquire this one, because you will have had experience with other people and their affairs. You will know the difference between experts who conduct their business rationally and the ignorant ones who do not. Understanding human affairs is important to living well.

9. Natural Science

Next highest under prudence is the excellence of natural science or the knowledge of nature (φυσική, *physikê*), which is a source of happiness for two reasons. First, a devotion to science requires us to exercise our reason, the best part of ourselves, and so we live as our best selves. Second, we apply our reason to the whole of existence, using it to "examine what everything is, why it is produced, what is possible according to nature, and what is not."[395] In this way our souls "inhabit the entire world," and we delight in our comprehension of it, and thereby approximate the knowledge and bliss of the gods and other superior beings.[396]

10. Citizenship

Next Plethon suggests that we develop the excellence of citizenship, civic virtue, public life, or political conduct and action (πολιτεία, *politeia*), which is at the middle rank under the virtue of justice and pertains to our relations to other people. He observes that in nature the higher and more perfect species associate with each other more than the lower, less perfect ones; the more advanced animals are the more social. Human beings, therefore, as the highest species, should have the best organized, most cohesive society. As animals are sensitive to their parts, so also are groups sensitive to their members and care for them.

---

394. Plethon, *Virtues* B.9.11.

395. Plethon, *Virtues* B.10.11.

396. Plethon, *Virtues* B.10.11.

Thus, virtuous citizens who truly apply themselves and live for the general interest will certainly not derive a meager advantage, because they will not only live in a more human way according to their nature, but, moreover, they will make themselves as similar as possible to the most perfect species.[397]

They will put the general welfare before their private affairs, since individuals flourish when public affairs are well managed; "when, however, private affairs separate themselves from the general interest, then both perish."[398]

11. Piety

The highest specific excellence under justice is piety or holiness (ὁσιότης, *hosiotês*), which pertains to our relation to the divine, specifically, to our worship of the gods and communion with divinity, both in public and private.[399] The truly pious person avoids superstition and understands that vows, rituals, offerings, prayers, and so forth give nothing to the gods, who need nothing, and will not affect them, for they are unchangeable. But pious people will do these things to change themselves, for these practices bring their souls into better conformity with the divine. The rites, invocations, and hymns suggested by Plethon were presented in detail in chapters 5 to 8; see also chapter 10 for a reconstruction of his doctrines on prayer, purification, and sacrifice.

12. Religiousness

Finally, the highest excellence under prudence, the supreme virtue, and the last to be fully developed, is religiousness or holiness and reverence and respect for gods (θεοσέβεια, *theosebeia*), which is the understanding of divinity and the contemplation of unbegotten beings.[400] The nature of the gods and the cosmos were explained in chapter 3, but your understanding of them will grow deeper through contemplating the divine and by practicing the rites and rituals.

---

397. Plethon, *Virtues*, B.11.12.

398. Plethon, *Virtues* B.11.12.

399. Plethon, *Virtues* B.13.12–13.

400. Plethon, *Virtues* B.13.13.

Plethon tells us that by practicing these excellences and by avoiding doing wrong, we will be "as happy and blessed as possible in this life," and after we die, we will be in a better state between our incarnations.[401]

---

401. Plethon, *Virtues* B.14.14.

X

Reconstructed Doctrines

~~~~

The material in this chapter, which is useful for understanding and practicing Plethon's religion, was discussed in some of the chapters of the *Book of Laws* that Scholarios destroyed. Fortunately, we can reconstruct what Plethon probably wrote on these topics based on his other writings and from his likely sources (especially those in the Golden Chain).

FATE

Plethon's chapter "Fate" (II.6, Περὶ εἰμαρνένης, *Peri heimarmenês*) was in the midst of the block of chapters burned by Scholarios, but it survives, probably because Plethon previously had circulated copies of this one chapter, and Scholarios could not destroy them all. Moreover, Plethon wrote about fate in his paper "On the Differences of Plato from Aristotle" and other places. You may be wondering, "If Plethon's chapter on fate survives, then what is it doing here, in a chapter of reconstructed, lost writings?" I have put it here because it is most relevant to Plethon's teachings on prayer and sacrifice, which were destroyed and are discussed later in this chapter.

Plethon takes a controversial stand on fate (εἰμαρνένη, *heimarmenê*), which takes some effort to understand; it is essentially the Stoic position, with which many Platonists disagreed. His teachings about fate are based on two axioms.[402] The first is that

---

402. Plethon, *Laws* II.6.1.

everything has a cause. The second is that a cause completely determines its effect. The second axiom implies that there is nothing random or indeterminate in the effect, since if there were, the random or indeterminate aspects would be causeless, contradicting the first axiom.[403] The implication is that our cosmos is completely deterministic, all things following necessarily from the first cause, Zeus. You will wonder immediately if Plethon denies free will (he does not), but we will get to his explanation a little later.

Plethon also argues that if the cosmos were not deterministic, divination would be impossible, but reliable divination *is* possible, and so the future is predetermined.[404] In addition, the gods sometimes give oracles concerning the future (the topic of one the destroyed chapters of the *Book of Laws*), which they would not be able to do if it were not predetermined. Plethon observes that the future cannot be changed, even if it is known through divination or an oracle, but we will have to consider these matters more closely when we discuss free will.[405]

We must remember that the gods exist outside of time, and so the entirety of the past, present, and future—which they cause!—lies before them in an eternal present. The gods have foreknowledge of everything that happens because they cause, directly or indirectly, everything that happens. The future established by Zeus is the best possible, according to Plethon, because he is himself the Good.[406] (This does not imply, of course, that we always will experience circumstances as good for us as individuals. Gravity is necessary for the earth to exist, even though it means we can fall down.) Denying fate is tantamount to atheism, writes Plethon, for either it denies the gods' ability to foresee the future, or it makes them the cause of what is worse, instead of what is best.[407]

Now we come to the complicated issue of "free will," since many suppose that fate, a strict determinism such as Plethon describes, eliminates any possibility of moral

---

403. The second axiom is inconsistent with contemporary quantum mechanics, at least as commonly interpreted, in which the collapse of the wave function into one of several possibilities is a purely random event. This does not change things much, since although events are not deterministic at the microscopic scale, they are still largely deterministic at the macroscopic scale (except perhaps for Schrödinger's cat!).

404. Plethon, *Laws* II.6.3.

405. Plethon, *Laws* II.6.4.

406. Plethon, *Laws* II.6.2.

407. Plethon, *Laws* II.6.1.

responsibility. Moreover, it is supposed to lead to fatalism, a depressing and defeatist attitude that nothing we do matters, for the future is completely determined. In fact, it long has been recognized that robust notions of self-determination, autonomy, and moral responsibility are not inconsistent with strict determinism; this is a philosophical position called **compatibilism** (because free will is compatible with determinism). The compatibilist position has been discussed since ancient times, but it is subtle and still debated today. This is not the place for a thorough analysis, but I will address issues that are important for understanding Plethon's ideas concerning moral responsibility in a deterministic universe.

To begin, it will be helpful to set aside the term "free will" for the time being; the ancients often put the question in terms of whether something is "up to us" (ἐφ᾽ ἡμῖν, *eph᾽ hêmin*), which is a more concrete and less loaded term. In ordinary language, a choice is up to us if we can make it on the basis of *our own* thoughts, beliefs, perceptions, desires, feelings, values, memories, knowledge, intuitions, and so forth. One way a choice is not up to me is if it violates the laws of nature; I cannot choose to fly by flapping my arms. Moreover, if someone pushes me off a cliff, my leap was not up to me. On the other hand, if someone holds a gun to my head and tells me to jump, it is up to me whether I do so or not. There are complications, such as addictions, compulsions, and coercion, in which people make choices that are inconsistent with more deeply held beliefs, values, and intentions, but they do not change the basic explanation of what is "up to us." If it arises from what is ours (beliefs, desires, intentions, etc.), then it is up to us.

From this perspective, even if these choices are a result of deterministic physical processes operating in *my* brain, the choices nevertheless depend on the beliefs, desires, intentions, and the like residing in *my* brain, and thus they are up to *me*. Again, the issues are complicated, but I hope I have at least made plausible the idea that some things are up to us, even in a completely deterministic universe.

Plethon considers how, if everything, including the gods, is subject to this fate (which is identical to Zeus), we can be considered masters of ourselves and free.[408] The answer is that the highest part of our souls, which he calls the *phronoûn* (φρονοῦν), the prudent, wise, or thinking part, has mastery over the other parts of our soul, such as the desires,

---

408. Plethon, *Laws* II.6.5.

appetites, will, impulses, and feelings. This higher part makes the choices that are up to us. But like the gods themselves, this part is subject to fate. The choices it makes depend on both its innate characteristics (received from the gods) and its education, for which it also must have an inclination, given to it by the gods. That is, its choices depend on both nature and nurture. Nevertheless, because it is *my* prudent part, with both its innate and learned characteristics, that makes these choices, they are up to *me*.

Moreover, I am responsible for the actions that are up to me, and I may suffer the consequences of my mistakes. Indeed Plethon tells us that there is a class of daimons who act as the gods' agents and are responsible for correcting us (see "Daimons" on page 217).[409] We should not think of these negative consequences as punishment for our (predetermined) errors. They are more like bad grades on an exam, criticism from a coach, or painful medical procedures, all of which are intended to make us better. They are the gods' way of causing (predetermining) a future in which we make fewer mistakes, the gods' means of improving us, of making us more godlike.

However, it may seem cruel to assume that calamities, illness, and suffering are a consequence of the sufferer's errors; it seems like blaming the victim. Nevertheless, it is often worthwhile to consider this possibility, at least as a hypothesis. What lessons can I learn from this unfortunate situation? Can I find in these circumstances some good either for myself individually or for the world at large? Regardless of whether the gods are actually trying to correct us, it may be beneficial to consider that possibility and reap some good from a bad situation.

Free will is much more of an issue in religions, such as Christianity, that believe in a vindictive god who will punish our mistakes, perhaps with eternal damnation. Such punishment would be cruel and unjust if we supposed we were forced to make those mistakes by that very same omnipotent god (or by other agents he has created, such as Satan). It is also difficult in these religions to reconcile an omniscient god, who can see the future, with the ability of people to make free choices, for which they will be generously rewarded or horribly punished.

Many people reject the idea of predetermination because they cannot tolerate the idea that they are bound by an inexorable fate, that they have no true freedom. This

---

409. Plethon, *Laws* II.6.8.

feeling is misguided, as we've seen, for in fact a great deal is *up to us*, properly understood, in particular most of the choices to which we attach moral responsibility. We *are* truly free if things are up to us.

Moreover, Plethon argues, we have the only sort of freedom that is worth having, for everyone wants to do well and be happy and therefore to be free to pursue those goals.[410] But since Zeus is the cause of the Good (that which anything acts to gain or keep), by conforming to the law of Zeus (which Plethon calls Justice), we will be living as well as we can. This is the only freedom worth having. We may go wrong, of course, mistaking some apparent good for the truly good, but then we may hope that the daimons will set us straight.

When all is said and done, you will have to make up your own mind about whether the universe is completely predetermined. Contemporary physics teaches there is an unavoidable element of chance (not subject to our personal choice, it should be noted). I don't think it makes too much difference to the practice of Plethon's religion whether every last detail is predetermined by Zeus or whether in his overall organization he has left some room for either chance or completely free choice. It should not affect our behavior much.

PRAYER

Plethon criticizes the notion that through our prayers we might change the gods' minds and influence them to do something different than what they intended.[411] In fact, he asserts that this opinion denies the providence of the gods. For if the gods have determined what is best for the cosmos as a whole (even if not for me as an individual), then I am praying that the gods do what is worse for the cosmos. Conversely, if I imagine that I'm praying for what is better for the cosmos, then I must suppose that what the gods had previously intended was worse. Therefore, the belief that prayer can influence the gods contradicts both the predetermination of fate and the goodness and providence of the gods.

For these reasons, we might suppose that Plethon thinks that prayer is pointless, but he does not. In fact, we've seen that he offers rather lengthy prayers to the gods (chapter 6), and so we need to understand why. Unfortunately, Plethon's chapter "Prayer" (*Laws* III.33,

---

410. Plethon, *Laws* II.6.6–7.

411. Plethon, *Laws* II.6.1–2.

Περὶ προσευχῆς, *Peri proseuchês*) was lost to Scholarios's wanton destruction, but we can get a good idea of what he taught from his chapter on fate (II.6) and from the writings of his Platonic predecessors, especially Iamblichus, the final link in the Golden Chain.[412]

Platonists generally agreed that the gods are impassible—not subject to emotions—and therefore not subject to such human emotions as anger, jealousy, revenge, fear, desire, pity, and love; nor are they swayed by flattery, adulation, threats, or gifts. The gods are sufficient unto themselves. Nevertheless, Platonists considered prayer to be essential, and Iamblichus asserts, "no sacred act can take place without the supplications contained in prayers."[413]

Since prayer cannot change the gods, its purpose must be to change *us*. Iamblichus tells us that dedicated prayer will improve our intellect and intuition and will increase our soul's receptivity to the gods, enlarging its "receptacles" for divine Ideas.[414] Prayer accustoms the soul's eyes to the divine light, so we can perceive the life of the gods, thus perfecting our ability to contact the gods "until it leads us up to the highest level of consciousness of which we are capable."[415] This is the meaning of the seventh Magical Oracle, which reads, "You must make haste to light, and to the Father's beams, / from whence was sent to thee a soul full-clothed with mind."[416]

Plato teaches us that love and desire for the gods grow the wings of the soul so it can ascend to them and enjoy their community.[417] Iamblichus writes that prayer kindles in the soul love (ἔρως, *erôs*) for the gods, perfects hope (ἐλπίς, *elpis*), and establishes trust (πίστις, *pistis*) in the divine light.[418] Love, hope, and trust (or faith) are the three "Chaldean virtues" of Neoplatonism, by which we may be drawn upward to the One.[419] Through prayer, we become "familiar consorts" of the gods.[420] Moreover, prayer

---

412. See especially Iamblichus, *On the Mysteries* 2.6 and 5.26.

413. Iamblichus, *On the Mysteries* 5.26 [238], 276–77.

414. Iamblichus, *On the Mysteries* 5.26 [238–39], 276–77.

415. Iamblichus, *On the Mysteries* 5.26 [239], 276–77.

416. Plethon, *Magical Oracles* 7.

417. Plato, *Phaedrus* 246d–e, 251a–c.

418. Iamblichus, *On the Mysteries* 5.26 [239], 276–77.

419. See MacLennan, *Wisdom of Hypatia*, chs. 10–12, on these three paths of theurgic ascent.

420. Iamblichus, *On the Mysteries* 5.26 [239], 276–77.

kindles the divine spark in our soul and purifies it of contrary influences, bringing it into greater conformity with the life of the gods.[421] Finally, it purifies our soul's aethereal and luminous vehicles of mortal influences (see "Human Beings" on page 78 and "Philosophical Purification" on page 99).[422]

Prayer is necessary, according to Iamblichus, because we cannot reach the divine by intellect alone.[423] We are mortal, bound in time and space, but the gods are eternal, transcending time and space. We are inferior to them in power, purity, and all else. Prayer opens us up to their benefactions and makes us more like them.

Iamblichus defines three degrees of prayer.[424] The first, **introductory** degree establishes contact and acquaintance with the gods, which leads to spiritual illumination. The second, **conjunctive** degree establishes a sympathetic link between the gods' minds and ours, which invites divine providence into our lives. Through this sympathetic attunement, our habits of thought conform to the gods', and we work together with them. Third, **ineffable union** roots the soul directly in the authority of the gods, which leads to the soul's perfect fulfillment in the divine fire. We are elevated toward the One, and our imperfection is embraced by divine perfection.[425] Union with the One is rare, according to Iamblichus, typically coming late in life after many years of spiritual practice.[426]

Ultimately, the prayers are sent down to us from the gods, awakening in our souls the symbols and ideas by which we are drawn up to the divine. A Magical Oracle asserts of our soul,

> But the Paternal Mind accepteth not her will,
> until she flee oblivion, and pronounce a word,
> inserting memory of the pure paternal sign.[427]

---

421. Iamblichus, *On the Mysteries* 5.26 [238], 274–75.

422. Iamblichus, *On the Mysteries* 5.26 [239], 276–77.

423. Iamblichus, *On the Mysteries* 1.15 [47], 58–59.

424. Iamblichus, *On the Mysteries* 5.26 [237–8], 274–75.

425. Iamblichus, *On the Mysteries* 1.15 [48], 60–61.

426. Iamblichus, *On the Mysteries* 5.22 [230–1], 264–65.

427. Plethon, *Magical Oracles* 6.

Plethon's explanation is that the Second God (Poseidon) will accept our soul's desire for the good if it detaches itself from material concerns ("flees oblivion") and utters either out loud or mentally some speech that recalls to mind a divine symbol.[428]

Proclus writes, "all things pray," and by this he means that all things (inanimate as well as animate) look back to their divine cause, the source of their being, in order to exist authentically.[429] Moreover, all things in the cosmos exist in lineages or chains of causation from the gods. These are the channels by which divine energies descend into the world, and they are the rays or lines of force by which we may be drawn back up and return to our divine origins. These provide the sympathetic linkages used especially in theurgy (chapter 11), but also the symbolic images and metaphors used in prayer. They are implanted in our souls by the gods, if we open ourselves to them and look within. This is the meaning, according to Plethon, of Magical Oracle 22, which reads, "Let lead the soul's immortal depth; / and all thine eyes extend quite upward."[430] We turn our knowing faculties upward, allowing ourselves to be led by the immortal depths of our souls, where the divine symbols reside.

How then should we pray? We can get a good idea by looking at Plethon's prayers (which he calls "addresses," προσρήσεις, *prosrêseis*) in chapters 6 and 7. They have been called "didactic" because a significant part of them is devoted to describing the gods, their functions, and their interrelationships. This is more than a theology lesson, however, for implanting these ideas in our minds fulfills the introductory degree of prayer, acquainting us with the gods, but also opening the receptacles in our souls for the divine energies. Because the gods are Platonic Ideas, by establishing in our minds individual ideas that are images of those universal Ideas, we strengthen the bond between us and the gods. Thus, a Magical Oracle states, "Learn the noetic, which exists beyond thy mind."[431] Plethon explains that although the Demiurge has implanted images of the noetic Ideas in our minds, they exist there only potentially, but they actually

---

428. Plethon, *Commentary* 6.

429. Proclus, *Commentary on Plato's* Timaeus 1.213.2–3, translated in Wallis, *Neoplatonism*, 155.

430. Plethon, *Commentary* 22.

431. Plethon, *Commentary* 29.

exist beyond the mind—in the realm of the Platonic Ideas—and that is where we can encounter them in reality.

Plethon's prayers also ask the gods for various benefits, generally improvement in our minds and souls: "Grant us to have an understanding of you"; "Strengthen our thinking and most divine part to be powerful and the master of our other faculties"; "Following you as much as possible in all our conduct, we will be associated with you by the identity of our actions."[432] In this way prayers help fulfill the conjunctive function: by aligning our thinking with the gods' (our ideas with their Ideas) we cooperate in their providential care for the cosmos, and thereby open our souls to their beneficence.

Ancient Greek prayers, and Plethon's too, typically have three parts, but they can overlap in various ways. You can use this as an outline for your own prayers. The first part is the invocation, which identifies the god by name and focuses our attention on him or her. For example, "O Zeus, greatest and most eminent of gods, O Self-Father, O Eldest Creator of everything, all-powerful and eminent king!" The second part is the narration, in which the god's functions and offices are recalled; this corresponds to the introductory function of prayer wherein we are reacquainted with the god, establishing a sympathetic link. While it is common to recall the god's cosmological roles in the great chain of being, it is also appropriate to recall times when the god aided you personally. The last part is the prayer proper, which is usually either a petition ("Grant me wisdom") or an expression of gratitude ("Thank you for the recovery of my health"); they may be combined (thanks for past benefits, requests for the future). This part serves the conjunctive function, since it reinforces cooperation between gods and mortals.

PURIFICATION

Plethon had a chapter "Purifications" (*Laws* I.23, Περὶ καθαρμῶν, *Peri katharmôn*), which was destroyed, but we can make reasonable conjectures about its contents. The preface to the *Book of Laws* claims that his rituals are "reduced to simple practices, without superfluity, and yet sufficient," and so we may presume that he advised simple purification rituals

---

432. Plethon, *Laws* III.34.8, 14, 18.

from the Hellenic and Platonic traditions.[433] According to Plato, purification (καθαρμός, *katharmos*) is "the science of division," especially the division of what is better from what is worse.[434] In religion, purification separates the sacred from the profane, sanctifying times, places, actions, objects, or people. It is a symbolic action that makes us conscious of this sanctification. (Like prayer and sacrifice, it affects us, not the gods.)

Purification can be understood in two senses, both relevant to Plethon. The next section, "Ritual Purification," teaches specific symbolic rituals that can be used to effect this separation of the sacred from the profane. A following section, "Philosophical Purification," explains the metaphorical notion of purifying the soul in Platonic philosophy.

Ritual Purification

Ritual purification uses physical substances and actions symbolically to align the soul with the higher, divine realities. Substances symbolize purification—the separation of the sacred from the profane—by increasing the sacredness of something, either transferring divine virtue to it or removing the mundane and everyday from it. A sacrifice (see page 200) is a good opportunity to consecrate for purification some substance, which may belong to any of the four elements.

Water is the substance most commonly used for purification in ancient Greece, and you are probably familiar with the "holy water" still used in many religious traditions. According to ancient tradition, such water should come from a pure and flowing source such as a spring or the ocean; in the modern world, tap water also works. The water may be blessed (consecrated to its purifying purpose) by a prayer such as this: "Lady Tethys, from whom all pure water springs, bless this water so it may purify whatever it touches. Be it so!"

Do so with confidence in your own connection to the deity (established through your prior purification, prayer, and sacrifice) and in the god's power to bless it. Immersion in sea water was considered especially purifying in ancient times—"the sea doth wash away all ills"—and so salt might be added to holy water to strengthen its symbolic

---

433. *Laws*, preface; A comprehensive purification treatment is Parker, *Miasma: Pollution and Purification in Early Greek Religion*.

434. Plato, *Sophist* 226d.

efficacy.[435] Another way to increase the purifying power of holy water is to douse in it a sacred flame, such as an incense stick or a burning brand from an altar fire, for both salt and fire are cleansing.

Holy water may be sprinkled on objects to sanctify them. In ancient Greece such aspersion might be performed with a sprig of laurel, which was sacred to all the Olympian gods; Apollo himself was supposed to have instituted the practice of sprinkling holy water with a laurel sprig. An olive sprig is especially good for purification; it was considered more suitable to the gods of Tartarus but might be used for any god. Holy water is also used for lustration (ritual cleansing); the usual method is to dip your fingertips or hands into it. It is a symbolic washing, not an ordinary washing. Afterward, the now "polluted" water is disposed of in the earth.

Fire can be used for purification. In ancient times torches were often used; now candles are more practical. Invoke Leto, the goddess of fire, to bless it. Move the candle around the object to be purified, and be careful! Incense combines the elements air and fire and can be used for fumigation. Usually pleasant incenses, such as frankincense and myrrh, are used to impart divine purity, but acrid substances, such as burning sulfur, can be used to drive out impurities; in Homer sulfur is a cure for anything bad. The earth substance most commonly used for purification is salt, which may be blessed like the other substances.

Purification is used for demarcating the space, time, and participants of a ritual. Plethon writes that worship services should be conducted in a consecrated temple or at least in a place free of human bones and excrement, which are spiritually polluting.[436] A permanent temple, once it is consecrated, does not need to be purified for every service, but if the ritual space is used for other, secular purposes, then it should be purified for each worship service.

In ancient times, sacred space was commonly demarcated by encircling it. A full consecration might use substances ascending though the elements: earth, water, air, and fire. The first circumambulation sprinkles consecrated salt around the boundary. In the second circumambulation we sprinkle holy water or carry a bowl of lustral water.

---

435. Euripides, *Iphigenia in Taurica* 1193.

436. Plethon, *Laws* III.36.1.

The third is a fumigation by incense. Finally, a candle or candelabra is carried around the space. With each circumambulation, invoke the corresponding elemental goddess (see chapter 3) to bless the purification. For example, "O Hestia (Tethys, Hekate, Leto), we pray that you purify this space by the power of your earth (water, air, fire)." This is a rather elaborate purification that might be used to consecrate a permanent temple or for the major holy day rituals. For everyday rituals, a circumambulation with water is sufficient. Remember, Plethon advocates simple rites![437] Normally, one location is designated as the entryway to sacred space, and no one tainted with impurity is allowed to enter (more on this later). As Plato wrote, "The impure may not approach the pure."[438]

The time of a ritual is also separated from ordinary time so that everyday concerns are set aside to focus on the divine. The beginning of a ritual may be marked by the delimitation of sacred time, including lighting any candles or incense, if that has not been done in advance. Entry into sacred space also helps us shift into a reverential mindset. Plethon's rituals are begun by a formal proclamation from the sacred herald. Another proclamation ends the ritual, which is also signaled by extinguishing any candles and by exiting sacred space.

Finally, there is the purification of the participants in a ritual, which involves personal purification and group purification. It has been suggested that you should think of this like going to a fancy dinner or other formal event. You would clean yourself up and put on special clothes as a sign of respect; the same for ritual. This does not have to be special ritual garb for the regular participants in the ordinary day rituals, but those participants who are more actively involved, such as the priest and sacred herald, may want symbolic robes and accoutrements. Similarly, for major rituals, such as on holy days, it is appropriate to take a ritual bath in advance. One bath is sufficient for the entire holy day, typically before the holy day eve service. For ordinary day worship services, it is sufficient to wash your hands when you enter ritual space (described next). In the *Iliad* Hector refuses to pour a libation to Zeus with unwashed hands.[439] The most

---

437. Plethon, *Laws*, preface.

438. Plato, *Phaedo* 67b.

439. Homer, *Iliad* 6.266.

important individual purification is your shift of mental focus from everyday matters to the divine.

In ritual space, the group is purified, which also binds it together in common purpose. Typically, this is a lustration. Many ancient temples had a bowl of **lustral water** (χέρνιψ, *chernips*), which is water for purification, near the entrance to the sacred precincts; entrants dip their hands in it, perhaps sprinkling themselves. Alternately, an officer might sprinkle participants as they enter. Another approach is to carry a bowl of lustral water around the circle so participants can sprinkle themselves or dip their hands. Participants can also be purified by incense (but be considerate of people with incense allergies or breathing difficulties!) or anointed with consecrated oil.

I should say a few words about spiritual pollution (μίασμα, *miasma*). In the Hellenic tradition this primarily results from encounters with death (e.g., attending a funeral, being involved in a fatal accident), or from having committed certain serious crimes. A person afflicted with these sorts of impurities is not permitted to enter sacred space and participate in the usual worship. They can, however, be purified, and a typical ritual would have them sit in the center of the ritual circle to be purified by each of the four elements. The priest and other participants pray to the gods (especially Zeus and Apollo) and the daimons that the subject be purified and restored to a healthy state.

Philosophical Purification

In Plato's *Phaedo* (69b–c), Socrates says that the cardinal virtues (chapter 9) are a kind of purification, and he adds,

> And I fancy that those … who established the mysteries were not unenlightened, but in reality had a hidden meaning when they said long ago that whoever goes uninitiated and unsanctified to [Hades] will lie in the mire, but [whoever] arrives there initiated and purified will dwell with the gods.[440]

He is alluding here to the ancient mysteries, in which initiation was in three stages: purification, illumination, and deification (or perfection); in each of these stages the

---

440. Plato, *Phaedo* 69c, in *Plato in Twelve Volumes*, vol. 1, trans. Harold North Fowler.

cardinal virtues are interpreted at a higher level.[441] The first step is purification because "the impure may not approach the pure."[442] In this case, the goal of purification is for the human immortal mind (the *nous*) to separate voluntarily from its mortal soul and body so it may approach the immortal gods, a sort of "dying before you die."

In the context of these purifying virtues (or excellences), fortitude is fearlessness regarding this separation of the mind from the body and the determination to pursue this spiritual discipline. Self-control consists in resisting disturbance from bodily needs and feelings ("impurities" in this context), so that attention is concentrated in the higher soul (*nous*). Prudence is the ability to live on the basis of reason and intuitive insight (noetic understanding), as opposed to bodily sensations and emotions, and justice subjects the entire soul to the governance of reason and the mind (*nous*) according to Platonic philosophy. Plotinus taught that when the soul is purified, it becomes a Form or Idea and wholly divine.[443]

SACRIFICE

The fourth-century Neoplatonist Sallustius writes, "prayers divorced from sacrifices are only words, with sacrifices they are animated words, the word giving power to the life and the life animation to the word."[444] Plethon wrote three chapters on sacrifices or offerings (the same word in Greek: θυσία, *thusia*), which discussed (1) the sacrifices that suit various gods; (2) the circumstances, manner, and gods receiving sacrifice; and (3) the predispositions with which one should sacrifice (*Laws*, III.37–39). All this was lost to the flames. To make a reasonable guess about what he wrote concerning sacrifice, we can look at the writings of earlier Platonists, in particular the last two links in the Golden Chain, Porphyry and Iamblichus.[445] We can also assume that Plethon's rites were "reduced to simple

---

441. On this, see Addey, *The Unfolding Wings: The Way of Perfection in the Platonic Tradition*, and MacLennan, *The Wisdom of Hypatia: Ancient Spiritual Practices for a More Meaningful Life*.

442. Plato, *Phaedo* 67b.

443. Plotinus, *Enneads* 1.6.6.

444. Sallustius, *Concerning the Gods and the Universe* 16.24–26, trans. Nock, 28–29.

445. Primarily Porphyry, *On Abstinence from Killing Animals* 2.24, 33–34, 37, 45, 61; Iamblichus, *On the Mysteries* 1.13; 5.11–15, 20, 24.

practices, without superfluity, and yet sufficient" and in particular "without exceeding the measure sufficient to mold our imagination."[446]

Porphyry tells us there are three principal purposes for sacrifice: to honor the gods, to thank them, and to request some benefit from them (thus focusing on present, past, and future). Of course, as we saw in our discussion of prayer, the gods are impassible, and so they will not be flattered or have their egos stroked by honor or gratitude, nor will they be coerced to change their minds from what is best to something more appealing to us as individuals. As with prayer, the purpose of sacrifice is not to change the gods but to change us. According to Iamblichus, sacrifice focuses our attention on the gods, reminds us of the benefits we receive from them and of their providential care for the cosmos, and makes them manifest in our lives by a sympathetic alignment of our souls with theirs.[447]

"The gods do not harm us because they are angered," explains Porphyry, "but because they are unrecognized"; in other words, we suffer by ignoring the gods and not living in harmony with them.[448] The gods are self-sufficient and do not need anything from us. Rather, according to Plethon, we make offerings to them in order to excite our own imagination, which is the faculty nearest to the divine part of our being.[449] In this way we train it, leading it to the beautiful and divine, and helping us guide our lives by divine providence and reason.

What should we offer? Iamblichus observes that creators are always fond of their creations, and therefore it is natural that gods prefer as offerings those things that are in their lineage, those beings of which they are the cause.[450] These are the things at all levels of reality in their chain or line of descent. Moreover, a proper sacrifice is of the same kind (συγγενής, syngenês) as both the deity and the soul of the offeror, so that it establishes a sympathetic link between them.[451]

---

446. Plethon, *Laws*, Preface, III.34.17.

447. Iamblichus, *On the Mysteries* 5.24 [235], 270–71; Shaw, *Theurgy and the Soul*, 149.

448. Porphyry, *Letter to Marcella* 18.28b, trans. in Sorabji, *Philosophy of the Commentators*, 374.

449. Plethon, *Laws* III.34.17, 54.

450. Iamblichus, *On the Mysteries* 5.24 [235], 270–71.

451. Shaw, *Theurgy and the Soul*, 153.

Being of the same kind as the deity means that the offering should be similar to the nature of the god. For example, deities of the material world, such as the celestial gods and daimons, receive material offerings (e.g., flowers, fruit, cakes, incense, and beverages). Supercelestial gods—who are eternal Ideas—receive intellectual offerings, such as poems and hymns. The ancient Platonic sage Apollonius of Tyana (15–100 CE) argued that the highest god, the Ineffable One, whom Plethon calls Zeus, can receive only immaterial offerings, and that even spoken words and hymns are too material. Therefore, "we shall worship him in pure silence and with pure thoughts about him."[452] Plethon's conception of the highest god is not quite so ineffable (see chapter 3), however, and we know that he offers Zeus both spoken prayers and hymns. Moreover, the gods' lineages extend through all the levels of being, from the eternal Ideas, down through the celestial spheres, into the material world, including daimons, embodied beings, and inanimate objects. Therefore, it is quite appropriate for a sacrifice to begin with material offerings and progress upward to less material ones.

The supercelestial gods are known in philosophy as the noetic or "intelligible" gods and correspond to the Platonic Ideas. Porphyry reminds us that we offer back to gods some of what they have given us to nourish us and sustain our existence; this is the basis of first-fruits offerings.[453] Therefore, since the intelligible Ideas are the nourishment of souls, the appropriate offering for intelligible gods is the singing of hymns. To the celestial gods, who have bodies, we should offer inanimate things, such as honey, barley grains, flowers, and other fruits of the earth, but especially fire, which is akin to these gods. These were the sacrifices of the earliest people. Material offerings are also appropriate for the daimons, but especially incense, since they have aethereal bodies that are invisible and warm like incense smoke.

Fire is a potent symbol in sacrifice. Incense, candles, and other offerings may be burned because, as Iamblichus explains, "the fire of our sacrifice imitates the divine fire."[454] For we see that fire transforms anything else into its own form, so that it becomes luminous and rarified and ascends heavenward. Such a sacrifice does not draw

---

452. Quoted by Porphyry, *Abstinence* 2.34.2, 69.

453. Porphyry, *Abstinence* 2.34.4.

454. Iamblichus, *On the Mysteries* 5.12 [215], 246–47, trans. in Shaw, *Theurgy and the Soul*, 150.

the gods down into matter, but elevates the sacrifice and the sacrificer to the "divine, heavenly, and immaterial fire."[455] The altar smoke, incense, and perfume all fortify the spirit (πνεῦμα, *pneuma*) in our aethereal bodies. In particular, the burning offering symbolizes the process by which our souls, which were originally fiery, become similar to the gods, becoming impassible, purified, liberated from matter. Thus, writes Iamblichus, "We are led up to the fire of the gods."[456] Being of similar substance to the gods, we participate in their friendship and sympathy.

It probably goes without saying, but offerings for the gods should be high quality, the best of whatever they are. On the other hand, ancient sources are adamant that offerings do not have to be expensive or onerous, but in order to be effective they should be offered with clear intention and commitment. (They affect us, not the gods.)

Although Plethon does not mention it in the pages that have survived, one of the most common sacrifices in ancient times was the **libation**, or drink offering. After praying to one or more gods, pour out a little of the drink while declaring "*spondê*" (σπονδή, which means "libation"). You may offer any beverage (especially water, wine, honey, or milk) or other precious liquids, such as olive oil or perfume. You may offer a few drops or more, pouring them onto your altar (see page 205), sacred fire, or the ground if it is just a little. If you are indoors, you can pour it into a bowl; dispose of it respectfully afterward (as explained later). If the offering is a beverage, you should drink the rest, thus sharing with the god.[457] When making the offering, it is customary to tip the vessel away from yourself, so that the drink does not pass over the place where you put your lips. Libation is an act that cannot be undone, and so it is a consecration and commitment to the gods. Libations are common with meals, but can be done at any time and often accompany other rites.

In addition to conforming to the god, an effective sacrifice, one that has an appropriate effect on the sacrificer, should conform to the soul of the offeror. Few people

---

455. Iamblichus, *On the Mysteries* 5.11 [214], 244–45, trans. in Shaw, *Theurgy and the Soul*, 149.

456. Iamblichus, *On the Mysteries* 5.12 [215], 246–47, trans. in Shaw, *Theurgy and the Soul*, 150.

457. Traditionally, a different sort of drink offering, the *choê* (χοή), was made to the *Chthonioi* (underworld deities, especially Hades and Kore), the heroes, and the dead, in which the entire offering is poured out into a pit in the earth. Given the rather different role that Pluto and Kore play in Plethon's theology (they are the supercelestial gods most involved with *living* people), I think the *spondê* is appropriate for all the gods.

will have reached the level of contemplative practice recommended by Apollonius. Most of us will need the crutch of material offerings, including spoken prayers and hymns, for we must be sufficiently absorbed in the rite that it activates the symbols and images implanted in our souls by the gods, for an Oracle asserts, "Paternal Mind implanted symbols into souls."[458] It is this kindling of the symbols in a god's line of descent that draws our souls upward to absorb that god's energy (recall Magical Oracle 6 on page 193). These symbols "preserve the power of the communion between gods and [people]," according to Iamblichus.[459] In fact, Iamblichus also teaches that it is counterproductive to attempt intellectual (noetic) worship before the feelings and emotions have been purified by material sacrifices to the daimons.[460]

Sacrifice binds the cosmos together in a great circle of love (ἔρως, erôs) and friendship (φιλία, philia), for the good emanates from Zeus, the One-Itself, proceeds down through all levels of being into the material world, and through our sacrifice ascends again through the levels to complete the great circuit of being. The first Magical Oracle states,

> *Seek thou the soul's way, whence or in what rank*
> *to serve the body; to that rank from which thou flowed,*
> *thou mayst rise up again; join act with sacred speech.* [461]

This means, according to Plethon, that our immortal souls have descended through the levels of reality into our bodies in order to care for them while alive. If we perform this office well, then we may reascend by this same path to the place of divine light from which we came. This is accomplished by a combination of divine worship (prayers) and religious rites (sacrifices).[462]

Enough theory. I think we can accept that something like the foregoing was Plethon's theory of sacrifice, but how is it practiced?

---

458. Plethon, *Magical Oracles* 28. In the Magical Oracles, Paternal Mind (*Nous*) refers to the Second God, specifically Poseidon, but more generally to all the supercelestial gods.

459. Iamblichus, *On the Mysteries* 5.24 [235], 270–71.

460. Iamblichus, *On the Mysteries* 5.15 [219], 250–53. See also Shaw, *Theurgy and the Soul*, 150–51.

461. Plethon, *Magical Oracles* 1.

462. Plethon, *Commentary* 1.

First, you will need to establish one or more altars (βωμοί, *bômoi*, sing. βωμός, *bômos*), which may be indoors or outside. Ancient altars tended to be permanently dedicated to a single god, but I suspect that Plethon worshipped several gods at each of his altars since his invocations address multiple gods. The altar may be any flat surface on which you can make offerings. Permanent altars are best, but if that is impossible, you can designate a temporary one by spreading an altar cloth on a table.

The sacrificial act is demarcated by purification, which, as we have seen, is a process of separation in time, space, and attitude. Normally both the altar and the ritual space are purified. At very least, your hands should be ritually cleansed. Porphyry suggests wearing white, which was the ancient custom of philosopher-priests.[463] This is obviously a symbol of purity, but even more important that outer cleanliness is inner purity: a lightness of soul that is not burdened with heavy foods or with feelings and thoughts that distract us from the divine.

Typically, a sacrifice begins with a prayer, for, as Iamblichus tells us, "sacrifice and prayer reinforce each other and communicate to each other a perfect ritual and hieratic power," and so there may be prayers at the beginning, at the end, or in the midst of sacrifices.[464] Prayers may themselves be considered offerings (especially if they honor or thank a god), and it is in fact common to pray while making other offerings (e.g., while sprinkling incense on the fire or pouring a drink offering). For example, a burnt offering might be accompanied by a prayer such as this: "As this offering is consumed by the sacrificial fire, so may thy divine fire consume in my soul any discord, any false opinions, any poisonous emotions, or anything else that obscures thy divine light."

As the offering is made, all the participants may touch the altar and say, "Be it so!" (εἶεν, *eien*) to share in the blessing.

One problem with determining suitable offerings is that the gods, as described by Plethon, have wide-ranging and somewhat abstract areas of responsibility. For Apollo we would want an offering symbolizing Identity, and for Dionysos an offering of Self-motion, but what might these be? As mentioned before, for these supercelestial gods, an intellectual offering is most appropriate, such as a poem, song, or prayer, perhaps accompanied

---

463. Porphyry, *Abstinence* 2.45.4.

464. Iamblichus, *On the Mysteries* 5.26 [240], trans. in Dillon and Gerson, *Neoplatonic Philosophy*, 232.

by burning some incense (frankincense being a good, general-purpose choice) or a fragrant candle. Plethon's hymns are examples.

As Porphyry explained, one common purpose for sacrifice is to request a god's aid, in which case you might vow some offering or action in thanks for that aid.[465] You should always fulfill your vows and therefore think carefully before you make them! Don't promise what you can't deliver; fulfilling a small vow is better than reneging on a big one. A small image of that for which you are either seeking aid or grateful can be placed near an image of the god. In ancient and modern times, people have offered images of healed or cured body parts, for example. Accompany your offering with a prayer; you can also light a votive candle or incense.

Another common kind of thanks offering is of **first fruits**, in which you offer the first of anything you have accomplished. These may be literal first fruit—from your garden, for example—or more abstract, such as the first performance of a new song. Also, it may be a symbolic representation of the thing if it is impractical to offer the thing itself (maybe you built a house!).

One important offering is our own excellence or virtue. We receive our excellence from the gods, which serves to make us like them, and therefore we can give thanks and honor the gods by striving to live up to this potential. For hints on how to do this, see chapter 9, "How to Be Excellent," and seek the gods' aid through prayer and sacrifice. Porphyry writes that we may offer ourselves as a sacrifice, by purifying our mind and understanding and by constructing a divine image within our mind to make a temple in which the god may dwell.[466]

Practical matters: If you make offerings of food or other perishable materials, you will need to clean them up (as they did in ancient temples too). The most respectful way seems to be to dispose of them in the earth or as compost. If that's not practical (e.g., you live in an apartment), then wrap them up neatly and dispose with other refuse (which will go to a landfill). If that bothers you, then stick to offerings that are immaterial or can be burned up on the altar.

---

465. Porphyry, *Abstinence* 2.24.1.

466. Porphyry, *Abstinence* 2.61.1.

POWERS OF THE SEVEN PLANETS

As explained in chapter 3, the seven planetary gods collaborate with the Titans to create our mortal nature. Although Plethon's two chapters on the planets (*Laws* II.14–15) were burned, we can infer his teachings on the planets' powers in our bodies and souls from his astrological sources (primarily Ptolemy) and from the writings of Vettius Valens and Marsilio Ficino, Plethon's follower in Platonic philosophy.[467] As our souls descend into incarnation, they acquire these powers to varying degrees depending on the time and place of our birth and our choices before incarnation (see "The Guardian Daimon" on page 224). Like all deities, the planetary gods are essentially good, but through their interaction with the imperfections of our souls and bodies, they can have undesirable effects.

The seven planets are a celestial image of the seven eldest supercelestial gods (Poseidon, Hera, Apollo, Artemis, Hephaistos, Dionysos, Athena), from which the planets receive some of their powers. They also acquire their powers from the elemental goddesses via the qualities **hot**, **cold**, **moist**, and **dry** (which must be understood symbolically; see "Goddesses of the Elements" in chapter 3). These result from the planets' interactions, which depend on their positions in the heavens, beginning with the Moon nearest Earth, and ascending through the spheres of Mercury, Venus, the Sun, Mars, Jupiter, and Saturn, which is nearest the sphere of the fixed stars.

The hot and moist powers, which correspond to the elements Fire and Water, are considered to be more active. These expansive and fluid powers together promote fertility, growth, and development. They both tend to separate things: moisture loosens bonds and rigid structures, and heat discriminates things (think distillation), sorting them out; both are essential for new growth, change, transformation, and progress.

The other two powers—the cold and the dry—are more passive. Coldness, which is characteristic of Air according to Plethon, is the power of connection, and dryness, associated with Earth, is the power of fixation and stabilization.[468] These powers tend to

---

467. Ptolemy, *Tetrabiblos* 1.4–8; Ficino, *Three Books on Life: A Critical Edition and Translation with Introduction and Notes*. A psychologically sensitive description of the planets in Ficino can be found in Thomas Moore, *The Planets Within: The Astrological Psychology of Marsilio Ficino*, Part II. Other sources are Vettius Valens, *Anthologiarum Libri*, book 1, and Macrobius, *Commentary on the Dream of Scipio* 1.12. A careful analysis of the planets in Valens, and in Hellenistic astrology more generally, can be found in Chris Brennan, *Hellenistic Astrology: The Study of Fate and Fortune*, ch. 7.

468. Plethon, *Laws* III.34.27.

keep things as they are, so they impede new growth and transformation. Nevertheless, they are essential for preservation, permanence, and stability.

The Sun and the Moon are called the Greater Lights or Luminaries and rule the celestial gods as images of Poseidon and Hera, the rulers of the supercelestials. They each head a "sect" (αἵρεσις, *hairesis*) of three planets with related powers: the solar sect is the Sun, Jupiter, and Saturn; the lunar sect is the Moon, Venus, and Mars. Mercury moves between the sects depending on the time of day. Ficino tells us that, except the gods, nothing lives except by means of the Sun and Moon.[469] The Sun is primarily responsible for the forms of mortal things, and the Moon provides the matter, but all the planets collaborate in the creation of mortal things, as explained later.[470]

Sun

The **Sun (Helios)** is especially hot and also drying, as you would expect. Therefore, it is fiery, and we must remember that Fire (or Aether) is the substance of the bodies of the celestial gods and daimons. This luminous solar power is characteristic of all the celestial gods. It is the cause of spiritual illumination from the planets (and parallels Poseidon as the Idea of Ideas). This is symbolized by the Sun's central position in the planetary spheres: ♄♃♂ ☉ ♀☿☽.

The Sun is the source of intellectual light and intelligence (φρόνησις, *phronêsis*), of keen perception and imagination; he is the power of the mind (*nous*). As Fire is the most spiritual element (with no material body and a drive to ascend), so the Sun is the most spiritual planet, a source of spiritual insights and illumination. He governs our interactions with the gods and therefore divination and other forms of theurgy (chapter 11).

The Sun is a source of judgment, good council, and authority; he confers great nobility, but it can harden into pride or flare into ambition. Due to his excessive heat and dryness, the Sun tends to rigid and fixed discriminations and structures, to dogmas and fixed ideas, which can lead to spiritual death and rigor mortis, for without moisture

---

469. Ficino, *Three Books on Life* 3.6.79–80 (*Opera*, 538), 268–69.

470. If you are familiar with Hellenistic astrology, you will know that Jupiter and Venus were considered benefic, and Saturn and Mars malefic. Each sect therefore contains one benefic and one malefic. As Plethon informs us, however, all the gods, including the celestial gods, are good (*Summary* 3); they all have characters that may benefit us or cause us trouble in particular situations.

there cannot be life and growth. Therefore, every evening the Sun sinks into the western ocean, where it is rejuvenated, reborn, and the governance of the heavens is turned over to the moist Moon and other planets.

Moon

The **Moon (Selene)**, who is called "the Other Sun," regularly approaches the Sun, receiving her light from him, and so she is somewhat warm, but she is especially moist because she is in the lowest celestial sphere where she absorbs moist vapors from the earth. Bearing the warm and moist powers, she is exceptionally active. She encourages us to wander and can bring inconstancy.

In the material world everything is in flux—continually coming to be and passing away—and so ancient philosophers symbolized our mutable world by water (recall the discussion of Rhea, the goddess of the elements, in chapter 3). The Moon is the most mutable planet as she moves fluidly between the opposites, full and new, tempering the extremes to achieve balance and peace. Her regular cycle of phases symbolizes the cycles in everything, especially in natural processes; all things wax and wane until they finally disappear. Being warm and moist, she is the fertile principle, bringing the disembodied ideas of the Sun and other planets into material manifestation; she is the power of conception and motherhood. She governs the unconscious processes of nourishment, growth, and development in our bodies; she supports the processes of life.

As the planet nearest to the earth, the Moon is most intimately involved in our embodied life and everyday experience. In particular, she governs our physical bodies and their natural processes. Therefore, she mediates between our soul and our body, a relationship that varies as she changes; as Ficino writes, "We have the heavens entire within us," and therefore "Luna symbolizes the continuous motion of soul and body."[471]

Since the Moon occupies the lowest celestial sphere, the one nearest to our world, she is especially responsible for channeling the powers of the other planets into our earthly life. She also brings their divine forces into our individual psyches and thus holds the key to the unconscious mind, to its archetypes and complexes. In particular, as the Moon reflects the light of the Sun, so the lunar part of the soul reflects the illumination coming from

---

471. Ficino, *Opera*, 805, my translation.

the solar part; therefore, the spiritual inspirations are mirrored as concrete images in the imagination, which brings them into our experience. She brings us dreams and visions.

The Moon is connected with magic because she stands at the gateway between mundane reality and the celestial and supercelestial realms, between the natural and the supernatural. "Just so," writes Ficino, "the safest way will be to do nothing without Luna's aid."[472] The ancients taught that Cancer, which is the domicile of the Moon, is the Gateway of Mortals, through which human souls descend into embodiment (and, as we will see, the opposite sign Capricorn, ruled by Saturn, is the Gateway of Gods through which human souls may return to the gods).

Saturn

Plethon calls **Saturn** by the traditional name **Phainôn**, which means shining, but also more generally illuminating, showing forth, revealing, and he is the celestial god of spiritual revelation. Saturn is primarily cold, according to Ptolemy, because he resides in the outermost planetary sphere, below the fixed stars and far from the Sun. For Plethon coldness is the principal quality of Air, which is opposed to the heat of Fire and the Sun.[473] Ptolemy also tells us that Saturn is quite dry due to his sphere, which is farthest from the moist exhalations of the earth. These properties—coolness, which tends to connect disparate things together, and dryness, which leads to rigid, fixed, stable structures—are central to Saturn's effects in our minds and bodies. He is characterized by contraction and restraint. Saturn's coldness and remoteness from the earth facilitate establishing many connections between abstract ideas, transcending distinctions and differences caused by the separation of heat. He governs abstract rationality and understanding.

For these reasons, and because he moves so slowly and is in the sphere adjacent to the fixed stars, Saturn is the planet that resists change. He is heavy and immoveable, like his metal, gray lead. Saturn withdraws the vital warmth and moisture from life, and so he is involved in melancholy and depression.

Nevertheless, because of his distance from the hot flux of everyday experience and emotions, and because of his nearness to the highest celestial sphere, the fixed stars, who

---

472. Ficino, *Three Books on Life* 3.6.17 (*Opera*, 537), 266–67, my translation.

473. Plethon, *Laws* III.34.27.

are images of the supercelestial gods and contemplate the eternal Ideas, Saturn's gift is deep religious contemplation and profound spiritual insight. As mentioned previously (under "Moon"), the Gate of the Gods is in Capricorn, which is ruled by Saturn, who reveals the way by which our souls can return to the gods through spiritual practices, such as theurgy (see chapter 11).

Saturn's cold, dry nature leads us to build theological systems, but they tend to be abstract—far removed from feelings, imagination, and life—and also rigid, too brittle to adapt and grow. He prefers stable systems and organizations and has a talent for administration. In general, the cold dryness of Saturn does not support new growth, development, and flexibility (which require warmth and moisture), and so Saturn inclines us to lean on the rigid structures of the past, a petrified conservatism devoid of life. Without the benefit of inspiration, growth, and fluid flexibility, Saturn is obliged to tinker with his old ideas, patching them up as best he can.

Cold, dry, remote, showing souls the way back to the gods: Saturn is the planet of old age and death, but he can bring rigidity of thoughts and habits, obstinacy, strictness, cynicism, ill-temper, misanthropy, and depression to people of any age. To gain the benefits of Saturn while tempering his excesses, we may cultivate other planetary influences, such as Venus (moderately moist) and Jupiter (moderately warm).

Saturn and Mercury are both involved in intellectual activities, but in different ways. Saturn lacks the nimbleness and adaptability of Mercury (described later), but compensates with a spiritual depth and seriousness unavailable to that flightier planet. No planet should be ignored.

Mars

Mars (**Pyroeis** = fiery) is especially dry, which is the power characteristic of the element Earth, according to Plethon, but he is also quite hot, because his sphere is next to that of the Sun (which is hot and dry).[474] Therefore, Mars brings the active, separating force of the warm power to the firmness and strength of the dry power. He governs what is hard and cut off.[475] As a consequence, Mars is a divisive planet, and from ancient mythology

---

474. Plethon, *Laws* III.34.27.

475. τὸ σκληρός καὶ ἀπότομον in Valens, *Anthologiarum Libri* I.i, 3.13.

we know him as a violent war god. And indeed he brings us an inclination to anger, verbal abuse, righteous indignation, hatred, disagreement, strife, competition, conflict, confrontation, arrogance, aggression, and hypermasculinity, for better or worse. We may think of these as negative tendencies, but of course it is also Mars who gives us the boldness and courage to confront injustice and anything else that is wrong and needs to be opposed. He helps us to defend ourselves and others against any kind of aggression or oppression. His gifts include constructive confrontation and productive competition. With an indomitable will and persistence, he fearlessly defends the truth.

The division sown by Mars need not be directed at others; it can arise in our own soul, as he can put one planet in conflict with another. This is an essential truth of polytheism: these celestial gods have their own inclinations and agendas, which may be in conflict, and it is our task to find an accommodation among them. This diversity of aims is according to the will of Zeus.

Jupiter

The sphere of **Jupiter** (**Phaëthôn** = shining, brilliant) is between the hot sphere of Mars and the cold sphere of Saturn; therefore, he is moderate, a well-tempered balance of these two powers. He strikes a mean between the power of division, discrimination, and separation and the power of connection, synthesis, and blending. He fosters benevolence, friendship, and fidelity.

However, Jupiter is also somewhat moist (and thus akin to the Moon and Venus), which combines with his warmth to make him a fertilizing power, stimulating new growth of all sorts. He is the power of fatherhood. Indeed, Jupiter is the mental power that implants the seeds or seminal principles into material reality, manifesting them; he doesn't just think, he acts. He is, Ficino writes, "the intellect from whom the universe is produced."[476] He brings profound knowledge (γνῶσις, *gnôsis*) and spiritual leadership.

Because of his moderate nature, Jupiter tempers the powers of all the planets, humanizing them, adapting them to each other, and making them more compatible with social life. For example, Jupiter moderates the overly spiritual tendency of the Sun, which may parch the soul, hardening it; Jupiter is more humane. On the other

---

476. Ficino, *Opera*, 935, my translation.

hand, Jupiter also tempers the more embodied aspects of the soul arising from the Moon and Venus (described later), again adapting them to social life. Therefore, Jupiter serves as a mediating power uniting the elevating but aethereal spirit of the Sun with the more embodied spirits of the Moon and Venus. "Mix into one the Solar things and the things of Venus," recommends Ficino, "and thus you will make a Jovial compound from both."[477]

Jupiter's temperate nature helps us adapt to living in communities and guides us in the formulation of the laws and constitutions that support civil society. Therefore, Jupiter is especially helpful to lawgivers "just as," Ficino writes, "Jupiter is the supportive father for people leading a common life."[478] He grants political wisdom, justice, a civic attitude, and stewardship, but his political ambitions can descend into tyranny.

Venus

Venus (**Eosphoros** = dawn-bringer or **Phosphoros** = light-bringer) is predominantly moist due to the relative nearness of her sphere to the moist vapors of the earth, but her moisture is more moderate than the Moon's. Venus is also moderately warm because her sphere is next to that of the Sun and because she always stays close to the Sun in the heavens. Because of this warmth, but especially her moisture, Venus promotes growth and fertility, and so she is also the power of passion, desire, love, and sex. She also promotes motherly behavior in people of any sex: nurturing and caring for the young, cultivating growth and development.

Venus is similar to the Moon but a gentler power, connected with the body, the senses, sensuality, beauty, and aesthetics; she grants artistic sensibility and skill and relishes adornment. Venus is also the power of the lower parts of the soul, which are more closely connected with the body. These include our emotions, which are fluid—ever changing—but also warm, making distinctions between love and hate, attraction and aversion, happiness and sadness, anger and fear. However, the ancients called her the laughter-loving goddess, and she inclines more to good cheer, laughter, pleasure, and friendliness; she likes to give and receive gifts.

---

477. Ficino, *Three Books on Life* 3.5.24–5 (*Opera*, 537), 264–65, my translation.

478. Ficino, *Three Books on Life* 3.22.38–9 (*Opera*, 565), 364–65, my translation.

The moist, embodied feelings of Venus tend to balance the fervent and parching spirituality of the Sun; they temper each other. For the same reasons, Venus and Mars temper each other: Venus softens the aggression, anger, and divisiveness of Mars, but Mars increases the burning desire in Venus's love and the heat of her other emotions. Ultimately, Mars is conquered by his love of Venus. "Mars in turn follows Venus, but Venus does not follow Mars," writes Ficino, "because audacity is the servant of love, but love is not, of audacity."[479] Venus brings good reconciliations.[480] In mythology, Harmonia is the daughter of Mars and Venus, but this harmony is not a bland lack of discrimination; it is much more like a melody: a system of contrasts that combine into a unified and emotionally satisfying whole. (In ancient Greek, a *harmonia* is a means of joining things together, an agreement, a musical scale or tuning.) Love and Strife are the two fundamental powers in the cosmos, according to Empedocles; all things come into being through their union.[481]

Mercury

Mercury (Stilbôn, from στίλβω, *stilbô* = to glitter or twinkle) is the most ambiguous planetary power, a kaleidoscope of ever-changing qualities. His sphere is next to the Moon's, and so he has some of her moist, dissolving power, ever in flux, the power of the element Water. However, his sphere is also near to the Sun's, and he is the closest companion of the Sun in the heavens, and so, Ptolemy tells us, he is also drying, which is the power that makes things fixed, stable, and determinate, the principal power of the element Earth.[482] As he moves quickly through the heavens, Mercury vacillates between these opposed characteristics of the Sun and Moon (and therefore, as previously mentioned, he moves between their sects).

The planets rule different faculties and parts of the body, and according to Ptolemy, Mercury is responsible for speech and thought.[483] Therefore, he promotes education,

---

479. Ficino, *Opera*, 1339, my translation.

480. συναλλαγὰς ἐπὶ τὸ ἀγαθόν (Valens, *Anthologiarum Libri* I.i, 3.19).

481. Empedocles, LM 22D73 (DK 31B17) in Laks and Most, *Early Greek Philosophy V: Western Greek Thinkers, Part 2*, 410–23.

482. Ptolemy, *Tetrabiblos* 1.4 [18], 38–39.

483. Ptolemy, *Tetrabiblos* 4.4 [178], 382–83.

reasoning, debate, interpretation, and communication. Ficino asserts Mercury causes remembrance when he stimulates the memory, speech when he stimulates the imagination, and interpretation when he stimulates reason in the soul.[484] He grants forethought and intelligence, supporting philosophers, prophets, and dream interpreters, but also ambassadors, speakers, teachers, and advisors, all those who must think precisely and express themselves skillfully (including mathematicians and computer scientists). Mercury is not above strategic use of rhetoric, ambiguity, and paradox, but he can use deceit as well. He is inventive. In fact, Mercury, in cooperation with the other planetary powers, supports many occupations and activities.

Mercury is closely related, of course, to the god Hermes, whose name (Ἑρμῆς, *Hermês*) is related to the verb *hermêneuô* (ἑρμηνεύω), which means to interpret, expound, or explain. These activities include the ability to translate from one language to another, and thus the ability to understand other people and other cultures (for Mercury and Hermes negotiate the crossing of boundaries). They also include the ability to see alternative interpretations or understandings of words, observations, events, and situations, to nimbly switch between them in order to find the best interpretation in a given context. Mercury's fluid creativity keeps the interpretations changing so we can grab the one that's best in current circumstances as it passes. But he can be capricious and destabilizing.

By understanding the hearer, Mercury also allows us to explain or state things in a different, more appropriate and effective way, quickly adapting to the situation. Therefore, he brings the skills of the expert communicator: eloquence, rhetoric, persuasiveness, wit, word play, creative expression. Ficino reminds us that in mythology Mercury uses his wand, the caduceus, to awaken or to put to sleep, and so he can stimulate the minds of ourselves and others, or he can lull them into inattentive dullness or distraction, as suits his purpose.

In contrast to the burning, parching spiritual elevation of the Sun and the cold, dark spiritual depths of Saturn, Mercury's intelligence is grounded in experience, either in shifting emotions (fluid, Water) or in the solidity of the embodied situation (dry, Earth). His imagination is concrete and practical, seeing the way through the situation at hand, ever ready to switch to plan B, or C, or D, or back to A.

---

484. Ficino, *Opera*, 912.

Correspondence with the Seven Elder Gods

The seven planetary gods seem to be images of the seven elder gods (Poseidon, Hera, Apollo, Artemis, Hephaistos, Dionysos, and Athena), but Plethon does not specify an explicit correspondence, except to note that the Sun and Moon are the rulers of the celestials as Poseidon and Hera are of the Olympians.[485] In each case the male is associated with Form and the female with Matter (see "Divine Gender" in chapter 3). However, we know that the order in which gods are generated is significant for Plethon, and in the two places where he enumerates the planets, he does so in the same order: Sun, Moon, Venus, Mercury, Saturn, Jupiter, Mars.[486] Aligning the two lists reveals a number of correspondences, which give us additional insights into the planets.

Plethon does tell us that the Sun and Moon, who are the causes of Form and Matter in the material world, correspond to Poseidon and Hera, who are the causes of Form and Matter in the realm of Ideas.[487] Next consider the gods of movement and change. Hephaistos, who is the cause of immobility and permanence, corresponds to Saturn, the cold planet who strives to keep things as they are; Hephaistos establishes the fixed relations among the gods, and Saturn maintains fixed systems of ideas, especially in spiritual matters. Athena is the Idea of external force and separation, and she corresponds to Mars, the power of division, conflict, and aggression; traditionally, both Athena (Minerva) and Mars (Ares) are connected with warfare and defense, but Athena's strengths are more intellectual; those of Mars, more physical. Dionysos, who is the Idea of self-caused or voluntary change, especially upward to perfection, aligns with Jupiter, an intellectual planet who tends to elevate material existence, organizing it more like the community of gods. This leaves two gods, Apollo and Artemis, and two planets, Venus and Mercury, to consider. Here Plethon seems to have reversed the order of the planets, for Venus most closely corresponds to Artemis and Mercury to Apollo. Artemis is the Idea of diversity and multiplicity, both among and within individuals, and Venus is the power of fertility and growth. Apollo is the Idea of Identity, especially among the Ideas, which gives them their exact meanings, and he is the patron of the arts and

485. Plethon, *Laws* I.15.14; Hladký, *Plethon*, 106.

486. Plethon enumerates them in the Second Address of the Afternoon (*Laws* III.34.34) and in Hymn 9, the Seventh Monthly Hymn, to the Celestial Gods (*Laws* III.35.9).

487. Plethon, *Laws* I.15.14.

sciences; Mercury is also an intellectual god, but his understanding is more contextual, more situational, better able to adapt to circumstances. As usual, the males Apollo and Mercury are more associated with ideas and form, while the females Artemis and Venus are more involved with matter and multiplication (again, recall "Divine Gender" in chapter 3).

Therefore, all the planets seem to correspond to the elder gods in the order Plethon listed them, except that Venus and Mercury are switched. Plethon does not state explicitly that the order in which he lists the planets is significant, so the switch might mean nothing, or perhaps there is something more subtle going on. If we had the destroyed chapters on the planets, we might know for sure, but alas we don't. I think they are switched, but the issue is not very important for understanding his theology or practicing his religion.

DAIMONS

As the divine beings nearest to us, it is important to understand daimons correctly. Plethon tells us that they transmit gods' benefactions to us and are the divine beings most responsive to us.[488] Sadly, Scholarios destroyed the four chapters that Plethon devoted to them (II.18–21), in which we suppose they were explained in detail. Fortunately, we can reconstruct what Plethon probably taught from his surviving remarks about them and from a fairly consistent Platonic daimonology.[489]

The Nature of Daimons

Calcidius defines a daimon as "a rational, immortal, sensitive, aethereal living being taking care of people."[490] He explains that it is a living being because it has a soul governing a body, rational because it exercises prudence, immortal because it has one body forever,

---

488. Plethon, *Laws* III.34.6, 35.14.

489. Principal sources are Porphyry, *On Abstinence from Killing Animals* 2.38–41; Hierocles, *Commentary on the Pythagorean Golden Verses* in Schibli, *Hierocles of Alexandria*, 192–96; and O'Neill, *Proclus: Alcibiades I. A Translation and Commentary*, 2nd ed., 47–8 [71–3]. See also Addey, "The Daimonion of Socrates: Daimones and Divination in Neoplatonism," in Layne and Tarrant, eds., *The Neoplatonic Socrates*, ch. 3.

490. Calcidius, *On Demons* (*Commentarius Ch. 127–136*), 7 [ch. 135a], 38.

sensitive because it has desires and chooses, aethereal because its body is made of aether, and that it cares for people by the will of the gods.

Daimons are intermediate beings, and their existence is required for the perfection of the cosmos. Consider the kinds of rational beings. On the one hand, we have the supercelestial gods, who are eternal—outside of time and space. As a consequence, they do not have physical bodies (which exist only in time and space), and they are impassible: they are not affected by events in time and space. On the other hand, we have human beings, who have immortal souls, but mortal physical bodies, which are passible: subject to events in time and space; we feel and experience. According to Pythagorean-Platonic principles, in order to have a unified cosmos, these opposites must be joined by a mediating principle, and that is provided by beings that are immortal and passible (thus sharing immortality with the gods and a passible nature with humans).[491] These beings have everlasting bodies—their aethereal vehicles—that exist in time and space and are affected by other bodies; these beings are the celestial gods and the terrestrial daimons. Recall (chapter 3) that both have very subtle aethereal vehicles—made of *pneuma*—but the stars' and planets' vehicles are fiery and therefore visible, whereas the daimons' vehicles are more like warm breath and therefore invisible. The other difference, of course, is that the celestial gods reside in the heavens whereas the terrestrial daimons reside on earth. (Humans also have invisible aethereal vehicles, which connect our souls to our gross physical bodies.) Like humans and the celestial gods, daimons have a mind (*nous*), soul (*psychê*), and body (*sôma*).

Recall that Zeus emanated two ranks of supercelestial gods: the Olympians, who are the Ideas of imperishable beings, and the Titans, who are the Ideas of perishable beings (his "high-born" and "low-born" children, respectively). Similarly, the celestial gods are the "high-born" children of Poseidon, and the daimons are his "low-born" children (recalling that there is no moral approval or condemnation implied by these terms).

As Plethon informs us, daimons have infallible correct opinions but cannot prove them scientifically.[492] This is in contrast on the one hand to higher gods, who have both

---

491. In this chain of being, according to Maximus of Tyre (Guthrie, *Pagan Bible*, 18), gods and daimons share immortality, daimons and humans share passibility, humans and (non-human) animals share sensibility, animals and plants share vegetative souls (whose function is nutrition and growth).

492. Plethon, *Laws* I.5.9, III.34.6.

infallible knowledge and scientific understanding, and on the other to us, who often have neither.

The Functions of Daimons

Porphyry explains that daimons are responsible for administering, under the gods' direction, much of our world, including animals and plants, and the conditions favorable to them, such as moderate temperature, rain, and weather.[493] They are the agents of the gods' providential care for us. This is because the gods, who are impassible, cannot feel joy or grief, but the daimons, who are passible, have these feelings. Therefore, they are empathetic with humans, feeling joy for good and honest people, but anger at the wicked, which they know by looking into our thoughts. Because they are empathetic, daimons heal us and correct wrongs. They carry our prayers to the gods, bring us divine aid, and inform us of the gods' will.

According to Synesius, as intermediate beings between gods and humans, the attention of daimons is divided between contemplation of the gods and care for earth and its inhabitants; sometimes they are looking upward, sometimes downward.[494] Therefore, we cannot expect them to intervene in every small matter. They are like mechanics, occasionally adjusting and tuning a machine that otherwise works on its own, or like the pilots of ships, who occasionally adjust the speed and heading of a ship to keep it on course.

Plato and Calcidius connect the word *daimôn* (δαίμων) to the word *daêmôn* (δαήμων), which means knowing or experienced in something, because daimons also govern knowledge and skills in many disciplines, including the liberal arts, medicine, and physical training.[495] They are experts, with prudent minds, sharp intellects, good memories, much wisdom, and obedience to the gods. Therefore, they are well equipped to help people in many matters. Daimons sometimes bring us images of the future, according to Plethon, usually in dreams, but sometimes by inspiring waking visions.[496]

---

493. Porphyry, *Abstinence* 2.38.

494. Synesius, *On Providence* 1.10.1, in Guthrie, *Pagan Bible*, 73.

495. Plato, *Cratylus* 397c–398c; Calcidius, *Demons* 4 [ch. 132], 28.

496. Plethon, *Laws* III.34.64.

There are various ways to classify the daimons. Proclus lists six ranks of daimons.[497] The highest two, the **divine** and **noetic daimons**, provide our guardian daimons, described later. The **psychic daimons** care for our souls, and the **corporeal daimons** care for our bodies. **Physical daimons** deal with the rest of living nature (φύσις, *physis*), and the **material daimons** handle all the processes in the material universe.

Each of the gods has daimons in their lineage, who assist their **leader god**, and according to Plethon, each planetary god leads a division of the daimons, sometimes called their "body-guards" (δορυφόροι, *doryphoroi*).[498] Therefore, there are solar daimons in the train of Helios, lunar daimons in the train of Selene, martial daimons for Mars, and so forth, who assist the planetary gods in their functions. Although the celestial gods are visible, their offspring daimons are invisible (due to their breath-like aethereal bodies). A daimon may be known by the name of their leader god, but most daimons are anonymous.

Another common classification, found in Hierocles for example, has three descending ranks of daimons: angels (ἄγγελοι, *angeloi*), daimons proper (δαίμονες, *daimones*), and heroes (ἥρωες, *hêrôes*).[499] In ancient Greek, *angelos* (ἄγγελος) means messenger, and that is their principal function: to communicate between the gods and us so that we can live well. They "bring to light and define for us the guidelines for happiness."[500] The second class, *daimones* in the narrow sense, are those knowledgeable and experienced in divine laws (as suggested by the derivation from *daêmôn*). To explain the third class, Hierocles connects the word *hêrôs* (ἥρως) to the word *airô* (αἴρω), which means to raise up, lift, exalt, or sustain; therefore, a hero can elevate us by means of love (ἔρως, *erôs*) from our earthly life to divine citizenship.[501] According to Plato, they also aid the ascent by the dialectical process of asking questions (ἐρωτᾶν, *erôtan*).[502] These heroes are divine and children of the gods, and they probably should be distinguished from

---

497. O'Neill, *Proclus: Alcibiades I* 71–72, 47.

498. Plethon, *Laws* III.34.6.

499. Hierocles, *Commentary on Golden Verses* 3.7, in Schibli, *Hierocles of Alexandria*, 193. He observes that informally any one of these terms may refer to all three classes.

500. Hierocles, *Commentary on Golden Verses* 3.6, in Schibli, *Hierocles of Alexandria*, 193.

501. Hierocles, *Commentary on Golden Verses* 3.6, in Schibli, *Hierocles of Alexandria*, 192.

502. Plato, *Cratylus* 398d4–7.

the heroes who are deceased illustrious persons and whom Plethon mentions gathered around Pluto.[503] The latter seem to be exceptional mortals that have been freed from the cycle of rebirth and promoted to the rank of daimons for their good deeds. Hierocles also mentions "earth-dwelling daimons," who are daimons with a corporeal body.[504] They were born as human beings, but their souls have become daimonic through virtue, wisdom, and especially knowledge and experience of the gods. These are truly holy men and women.

Although it is not clear that he intends it as a classification, Plethon's Hymn 14 (the Twelfth Monthly Hymn, to the Daimons) lists five functions that daimons perform for us.[505] First there are *purifiers* (καθαιρόντες, *kathairontes*), who aid in the process of purification described previously. We may assume this includes both ritual purification and purification of the soul, which also includes purification as the first stage of philosophical ascent. We have seen that purification creates a distinction, and these daimons may be invoked to create or maintain such a distinction, for example separating the sacred from the profane. One may also need cleansing from what is impure, from *miasma* or spiritual pollution, perhaps resulting from some misdeed or trauma. This is an emotional pollution, which may infect us and can be cleansed with the aid of purifying daimons. The same applies to other emotional blocks or malaise, to obsessions, or to anything else preventing us from living well. This sort of purification blends into philosophical purification, the separation from too intense involvement with bodily pleasures and pains, in order to purify the soul for the ascent to the divine.

Next Plethon mentions *elevators* (ἀναγόντες, *anagontes*), who are daimons concerned with raising us up toward the gods, returning our souls to the divine realm, which is their home. These are the daimons who reconnect us with the gods, and so they also oversee prayer, sacrifice, and theurgy. They also help to restore the soul after the purifiers have cleansed it.

The **guardians** or **watchers** (φρουρεῦντες, *phroureuntes*) aid us on both the mundane and spiritual levels. On the mundane level they look out for us and warn us.

---

503. Plethon, *Laws* III.35.20, 36.21.

504. Hierocles, *Commentary on Golden Verses* 4.2, in Schibli, *Hierocles of Alexandria*, 196.

505. *Laws* III.35.14.

Since they have true beliefs, they give inklings that something is not right or that we should pay more attention. They also help us to watch for opportunities and for the opportune time for something. The watchers also help us to recognize and avoid temptations that don't suit our living well. In our spiritual practices, these guardians help us to avoid traps, such as ego inflation and distraction by irrelevancies; they bring spiritual discernment, helping us to distinguish the true from the false—or the good from the bad—in spiritual matters. They assist in theurgy (see chapter 11).

The **saviors** or **preservers** (σώζοντες, *sôzontes*) are the daimons especially devoted to keeping us safe and preserving our lives. They also keep our souls safe, preserving them from corrupt influences and errors. By doing so they help ensure that we have a good condition after death and in our next incarnation. The saviors also rescue us if we have got into some difficulty, either mundane or spiritual, and bring us to a better state.

The **rectifiers** (ὀρθοῦντες, *orthountes*) are the daimons who can easily straighten our mind (*nous*) so that we think clearly but also intuit matters correctly. In this way they guide us to health, safety, and happiness. Daimons have true beliefs and guide us to the truth, especially about divine matters. Therefore, the rectifiers also correct our errors, fallacies, and failures to see the truth. The rectifiers also set us upright, directing our mind upward and leading it back to the eternal Ideas.

"Evil" Daimons

Plethon insists that all daimons are good, as evident from the titles of two destroyed chapters: "That the daimons are not bad" and "Rebuttal of slander against daimons."[506] In this he agrees with Pythagoras, Plato, and most Platonists, with the notable exception of Porphyry. As explained in chapter 3 ("Terrestrial Daimons"), as an emanation of Zeus, the entire cosmos, including the daimons, is good. Certainly, however, bad things happen to good people, which calls for an explanation, and ancient people often blamed evil daimons.

In my discussion of Plethon's theory of fate, we saw that harm, pain, and other difficulties might come to the individual if it serves the greater good of the cosmos, as

---

506. Plethon, *Laws*, table of contents.

determined by Zeus and fate. In particular, daimons might cause these undesirable situations as part of their care for the world in service to the gods.

Moreover, as both Plutarch and Hierocles wrote, daimons are responsible for retributive justice: punishing us so that we learn to behave better.[507] They serve as avengers of crimes and impiety, and enforce the laws of divine justice. Proclus agrees that daimons are essentially good, though they may cause apparent harm.[508] They are like teachers, who sometimes punish students in order to improve them, and do not permit them to advance until they are ready. And they are like the guards who stand in front of temples and bar defiled persons from the sacred precinct. By admitting the undefiled person and barring the defiled, they are doing what is right. So also there are daimons who lead our souls up to the gods, but others who bar those who are not ready; they are not evil, but just and good.

Porphyry, in contrast, thought there must be bad daimons (which he called δαίμονες φαῦλοι, *daimones phauloi*: inferior, common, or vile daimons) because harm can't come from what is good.[509] However, we've seen that situations may be good overall in spite of being harmful to us as individuals. Moreover, an apparent harm may be for our correction and hence for our ultimate benefit. Porphyry thought the difference between good and bad daimons is in how much attention they pay to their aethereal bodies.[510] A good daimon's rational mind dominates its bodily *pneuma*, whereas a bad daimon is excessively influenced by its bodily feelings and passions. They in turn inflame our souls with greed, ambition, lust, and desire for pleasure and power.

Similarly, according to Synesius, the bad daimons predominantly affect our body and lower soul, the part responsible for sensual desire, hunger, greed, anger, fear, and other passions, which—while not harmful in themselves, and providing some benefits—can interfere with living well if they are ungoverned.[511] Therefore, we are shielded

---

507. Plutarch, *Obsolescence of Oracles* 13.417B, in Plutarch, *Moralia V*, 388–9; Schibli, *Hierocles of Alexandria*, 132, 160–62.

508. Proclus, *On the Existence of Evils* 17.8–27 in Sorabji, *The Philosophy of the Commentators*, 407–8.

509. Porphyry, *Abstinence* 2.41.

510. Porphyry, *Abstinence* 2.38.

511. Synesius, *On Providence* 1.10.2, in Guthrie, *Pagan Bible*, 75.

from the effects of the bad daimons to the extent that our higher soul—the *nous*—governs our lower soul. So far as we accomplish this, we live a tranquil life akin to the gods'.

There is, I think, some truth in Porphyry's position. The daimons serve the gods in the administration of the cosmos, and to this end each of us is accompanied by personal daimons (οἰκεῖοι δαίμονες, *oikeioi daimones*) who guide our behavior in accord with the interests of their leader god. Their interests and opinions are limited, however, and therefore daimons may be in conflict with one another. Moreover our personal daimons are subject to the same experiences as we are, and so they may incline us to behavior that has helped us cope in the past but might not be helpful overall. Therefore, it is worthwhile to seek higher guidance from our guardian daimons.

The Guardian Daimon

The idea of a guardian daimon, angel, or spirit is found in many spiritual traditions. A principal source in the Platonic tradition is the "Myth of Er" in book 10 of Plato's *Republic*.[512] In this myth, the souls awaiting reincarnation are selected by lot to choose the kind of future life they will live. (This choice absolves the gods, according to Plato, from any blame if the person chooses a blameworthy life!) Once they have made their choice, they are assigned, from among the daimons who preside over the ascent and descent of souls, a guardian (φύλαξ, *phylax*), who will accompany them through the coming incarnation. When eventually they die, according to the myth, this guardian daimon will be a witness to how they lived, which affects their fate in the afterlife and the next incarnation.

While we live, according to Proclus, the guardian daimon guides our life according to the dictates of fate and gods, bringing the gifts of providence and ordering our affairs to help us to live well.[513] The guardians are the divine judges who ensure that we experience the results of our choices, according to Hierocles, thus implementing a fate that is always just and that has been established to order our souls in conformity with divine providence.[514] The guardian strives to prevent us from making mistakes that would lead to later suffering.

---

512. Plato, *Republic* 10.614–21.

513. O'Neill, *Proclus: Alcibiades I* 77–88, 51.

514. Hierocles, *On Providence* codex 251.8 [462a], in Schibli, *Hierocles of Alexandria*, 342.

This daimon organizes all our affairs, improves our mind, moderates our emotions, and maintains our body. If we listen to our guardian, we will be saved; if not, we will suffer misfortune. The second-century Platonist Apuleius of Madauros summarizes this daimon's benefits:

> [The guardian daimon] is our forewarner in uncertainty, our [counselor] in matters of doubt, our defender in danger, and our assistant in need. He is able also by dreams, and by [signs], and perhaps even openly, when necessity demands it, to avert you from evil, to increase your blessings, to aid you when depressed, to support you when falling, to [illuminate] your darkness, to regulate your prosperity, and to [correct] your adversity.[515]

He writes that the guardian resides in "the most profound recesses of the mind" (in the unconscious mind, as we would say now) and therefore knows our inmost thoughts.[516] Platonists sometimes call it the "supreme flower" (ἄκρον ἄνθος, *akron anthos*) of the soul, and it is in fact the image in our individual psyche of the One—that is, of Zeus: "There is a notion known by just the flower of mind."[517] Though our guardian will communicate with us by dreams and signs, we can also contact it directly by means of theurgy (see chapter 11).

Both daimons and humans have aethereal bodies, and our guardians communicate with us by illuminating our aethereal vehicles, which support our reason, imagination, and perception. Therefore, we hear our guardian, not through external perception but through inner awareness (our spiritual ears). Although daimons use our aethereal vehicles and souls as instruments to communicate with us, and we hear them in our minds, they are independent beings.

Plutarch writes that the reason many people have difficulty hearing the utterances of daimons is the restlessness and disharmony in their souls; the daimonic voice is lost in the noise.[518] A philosophical life helps us hear our guardian. Those exceptionally virtu-

---

515. Apuleius, "On the God of Socrates," ch. 16, in Apuleius, *Works*, 367.

516. Apuleius, "God of Socrates," ch. 16, in Apuleius, *Works*, 365.

517. Plethon, *Magical Oracle* 30.

518. Plutarch, *On the Daimonion of Socrates* 589D–E, 592C, in Plutarch, *Moralia VII*, 456–57, 474–75.

ous people with a quiet temperament, who can still their lower souls, can respond to the "sympathetic vibrations" of the daimon's voice and sense it; they are the ones properly called holy and divine persons. Some people are born responsive to the daimons; they are the ones we call prophets. He writes that the gods and daimons choose these people as an expert horse-trainer might select the best horse from a herd for a special training.[519] Such a "horse whisperer" will train and control that horse, not with bit or bridle, but by symbols that the common herd cannot perceive or understand.

I mentioned that guardian daimons come from the two highest classes in Proclus's classification: the divine and noetic daimons. Most of us have guardians from the noetic class, who care for our intuitive mind (*nous*) and are responsible for ascent and descent—in other words, for guiding us into incarnation, through life, and back to the heavens. Proclus writes that the divine daimons are closest to the gods and often look like them.[520] They are assigned to "perfect souls" such as Socrates and Plotinus, souls who, through their self-knowledge, are identified with their own essential nature and have united with their leader god. They have already ascended, and have earned a divine guardian who accompanies them through successive incarnations.

Socrates was famous for his "little daimon" (δαιμόνιον, *daimonion*)—in fact a divine daimon!—that warned him away from things he shouldn't do. Unlike the noetic daimons that most of us have, Socrates's guardian didn't need to urge him to do what was right. As Proclus writes, his soul was overflowing with goodness, and so if he made a mistake, it was by acting when it would be better to wait or refrain entirely.[521] Thus, his guardian's job was to restrain him. Discerning the appropriateness of action is difficult for people, according to Proclus, but not for daimons.[522] With this assistance, Socrates functioned as an **earth-dwelling daimon** (a daimon with a human body), whose duty was to guide others (such as Alcibiades). He was an instrument of divine providence.

---

519. Plutarch, *On the Daimonion of Socrates* 593A–B, in Plutarch, *Moralia VII*, 478–79.

520. O'Neill, *Proclus: Alcibiades I* 71, 47.

521. O'Neill, *Proclus: Alcibiades I* 80–81, 53.

522. O'Neill, *Proclus: Alcibiades I* 82, 54.

XI

Theurgy

Theurgy (θεουργία, *theourgia*) is a Neoplatonic term for ritual practices for interacting directly with gods and daimons. The etymology of the word is "god-work" (θεός + ἔργον, *theos + ergon*), which contrasts it with "theology," or "god-talk" (θεός + λόγος, *theos + logos*). Although theurgical techniques have been practiced since prehistoric times and have their roots in shamanism, the term appears to have been coined in the late second century CE by Julian the Chaldean and his son, Julian the Theurgist. Many Neoplatonic philosophers, and most notably Iamblichus and Proclus, considered theurgy to be essential to their religious practice. This is because theurgy provides means to communicate directly with gods and daimons: to ask them questions and to receive answers, even to negotiate with them. In this way theurgists can receive personal guidance and advice but also more general theological knowledge and insight.

Plethon does not mention theurgy, and this has led most scholars to assume that he was against it, or at least uninterested in it. He is supposed to have been more of a philosopher than a ritualist. In fact, the preface to his *Book of Laws* states that it teaches "ritual reduced to simple practices, without superfluity, and yet sufficient."[523] As you have seen (chapter 5), his rites are quite austere and even academic. This is perhaps why Plethon does not include Proclus, who was notorious in the Middle Ages for his Pagan theurgy, in his Golden Chain. (Plethon's enemies accused him of plagiarizing Proclus,

---

523. Plethon, *Laws*, preface.

but that is incorrect; his philosophy has more in common with Plotinus and others in the Golden Chain.) On the other hand, Iamblichus is in the Golden Chain, in spite of his having written the best-known surviving book on theurgy (*On the Mysteries*).

It is interesting, however, that some of Plethon's explanations of the Magical Oracles betray an interest in theurgy and apparent approval of it.[524] Therefore, another possibility is that Plethon practiced some form of theurgy but didn't write about it. Theurgy was also called "the priestly art" (ἡ ἱερατικὴ τέχνη, *hê hieratikê technê*) and might be considered specialized knowledge for the priests of his religion. He also approved of Plato's statement that some knowledge should be communicated only orally.[525] Certainly in Plethon's time the punishments for performing Pagan rituals were much harsher than for teaching Pagan philosophy, for in the latter case one could claim to be teaching the history of philosophy without believing it. In any case, regardless of Plethon's attitude about theurgy or his practice of it, theurgy is a useful tool for modern Pagans and can help us to fill in the gaps in Plethon's mutilated book. That is why I am teaching the basic technique in this chapter.

Although theurgical ritual can be elaborate, the basic operation can be quite simple and effective. The technique is based on the fact that the gods—as Platonic Ideas—have emanations or images at all lower levels of reality, down into the material world. Things at lower levels, therefore, have imprints or signatures of the various divine energies that have produced them. By making use of material objects, substances, words, sounds, images, and so forth, we can tune our soul like a radio to a particular divine energy and come into communion with it. Material things used in this way are called symbols (σύμβολα, *symbola*) and signs (συνθήματα, *synthêmata*). You can see how theurgical rituals could become quite complicated, but it is best to start simple. The simplest rituals are often the most effective. As the first Magical Oracle instructs, "join act with sacred speech."[526]

One final important point before we get to the technique: We must remember that the supercelestial gods are outside of time and space. Therefore, while we can be

---

524. His *Commentary* (in appendix C) on oracles 6, 7, 9, 11, 18, 19, 22, and 24–30 may be mentioned.

525. Plato, *Phaedrus* 276d; Plethon, *Contra Scholarii pro Aristotele obiectiones* 983 D.

526. Plethon, *Magical Oracles* 1.

inspired by their eternal Ideas, we cannot expect them to "hear" us; for that would be an event in time, and they would be different after hearing us. The gods, however, emanate daimons, who do exist in space and time, to act as their ministers and assistants (see chapter 10), and, as Plutarch has explained, we often invoke these daimons by the names of the gods they serve.[527] Since daimons exist in space and time with us, they can hear us and interact with us more directly. Therefore, in theurgy we are most commonly interacting with daimons rather than supercelestial or even celestial deities. This is in fact the daimons' job in the cosmos.

TECHNIQUE

Preparation

Here is the basic theurgical technique for a meeting (σύστασις, *systasis*) with a god or daimon. It has the general structure of a sacrifice, so review the material on prayer, purification, and sacrifice in chapter 10. Do your theurgy in a place where you will not be disturbed. Evening or nighttime is often best, but operations can also be scheduled astrologically. Theurgy is best done alone so that you will not be disturbed by others' reactions. Have localized lighting, such as a candle or oil lamp, so your attention remains focused. You may find it helpful to have an image (a statue or picture) of the god you intend to invoke. To record your operation, have a notebook handy. (You can use a computer if you can type quickly and won't be distracted by stuff popping up!) You might find that burning a little incense—frankincense is a good choice—helps put you in a contemplative frame of mind. You might also find it helpful to don some special garb to help shift your mind out of the mundane realm and toward the gods. It doesn't have to be anything elaborate or traditional; what matters is that it signals your mind that it is engaged in divine works (θεῖα ἔργα, *theia erga*).

When everything is ready, you can begin the operation. You can use the purification procedures in chapter 10 to prepare sacred space and begin the ritual, or simply declare your intention to devote your attention to the gods for the duration of the ritual. Take a

---

527. Plutarch, *The Obsolescence of Oracles* 21.421E, in Plutarch, *Moralia V*, 412–13.

few deep breaths, ground and center yourself, and clear your mind of everything except the object of your ritual.

Invocation

The next step is to call on the deity or its attendant daimons. The simplest approach is to call them by name: for example, "I call on thee, Aphrodite, goddess of perishable matter, who grants its unending continuation, to come to me and answer my questions, to grant me your aid and inspiration." Of course, a timeless, spaceless goddess cannot literally hear you or come to you; she is present already; it is a metaphor for attuning your soul to her divine energy. By doing this, you are dialing in her daimons as well.

You can make the connection better by using the attributes of the deity, especially those mentioned in Plethon's hymns and invocations. For example, Athena might be invoked as "you who rule and govern form," "source of every motion caused by another," "dispeller of the superfluous," "thou who rouseth our hearts to duty with good sense" (cf. Hymn 10). You can also use traditional images and attributes of the gods, but make sure they are consistent with the deity you intend to invoke (for example, Athena's shield and spear are good). Hold the image in your mind while you repeat the invocation.

Sometimes you don't know the name of the deity to invoke. Perhaps you are seeking aid for a specific problem or requesting inspiration for a project. In this case, you should focus on the issue at hand while calling on the gods in general for aid (see Plethon's "Prayer to the Gods of Learning" in chapter 2 and *Laws* I.4 for an example). See who shows up. They might not be whom you expected, but they will almost surely have something important to discuss.

Another possibility is that some figure, such as guide or teacher (and probably a daimon), has appeared in a significant dream or fantasy, and you want to communicate with them. You can imagine them as they appeared in your dream while you request them to appear.

In all these cases you are using some mediating being (in theurgy called an *iynx*, ἴυγξ, sometimes written "jinx"!) to connect you to a deity relevant to the matter at hand.[528] A Magical Oracle alludes to this: "The Iynges, thought by Father, also think themselves,

---

528. Majercik, *Chaldean Oracles*, 9–10.

/ by his unutterable counsels moved to understand."[529] Plethon explains that the *iynges* (ἴυγγες, plural of *iynx*) are Ideas conceived by the Father (Zeus), but are also themselves minds that conceive ideas. The immutable relations among the eternal Ideas move the *iynges* to stimulate corresponding ideas in our souls, thus binding us to the gods.

You may find it helpful to visualize some special entrance or pathway to the divine realm—for example, a temple, cave, or grove. The pathway, which may be just for you, may appear spontaneously in your imagination or be given to you by a god. In the meantime you can design your own and see how well it works.

Meeting

Then you wait. Usually some figure will appear in your imagination—an image or voice—but not necessarily whom you expected. Often the atmosphere around you will seem to be charged or animated in some way, and that is a good indicator that a deity has arrived.

You can ask them who they are, and it is polite to ask them how they would like to be addressed, for even if you have called them by name, they might prefer a different form of address. You can ask them how they prefer to be invoked; they might give you a special phrase (a spell), a gesture, a visualization, or ritual to invoke them more directly, and you should record it in your notebook.

You should always be polite, as befits addressing a deity (even if "merely" a daimon), but your human soul is also divine, and so you should not abandon your moral authority as a human being, a descendant like them from Zeus. Maintaining your moral autonomy is critical as you negotiate with the deity, for they might have demands of you for their own purposes (under the will of Zeus) or in return for your requests, but you are not obliged to obey them if they are morally unacceptable. They might have harsh or unpleasant things to say to you. And so the negotiation continues, with the goal of satisfying the desires and needs of both of you.

Like all good negotiations, the goal should be a win-win outcome. You should neither think you are in absolute control (like some foolish medieval sorcerer thinking he could command the demons), nor should you blindly cave in to their demands. Although, as emanations of Zeus, the Good Itself, they are charged with the providence

---

529. Plethon, *Commentary* 33.

and governance of the universe, there are—especially for daimons—many ways this can be accomplished, and so we should strive to ensure the path conforms with contemporary ethics and your own morality.

Your meeting with the deity might not be all talk, as suggested so far. They might lead you on quests, show you mysteries, transform you, heal you, or engage in many other activities in your imagination. (Remember, your imagination is the highest part of your soul next to your *nous*, and it is your medium of communication with the divine.) In all this you should remain yourself internally (with your own knowledge, beliefs, values, and feelings) even if, in this imaginal realm, you are transformed externally. The key to making all this work is to accept seriously its complete reality throughout the theurgical operation. Record in your notes the discussions and everything else that occurs as it happens; you can add additional detail later.

Agreement

Often your negotiations and other interactions with the deities will result in some sort of agreement: mutual obligations on the part of you and the deity. Therefore, it is important to take these negotiations seriously. Although you might be able to negotiate a change in the terms of the agreement, you should expect to have to fulfill your obligations. Think twice before you agree to anything!

Dismissal

When you reach the end of your operation, you may want to make arrangements for future meetings, if you have not done so already. Thank the deity for meeting with you and ask them to return to their realms so that you can return to ordinary life. If you have taken some pathway into the divine realm, then retrace your steps, unless the deity has given you different exit instructions.

It is wise to reground yourself in ordinary reality. Extinguish candles, lamps, incense, and so on. Remove any special garb. Stamp your feet. Clap your hands. Drink some water and eat some food. If you don't feel like you are back to mundane reality, insist out loud that the deity depart so that you can return to your mundane activities. If you know a formal banishing ritual, you can use it; otherwise, do a purification to separate yourself from the divinity.

Follow-Up

After your theurgical operation, you should recopy your notes into your journal so that they are easier to read. Correct your spelling and other obvious errors and insert descriptions or explanations of what took place, but try to keep to a true and accurate account of the operation. When you review and contemplate your record at a future date, you can add further interpretation and discussion of the results of the operation. You may want to transcribe your theurgical experiences into a nice journal, as befits your interactions with divinity.

In addition to recording your operation in your journal, it is often valuable to take some concrete action to solemnify your agreement with the deity. This could be a simple offering or ritual action that symbolizes your agreement. In fact, you might have vowed to take this action as part of your agreement. (See chapter 10 on sacrifice.)

Personal Gnosis

You will receive many important insights and answers from your theurgical operations, and you may feel compelled to share these valuable truths with the world, to be the prophet of a new revelation. Please don't. In psychology this is called an "ego inflation": getting puffed up with a feeling of your own importance.

In theurgy it is important never to forget that all our interactions with deity are via our individual souls, in particular our imaginations, which may distort or contaminate the message. Moreover, many of our interactions are with personal daimons, and what they have to say may apply only to you as an individual at a particular point in your life. Do not assume it is the same for everyone. Of course, you can ask the deity if it is, and they will give the answer appropriate for you.

Plethon tells us that daimons have true opinions, but they do not know the scientific or logical reasons for those true opinions. I will add that daimons may be very specialized, dealing only with very specific matters or individual people, and so their opinions, while true, might not be generally applicable. Moreover, due to their narrow focus, they might not even realize that their opinions are not generally true. So you must always use your own judgment and not assume you are learning universal truths.

The insights received in theurgy are sometimes called "unverified personal gnosis," that is, personal revelations that are not known to be true for others. Sometimes they can become "verified personal gnosis" if they are confirmed in external events. Similarly, if many people independently receive the same revelations, they can become a public gnosis of more than personal significance. Therefore, obtaining divine revelations of general applicability can require collaborative work of multiple theurgists. It can come from an individual who has a track record of verified personal gnosis, but it is difficult to exclude the possibility of personal contamination in any particular case.

To sum up, we don't know if Plethon used theurgy in his private practice or in formulating his theology, and we don't know if he taught it. Nevertheless, it can be a valuable tool in your own spiritual practice if you understand what it can do and what it cannot.

Conclusions

—————◦∞◦—————

Now you know the Neopagan religion of Renaissance philosopher George Gemistos Plethon, a religion based in ancient Greek Pagan religious practice and in the most mature Neoplatonic Pagan theology and philosophy, but descending from ancient wisdom traditions. You understand how a philosophical analysis of reality reveals several orders of gods, whom Plethon has named after the gods of traditional Greek Paganism. Highest is the One-Itself, or Zeus, the ineffable first principle that emanates all of existence. Next in order of existence are the twenty-two supercelestial gods, divided into the Olympians, who are responsible for imperishable beings, and the Titans, responsible for perishable beings. Below them are the celestial gods, visible manifestations of the cocreators of material existence. Lowest in the orders of divinity are the daimons, who are the mediators between humans and other divinities.

You have also learned how to worship the gods using rituals rooted in ancient Pagan practice but adapted to Neoplatonic theology and the modern world. Plethon has provided us with invocations, prayers, and hymns that connect us with the gods according to Neoplatonic principles. He has provided us a calendar to organize our rituals and holy days in a sacred year that follows the natural cycles of the sun and moon. All this is sufficient to organize the regular practice of a Neopagan religious community but is also easily adaptable for a solitary practitioner. This is because Plethon's religious practices, though inspired by ancient practice, are grounded in Neoplatonic philosophy and theology, not in a fundamentalist adherence to this or that ancient practice.

Although a religious bigot destroyed much of Plethon's *Book of Laws*, important missing parts of it can be reconstructed from his other writings and from the writings of the sages, lawgivers, and philosophers in the Golden Chain leading down to him. Therefore, you now understand how prayer, purification, and sacrifice operate; what are the powers of the seven planets; and what is the nature of daimons. You also know basic theurgical operations—taught by Neoplatonists and perhaps by Plethon—to communicate with gods and daimons.

Although Plethon lived six hundred years ago, he has given us the best image of what Hellenic Paganism might look like if it had survived the persecution and suppression by Christian emperors, laws, and religious organizations. As such I hope you will find it to be a practical basis for your own religious practice, as I have. It is a basis only, however, and Neopaganism is a living religion, and so it should continue to evolve and adapt like any living thing.

APPENDIX A

Plethon's Summary of the Doctrines of Zoroaster and Plato

Translated by John Opsopaus

[1]   Here are the most necessary principles to know for whoever wants to think wisely.

[2]   (1)[530] First, concerning the gods, we must believe that they really exist. One of them is Zeus, the king, the greatest of all and the best possible. He presides over the Whole; his divinity is of an order quite exceptional; he himself is in all respects and altogether uncreated; at the same time he is the father and the first demiurge of all beings. His oldest son, motherless and the second god, is Poseidon. He has received from his father the second place in the government of all things, and in addition the right to produce and create the heavens, but with the help and the ministry of other gods, some of whom are his siblings, these all being motherless and supercelestial: the Olympians and the Tartareans. Others are engendered by himself with the help of Hera, the goddess who produces matter; they are the gods who live within the heavens, namely, the celestial race of

---

530. I have numbered the twelve principles to make them clear.

stars and the earthly race of daimons, who are next to us in nature. Poseidon has entrusted Helios, his eldest child, with the government of heaven and the generation of mortal beings therein, and this of course with Kronos, brother and head of the Tartarean Titans. A difference between the Olympian gods and the Tartareans is that the Olympians produce and govern all immortal things in the heavens and the Tartareans preside over mortal things here. Thus, Kronos is leader of the Tartareans or Titans and presides over every form of mortal. Hera, who among the Olympians is placed second after Poseidon, furnishes for his works the primordial, indestructible matter over which she herself presides. As for Poseidon, he governs all kinds of immortals and mortals; he is the leader presiding over everything, and indeed he is himself coordinator of all things. For Zeus alone, by his exceptional divinity, dominates the All exceptionally.

[3]   For the first principle, this is the most exact summary of what to believe. (2) Moreover, these gods look after us, some acting immediately by themselves, the others through the inferior [gods], but always according to the decrees of Zeus, who rules everything. (3) They are not the cause of any evil, neither for us nor for any beings; on the contrary they are essentially the causes of all good. (4) In addition, it is according to the law of an immutable fate, inflexible, emanated from Zeus, that they perform all their acts in the best possible way. These are [the principles] concerning the gods.

[4]   Concerning the All: (5) First, the All, including the gods of the second and third orders, was created by Zeus, is everlasting, and has had no beginning in time and will have no end. (6) It is assembled into one from all the many things. (7) It was created in the most perfect way by the most perfect worker of all, who left nothing to add. (8) In addition, it is always preserved immutable in its established form. These are [the principles] concerning the All.

[5]   Concerning ourselves: (9) First, our soul, being akin to the gods, remains immortal and everlasting in the heavens for all time. (10) Always attached to a mortal body, sometimes to one, sometimes to another, it is sent by the gods, for the sake of the harmony of the All, so that the union of mortal and immortal in human nature contributes to the unity of the All. (11) Because of this kinship with the gods, we must consider the good to be the end that suits our life. (12) Finally, the gods, by fixing the laws of our kind, placed our happiness in the immortal part of our being, which is also the most important [part].

[6]   Here together are the twelve principles, on the gods, on the All, and on our nature, that must be known and accepted if one wants to have exceptional understanding and really to be wise.

Appendix B

Plethon's Book of Laws

Translated by John Opsopaus[531]

[**Preface**]   This book contains:

Theology after Zoroaster and Plato; the traditional names of the gods of our Hellenic ancestors have been preserved for the gods recognized by philosophy, but by restoring each of these names from the less philosophical meaning that each has taken in the fictions of poets to the best sense of philosophy;

Ethics according to the same sages, and in addition according to the Stoics;

Politics on the model of that of Lacedaemon [Sparta], by removing on the one hand the excessive rigors that the greater number would not support, and by adding on the other, especially for the use of governors, the philosophy, which establishes the principal merit of the Platonic institutions;

Ritual reduced to simple practices, without superfluity, and yet sufficient;

Natural Science largely according to Aristotle.

This work also touches the principles of logic, Hellenic antiquities, and some points of health.

---

531. Because there is as yet no complete English translation of Plethon's *Book of Laws*, I have prepared this working translation. It is no doubt imperfect in many ways, but I have checked it against the partial English translations and paraphrases in Hladký, *Philosophy of Gemistos Plethon*; Woodhouse, *George Gemistos Plethon*; and Anastos, "Plethon's Calendar and Liturgy"; and against the French translation by A. Pellissier in Alexandre, *Pléthon: Traité des Lois*.

TABLE OF CONTENTS

Book I

---

532. Chapters surviving in whole or in part are marked with an asterisk.

Book II

Book III

6. The form of government

7. Fortitude

8. Things that are and those that are not in our power, according to the theory of fortitude

9. Various kinds of fortitude

10. Self-control

11. Measure and symmetry*

12. Various species of self-control

13. Strength, according to the theory of the various species of self-control

14. Prohibition of intercourse between parents and their children*

15. The generation of gods, according to the principle of the prohibition of intercourse between parents and their children*

16. The union of one man with several women

17. The use of public women

18. The eating of meat

19. The unity of the property in the same household

20. Not squandering the property of someone who has died

21. The mode of existence

22. Zeus: that there exists in him no division, even nominal

23. The All, a plurality that is one

24. The difference of goods

25. Justice

26. Various kinds of justice

27. Comparison of the various species of virtue

BOOK I

Chapter 1: The diversity of opinions among people on the most important matters

[1]   This book deals with laws, institutions, beliefs, and practices that can assure people, in private life and in public life, the best, the most beautiful, and the happiest possible fate. Indeed, such is human nature, that people tend before and above all to happiness; it is at once the unique and common end of humanity, and the peculiar aim of each one's life; it is in order to achieve this that we pursue and practice all other things. All are carried away toward this common goal, but not all go the same way; that is where they separate. Some think to find happiness principally in pleasure; they do everything in view of pleasure alone; they want, as much as possible, to taste it all, in all its forms, of whatever nature, whatever source it comes from. Others place happiness in the possession of riches; the only job of all their life is to get richer and richer. Others run after glory; they have no other ambition than to have the praise and admiration of the crowd. Others, finally, neglect all the rest to consecrate their whole life to goodness and virtue, persuaded that virtue alone can give true happiness.

[2]   Virtue itself does not have the same characteristics for all; we see that good and evil change according to opinions and usages. Thus, some

believe that study and knowledge are of no use to virtue; there are some who scrupulously flee all exercise of mind, some sophist impostors having persuaded them that knowledge is only evil and corruption. Others, on the contrary, regard knowledge as the principle of all virtue; they make every effort to acquire as much knowledge and wisdom as possible. Some devote all their effort to multiplying sacrifices and religious ceremonies, and some condemn all these practices; others admit one and reject others, but with so little agreement among them that the same practices appear to some religious and to the other sacrilegious. Some place in celibacy and in the complete abstinence from sensual pleasures the noblest and the most divine life; for others, it is nobler and more divine to marry and have children. Some make a choice among the foods that people are accustomed to eat; they decide that some are forbidden and that it is a crime to eat them, while others are allowed. Others allow complete liberty in this respect; there is no food whose use seems to them to be prohibited as impious; it is in moderation alone that they place the good. Some consent to languish in a repulsive filthiness; others find some merit in cleanliness and seek it. Some extol poverty and indigence; others admit wealth to a certain extent. Some display extreme shamelessness; others respect modesty and the general laws of propriety; they prefer decency to indecency in all things. There are some who, in principle, establish the pursuit of virtue, not for itself, but in view of some reward that the gods would bestow upon them; according to them, virtue alone does not suffice for happiness. Some think they ought to seek virtue for itself, and not in the hope of a reward. Others, finally, pursue virtue for itself and for the rewards which the gods bestow on those who practice it.

[3]   When we see that on these points and still others people behave according to principles so contradictory, so confused, it is clear that if we want to choose for sure the best rule of conduct and not to deviate from the common goal that all pursue, namely happiness, we must not take at random the first road encountered, but first consider carefully what is the best kind of life of all, where true happiness is found, then fix our choice. But before

that, it will be necessary to examine what human beings are, what is their nature, and what are their faculties. Without this preliminary study, we could not know what it is better to do, to know what job we should do with our faculties. For it is so with every instrument and every object, that, if we know neither its nature nor its properties, we cannot make proper use of it. Now it is impossible to know what a human being really is if we have not begun to study thoroughly the nature of things, if we have not recognized what is the first principle, what is the second, third, and last order, and what is the function proper to each of these beings. It is after having examined them all that one can legitimately study the human being in the midst of them, to find out to which beings it is similar and in which respects, from which ones it differs and to what degree, and what are the elements of which it was formed; finally, given its nature, what is its power. It is after having sufficiently clarified these questions that we can draw the rules for human life; then we will know what is the best and most useful conduct, and that easily and without difficulty.

[4] But the question of the nature of other beings is not subject to less disagreement. Some think that there are absolutely no gods; others believe that the gods exist, but that they do not watch over human affairs; others, finally, that they watch over human affairs and all things. But among these, some think that gods are the authors of evil as well as good, others that they produce only good and never evil. Some admit that they can let themselves be swayed by the prayers of people and divert things that in their wisdom they thought they should do; the others that the gods are absolutely inflexible, and that, always faithful in their thought in conformity with the decisions of fate, they lead everything to the greatest perfection possible. Some believe that there is only one god, and nothing else seems to them worthy of being respected and honored by people; others recognize several gods resembling one another and the same in divinity; according to yet others, there is a god par excellence, a supreme god, the first principle of all things, and other gods placed on a second and third rank.

[5]   Some think that, excepting the one creator god, everything has been created in time as by a cause and that everything must one day perish and disappear; others, that the world was created but that it will endure forever; others, finally, that one part of the world is formed and born while another dissolves and perishes, in never-ending succession. Some argue that the universe is the effect of a cause, but that it was not created in time, and therefore it is eternal and cannot undergo any change from the god who produced it and watches over it, because this god has an immutable nature and never rested, but worked unceasingly, and according to unchanging principles, to the production of the All.

[6]   Disagreement is not less about human nature. Many think that it is like that of all other mortal beings and animals, that it is neither nobler nor more divine; others allow people to raise their hopes to the perfect purity of the divine essence. Some assign to human nature an intermediate place that it must always occupy; they regard it as a mixture of divine and eternal nature with mortal nature.

[7]   In the midst of the uncertainty and confusion that obscures these problems, if we do not carefully examine every opinion and cannot distinguish once and for all which side has the best reasons, in order to find the truth and to secure its possession, then we will not know how to regulate our life, we will hesitate on the manner of direction we will embrace, and we will follow at random any party that will present itself. In short, one will become, without suspecting it, of all people perhaps the most miserable, instead of being happy as one hoped for.

Chapter 2: The best guides in the search for truth

[1]   What is the manner of proceeding in the examination of these opinions? What guides should be followed in this study? For these subjects have been treated by a throng of poets, sophists, lawgivers, and philosophers. But poets and sophists can be regarded rightly as bad guides in such matters. Poets are very inclined to flattery; they have no other purpose than

to please people and to cheapen the truth and the good. And sophists turn in many matters to sleight of hand and seek fame at every turn, and some even raise their claims above human nature. As for the truth, they have no concern; they even seek a thousand expedients to disguise it. Both of them diminish the gods to the human, raise the human to the divine, upset all things, and thus do the greatest harm to those who listen to them. Such are the poets and sophists for the most part. But lawgivers and philosophers can do no better than to express some sensible opinion on the subjects that occupy us. In fact, since lawgivers always propose the common good, it is unlikely they will deviate from it; and the philosophers, believing that truth is the principal element of happiness and pursuing it in preference to all treasures, will probably find it better than anyone else. However, as most men are by their nature unable to fully attain knowledge and possession of the greatest things, there are two things to fear: on one hand, that even among philosophers and lawgivers there are some who have been too weak to discover the good and the true, and, on the other hand, that we are not mistaken in taking as wise lawgivers or philosophers some sophists or some poets who are adept at seizing the ignorant mind of the vulgar.

[2]   As for us, here are the guides we choose among the lawgivers and the wise. It is first the oldest whose name has come down to us, Zoroaster, who revealed, with the greatest brilliance, to the Medes, the Persians, and to most of the ancient peoples of Asia, the truth about divine things and most other great questions. After him come, among others, Eumolpus, who established among the Athenians the Eleusinian mysteries to teach the doctrine of the immortality of the soul, Minos the lawgiver of the Cretans, and Lycurgus of the Spartans. Let us add Iphitus and Numa, the first of whom, together with Lycurgus, founded the Olympic Games in honor of Zeus, the greatest of the gods, and the second gave the Romans a great number of laws, many of them relevant to the gods, and especially to religious ceremonies. Among the lawgivers, these are the ones we prefer.

[3]   Among the other sages we choose, from the barbarians, the Brahmans of India and the Magi of Media. From the Greeks, among others, especially the Kouretes, whom tradition lists among the most ancient lawgivers; it is they who reasserted the doctrine about the existence of the gods of the second and third orders, the immortality of the creations and children of Zeus, and of the entire Whole, doctrines that had been destroyed in Greece by the Giants, those godless beings who fought against the gods. By the force of invincible reasoning, and by the war which they made against the Giants, the Kouretes triumphed over their adversaries who claimed that everything is mortal, excepting only the creator, the ancient principle of all things. After them we will quote the priests of Zeus at Dodona and the interpreters of his oracles, and several other inspired ones, especially the diviner Polyidus, whom Minos himself cultivated for his wisdom, Teiresias, who gave the Greeks a great deal of high knowledge and who developed with the greatest brilliancy the theory of the ascent of the soul and its endless return to the earth, and Cheiron, tutor to a great many heroes of his time, to whom we owe much knowledge and important discoveries.

[4]   Let us add the seven sages who flourished with brilliance at the time when Anaxandridas and Ariston reigned in Lacedaemon: Chilon of Sparta, Solon of Athens, Bias of Priene, Thales of Miletus, Cleoboulus of Lindos, Pittacus of Mitylene, and Myson of Chenai.

[5]   To all these masters we must add Pythagoras, Plato, and all the distinguished philosophers who arose in their school, and of whom the most illustrious are Parmenides, Timaeus, Plutarch, Plotinus, Porphyry, and Iamblichus.

[6]   Since all these agreed on most of the questions, especially the most important, they seem to have expressed the best opinions, according to the more sensible people who succeeded them. We will therefore follow them, without ourselves seeking to innovate on such great subjects and without receiving any of the modern innovations of some sophists. There

is this great difference between the sage and the sophist, in that the sages express opinions always in harmony with the older beliefs, so that, even by their antiquity, the true doctrines outweigh the erroneous propositions that have been or still are advanced, while the sophists always aim at the new, the only object of their ambition. It is, indeed, the best way to achieve this vain glory for which they are excited. For us, we will adopt the doctrines and the words of the most sensible people of antiquity. Then, with the aid of reasoning, the most powerful and the most divine of our means of knowing, we will compare as exactly as possible all the systems to judge what is the best opinion in all things.

[7]   For the great vice of poets and sophists is never to give any valid reason for the opinions they put forward; it is to a prophetic inspiration from the gods, who no doubt came to visit them, that they both pretend to owe this knowledge. Thus, the poets, adorning their words with the charms of expression and rhythm, seduce those who listen to them and mislead souls who do not know how to distinguish the pleasure of style and harmony from truth or falsity of ideas. For the rest, poets care little about persuading their listeners, it is enough to amuse them, whether they persuade them or not; but there are people on whom they act more than they seek. For the sophists, some employ false reasoning instead of right and true arguments, and thus deceive ignorant minds. Others, the most charlatan of all, pretend to perform certain miracles and seem to accomplish great things by a divine power, but in reality, means, and results, all is imposture. Yet they affect minds that are weak and uncritical, and then their lies, enlarged by later speeches and writings, mislead many others. Last, these doctrines are accustomed to be heard repeatedly from infancy, an authority that does the greatest harm to society by accrediting a thousand absurd principles, which have the gravest consequences for the conduct of human life.

[8]   On the contrary, well-reasoned arguments clearly teach the truth about the topics under examination and, offering themselves to the discussion

of careful criticism, they lead the latter as well as the former to personal knowledge, not borrowed, against those who, deceived by the teachings of sophists, blindly borrow their persuasion from those who let themselves be persuaded before them.

Chapter 3: The opposite doctrines of Protagoras and Pyrrho

[1]   These two doctrines, quite opposite to each other, but equally vain and pernicious, must also be rejected. One [Protagoras] says that everything is true, that the human is the measure of all things, and that what anyone imagines exists for that very reason. The other [Pyrrho] argues that nothing is true, that people are incapable of being judges of anything, and that we must not even believe the testimony of things. Their two propositions are easy to overturn and consequently to refute. If one says that everything is true, one will be forced to grant the truth of the opposite opinion, which is that of most people, namely that not all things are true. If we say that nothing is true, we agree that this affirmation itself is not true. Moreover, most people recognize degrees in knowledge and ignorance; they will seek lessons from scholars and accuse the ignorant of not possessing well enough what they claim to know. Would it be so if people believed that truth is everywhere or nowhere?

[2]   Neither can it be said that two contradictory propositions are both true or both false at the same time; it is an opinion that nobody will entertain. Thus, everyone will say that this proposition: "the universe is eternal," has for a contradictory this one: "the universe is not eternal," and that it cannot be that these two propositions are both true or both false. In all similar cases, only one of the propositions is true and the other is false. Similarly, for the future, no one will argue that all facts will necessarily justify their predictions or that all will come to deny them, but everyone knows in advance that some facts will contradict them, while others will agree with them, so that some forecast will have been true and other false.

[3]   Thus, these two doctrines are equally convicted of falsity and absurdity. Nor should we take into account this other opinion, that, if we were able to attain something in the knowledge of truth, it would not be for us, as mortals, to pursue our research into divine matters because of the inferiority of our intelligence and because the gods do not want their nature to be the object of an indiscreet curiosity. Indeed, the gods would not have given us in vain the desire to study their nature if they had wanted to forbid us this study and to refuse us the faculty to acquire some clear notions of them.

[4]   Moreover, it would be equally absurd to believe that we must either have no idea of these things and live like the brutes, or accept at random and without examination all the imaginations that arise, for we would not achieve the happiness we pursue. In fact, even if, by a divine chance, someone, without the help of reason, encountered the truth on these matters, having thus acquired it, they would never possess it surely, and they could not pursue it to enjoy either perfect happiness nor even a little happiness, having neither the reason nor the knowledge necessary to shed light on the most important questions, and ignorant even whether they are happy or not. Because it is not enough to imagine being happy, which can happen even to madmen, it is still necessary to know in what way and how one is happy, what is good for a person and what is bad, and why.

[5]   Moreover, divine things do not contain any vice that could compel the gods to hide themselves, and the gods are incapable of a feeling of jealousy that would prevent them from joining with their other benefits that of being known. And although the divine nature is far above human nature, we cannot say that humans are condemned not to know it, because they also have reason and faculties that are not at all foreign to the divine nature. Finally, if the gods have disposed us to seek their nature, it is precisely for us to seek it, to know it, at least in part, and to derive from it the greatest advantages. In fact, taking for principles the ideas and revelations concerning the divine nature given by the gods to all people in common,

or at least the ideas of the greatest number and the most virtuous, establishing them securely, and then, by rigorous reasoning, drawing from these principles the consequences to which the wise will open the way for us, with the help of the gods, we cannot fail to have the best beliefs concerning everything. It is therefore to the guardian gods of reason that we must, before going further, address our prayers so that they may encourage this work by their inspiration.

Chapter 4: Prayer to the gods of learning

[1]   Come to us, O gods of learning, whoever you may be, in whatever number you may be, you who preside over understanding and the truth, who distribute them to whomever you please, according to the decrees of the almighty father of all things, King Zeus. Without you, we would be unable to accomplish such a great work. Come guide our reasoning, and grant this work to obtain the best possible success and to be like a treasure always open to those people who want to lead the most beautiful and best conduct in public or private life.

Chapter 5: General principles on the gods

[2]   Here are the beliefs that can best be said to have been transmitted to us by a succession of divine men. The gods are all the beings of a higher and happier nature than human nature. They provide for us from their overflowing happiness; no evil can come from them, but they are the authors of all good; by an irreversible and immutable fate, they attribute to each the best possible dispensation. There are many gods, but with different degrees of divinity. One of them, the greatest of all, is the supreme god, King Zeus, who indeed infinitely surpasses them all by his majesty and the excellence of his nature; he has existed from all eternity. He is not born of any other, he is Self-Father, and, as the only one of all beings that has no other father than himself, he is the father and the eldest demiurge

of all things; he is supremely essential essence, absolutely one, supremely identical to himself; he is the Good.

[3] The other gods are divided according to divine nature into the second and third orders, the first of which are the children of Zeus, his creations, and the second are the children of his children, the creations of his creations. These are the instruments by which King Zeus governs all things and especially human affairs; each of them is set over a greater or lesser part of this universe, but all are governed by great Poseidon, the eldest and most powerful of all Zeus's children, the most beautiful of his creations and the most perfect.

[4] The gods born immediately from Zeus himself are the supercelestial gods; they have a divinity of the second order, free from all connections to bodies and matter; they are essentially pure Forms, immutable intellects, always and in all things acting by the sole force of their own thought. Each of them derives from Zeus himself an essence, an indivisible from the indivisible, but which contains in itself, in a manner at the same time collective and individual, everything under itself of which it is the cause. As to their attributes, all these gods, except Poseidon alone, the oldest of them, receive them from each other, their king and father having established among his children a community and a reciprocity of benefits, the most beautiful gift that he granted them after participation in his essence. But Poseidon, ruled by Zeus alone, governs all the others. Among the other gods, those are higher who have the fewest superiors and who do more and greater things in the universe; lower are those who do lesser things and who recognize more superiors.

[5] Other divisions are still to be found in this class of gods. According to the most important, it is divided into two great families: first, that of the legitimate[533] children of Zeus, whom their father endowed with the faculty of also producing immortal beings. The other gods, who form the

---

533. γνήσιος = belonging to the race, born in wedlock, legitimate, lawful, genuine, qualified. In this context, belonging to the superior family of Olympian gods.

illegitimate[534] family of the Titans, produce only mortal and perishable beings; they are like the first gods in the community of origin, but they are very inferior to them in power and grandeur.

[6]   All these gods are in all respects out of time, because they always remain and are absolutely immutable. Indeed, time is the measure of change, and they have eternity as the measure of their life. For them there is neither past nor future, neither before nor after; for them everything is eternally present. Neither can they be circumscribed by location in space, for it is proper for bodies to be so circumscribed in a place, but they are pure essences without bodies. However, they have their proper place, in the sense that they are classified in a definite order, so that each of them holds the middle between the one who precedes and the one who follows.

[7]   Therefore, the whole supercelestial realm is shared among these gods, but the main division of this upper world is a division into two parts which correspond to the two families of gods, and are the particular seat of each of them: the legitimate children of Zeus inhabit Olympus, the highest and most pure region of the heavens; the illegitimate race occupies Tartarus, a region inferior to the other.

[8]   These two distinct families, that of Olympus and that of Tartarus, form a great and holy group, an intelligible and supercelestial world ordered by King Zeus, an eternal world, rich in all wealth, containing all these second-order gods sufficient and lacking nothing to form a complete set. These gods, separated from each other in the most exact manner, so that each of them is in his attributions the most perfect and self-sufficient as possible, are at the same time united by the community of goods and the bonds of a reciprocal affection. For, while they have an individual character, yet they form a whole, as is appropriate for beings who proceed from the same principle and tend to the same end, namely, their father, their creator, the great Zeus, absolutely one and all-powerful. To him all things are

---

534. νόθος = bastard, illegitimate, baseborn, spurious, not genuine. In this context, not of the superior family of Olympian gods.

subject and devoted, without struggle, without opposition, without ill-will; but these gods especially accept his domination with good-will. They are united by customary and friendly relations and think the same. On the one hand, they direct the gods that are less powerful and younger than themselves; on the other, they let themselves be guided by the older ones, for in this superior world there reigns in all things a perfect harmony and order. This is the constant state in which all these gods hold each other.

[9]   Poseidon and his legitimate siblings, the Olympians, have children who form gods of a third order; these gods inhabit the heavens, they are rational and immortal beings, they have unerring souls and bodies that escape old age and corruption, and their nature cannot admit any harm. Their creators have also divided them into two classes. One is the legitimate and celestial family of the stars, whose souls are of the purest kind and attain everything by their understanding, and whose bodies are the most beautiful and active; they are gods who move and wander but follow regular orbits.

[10] Then comes the illegitimate and earthly family of the daimons. Their bodies do not have the same virtue, nor do their souls, which are of an inferior kind and do not attain the understanding of all things, although they conceive many things by conjecture only, but always with accuracy, because they always can follow in the footsteps of the gods of the higher class and, thanks to these, remain infallible always and in all things. This class is charged with executing the orders of the other gods, and immediately touch on human affairs.

[11] We thus distinguish four classes of gods: the first two are supercelestial: one inhabits Olympus, the other Tartarus; the last two inhabit the heavens: one is celestial, the other is terrestrial. All these gods are begotten in the sense that they proceed from one cause and have received existence from another, but they are uncreated and imperishable in time, for they proceed from Zeus, who is eternally active, who is not and has never been confined to mere potentiality without action; that is why they have neither beginning nor end.

[12] In this god [Zeus], essence and action are identical; there is no distinction between them, for this god is essentially one, never different from himself. In the *nous*, action is already distinct from essence, but action is continuous, never at rest. Also the creatures that the *nous* produces without the concurrence of any being of another class are immortal. In the soul we distinguish in the same way essence and action, but although the soul is active in part, most often it is limited in its action and reduced to the role of pure potentiality. Finally, in the body, besides all this, the essence is divided into form and matter, matter which is not only mutable, but also decomposable and infinitely divisible.

[13] Here is another difference and the most essential among beings. The supercelestial gods are not only uncreated in time but also by their permanence, because they are absolutely immutable and eternal, there is nothing in them that has not previously existed, and, finally, they are generated only subject to a cause. Indeed, everything that derives its existence from a cause is generated in that it continues to receive the being of another power and is incapable of being sufficient for its own existence. The celestial gods are also begotten with regard to the cause, for in relation to the essence of their soul they are uncreated, since their souls are immutable and therefore eternal, but as to the action of the soul and of the nature of the body, they are truly created, for they are subject to movement, to continuous renewal, and to divisible and measurable time.

[14] Indeed, time begins from this soul that governs the heavens; it is first the ever-moving measure of the soul's action. Then time spreads within the nature of all souls and bodies. It is the image of eternity,[535] always already past and no longer, about to be and not yet. In the moment it is always and now, but different and always becoming different; it divides time into past and future.

---

535. Cf. Plato, *Timaeus* 37d.

[15] As to place, these same gods may also be circumscribed in a certain part of space, because they are united with bodies, which is why we may call them "celestial," while the other gods are called "supercelestial" and cannot be located in a body or in any place. In grandeur, the Olympians rise above all other gods, whatever their origin, but in number, they are the most limited. It is the same for the daimons; those who are actually closer to Zeus, who is pure unity, are also less numerous, but those who are more distant are more numerous; thus, some are closer, the others farther away from his unity. But above the gods of Olympus and of this universe is placed Poseidon, to whom King Zeus has entrusted the government of all things after him, as to the most powerful, the greatest, the eldest of his children. However, Zeus did not make him equal to himself, because it would be inequitable to place in the same rank as a self-sufficient being one who has his existence through another … [Here the chapter breaks off.]

Book II

Chapter 6: Fate

[1]   Are all future things determined and fixed in advance by fate, or are there any things which have not been determined and which occur without order or law, as chance brings them? Without doubt, all things are subject to law, for if some event occurred without being determined by a law, either it would have no cause, and then there would be a fact that would occur without a cause, or the cause which produced it would act without determination, without necessity, and then there would be a cause that would not produce its effects necessarily and in a definite way. The two things are equally impossible. But it is still far less possible that the gods change what they have resolved for the future and do something else than what they have decided, determined to change by people's prayers, by certain gifts, or by some another similar reason. In fact, by denying the necessity and the predetermination of the facts to come, one exposes oneself to denying entirely the gods' providence over human affairs, or to accusing them of being the authors of what is worse, instead of the best possible, since things that they have decided second must necessarily be worse than those decided first.

[2]   Those who absolutely deny fate therefore fall into one or other of these impieties. But these two suppositions are quite impossible. All future events are fixed from eternity; they are arranged in the best possible order under the authority of Zeus, the sole and supreme master of all things. Alone of all beings, Zeus knows no bounds, since there is nothing that can limit him (for something can be limited only by its own cause), but Zeus is too great to be bounded and remains eternally and perfectly identical to himself. He has for his essence the greatest and most powerful necessity, which is by itself in an absolute manner and does not derive from any different power. For what is necessary is better than what is contingent, and the greatest necessity is to be essentially good. To those who proceed immediately from him, Zeus communicates the same attribute to a lower degree, for the beings he produces are necessarily of the same nature as himself. He determines these things and all the others because of himself, and there is nothing so great or so small that he himself cannot assign its limit, because there is nothing of which he is not the supreme cause.

[3]   Moreover, if the future were not fixed, foreknowledge would be impossible, both for people and even for the gods; for we cannot know with certainty the indeterminate, of which we cannot say exactly in advance whether it will or will not be. Now, the gods know the future, since it is they who fix it, and they are present in it as the cause even before it has come into existence. They know it only because they determine and produce it, for they cannot know something by being themselves affected by it. Indeed, it is repugnant and impossible to admit that the gods are affected by things of an inferior nature that do not even exist yet. Thus, those who think that the gods exist and who at the same time refuse them the foreknowledge and predetermination of the things here are led to deny them knowledge. For they could not know them by being subject to the action of these things [here], since the inferior cannot act upon the superior, nor could they act upon them, because they would not even be the causes of them. It is necessary, in fact, that what knows be connected with the known thing, either as a participant by undergoing

its action, or as a cause by acting on it, all knowledge being impossible in any circumstance other than on a relation between the knowing and the known. And even if the gods were the authors of the things of this world, but not in a determined and necessary way, they would never know what they should do one day, since they could not fix it necessarily and from all eternity in an immutable way.

[4]   But the gods know the future, and among people they choose some to whom they make it known to a certain extent. Some people wanted to make use of this forecast of part of the future to try to escape it, but, like others, they discovered the necessary and inevitable determination of fate. It is even the case that, by this forecast of their fates and by their efforts to escape them, they have brought about their fulfillment, that very thing being in their fate. There is therefore no way to escape or to avert things once decided by Zeus for eternity and fixed by fate.

[5]   But, it will be said, if all is determined in advance, if no present or future fact escapes necessity, that is the end of human freedom and divine justice because, on the one hand, people will act under the rule of fate, they will not be masters of themselves, and they will not be free; and on the other hand, the gods will completely renounce punishing the wicked, for they would not be just in punishing them, since their wickedness is destined and involuntary. But people are masters of themselves, not as having no one who governs them, either among other beings or among the gods themselves, but as having in themselves a single principle that commands—that is to say, the understanding—and all the rest of the faculties obey it. It is this unique principle, the best of our nature, that controls all the rest, but nobody would dare to maintain that this understanding itself undergoes no domination. First, it is obviously subject to the impression of external things. Moreover, even if it is true that in different people the understanding is not subjected in the same way to the same influence, it would be no less absurd to think that it does not undergo these influences necessarily, since obviously it depends on the particular character of each individual understanding and

also on its training. In fact, the same event, coming to act upon several different people, will necessarily produce different impressions on them, for their understanding differs both in nature and in training. Now, the nature [of the understanding] depends on the gods, and training depends on the prior intention of the one who practices it, an intention which cannot be born in a person without the attendance of a god.

[6]   Thus, people are masters of themselves by governing their conduct, although this domination is subject to superior domination, and it can be said that they are free and not free. Indeed, it would obviously be a mistake to say that freedom is the opposite of necessity, for slavery would then be called necessity, but slavery presupposes domination in which the slave is subjected in their capacity as slave. But this first necessity, which alone exists absolutely and by itself while all things exist through it, this necessity that we call the absolute Good, Zeus, to what domination will it be subjected? For surely, that which is domination cannot be at the same time slavery. If, on the other hand, slavery is called submission to a superior, and liberty is the liberation from all domination, there will not be one free person, or even one of the gods, except Zeus, for every inferior will be the slave of whoever governs them, and all will be slaves of their common master, Zeus. In this way, the servitude would not be painful or something to flee. In fact, slavery under a good master cannot be unpleasant; more than that, it is profitable and gentle to the slaves themselves, because one experiences only good under a good master.[536]

[7]   But if we do not accept this definition of slavery and liberty, if instead we say that these two states consist in being prevented or not from living as we wish, then because everyone wishes to live well and be happy, whoever is happy will at the same time be free, whether they have a master or not, since they live as they wish; the unlucky person, on the contrary,

---

536. Most of us will find this statement false and offensive. Our modern insistence on personal liberty inclines us to rebel against compulsion even if it is in our own best interests. In any case, Plethon is not advocating slavery; he is building an argument that we will live most happily if we choose to live in conformity with divine providence or the will of the gods, which is fundamentally good.

not living as they would have liked, will not be free. Now people can be unhappy only when they are wicked; thus, no one wants to be wicked, since no one wants to be unhappy. It is therefore against one's will and by mistake that one becomes wicked; consequently no wicked person is free, which is the privilege of honest and virtuous people.

[8]   If the gods chastise the wicked, the goal they propose to themselves and to which they lead, is not the punishment itself, but the correction of the faults. In fact, it is impossible for people never to err, since they are composed of two natures, one divine, the other mortal. Sometimes they are led by what is divine in themselves to the imitation of this perfection in which they participate; then they are virtuous and happy. But sometimes they are carried away by their mortal instincts and they turn out badly; it is then that the gods come to their aid and seek to correct them by punishments. The gods want the punishments inflicted upon them to deliver them from their wickedness, just as bitter and painful remedies deliver our body from sickness. They intend that people be thereby brought to a better state and pass from slavery to liberty, when the gods judge that, because of their bad nature, means of sweeter correction cannot reach them. Thus, nothing prevents someone from being punished, although their wickedness is involuntary, since the punishment, far from adding to their ills, gives them a benefit.

[9]   In short, there are gods, they watch over people, and they are not the cause of any evil. Finally, according to the inevitable law of fate, they give each one what is best for them. In order not to exceed our limits, we will stop here.

Chapter 26: Reasonable action of some animals

[1]   The acts of certain animals seem to attest an inspiration of reason, such as among a thousand others, these that are the best known: the government of the bees, the foresight of the ants, and the hunting of the ingenious spider. If they use an individual reason, then it must be superior, inferior, or equal to that of humans. If these animals had a reason more enlightened than ours, then in all or almost all circumstances they would act

better than humans, but it is apparent that most often they remain below us. If this reason were inferior, each of them would not attach itself exclusively to a single work to bring it almost to perfection, for it seems to be the characteristic of an accomplished intelligence superior to human intelligence to always apply to a single work to render it as perfectly as possible. Finally, if their intelligence were equal to human intelligence, they would not concentrate thus on a single work, only to show themselves inferior to human works in everything else. It is evident then that animals obey not an individual reason, but the influence of that soul that governs the heavens and of the separated intelligences that preside over each of these things, and to which that soul attaches each of them.

[2]   It is thus not only with animals, but also with inanimate things. Among others we may mention the tendrils of the vine and the pumpkin, which, if they do not meet anything with which to hug, remain straight, but if a branch presents itself, they roll up at once. By the action of this same soul, the magnet attracts iron, and mercury in contact with gold, or with some other metal of the same kind, attaches to it in a marvelous manner and is uplifted;[537] all similar phenomena must be related to the same cause. It is this soul that embraces our world below, which, by its power, governs all the parts, accomplishes everything according to reason, and brings together those other things that have some affinity.

[3]   When Helios and Kronos finished this last mortal creation according to the plans of Poseidon, head of all that exists, then not only was our world completely finished by Poseidon himself, but also, by the power of King Zeus, this entire creation composed of a multitude of different beings—eternal, temporal, immortal, mortal—formed one complete system as beautiful and as perfect as possible.[538]

[The remainder of book II was destroyed.]

---

537. That is, the mercury amalgamates with the gold or other metal.

538. Alexandre, *Pléthon: Traité des Lois*, 82, incorrectly takes this paragraph to be the beginning of II.27, but it is the last part of II.26 (Masai, *Pléthon*, 398, n. 8).

Book III

Chapter 11: Measure and symmetry

[1] Beauty, of which we have spoken, must be sought in measure and symmetry; it needs a fixed limit and cannot be either unmeasurable or indefinite and constantly increasing. However, this objection may be made: if the greatest existence is at the same time the best, why is it not that which increases indefinitely but that which remains in measure that is beautiful and good? It is that it is neither the most in number, nor the most in volume, nor in a word the most in quantity which exists in the highest degree, but rather what is best endowed to last forever, and that which is best able to last forever is unity and what comes closest to it. But the simple is more unified than the compound, the symmetric more than the asymmetric, and the proportionate more than what is not. Indeed, common measure or identity of proportion are precisely what makes a unity of things symmetrical or proportionate. But that which has neither measure nor proportion, either between its own parts, or with the things to which it relates and of which it is itself a part, lacks unity and consequently cannot last forever. Thus, the greater existence, beauty, and goodness are in definite measure and not in the ever-increasing and indefinite. That is enough on this subject.

Chapter 14: Prohibition of intercourse between parents and their children

[1]   The use of public women, the eating of meat, the unity of property in a single household, and not squandering the property of someone who has died[539]: each of these will be considered in the appropriate place, whether some of them are rightly legislated, and for others that are right insofar as they are equally customary among nearly all people, for what reason they are right.[540] But first of all, we must focus our attention on the prohibition of intercourse between parents and their children.[541] Not to mention the suitability of this law, its universality and its invariability suffice to show that it was the gods who imposed it on people, and since it comes from the gods, it is right. Without doubt, when human laws are in conflict, it is up to us to look for the best of them, but when they all agree, it is not permissible to question the justice of their decision; it is necessary in this unanimity, whatever its object, to recognize the mark of a divine revelation. But the search for motives is a study worthy of the one who wants to have thorough knowledge of the laws, for there are many [laws] whose reason escapes the vulgar. Thus, people have always been unanimous in banning intercourse between parents and their children, but very few could say why this opinion is right; this research will not be without interest.

[2]   First it will be admitted that the sexual act was instituted by the gods to perpetuate the race of mortals and also to give it a kind of immortality. In the second place, on the part of the ones who perform it, this act is the efficient cause that produces beings like themselves. Last, these two

---

539.   τελευτὰς, a correction of τελετὰς in the manuscript.

540.   The part of this paragraph to this point is from manuscript *Bruxellensis* 1871–1877, fol. 66r (ed. F. Masai, *Pléthon*, 125, n. 1) in Hladký, *Plethon*, 320.

541.   Although it is relevant to the legislative function of his *Book of Laws*, Plethon's focus on the incest prohibition may be surprising, but as is explained in the next chapter, it is based on the same reasons as his rejection of incestuous relations among the gods in Greek mythology.

things, immortality and the procreation of a self-like being, are essentially suited to the gods, for all the gods are immortal, and those who are more powerful than the others produce beings like themselves, immortal like them, or mortal like those here below. Therefore, for this act to be well done, it must be as close as possible to the mode of generation that belongs to the gods; this is an argument that the weakest intelligence must understand and accept.

[3]   It is no less evident that the more important an action is, the more we must endeavor to do it well, and we cannot deny the importance of this act, which in our mortal nature is the imitation of the immortality of the gods and of their manner of procreation. For it would be a mistake to believe that if we do not perform this act in public, it is because it is something shameful. Indeed, many people do not want to do in public the religious acts that they regard as the holiest; to celebrate their greatest mysteries, they hide themselves from the crowd, fearing that some spectator, for lack of being sufficiently prepared to attend, may make them a laughingstock. Regarding the procreative act, if people do not perform it in public, it is for fear of disturbing those who witness it, because human weakness makes them easy to inflame, if not into desire, at least up to the imagination of such an act, and that for the least pretext. How, then, could it be good for the man who shares his bed with a single woman to expose it to all eyes? The spectators, men or women, having no part in this act, would be agitated, if not by desire, at least by the imagination of a pleasure illicit for them. Men would like to share the favors of the same woman, and women would like to give themselves up to the same pleasures with the same man, although neither could accomplish this action without crime. Now, the imagination alone of illegitimate actions is wrong, and it would be even more culpable to awaken such desires in others. Such are the reasons that sexual intercourse is hidden.

[4]   Another proof that it is not because people regard it as shameful, but that they surround it with mystery, is [provided by] the publicity they give to

marriage. They summon to it the most people they can, as if to a grave and solemn act, and make them witnesses of the bridal union, when all know what is the purpose of this union.

[5]   Thus, the act of which we speak is one of the most important that is given to people to do and deserves that its accomplishment be as perfect as possible. Indeed, nothing is more shameful than an important act that is badly done. It is one thing to play a simple game badly, but something else not to bring to an important act the care it requires. Then, therefore, as it must be as perfect as possible, it will be necessary, as we have said, that it be an image of the generation of the gods.

Chapter 15: The generation of gods according to the principle of the prohibition of intercourse between parents and their children

[1]   First, one must consider the generation of the gods and the way in which they procreate, so that we may understand their generation and see that if the parents had intercourse with their children, they would perform acts contrary to the laws of [divine] procreation. Zeus, the supreme king and eldest father [of the gods], produced without a mother the gods to whom he gave birth; in fact, there was no being that could contribute as a mother for the production of what he created. Moreover, in the absence of a participation of this kind, matter is absolutely irrelevant to the creation and life of beings who proceed immediately from Zeus. For in every generation the female principle is the one that contributes to material existence, so that the beings to whose production no female principle contributes cannot receive it from without, nor have anything material in themselves. When Zeus makes use of his creations for the generation of new creatures, he uses each as a model and not as a female principle.

[2]   Thus, he engendered without intermediary, in his own likeness, the most powerful of the gods, whom we call Poseidon. All others he has produced through others by creating each of them in the image of the other gods

he created, roughly, if we can assimilate this great work to a trivial matter, as images are reproduced and multiplied with the aid of several mirrors. Indeed, the body that is reflected, producing an immediate image of itself, creates at the same time all the other images, which are reproductions of each other.

[3]   And if we say that at least we need several different mirrors for this production of images, let us take as another example the unit, which of itself generates all the numbers by adding them successively without needing any other element. However, this production [of numbers] still differs in several respects from that of the supercelestial gods generated by Zeus, in particular because the former proceeds potentially to infinity, while the second is potentially and actually limited to a certain number of beings. Indeed, the unit joins a number as it occurs to form another [number]; it is thus that it itself perpetuates the production of numbers to infinity, since it can always add to the last formed. But Zeus, instead of adding to a being already created, divides it; he brings out from each of them the elements that were implicitly contained in them; he removes one and leaves the other. Thus, he effects the creation of new beings. Now, as these divisions proceed by means of opposites without ever having a middle, they cannot repeat themselves to infinity and must finally cease. Thus, Zeus produces a bounded number of beings, and of all these different beings he composes a single system.

[4]   Now, that this is the way he engenders the whole class of supercelestial gods, and not using one to create the other, that is what we have to prove, since we have come to talk about the generation of these gods by Zeus. The class of generated substance[542] is threefold and is not originally divisible into more [than three species]. The first is entirely eternal and always immutable; it admits neither past nor future, but it exists from all eternity. The second exists in time and is essentially subject to change; yet it

---

542. Or "essence."

is everlasting, has had no beginning, and will never end. The third is both temporal and mortal; it has a beginning and an end in time.

[5]   As there are three species of substances, there must be three modes of generation, and if the substances differ from each other, this difference must be found also between the modes of generation, because generation must be in relation with substance, and substance with generation. Therefore, if one of the beings belonging to the eternal substance comes from Zeus, who is pre-eternal and who alone of all beings exists by himself, all beings of the same substance will have to proceed also from Zeus alone. For, being entirely eternal, they could not proceed partly from the pre-eternal principle and partly from another, non-pre-eternal principle. Rather, pre-eternal Zeus created all eternal substance himself. He has entrusted to this eternal substance the production of temporal and everlasting substance, and to the latter the production of that which is at once temporal and mortal, so that each substance is produced by the generation that suits it, and each comes out of the source from which it must emerge—namely, from the substance that is immediately superior to it.

[6]   If the beings belonging to the eternal substance were all equal to each other, and none of them made superior or inferior to another, all this substance would be from Zeus himself. But nothing of the sort could have happened, and it has not happened, for it was necessary first that this substance should contain all the most diverse forms in order to possess the perfection of variety, then that these forms were themselves each one and unique, and that the system be a community and a kind of whole comprising them all, so that, in each of its parts and as a whole, this substance was as similar as possible to its creator, who exists by himself.

[7]   Since things are necessarily so, Zeus begins by generating of himself a single being in his image and makes of it the most noble and the most beautiful of all created substances; then he makes another image of that one, and finally all the others in the image of each other, their perfection always decreasing, as suits images. He is almost like a man who would

engender one of his children as similar as possible to himself, then others like that one, and others like them.

[8]   But when this takes place for man, it is always because of the strength or weakness of the emitted sperm. Indeed, if this sperm is emitted in all its strength, thanks to a sufficient maturity, it produces a male quite similar to his father; when it is less powerful, its product is female and similar to the father, or male and mother-like, or mother-like and at the same time female, or without resemblance to either the father or the mother, but with some other member of the same family, according to greater or lesser maturity.[543] Or this offspring does not even resemble a parent, but simply a human, or least of all the offspring is not exactly like a human but sometimes turns to another nature when [the father] does not abstain because of an absolute lack of maturity. For generation is not subject to human intention; no doubt the procreative act depends on one's intention, but generation depends on nature, which puts the mortal body in this or that disposition.

[9]   But for the perfectly simple nature of Zeus, to generate is not one thing and to create another; there are not certain creatures that he generates and some others that he creates; to generate and to create are for him the same thing: he generates by the intelligence that he has of what it is appropriate to generate, and he creates by his nature, which is always to produce. Thus, people cannot generate children as they wish, but they can build their homes and create the accessories as they like and when they want. Zeus, on the other hand, whose eternal essence is the identity of will and power, produces all the beings that he judges fit to contribute to the perfection of his entire work; he simultaneously creates them and generates them. He makes each being one and unique in its nature, for he does not do anything superfluous, and he gives all possible unity to the whole that results from his creation. Now there was no other possible unity here than that of community, and no community is better suited

---

543. Obviously, this analogy is based on incorrect prescientific theories of sexual reproduction.

to these things than to be the image of one another, for each thing has its own separate existence, and at the same time there is a certain community between the image and the model. Not only are the species the images of the genera, but they are also images of the other species that issue from the same genus by successive division and that are always divided into more perfect and less perfect, the less perfect being the image of the more perfect, the temporal essence of the eternal essence, the mortal nature of the immortal nature, the irrational of the rational, and so on.

[10] In this community of [species], the inferior beings possess, as appropriate, whatever attributes they have from those superior to them, from which comes a new link of affinity between the beings, since by their state of subordination, they are intimately connected with those who precede them, as the one who receives must naturally be to the one who gives. In fact, the lower natures must be simultaneously subordinate and not entirely different from those from which they receive anything. Zeus, therefore, by himself gives existence to each of these eternal substances, and those he has produced are used by him only as models for the creation of others, in order to maintain the mutual union of these beings, the images being found in the models and the models in the images by both their resemblance and distinction; each of these beings is necessarily in the relation of effect to cause,[544] and all have Zeus for a common cause. He in fact produces, by himself and alone, a single being, then on the model of this one produces another, and according to the latter still another, and so forth, until the completion of the whole, complete system. Having thus given them existence (since the creation of the higher [substances] that form the whole eternal substance belongs to him), he leaves to them the adorning of the others with their attributes, by which the higher beings must adorn those below them. The purpose and the end of this community among the gods is to form from their meeting a single system, a single cosmos, the most beautiful possible.

544. Or "a difference always being the cause of a difference" (cf. Hladký, *Plethon*, 93).

[11] It is thus that our souls are obviously adorned with their attributes by the divine souls, which are superior to them, not that they are produced by them, but they emerge from the same source, being like them of an immortal substance. Now, if it is so with our souls, so must the gods up there receive their existence in the way we have said, so that there is an analogy and a relationship between things on earth and those above, and from things up there to those here below. However, the motherless generation of Zeus's gods cannot be exactly compared to the generation of people; it has more to do with the generation of other immortal and mortal beings by these same gods and their children.

[12] In fact, the eldest of Zeus's children, Poseidon, although he is really a Form, is not the Form of this or that, but he comprehends in himself as genus all the individual Forms, and he is after Zeus the supreme cause of the Form of the All; hence, he is the supreme male principle of the gods, for he is the male principle that gives beings their specific characters.[545] His image, created like himself by Zeus and the eldest after him, is Hera, who also contains all Forms, but who, however, does not possess power equal to that of Poseidon. For he [Poseidon] possesses in himself all Forms in actuality, and is himself in actuality the cause of the Form of all the things of the All. She also possesses them all in actuality, but does not actually become the cause of the Form of anything; she produces only the primary matter that contains all the Forms potentially, not in actuality, for in fact, far from containing all of them, it does not possess any.

[13] Thus, this divinity [Hera] is a female principle and the first principle of this kind. Such, indeed, is the nature of the female principle: it furnishes to all beings matter and nourishment. Between these two divinities, there is nearly the same correlation as between semen and menstrual blood, which both contain, not in actuality but potentially, a being to come. But semen has more to do with the productive force; it gives rather the form.

---

545. See "Divine Gender" in chapter 3 for a discussion of this issue and its relation to prescientific theories of sexual reproduction.

While menstrual blood, less endowed with the productive force, is rather the matter proper to form the new being. Thus, these two divinities actually possess all Forms in common; Poseidon is the actual productive cause of Form, Hera of Matter.

[14] Thus, our comparison, although imperfect and unworthy of divine purity, gives a good account of the mutual relation and the respective action of these two divinities. By their union, they produce immortal beings. The two most powerful children, Helios and Selene, are united together by the same relations, and in the same way that these gods were themselves produced, they in turn produce mortal beings. In fact, Helios gives to these beings the form which he borrows from higher beings—that is to say, from the Tartarean gods; Selene furnishes them with matter specially placed under her influence. Helios is the eldest of the male gods who inhabit the heavens, Selene the eldest of the female.

[15] With these two, for the creation of mortal beings there are, among the eternal gods, Kronos and Aphrodite, who are in the same relations among the gods of Tartarus as are Poseidon and Hera among the gods of Olympus, and who create mortal beings in the same way; Kronos gives each one form, Aphrodite matter. Certainly, it is not the primary, imperishable matter, but a matter extracted from the eldest bodies and other elements, able like them to assume the forms found in these bodies from which it is extracted, but already acquiring the perishable state, and thus becoming the proper material to form mortal bodies.

[16] But the generation of mortal beings is not confined only to the gods around Helios. There are some of the eternal gods, those called Titans and Tartareans, led by Kronos, who cooperate with them in the generation of mortals, as we know by reasoning. For one might think that Helios, having in his mind the forms of mortal beings still purely intelligible and not actually existing anywhere, gives birth to each of these beings in the same way that artists have ideas of their artifacts, but we see that the works of artists are not completed in the same way as the natural

creations of mortals by Helios. Indeed, we see that all the artifacts of artists advance toward perfection only so long as they are in their hands and they work on them, but if they are abandoned half done, they make no further progress. In short, they never perfect themselves except in proportion to the work the artists give them. In contrast, the creations of nature are not necessarily subject to the advance or retreat of Helios with respect to their development and life. Otherwise, all would be daily or annual, and moreover during the night nothing would progress toward perfection, while we obviously see that plants and fruits develop even during the night.

[17] Now, it cannot be Helios, both advancing and retreating, that leads them to their perfection, for it is not permissible to attribute this effect to the action of his mind separated from his body. In fact, participated minds cannot act without their bodies on the other bodies, and, as for all those bodies, to act on the others they need to be in this or that position in relation to those on which they act. It will not be said that these things are perfected by themselves, for no potentiality comes to actuality without being moved by the action of an earlier force. Hence, that which is potentially perfect would never become perfect in actuality if it were not impelled to perfection by another essence that already possesses this perfection in actuality. It is not the heat received from Helios or any other affection absorbed by each mortal thing that could lead them to perfection in the absence of Helios; for what completes must always be prior to what owes it completion, and no modification of any form or substance may be prior to the modified object.

[18] It therefore remains to admit the necessity of certain Forms that remain by themselves in the supercelestial domain. They are incapable of producing, alone among themselves, whatever is produced here below. Thus, for example, the eldest of them may have produced Helios and Selene and the other immortal beings existing here [within the heavens], but to form here below the beings whose production concerns them, these deities

need the help of Helios and the other gods around Helios. However, once the creation is finished, when the object has already taken some structure, then they can by themselves complete it and preserve it for some time, the more perfect of them probably using this faculty more fully and longer than those who are endowed with a lesser perfection. This is why the perfection and the preservation of mortal things are not in proportion to the approach or retreat of Helios.

[19] Something analogous happens with thrown bodies, for they would not be thrown if nobody threw them; however, once thrown, they continue to move because the air seizes them and bears them for some time by the very effect of its resistance, without the thrower continuing to touch or to move them.[546] Thus, the works of people are preserved as much as nature preserves them, because they are all formed of natural elements, but they can only be completed in proportion to the work that artists devote to each of them, unless some of their parts, needing a certain maturity, be entrusted to the care of nature. But, in general, they advance to perfection only to the extent that we have said, for nothing can take them back and complete them. In fact, with the departure of the artists' hands, the forms in the artists' thoughts, which furnished them with models, also depart.

[20] Indeed, there is no form here below that exists by itself; they all exist only in the god Pluto, who presides over every human form and contains in himself all human affairs in their entirety and in each of their parts, while the artists hold them in their minds only one by one and separated from each other. The same is true of mathematical numbers and mathematical magnitudes,[547] both of which exist in a kind of unity in the god Hera, who in fact presides over their infinity, since she presides over Matter in general, and which are then received by the human soul in an extended

---

546. This analogy is based on a pre-Newtonian understanding of momentum but is nevertheless informative.

547. That is, discrete and continuous quantities.

form, shadows and phantoms, in a sense, of divine things, but nevertheless capable of leading people to an exact knowledge of them. Such is the way in which the works of people are perfected.

[21] As for the natural substances, which are formed from models that exist by themselves, it is clear that their perfection must not also depend on the approach and the retreat of Helios, because they have for support these models, some more perfect, others less, the former better able to perfect their works, the latter less endowed with this faculty.

[22] Nothing is more rational, in fact, than that the different classes of substances partake of their proper causes. The first, eternal class is from Zeus alone. The class that follows it, already existing in time but everlasting, is from his children, who are many but all siblings of each other, since they proceed from Zeus himself, but we specially attribute this creation to Poseidon, their chief, as to the architect the construction of a building, and to the general the victory in a battle. The third and last substance, which is both temporal and mortal, does not owe its origin to gods who are all siblings of each other, but some of the gods who produce it are children of Zeus himself, the others of Poseidon. In general we attribute its generation to Kronos and Helios, the leaders of the gods who produce this kind of substance. But enough is enough about the generation of gods; now let us return to our first subject.

[23] We have shown that gods are divided into males and females, that males provide form to beings that come from them, and that females give matter. It is evident, then, that all the gods must belong by their nature either to the male or the female, because the creative gods must necessarily be for their creations either the cause or the form that specifies them, or else the matter and its properties. Those who are not creative, such as most of those within the heavens, must necessarily have some occupation and cannot remain entirely idle, for absolute rest is not a life. Since each of the gods must have a task to fulfill, this task will have something to do with either the male or female principles. For necessarily they must play

an active or passive role, and of these two roles, the one obviously suits the male principle, the other the female. Form, which is the cause and the necessary element of the male principle, represents action; Matter, which is the element of the female principle, essentially represents passivity. It is therefore not only the gods who by nature belong either to the male or to the female, but also among all beings those in whom form and action predominate are chiefly attached to the male nature, and those in whom matter and passivity predominate are related to the female; consequently, it would be very difficult to find an ambiguous being balanced between these two natures.

[24] All beings, whoever they may be, thus have a mutual intercourse according to their differences; this intercourse, for some, presents only an image of the intercourse between male and female, but for material beings, when they work for the production of other beings, this is intercourse in the proper [sexual] sense of the word. In this intercourse, however, no gods unite with those whom they produce. Indeed, Zeus does not have with Hera, any more than with any other divinity, the intercourse of male with female; he uses her only as a model for the production of the divine beings who need this goddess to contribute as a model for their generation. The same can be said of Poseidon with Selene or of Helios with Hera...

[The remainder of the chapter was destroyed.]

Chapter 31: Judgments

[1] Animals act without reason, not according to their own intelligence, but under the direction of the soul that governs our heaven—I mean the soul of Helios—and also under the direction of Kronos and other minds who are separated [from matter] and governors [of the cosmos]. These, borrowing everything from Helios, who is the principle of generation and life for animals, govern them according to the power which has been

given to them, a power that for them is one, but divided among the different beings subject to their action. Thus, guided by these more divine beings, animals cannot do anything they should not do. (It could not be according to their own intelligence, for they have none; nor could it be by the external influence of these divine intellects, for it is not permissible to suppose this.) It is for this reason that they perform their acts, and in particular that act [procreation], more correctly than people. For people, under the influence of their own intelligence and fallible opinion, are often mistaken, both in this act and in all the rest, and make use of their faculties sometimes in conformity with nature but needlessly, and sometimes even, which is much more shameful, contrary to nature. But animals cannot commit any similar fault, so that if one of them unites with different species, but similar to its own, one must believe that it is due to the physical relations of species to each other.

[2] Moreover, if the ardor of the senses was less strong among people, we would not need such severe legislation. But the gods knew that people are governed by an imagination prone to error and that some would, therefore, misuse sexual indulgence, while others would abstain from it entirely, either judging it as wholly impure or as less perfect than abstention; that others, by the misanthropy of their character, would be reluctant to feed a woman and children; that others, finally, being unable to bear losing their children, would prefer not having children to losing the ones they had, instead of relying in this respect on the will of the gods and performing the duty imposed on us to contribute to the propagation of the species and the preservation of the All.

[3] The gods, therefore, knowing all this and that the weakness of the judgment of people would lead to all these errors, as we have examples around us, did not want too many people to abstain from sexual indulgence and to fail in the providence by which Zeus maintains a link between mortal and immortal beings through the intermediary of the human species. That is why they have inspired people with such a desire that it

prevails over all the others and is very difficult to triumph over unless it is opposed by the force of a still more powerful opinion.

[4] But they knew that the opinion that one must abstain completely from sexual pleasures would, in the end, find few partisans, and that if it entered a few minds, most of the time it would not be strong enough not to yield easily to the incessant persecutions of the most powerful of all desires. But much more than abstinence of sexual pleasures the gods [feared their depraved use][548]. . . . because people, among the other duties of their nature, must live as citizens, as sociable people, not loners. That is why we punish by death most of those who are degraded by such actions;[549] at the same time we want to deliver them from this miserable state and to save their country from such shame.

[5] Those who commit acts against nature—for example, those who are convicted of the crime of sodomy or bestiality, or of any of those things that are only found among the most corrupt people—these must be punished by fire, and one must at the same time burn the criminal and his victim, or if he has exercised his brutality on some animal, burn the animal with him. It is also necessary to burn adulterers, and those men or women who will have led or helped them to commit this crime. As for the adulterous women, they will have their hair shaved and will be delivered to the inspector of prostitutes to be abandoned to prostitution, so that if they could not keep their fidelity to the one to whom they owed it, they serve at least to maintain other women in conjugal fidelity, by offering to the passions of men too inclined to lust a remedy tolerable in the eyes of the law. Likewise burned will be anyone who violates any woman, unless she is a prostitute, even a courtesan if she did not publicly make

---

548. There is a lacuna in the text; the translation here follows Pellissier (in Alexandre, *Pléthon*, 125) and Woodhouse's paraphrase (*Plethon*, 343).

549. It will be apparent that Plethon's punishments are excessively harsh, which may reflect the late medieval culture in which he lived.

a profession of her body, and even a prostitute if she is done violence at the times when nature forbids the approach of this sex [i.e., during menstruation].

[6] All those who are defiled by these crimes, the most infamous of all, will be burned in the enclosures designated to contain their remains, and not in the common cemeteries. For there will be in each place three cemeteries separated by very visible fences: one for the priests, another for the common citizens, a third for these great criminals, and it is also in the latter where will be burned alive the sophist who dares to attack our beliefs.[550] This same punishment is reserved for those guilty of incest with a mother, a sister, or any relative in ascending or descending direct line. If a man is convicted of intercourse with some other relative to a prohibited degree, he will be punished by loss of civil rights until he is sufficiently purified, and in addition, access to sacred things will be forbidden to him. In the cemetery of the impure and infamous will be burned anyone who is judged by the magistrates to be guilty of a murder subject to expiation. If anyone is convicted of intercourse with a virgin girl, or with someone who, without being a virgin or being betrothed to anybody, would still be in guardianship, the culprit will be punished with death, even if this young girl would have given herself voluntarily to him, but burned and buried in the common cemetery, which will also be used as the burial place for one guilty of a murder not subject to expiation. Moreover, rape and adultery will not be punished only when they have been accomplished, but the very attempt will also be punished when it has failed, because for these crimes the attempt is regarded to be as criminal as the action. As for the man who would feel violently in love with someone who is betrothed or married to another, we want him to go immediately to find the advisor on sacred matters, to reveal to him the illness of his soul and to ask him for a means to

---

550. This is presumed to refer to Christians, whom Plethon calls "sophists" because they use subtle and misleading arguments to instill false beliefs.

purify it or for a restraint against the greater evil that would befall if passion triumphed over his soul. So, approaching the holy places … [551]

[7]   … and therefore punish him with death. But when the crime is not obvious, the accused is judged by a majority of votes, and in that case, it will be right to absolve him not only if he has only the minority of votes against him, but also if they are equally divided.

[8]   Add to this chapter on judgments a last article. If a man convicted by the court of one of those crimes that are punished with death proves that he has previously done some good deeds whose importance or number seems to exceed the magnitude of his fault, he must be considered as being neither incorrigible nor naturally perverse, but as having been the victim of some unfortunate circumstance beyond his nature, for example, of the inadequacy of his education, and then, instead of punishing him by death, it will have to be corrected by a temporary prison term. But this is enough to say on this subject, for if we have left some gap, the lights diffused in the course of this work will suffice, with the help of the gods, to put our magistrates in a condition to perfectly clear up for themselves the points that we have left in the dark.

Chapter 32: Names of the gods

[1]   We still have to deal with the religious rituals for the gods, and certainly it is not unimportant whether we worship the gods rightly or not, for if rituals are in harmony with religious beliefs, they can strengthen them, otherwise shake them. Now, if we have any sense, we will easily recognize that the entire conduct of our life and all our actions, whether good or bad, depend on our religious beliefs. This is a subject that we must deal with thoroughly.

---

551. According to Woodhouse, *Plethon*, 344, this paragraph, which breaks off at this point, is in Plethon's handwriting (in manuscript Marcianus gr. 406 in Venice), but the following paragraph is in a different handwriting. Since its topic is somewhat different, it might have been copied here from the otherwise lost chapter I.24, which has the same title.

[2]   But we must first speak of the names of the gods and prove that we were right in preserving the names of the gods of our ancestors, whose philosophy has made us recognize their existence. We should not designate each god by a periphrasis instead of a name, which would be difficult for many people, nor lay down new names, nor apply barbarian names to them, when we can use those used by our ancestors. However, it will be said, these names have been defiled by the poets who distorted the revelations of philosophy about the gods into false fables, and as such they should never be used. But one cannot say it is the nature of names that once defiled, they remain defiled forever. Their nature is to be defiled when they are employed in a base and accursed sense, but as soon as they are taken in a pure and healthy sense, they immediately become undefiled for the person using them. Indeed, it would be difficult to find a name so pure that it has never been defiled by anyone. Because one could say that it happened to the very name of God, when some people filled with many crimes have ... [552]

Chapter 34: Addresses to the gods

[1]   Thrice each day address the gods: first, either rising exactly at dawn or at daybreak but still rising early, then in the afternoon after engaging in business but before supper, and finally in the evening before bedtime. Further, use the longer addresses on the holy days, but the shorter ones on secular days. Let these be the addresses. [553]

Morning Address to the Gods

[2]   O King Zeus, Being-Itself, One-Itself, Good-Itself, you are great, great in reality, and supremely great. You have not been produced by anything, you

---

552. The rest of the chapter was destroyed, presumably because it criticized Christians for incorrect claims about God (i.e., Zeus). Cf. Woodhouse, *Plethon*, 345.

553. This paragraph is not in Alexandre's text (*Pléthon: Traité des Lois*) but is preserved in British Library Manuscript Add. 5424, fol. 101.1–7 (Hladký, *Plethon*, 311).

do not proceed from any cause, nothing is or has been before you. For you alone are pre-eternal; alone of all things, you are entirely uncreated, while you are the first cause and founder of all that participates in being. Through you and from you everything comes, everything is born, everything is established and maintained in the best possible order, both those that are eternal and supercelestial, and those who live in our heaven and exist in time, some immortal, others mortal and so placed in the last degree of beings. The first [eternal and supercelestial] you yourself create and provide with all benefits, and to the latter [temporal] you give other benefits by means of the various beings born directly from you, and you make sure that they are as perfect as possible, not only in themselves, but the most useful in relation to the order of the All, which is your supreme goal.

[3]   After Zeus, you are also great, O Lord Poseidon, the greatest and firstborn child of the greatest and first father, yet motherless, the most powerful and most perfect work of your father. You are the leader of all others after your father, the second father and second creator of this universe. After him and with him are you, O Queen Hera, first daughter of Zeus, wife of Poseidon, mother of the gods within the heavens, leader of the procession into multiplicity of inferior beings. And all you in turn, O Olympian gods, motherless and legitimate children of great Zeus, you together create all the immortal beings within the heavens, in common with Poseidon, your leader and eldest brother. Your place is with them, O Lord Pluto, protector of our immortal principle.

[4]   You too are blessed, O Lord Kronos; among the illegitimate children of Zeus, motherless like all those born of Zeus himself, you are the eldest and preside over all of mortal nature. After him and with him are you all, O Titans, O Tartareans, cocreators of portions of this same mortal nature together with Kronos, your leader and eldest brother, although your own substance is eternal.

[5]   You too are blessed, O Lord Helios, the eldest and most powerful of the legitimate children of Poseidon and Hera. Poseidon, having received

from his father Zeus this brother intellect younger than himself, has himself and with this brother intellect created a soul, but he has created a body with Hera, and especially with her, since this goddess produces matter. [They are] the most beautiful, good, and perfect soul and body of all souls and bodies, and of his creations. Then uniting them to this intellect itself, and submitting the body to the soul and the soul to the intellect, he has formed from this assemblage a sort of common boundary and bond between both parts, the supercelestial and that within the heavens. You [Helios] are leader of all the heavens and creator, in common with Kronos, of the entire mortal nature within it.

[6]   After Helios and with him, we greet the rest of you, O wanderer *Asteres* [Planets], you whose origin and composition are similar to those of your leader, your eldest brother. You share with him sovereignty over affairs of mortal nature and also over the race of earthly daimons, according to the division assigned to each of you, as well as [sovereignty] over our souls. After them, we address you, O highest *Astra* [Fixed Stars], you who were created to contemplate beings with an exact knowledge of all things, and especially to produce the great hymn to Zeus. Last, I invoke you, O blessed terrestrial daimons, gods of the last degree, who, serving the other gods, immediately touch our life and nature, but who are, like all gods, infallible and immune to evil.

[7]   May all the race of blessed gods favorably and kindly accept this morning prayer. It is you, O gods, who, under the direction of Zeus, administer and watch over human things. It is you who, among other suitable things devised for us, have separated our life into sleep and wakefulness, which is necessary for the preservation of this mortal body for the duration assigned to it. So from that moment when we wake up and leave our bed, grant us to live rightly and well—in the way that suits you best—as we pass this day, this month, this year, and the rest of our lives. You have the right to communicate, without envy, a part of what is yours to whomever it is possible. So grant it to us, who have a nature that is immortal

but mixed; and because you have attached us to this mortal part for the fullness and harmony of the All, so that there is a boundary and bond between the two parts, yours immortal and completely pure, the other mortal and perishable, at least [grant] that we are not completely dominated by the mortal element. May the ruling and excellent part of our nature, which is akin to yours, follow you as much as possible in everything and everywhere. May it dominate and govern our inferior part, and to this end [O gods], support us as far as possible. Assist us in all the actions, all the works that we undertake, to be directed according to your reason and your wisdom, that the mortal and non-rational principle not dominate us, and that we not be removed far from you by being carried away by the erring part of our nature. On the contrary, let us exercise the most authoritative part of our being, the immortal essence akin to yours, to follow you unceasingly, as much as possible, and to draw closer to you, who are always good and happy, to maintain with you, as much as possible, an intimate alliance, a familiar communion, adapting each of our actions to be especially fitting to this kinship, so that, as far as possible, we might regulate our mortal nature and, to the extent of our strength and by this communion, fare most happily.[554]

[8]   Above all, grant us, O gods, both now and always, as a first favor, to have an understanding of you; it will be the source of all goods for us. For there can be in us nothing more beautiful nor more divine than thought in general, which is the most divine act of our most divine part, and no use of thought could be more beautiful nor more blessed than that which relates to you and to the great Zeus, since it is impossible, without our knowing Zeus, to get a correct idea of you, nor without our knowing you, to get a correct idea of Zeus. Indeed, one does not comprehend his supreme goodness if one does not consider him as the creator of you, as good and blessed ones produced from him. For this king of all things, who is supreme goodness itself, wanted to be the principle and the cause

---

554. Beginning of holy day supplement.

of powerful and excellent ones similar to himself, and so he engendered you as the second rank of the gods. Then he gave the highest among you the power to produce a third order of divinities, in order to make you, as much as possible, yet more like him in this respect.

[9]   Thus, divinity is composed of three divisions of which the first, the greatest, and the most august is that of Zeus; the other two emanate from him: this one immediately, that one by the intermediary of the second; thus, he made the fullness of benefits. But it is King Zeus, completing this admirable whole, who has made it perfect and one. He composed it of both immortal and mortal beings, the generation of whom he shared with you. Moreover, he crafted a bond in it between the two parts, your race and the human race.

[10]   So you, executors of the purpose of Zeus, you have given us a place among beings, you have united an immortal form akin to yours, namely our soul, with a mortal nature, and you have fixed our happiness first in our immortal principle, then in the good and in participation in the good, which you have allowed to come to us—that is, in the imitation of yourselves—in which absolute goodness resides primarily. But the contemplation of beings is for you one of the greatest benefits, so it must also be for us the best of actions and the height of happiness, especially when we raise our thought toward what is greatest and most noble among all beings—that is to say, toward you, and toward Zeus, who commands you and all things—then toward the whole universe, and finally to the knowledge of ourselves who are in it. To obtain each of these benefits and all others to which we can aspire, help us, O gods, without whom no good is possible.

[11]   But, as the first of all benefits, establish in us the preceding doctrines and others like them, and since you have deigned to instruct us about our origin and the place we occupy in the All, keep us free so far as possible, safe from the misfortune and humiliation due to our lower part, and prevent us from being disturbed by whatever happens contrary to our purpose.

For in the first place these things must be nothing to us, since they reach only our mortal nature and not the upper part of our being, which is immortal and in which you have fixed our happiness. And second, it is not possible that things are always given to us as we would like them to be, for there would be nothing mortal in us if we did not suffer such accidents, and we would no longer be a compound of two parts, one immortal, the other mortal. And finally, you wanted us to be in [the middle of] the All.

[12] Then, to the extent of our condition and what you have given, we must use [what you have given], so grant us to use it with constancy and freedom, which you have provided with this superior reason, as a weapon against such awful things, [a weapon] which we are fortunate to have in each occasion. For we would be foolish to rebel against those more powerful than us; it would be unjust to seek what our masters have not given us instead of being grateful for what is already granted, which certainly is not contemptible. May we never blame you for any of these things, nor desire other than what you have given, but, yielding gently to what is fated, and knowing that you treat us always as favorably as possible, and sharing, among other things, our intelligence with yours, let us share also in all that you will.

[13] Let us never have any resentment against people, who after all are born to act as they themselves think, and who cannot affect us if we know how to turn our attention to ourselves and know to desire the most appropriate benefits. Let us not recoil before what is good and dear to you, in a matter coming down from you, being hindered by fear either of the labor, or of losing some of what is not really our own, or of disapproval from ignorant people.

[14] Strengthen our thinking and most divine part to be powerful and the master of all our other [faculties], as much as it can, regulating the others according to nature, the superior over the inferior, so that it imposes limits on each of them. As for the pleasures of the body, let us cling to them as moderately as possible, insofar as they do not seem to be able to

harm the good state of our body and soul, even if they do not contribute to making it the best possible. Let not a deceitful and extraordinary pleasure make our soul bad, and perhaps our body too. Let us consider riches, instruments [of these pleasures], only as a means of satisfying the reasonable needs of life, and take care not to allow desire to grow without bound in us, an inexhaustible source of ills.

[15] As for opinion, let us take into account only that of noble, good people, sure of finding in them witnesses and supporters of good actions. For those people who, on the contrary, have only false ideas about the noble and good, let us pay them no attention, and let us seek their esteem only so long as it never distracts from virtue wherever duty is involved. Thus, may we never be conquered by a vain opinion harmful to virtue.

[16] Of the bonds and relations that you have established between us and each of those with whom we participate, grant that we preserve them inviolate by rendering to each what is due them by virtue of these [relations], and especially to those with whom we are in community, beginning with the founders of our families, who are for us your own images and whom indeed you have established as the cause of our mortal part. Let us be trusty in procuring for everyone all the good proper to our relations with each of them, and let us never be voluntary causes of an evil, and never play the role of a destructive, awful, and unsociable being. May we, devoted to the common good of the city and the family of which we are a part, always hold this good before our own, thus following you, O gods born of the great Zeus, the great Good-Itself, entirely One-Itself, who has created and produced the All in its totality and in its parts: in its parts, each of which is the best and most beautiful possible; in its totality, one and multiple at the same time, itself a consonance with itself, of what has proceeded and perfected itself, to be even better and more beautiful. And you [gods] are ever the causes of good things, both among yourselves and for the other beings that you preside over and govern, for

the parts as for the whole, always and everywhere preferring the common good of the whole to the share of each individual.

[17] Let us fulfill your sacred rites as best as possible and especially as is appropriate to you who, as we know, lack nothing, for [these rites] are a means of molding and impressing our imagination, the faculty closest to the divine part of our being, to bring it up to what is good and divine, and at the same time to make it more submissive and obedient to our most divine part. Let us make holiness and piety consist in not neglecting anything in the rites consecrated to you, but without exceeding the measure sufficient to mold our imagination. Make us in all things as perfect as possible, and in our actions keep us safe from mistakes by these laws and other similar rules useful for life. If we fall into some fault, swiftly bring us a sufficient correction by setting before our minds a healthier reason, an exact discernment of good and bad, the surest way to cure our soul of mistakes and vice. In this way, allied with you to the extent of our strength, we will enjoy, as much as we are allowed, the greatest goods that exist in you, where envy can find no place.[555]

[18] Following you as much as possible in all our conduct, we will be associated with you by the identity of our actions. In our hymns in your honor, we will borrow the holiest images of you from the highest part of our being, and with you, and above you, we will celebrate great Zeus, in the contemplation of whom all who can share in it find the most perfect and most blessed state.

[19] O Zeus, the greatest and most eminent of the gods, O Self-Father Father, O eldest creator of everything, all-powerful and absolute king, by whom all dominion and all power over all other beings is established, directed, and governed, under you and under your supreme authority, O master most sovereign and at the same time most gentle, to whom all things are subject in all righteousness and for their own good, if these things are born and if

---

555. End of holy day supplement.

they exist, it is by you, it is also for you, who lack nothing, but who, being supremely good, wanted to make all things as good as possible.

[20] Of all good things, you are the first and the last, so that you do not seek good elsewhere than in yourself, for you are the Good. You are for the blessed the unsparing sponsor of their blessedness. You are the benefactor who lavishes on all beings the greatest goods and those most consistent with the good of the Whole.

[21] Everything is full of your glory. To thee sing all the classes of gods and regard this worship as the most excellent and most blessed of their acts. To thee also sings Poseidon, your first and most powerful child, who presides over other beings for all good things and above all others. To thee sings Hera his wife, Motherless Mother of all the gods within the heavens. Likewise sing all the other Olympian gods. To thee sing Kronos and the Titans, who rule mortals. To thee sings Helios, leader of heaven, as well as his siblings and subordinates, the planets, and the entire choir of the higher stars. To thee sings the entire earthly race of daimons, who are nearest to us, and finally to thee sing we in the last rank, the human species. Each of these [beings sings] according to their power.

[22] We too sing to you, and we beseech you to distribute to us the greatest goods possible. Be propitious and preserve us. Govern us in the midst of the All and grant us finally what you have judged is best for us and is, at the same time, fixed from all eternity.

[23] This address must be recited on each of the three days—New Moon, Second, and Third Waxing—that begin the first month, with the part concerning the month and year. On other new moons, [recite it] with only the text[556] concerning the month, omitting that about the year.

---

556. Alexandre (*Pléthon*) has ῥῆσιν, whereas MS Add. 5425 (fol. 107.6) has φᾶσιν; the meaning is about the same.

On the other holy days and also on the secular days, omit the whole about these two, namely, the month and year.[557] Finally, during the secular days, shorten the address; after this passage: "so that, as far as possible, we might regulate our mortal nature and, to the extent of our strength and by this communion, fare most happily." We must skip all the following [paragraphs 8–17] and resume at "Following you as much as possible in all our conduct," and [include] the rest up to the end of the speech.[558]

First Afternoon Address to the Gods

[24] O Lord Poseidon, of all the children of most great Zeus, you are the oldest and the most powerful. You were born of the absolutely uncreated self-father, and you yourself are not entirely uncreated, since you proceed from a cause, but you surpass all created beings by the greatness and the dignity of your power. Thus, your father has entrusted to you the authority over all things, to you who are essentially Form-Itself, Limit-Itself, Beauty-Itself, from whom all beings receive form and limit with the share of beauty that suits them. You are, after the great Zeus, the father and the oldest creator of the gods of the third class, of those enclosed within the heavens.

[25] After you comes Queen Hera, born of the same father as you, but inferior to you in dignity as in nature, for it is necessary that in the supercelestial regions where you reign there not be several equal divinities; each one must be of its kind, so you each might have similarities par excellence with the One-Itself, who has engendered you. It is her [Hera's] origin and nature to be responsible for presiding over the procession, the increase, and the infinite multiplication of things of a lower order. This is because, proceeding

---

557. In fact, there does not seem to be any "part concerning the month and year" in this address (unlike in the "Evening Address to Zeus after the Fast"). Pellissier (in Alexandre, *Pléthon*) interprets this to refer to hymns for the month and year, but this does not seem correct to me (since the text has κώλῳ, κῶλον, not ὕμνος). Perhaps Alexandre omitted this part; we will have to await a better edition.

558. The complete version of the speech takes about 20 minutes to recite and 10 minutes when shortened.

originally from you, the most perfect of things created, she created in herself the plurality of beings, and cohabiting with you in a chaste and divine manner, she became the mother of your divine children.

[26] Then, in their order come all the other Olympian gods, your brothers and sisters, the legitimate children of King Zeus; their nature varies, superior in some, inferior in others, but all have received in all things appropriate portions, which they rule under your authority.[559]

[27] Apollo [has under his law] identity; Artemis, diversity; Hephaistos, immobility and remaining the same; Dionysos, voluntary movement and attraction leading upward toward perfection; Athena, movement and impulse caused by something else and the repulsion of the superfluous; Atlas, the stars in general, his legitimate children; Tithonos, in particular, that of the planets, and Dione, that of the fixed stars; Hermes, authority over terrestrial daimons, the last class of subordinate deities; Pluto, over the most elevated part of our being, which constitutes our immortal nature; Rhea, over primitive bodies and elements in general; but in particular, Leto presides over the aether and the heat, which separates the elements; Hekate, over the air and the cold, which brings them together; Tethys, the water and moisture, which makes them fluid; Hestia, the earth and the dryness, which makes them compact. All these gods, legitimate and most powerful children of King Zeus, occupy Olympus, which is to say, the summit of the supercelestial region, the holiest of all; it is from there that, according to their attributes, they govern under your direction the mutable universe, which can be called created because it is the product of a cause and is the object of a creation, continually changing, but uncreated in time.[560]

[28] You, subject to King Zeus alone, are the guide and chorus leader of all others; it is you who marks the limit of their action and who orders

---

559. Beginning of holy day supplement.

560. End of holy day supplement.

the All. Thus, it is you whom we first address, since you attend to our most authoritative and immortal part, the creation under your direction.

[29] We honor you and thank you for the goods you have given us and that you give us. We sing hymns to you, and after you and with you we celebrate your brothers and sisters, the Olympian gods. O you divinities eternal and superior to time, for whom there is neither past nor future, but for whom everything is present and actual, receive favorably <u>and kindly</u> our afternoon address, which we offer from the lowest degree where we, <u>in time and withdrawn from eternity</u>,[561] are placed, at this hour when already the greater part of the day has passed, so that, if there is in us some suitable disposition, it is strengthened by the remembrance of you, and that we do not let perish, by the succession of days, months, and years, what is divine in us, but on the contrary, thanks to you, we preserve it imperishable and uncontaminated.

[30] O Lord Poseidon, and you, O Pluto, who watch over us, and all of you Olympians, without you we are not permitted to enjoy any good. Help us make virtue easy for ourselves, and help us in good deeds, which assure us, too, a share of happiness. All are worthy of your assistance, but above all, those who contemplate and celebrate great Zeus, to whom we turn last, the one who is for us, for you, and for all beings the dispenser of all graces, and the very first chorus leader for us as rational beings, and who grants, as far as attainable by each of us, the contemplation of his essence, and thus puts the finishing touch on all his benefits.

[31] In this address on secular days, after this passage: "but all have received in all things appropriate portions, which they rule under your authority," we must suppress the following [paragraph 27] and resume with "You,

---

561. Underlined text is from British Library MS. Add. 5424, fol. 108v.1–3 (Hladký, *Plethon*, 311) and fills a lacuna in Alexandre, *Pléthon: Traité des Lois*.

subject to King Zeus alone, are the guide and chorus leader of all others," and continue the speech up to the end.

Second Afternoon Address to the Gods

[32] O Lord Kronos, you are the first of all the Tartarean race of gods, illegitimate children of supreme Zeus; that is why you have received authority over them. With Helios, leader of our heavens, you have been responsible for the creation of mortal nature. Aphrodite, your companion, presides over the transmission of perpetuity into mortal things by succession. Under you are all those appointed to govern this nature according to the various portions they have received:[562]

[33] Pan reigns over the whole class of non-rational animals, Demeter reigns over plants, and all the others have received different parts, some greater some lesser, of mortal things. Among them is Kore, the god who directs our mortal part. Pluto, who presides over our immortal nature, has carried off this goddess as his wife; thus, an Olympian god, in love with a Tartarean goddess, establishes a link between Tartarus and Olympus by the decrees of Father Zeus.[563]

[34] And you, O Lord Helios [Sun], [born] of both great Zeus by the divine intellect that is in you, and also of Poseidon by the nature of your soul and body, his oldest and most powerful son, you are the common boundary between the supercelestial gods and those within the heavens, and you have been established by your father Poseidon as leader of this entire heaven. You and your six siblings and attendants—Selene [Moon], Eôsphoros [Venus], Stilbôn [Mercury], Phainôn [Saturn], Phaëthôn [Jupiter], and Pyroeis [Mars]—travel around, and you all, together with Kronos and the other Titans, perfect the whole of mortal nature. It is you [Helios] who, in the highest regions of our heavens, conduct this magnificent and numerous choir of celestial bodies. Under you also comes

---

562. Beginning of holy day supplement.

563. End of holy day supplement.

the earthly race of daimons appointed to serve the other gods. Finally you preside over our immortal part, and with the help of Kronos and the Titans under him, you form our mortal part, and you preserve us, as much as fated each of us. This is why, after Poseidon and the other Olympian gods, we also worship you and thank you for the goods we have from you.

[35] We pray to those of you who lead us to guide our immortal nature toward the good and beautiful, and so far as possible to render our mortal nature tractable and useful. <u>Grant, O gods, now that we have spent most of the day fulfilling our duties, to take the nourishment necessary for our mortal body with virtue—that is, having obtained it rightly—and with good will for those preparing it and equally for our dinner companions, and with temperance</u>[564] <u>and useful for our health, and further, with purity and vigorously.</u>[565] Grant us to use the rest of this day and our life in the best and most beautiful way in our power. Help us at last to contemplate and to sing hymns to King Zeus whenever necessary, but especially at this moment, so that we celebrate him as worthily as possible.

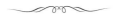

[36] In this address, on secular days, after this passage, "according to the various portions they have received," we must suppress the following [paragraph 33] and resume at "And you, O Lord Helios"; then continue up to "You and your six siblings and attendants." Take out the names of the six planets [underlined text in paragraph 34] and go to "travel around, and you all, together with Kronos and the other Titans"; continue to the end of the prayer. In days of fasting, nothing must be cut out; we will only

---

564. Sophocles, *Greek Lexicon of the Roman and Byzantine Periods*, s.v. "ἐγκρατής."

565. Sophocles, *Greek Lexicon of the Roman and Byzantine Periods*, s.v. "ἀθρύπτως." Maybe "unpretentiously" (cf. Pellissier translation in Alexandre, *Pléthon*, 167). This sentence is omitted on days of fasting because the meal comes later.

delete the passage relating to the meal [underlined text in paragraph 35], since it must take place only later.

Third Afternoon Address to the Gods: The Most Important of All, Addressed to King Zeus

[37] Being-Itself, One-Itself, Good-Itself, O Zeus, you alone owe existence to no other cause than yourself, you alone are a really essential essence and an absolute unity, not a multiple unity. For neither could several similarly uncreated beings come together in one whole, since they would need another being more powerful to assemble them, nor could one uncreated being merge with others proceeding from himself, because there would be no common nature between this self-existent principle and the beings who, having proceeded from him, would be distinguished from him by this difference. But only you are the unity; you are always and in everything identical to yourself. You are the Good, you are supremely good in yourself, and you have an immeasurable superiority over all other beings, which are [descended] from you and perfected by you. O Father of Fathers, Self-Father, Demiurge of Demiurges, Uncreated Creator, King of Kings, who rules over all rulers, you alone are absolute master and independent, nothing can be against you, but, commanding all of them, great or small, you fix for each their state and dispense their laws; you direct and set them straight by your most upright and unchanging will. O Master, greatest and highest Master, at the same time most gentle of all masters and lords, to you everything, from the first to the last of beings, is connected as to its original principle to serve in a just servitude, which is the supreme good for them, for it is through you that they were created and exist, by you and for you who had no need of them, but who wanted to satisfy your supreme goodness by producing all the benefits possible to the most perfect degree possible.[566]

---

566. Beginning of holy day supplement.

[38] That is why we celebrate and praise you, all of us, though our lot is the last degree of rational nature; we honor you and offer you the most pious homage in our power, for our every [religious] exercise concerning you is the most blessed of acts. The intelligent and reasonable nature of the gods celebrates you much better than we do.

[39] For indeed, O God pre-eternal and in all ways uncreated, in the supreme goodness of your judgment, you have not disdained to be both father and creator of generated gods, some by yourself without a mother, the others through the oldest of those same gods produced from you. For you are the author of the class of beings closest to your nature, both immutable and eternal, and, without the concurrence of infinitely divisible matter, by yourself you are the creator who produced beings existing in themselves, gods more than others like you, the supercelestial gods. None of them is equal to the other, but some are relatively inferior to others, so that each of them, being one in individuality, is thus like you as much as possible, but collectively they form a sufficient number and a great and perfect system, the entire supercelestial order, so that each in their individuality might be altogether one in common.

[40] You divided these gods into two families; one is made up of your legitimate children, the Olympian race of gods; the other is the Tartarean race of Titans, your illegitimate children, who share an origin from you, but are limited to a lesser power and dignity. Kronos is the oldest of the Titans and their leader.

[41] The oldest and most powerful of the Olympians, and at the same time of all [the gods], is the great Poseidon, whom you made the most perfect image of yourself possible, the limit of perfection in the entire generation of beings. To make him even more like yourself, you have given him sovereignty and leadership over everything, and moreover the faculty of producing and creating all beings enclosed in the heavens, but by summoning some of his siblings for each of these [creations]. Then, to organize the heavens for you and by your example, and plan to perfect it to contain the

most beautiful things, he begets a third nature of gods composed of body and soul in order to more closely preserve and order things.

[42] Now, as [Poseidon] begets them, taking as his model his own and the entire essence around him, entirely separate from matter, he also creates forms for our heavens and makes it out of them, but forms in no way separated [from matter]. On the contrary, he unites them to the matter provided by Hera, his sister and his wife, so that they are images and modeled on those [higher forms]. He forms a double class. One is entirely inseparable from matter, depending on it; they are all the non-rational species. The other one is in no way not dependent on [matter], but on the contrary keeps it dependent, and, although not actually separated, it is potentially separated and thereby more akin to your supercelestial nature; it is the rational soul.

[43] This soul is divided into three species. The first, which [Poseidon] made with scientific understanding of everything, are his legitimate offspring, the race of celestial gods, the stars. The second, which does not have scientific understanding of everything, but has right opinion of everything, are his illegitimate [children], the terrestrial race of daimons, the last race of gods, whom [the daimons] must assist. The third does not have a correct opinion of all things, but is fallible and is not the most perfect of his productions; it is our human soul, which comes immediately after the race of daimons.

[44] As for the other, non-rational substance, [Poseidon] made four principal species of body: fire, air, water, and earth. Choosing the most beautiful of these, the one which contains the least matter with the greatest volume, namely fire, he made vehicles for souls: of its bright and fiery part [he made the vehicle of the souls] of stars, and of the invisible and aethereal part, [the vehicles] of the souls of daimons and of us. Thus, always uniting a soul to a body, he has composed the three lower classes of immortal and rational living beings. However, he employed his siblings, the other Olympian gods, as assistants, each taking their part in the generation and

creation of the immortals here [within our heavens], namely of the three living species and of the four principal [species] of bodies.

[45] Of the stars, [Poseidon] made one class numerous, motionless, busy contemplating beings and glorifying you. But he also perfected seven planets, each corresponding to its particular eternal Idea. First, he united each of them to its own Idea or Intelligence, and then he combined the eternal intelligence, a soul, and a body into a certain triple nature, which serves as an association and a bond between the supercelestial order and the heavens, an admirable relation established by his all-powerful laws. He made the most beautiful and the best of them, Helios, the supreme limit of the perfection of the powers in the heavens. He united him to the most powerful of the participated intelligences, and charged him with the government of the whole heaven, because the All must also have its share of mortal nature, so that it is in fact entirely complete.

[46] You entrust the creation of these things to Helios and also to Kronos, the eldest of your illegitimate children. Both, charged with this mission, produce animals and plants of all kinds, and everything akin to them, each helped in this [creation] by his siblings, the one by the Tartareans, the other by the rest of the planets. These latter, in their movement and revolution, now approaching, now withdrawing, rearranging themselves, thus make mortal creatures, for the other creators of these [mortal creatures], the Tartareans, who abide, are incapable of accomplishing their creation without the partnership of [the planets]. They receive our souls, which Poseidon has made immortal but not quite pure, and they attach them, during the time prescribed for each of us, to a mortal nature and later free them from this place. In this way they construct from these substances, according to your laws and under the orders of their leader Poseidon, a bond between the two parts of the universe, the immortal and the mortal.

[47] Thus, all of the beings created by you are divided into three natural orders: the first, immutable and eternal, of which you yourself are the

creator; the second, everlasting, but mutable and temporal, over the generation of which presides Poseidon, the most powerful of your children; the last finally, inferior and entirely mortal, whose creation Helios and Kronos together administer. You have united these [three] classes, the first to the middle by the system formed by Helios and the other planets, and the middle to the last through the establishment of us and our affairs. You have made a unified and perfect whole holding the fairest things, an immortal generation, neither earlier nonexistent and later suddenly returning whence it came, nor sometime to be destroyed again. At the same time you perpetually preserve an immutable form, for neither could you not do what is most righteous, nor again not remove what is worse than the fairest possible.

[48] In this All you have given to all rational nature a sublime privilege: the faculty of knowing you and contemplating you, which you have granted to us in the last rank [of nature]. So, in concert with all the races of gods, we celebrate you as we are able and under the direction of great Poseidon, who also presides over this act and all that is beautiful.[567]

[49] You are truly great and immensely great, you who, being the extreme and supreme limit of all dignity, dispense to each of the other gods and of all kinds, the share of dignity that is rightly theirs and best befits the whole. Thus, you made us a boundary and bond between the ordained parts, the immortal and the mortal.

[50] This is the place you have chosen to assign to us in the All, and for us, as for the gods, you made happiness consist in the good, giving more to some, less to others, always in view of the general harmony. At the same time, you have made it possible for wrongdoers to correct themselves, easier for some, more painful for others. Thus, you have disposed all for the greater good of each being and for the greater benefit of the entire Whole, delivering all things to an eternal, inevitable fate, and fulfilling all

---

567. End of holy day supplement.

this by the gods to whom you have entrusted this care. So be propitious, save us, and lead us with this All, in the manner you have judged is best concerning us and fixed from all eternity.

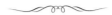

[51] In this address, in the secular days, after this passage "by producing all the benefits possible to the most perfect degree possible," we must suppress the following [paragraphs 38–48] and resume with "You are truly great and immensely great," and continue the speech up to the end. [568]

Evening Address to the Gods

[52] O King Zeus, we thank you, first and especially you, for all the benefits we ever have possessed, that we now possess, or that we ever will possess. Being the Good yourself, there is no other good beside you, for you are at once the first and the last for all beings, in a word, the supreme principle of all good things. After [Zeus], it is you, O Poseidon, and all of you gods, who transmit to us the benefits from Zeus; it is you that we thank always and on every occasion for all your gifts,[569] but especially for the following, the greatest and the most perfect of those we enjoy or can enjoy.

[53] First, you have placed us in the middle, between your immortal nature and mortal nature, and you have honored us as the common boundary and bond of these two parts. You have raised us above all that is mortal by our kinship with you, by participating in your immortality and by this glorious blessedness, which resembles yours, but in a much lesser degree. Again you grant us to be involved with you in other ways, first of all by our knowledge of you, then by grasping the remaining beings with

---

568. This paragraph, which is omitted in Alexandre, *Pléthon*, is found in British Library Manuscript Add. 5424, fol. 114v.2–7 (Hladký, *Plethon*, 311–12).

569. Beginning of holy day supplement.

our reason, sharing this ability especially characteristic of you, which you have deigned to share with us, and finally, by our knowledge of ourselves, for by this faculty, which you have given us, we are close to you, who especially know yourselves. That is how you have arranged that the best in us be appointed to command all the rest of us.

[54] Besides, you granted that the faculty that comes first after the most superior in us and dominates all the rest, the imagination, be useful to us for rituals, forming and modeling itself as much as possible on what is best in our superior part, to be more obedient to reason and enjoy the good and divine nature.

[55] You have also granted us, through our goodness toward our family and toward the whole human race, to imitate you, who are always the cause of good and never of evil. You have granted that we associate in this civic community with one another, which brings us closer to you, assimilating us as much as possible to you, who are children of the same father, King Zeus, who is Unity-Itself, and you have united and formed the closest possible community. In addition, you grant that the part of our soul that leans on opinion be ruled by the best part of us, treating as unworthy what is vain according to it, but esteeming in no way slightly what alone is useful to it and in some way advantageous for virtue.

[56] Thus, you did not allow us to be entirely subject to our mortal part, but have granted us, if we understand what is better, the power to govern ourselves by our superior part, enjoying pleasures when permitted by it, without enjoying them to the point of license, but by imposing upon them order and a proper bound, taking as a measure of [the enjoyment of] these strong needs the reasonable needs of the mortal part, so as to be free, even while remaining here [on earth], and not to regard as terrible what can happen to this mortal part contrary to our intention, when it is your [decision] to remove us from participation [in your happiness], either through the daimons, the subordinate class to you, their masters, or through [the fault of] our family and this human race, either for our

purification and care in the first case, or in the other by those exhibiting reckless ignorance about the soul. Often you even grant that we choose, much more, to seek what must hurt this lower part, to the point of sacrificing it sometimes entirely for the sake of the good and for the utility of our superior part, so much have you granted our immortal part to govern the mortal. Such are the great and good gifts with which you have favored us, raising and embellishing our stronger and sovereign part by the reasonings with which you inspire us on every occasion.

[57] You have given faculties to our mortal part so as to serve our immortal part, to profit from its assistance, and to taste certain pleasures that are proper to us, blameless and without danger for our superior part. Among not a few others, eyes endowed with sight are the most useful of our senses for the observation of many other things and principally for inspection of those celestial bodies by which we learn so many beautiful things, especially the numbering of the days, months, and years, by which we can measure our life so we conduct our affairs with regularity and good order. Likewise, the ears were furnished for hearing, and the mouth for the voice; they are indispensable organs for associating with others through what we each think in our soul, so that our bodies do not completely prevent a commonality of thought. [You have also given us] the sense of smell in our nostrils to enjoy the innocent pleasure of fragrances and to distinguish healthy food from harmful, often from afar even before trying it, according to whether it is pleasant or unpleasant. [You have placed] the sense of taste in our mouth to judge the flavors that are healthy for our nourishment, often with pleasure, as soon as we touch them. All in all, you have granted these faculties by which we are able to choose the nourishment of our life, a necessary offering to our mortal part, indispensable food for replenishing the matter that, ever changing, comes and goes so long as it is granted us to be preserved by you.

[58] It is still in view of this mortal and perishable part that you have granted intercourse of our male and female kinds, so persuasive by pleasure. By this

institution the whole of the species is always maintained in the same state by an uninterrupted succession of births, each filling the place of one leaving since a fixed number of souls is allowed, and at the prescribed periods of time you assign them a community of bodies for the same, so you do not lack their service.

[59] In addition, you have granted us to compensate for the insufficiency and weakness of our physical part by the techniques of the arts, varied according to their object, and for that you have given us hands, instruments suitable for preparing so many works of all kinds. You have granted us to use the strength and the particular aptitudes of non-rational animals for our purposes, and to appropriate to ourselves the advantages of their nature.

[60] For all these goods, it is to you, O King Zeus, first and foremost, that we must give thanks, as to the first and most powerful of our benefactors. After him, it is you, O gods, through whom these goods come from Zeus, and we have the most proper and deepest gratitude toward you, by whom, without any obligation and without any hope of return, we have been granted and we are still granted so many benefits, and to you who, good in yourselves, so want to spread the greatest abundance of goods, to share them as much as possible. Thanks be to you for all your benefactions in general,[570] but especially first and foremost for those by which you bring our soul to the rationality of virtue and goodness. For these are the most excellent of all goods, and you bestow them on the sovereign part of our being; there are none of them that do not come to us from you or through you. For it is you, the first and second [ranks], who [receive] the goods emanating from Zeus, some of them eternal in duration, the others not eternal but everlasting, and all alike unmixed with evil.

[61] After you and by you, we in our turn receive [the benefits], but [they are] intermittent and no longer perfectly continuous, yet still everlasting

---

570. End of holy day supplement.

because of their perpetual renewal and the immortality of our soul. For you give all your solicitude to this intelligence, our most divine attribute, which binds us to you by a kind of kinship; you are constantly pushing us toward goodness and we are heading in the right way, knowing that we too will fare especially happily and blessedly as long as we are able to follow you and reach your goodness.

[62] But when, yielding to the association with our mortal part, we move away from you, when we depart from you and don't think what we should, we fall, as a result of this abandonment, into faults, into error, and into a state both wicked and worthless. You, then, raise us up and straighten us, either immediately by the inspiration of better thinking, or by imposing various judgments if our bad dispositions prevent us from yielding at once to the wisdom that inspires us. In every way you bring us back again to goodness, either while we remain here or depart thither. When you happen to punish us, it is to correct our mistakes and to heal vices, of which it is impossible for us not to have a share because of our mortal part, which you have associated with the other [immortal part], thus mixing in us these disparate parts, mortal and immortal, first of all because it seemed necessary to you for the universal harmony, then because in this general society of beings you destined us to roles that are certainly not useless or despicable. We give thanks to you, who punish only for the sake of kindness and our good, and who have created us immortal in our stronger and most sovereign part and provided us everlasting [blessings] by your perpetual renewal.

[63] Hear, O gods, our nightly evening prayer, which we send you. If in this day we have failed and transgressed your laws, or in our past life if we have failed and have not yet corrected our mistakes, grant us deliverance and uprightness again. Prepare us with better judgment for good deeds, and give us reason to distinguish good from bad decisions, and cleanse us of the evils attached to us. Grant the growth of the good on each occasion, but with both prompt deliverance and correction of past and present mistakes until one day, after having fulfilled the time that you have

assigned to this life, we may come to that other, happier, and more divine life, in which we shall be delivered from the troubles of our mortal body. For if you have bound us to mortality for the sake of the community of the Whole, you have also assigned us a time after which our divine part returns, and each time its turn comes, it will enter into a life more divine and more in conformity with its nature. It will go to celebrate with those who have departed before, will engage more intimately with those of you whose nature is closer to ours, will learn from them what it is necessary [to know], and will enjoy in all ways a better and more beautiful lot, so that it is not always filled with the miseries of this mortal [body], but that it also might have a much better and more divine life, surpassing the other [life] in all respects and especially by its much longer duration.

[64] Since you produce the better from the worse, so far as possible, you are disposed to impart longer lasting [goods], and goods altogether much more than the evils, especially when you grant that we will understand much clearer and better everything that concerns us, to remember to the greatest extent each past life, either here or there, and to connect them together in our memory, those [memories] seized now by a profound forgetting because we have, during the first age of this life, crossed the River Lethe, and during the rest of the time we remain in the gloom of our mortal nature. Moreover, we will then have a clearer foreknowledge of the future, of which now we have but a scant image, which comes to us from the daimons, the race closest to ours, while sleep rids us of the tumult of sensations, or which even is revealed sometimes to those receiving a vision by a certain more divine extension of their thinking.

[65] And you, O blessed heroes, whose nature surpassing ours is closest to divinity, you who, during your life among us here, are for us in common the sources of the great benefits that he [Zeus] sends us through the gods, hail to you! And you, our ancestors, our parents, who are images of divinity for us and the immediate origins of our mortal nature, and you also, housemates and comrades, clansmen and kin, you who, older or younger,

have arrived first in that more divine and blessed life, and you too, companions and friends, and you, our fellow citizens, especially you who have presided over our common good, and especially you who have lost your life for the freedom of the community with the same belief, either for the preservation of their existence and well-being, or for the righting of disturbances that are not right: hail to all of you! And when the fate from the gods will call us, as they have called you, give us a gracious and kind welcome when we come as friends among our friends.

[66] And all of you daimons, especially those of you who are nearest us, and above you, Pluto, our protector, be kind to us, attend us here below so that we become good and honest, and when we go thither at the appointed time, welcome us kindly. All of you, O gods who watch over us, care for us now and always, so we might fare well and honorably, and [this night] grant us the rest necessary for our mortal part in a pure bed, free from any foul acts. Inspire us kindly while we sleep, guide our soul in a dream to your company, and awaken us whole and free of evil, willing to walk in this straight way that will lead us to the good and to all that pleases you. Grant us to do all that is good, and to sing your praises properly, and with you and in addition to you to celebrate great Zeus.

[67] O Self-Father Zeus, father and immediate origin of all motherless gods, the supercelestial gods, O eldest demiurge of all that exists, even by mediate procession, O truly supreme and sovereign King, who alone and independently hold all the powers under your control, O absolute master of all things, you are truly great and immensely great, all things are full of your power and magnificence. Be propitious, preserve us, govern us with the All according to what you have judged is best for us and what is also fated from all eternity.

[68] In this address, on secular days, after this passage: "but especially for these, the greatest and the most perfect of those we enjoy or can enjoy," we must suppress the following [remainder of paragraph 52] and resume with "but especially first and foremost for those by which you bring our soul to the rationality of virtue and goodness" [in paragraph 60], and continue the rest up to the end.[571]

Evening Address to Zeus after the Fast[572]

[69] O King Zeus, you are One-Itself and entirely uncreated, supremely One and in no way different from yourself. You are the first and last of good things, and in no way different from the Good, but you yourself create the Good and the All, produced by a cause from yourself, which is always whole and neither comes to be in time, nor ever will end. You organized a unity out of the many with agreements among them. Furnishing yourself with the best of beings, you made them one in the best way, preserved by you through all eternity. You are perfect in your highest singularity and possess nothing in yourself better or worse than anything else, indeed nothing entirely different, but you yourself completed and perfected this All by filling it with all kinds of Ideas, some higher, some lower, and entirely whole.

[70] You begat great Poseidon in the All, the most perfect of your creations and the most similar to you, and you entrusted him with leadership of everything, nor will he abandon providence for the very uttermost of beings. You bestowed power on him and a similar nature on the others, and granted him to guide this power and moreover to produce whatever you might need from them; in all respects, he manages their tasks well. You set up the entire intellectual and supercelestial order by yourself, and filled it with all kinds of Ideas indivisible in their essence, all of them

---

571. This paragraph, which is omitted in Alexandre, *Pléthon*, is found in British Library Manuscript Add. 5424, fol. 118v.21–119.3 (Hladký, *Plethon*, 312).

572. This address, which is missing from Alexandre, *Pléthon*, is found in British Library Manuscript Add. 5424, fol. 119.3–123.17 (Hladký, *Plethon*, pp. 312–18).

immutable minds, all these beings together and actually in one mental act of mutual contemplation, in a second divine order of all these gods. You united them under their chorus leader Poseidon into one, most beautiful cosmos, and gave it eternity as its measure of life; you put in it nothing passing, but all things existing forever and remaining as they are.

[71] Also by your arrangement these heavens are organized under great Poseidon and your other creations, the gods, as an image of your intellectual and eternal order, and these [heavens] are composed now of mortal and immortal things, so that the All might be completed perfectly for you, containing all things that it was possible to have in creation. Moreover the entire, endless time conferred a measure of life on it and became your image of eternity. It is already past or yet about to be; it does not exist and exists not yet; it is always in a present moment, which is always becoming one thing after another; it divides past and future time.

[72] In it great Poseidon, obeying you, placed the divine race of stars, combining the best form of soul with befitting bodies. Among them he placed great Helios, joining him with the divine mind of those produced in your eternal order, in order to bind in it two substances, eternal and temporal. And he appointed [Helios], the strongest of the gods in the heavens, to be their leader and the creator of all mortal nature with Kronos, its especial archon and ruler. He also gave [Helios] six other helpers for these tasks and provided them a similar constitution, but in no way his equal.

[73] Moreover [Helios] does not cease, through day and night, from measuring time for us by his unending cycles, completing each of them together with the revolutions of the entire aether. During the day, light is provided fully and beautifully for the eyes of those above the earth, and during the night for those below the earth, each making way for the other, and by these increases and decreases there is equality in the cosmos, the two depriving and bestowing on each other in turn. The creator of these things organized the month by each meeting of Helios and Selene, who is second to Helios in power. She takes a secondary light from him, and

she appears to us each night, as many times and whenever she will come. [Helios] kindly provides the year by his cycles around the zodiac and the ecliptic and [provides] the hours by his coming and going.

[74] Your eldest child Poseidon, guiding the creation of these heavens by your laws, placed in it the race of daimons, the last race of gods, standing midway between the stars and us. For after these races of gods, by your providence Poseidon himself placed our souls within the vault of heaven as a necessary boundary between, on one hand, everlasting things and the always perpetual goods of the races of gods and, on the other, those entirely subject to death. [Our souls] are also everlasting and enjoy goods resembling those of the gods, not perpetually, but intermittently, as they are lost and restored again, for you needed such a species in the All so that it might be finished complete and sufficiently perfect. Moreover, it is one, each part joined to another, not full of various separated kinds, but gradually changing little by little, each sharing with those in between them. Such are our souls, assembled by you, which became entangled with these mortal bodies. The separated mortal and immortal parts were brought together in us and bound together into one, so that these two natures would not be separated, but there would be some mixture of the mortal with the immortal things nearest them, through a discontinuous participation in good things, at some times clothed in a body and at other times set free and living by itself, and thus always withdrawing by turns through the whole of unlimited time, so that there is only such a conjunction as there is.

[75] By means of Poseidon and your blessed children, the gods, you have placed us here in the All, wherefore let us be pleased with our position, and let us be completely grateful to you for such as we are and for every other benefit of any kind that you have given us or might give us from time to time, and most especially for the share of divinity that you have given us. Since we make mistakes because of this position, in each

instance you have assigned a correction and actions to raise us up and bring us close to divinity.

[76] And now, on this day when we celebrate again the boundary between the departing month and the new one arising, when the two gods draw together, <u>and in addition [the boundary] between the completed year and that beginning, precisely when Helios turns during the winter</u>[573] and during this day of Selene's conjunction, when she grows again from being smallest, on this very day they have made a certain examination of us and our lives and judged the mistakes we have made, how we have fallen short, and the wrongs we have committed. From these we beg our deliverance and correction.[574]

[77] Having accepted our evening prayer, our kneeling, and our all-day fast, which we have established for ourselves as symbols of our love for you and as a service that is especially proper, but also most useful for those serving, release us from the evils that come to us through thoughtlessness, and in their place grant us what is good, making present goods better and granting those that we lack but are proper.

[78] You have offered us correct thought and judgment about what is good and bad according to the gods, to whom such things have been entrusted. You are indeed the mightiest purifier of faults and bad souls and the mightiest provider and guardian of what is good. So grant us, with the circuit of days, months, and years, the growth of the good each time, but also prompt deliverance from past and present wrongs, and our restoration to what is proper.

[79] We know happiness and blessedness are granted us through virtue and goodness, until one day, after having fulfilled the time that you have assigned to this life, we may come to that other, happier, and more divine life, in which we shall be delivered from the troubles of our mortal body.

---

573. Underlined text is omitted except in the last month of the year.

574. This paragraph is omitted except on Old-and-New-Moon.

For if you have bound us to mortality for the sake of the community of the Whole, you have also assigned us a time after which our divine part returns, and each time its turn comes, it will enter into a life more divine and more in conformity with its nature. [Our superior part] will celebrate with those of its kind who have already departed, whom we ourselves remember now and hereafter, and will engage more intimately with the gods closer to us, will learn from them what it is necessary [to know], and will enjoy an entirely better and more beautiful lot, so that it is not always filled with the miseries of this mortal [body], but also that it might have a much better and more divine life, surpassing the other in all respects and especially by its much longer duration; seeing that you produce the better from the worse, so far as possible, you are disposed to impart longer lasting [goods], and goods altogether much more than evils.

[80] But, O Master, grant us when we arrive there, O Master of Everything, to mingle with the gracious and kindly heroes there, whose nature above ours is closest to divinity, those who, during their lives among us here, were for all of us in common the sources of the great goods you sent to our ancestors and parents, who are images of you and the gods, and also to our housemates, comrades, kin whomsoever, who happen to have arrived in that more divine and blessed life, and also to companions, all fellow citizens, and others presiding over our common good, and especially to those who lost their life for the freedom of the community with the same belief, either for the preservation of their existence and well-being, or for the righting of disturbances that are not right; you have united us with the good and honest among them, and granted us to celebrate and to encompass everything under our protector, Pluto, and the other gods in charge of us. The most beautiful and most divine of the feasts and festivals that there are is the manifest contemplation of you, the eldest cause of all.

[81] In the present, may you grant us to be released from erring, first purified of guilt and acceptable to you and your gods, which is a sacred service that you perform, and afterward may you bring about that we eat our modest meal and go to sleep in an undefiled bed, which is indispensable for the preservation of our mortal [body] for the duration you have assigned it. And may you send us dreams from [the gods] for the sake of meetings with us, guiding our souls, and raising us out of evils without suffering, to celebrate your holy festivals in a holy way, and to pass through <u>this month and year at which we have arrived and</u>[575] our remaining life as blamelessly as possible and thereby especially dear to you, and also to accomplish other good things, both honoring the gods, your children, as is fitting, through whom, so far as it concerns you, human affairs are arranged, and then celebrating you as first principle of everything.

[82] O Self-Father Zeus, father and immediate origin of all motherless, supercelestial gods, O eldest demiurge of all things, both directly and by means of those born of you, O truly supreme and sovereign king, who alone and independently hold all the powers under your control, O absolute master of all things, you are great, truly great, and immensely great. All things are full of your power and magnificence. Be propitious, preserve us, govern us with the All according to what you have judged is best for us and what is also fated from all eternity.

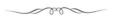

[83] Go through this address on all Old-and-New [Moons] and fasts, and, except in the first month, remove the part about the beginning and end of the year [underlined text in paragraph 76] and in addition this part: "this month and year at which we have arrived and" [underlined text in paragraph 81], the text about the year. On the two fasts of the last month

---

575. Underlined text is omitted except during the last month.

that are before Old-and-New, remove the whole earlier part concerning the boundary day of the two months [paragraph 76].

[84] Let these addresses to the gods be sufficient. Of the afternoon ones, the most authoritative is the third, which is to King Zeus, after which is this Evening Address to Zeus after the Fast; [then] either the morning [one], or the daily evening, or the first of the afternoon; there after the second afternoon.

Chapter 35: Hymns to the gods

[1]   *Hymn 1: First Perennial Hymn, to Zeus*

Zeus, Father, thou Self-Father, eldest demiurge,

All-Father, King, the highest and most great of all,

all-powerful, the One-Itself, the Good-Itself,

and Being-Itself, who made all things since endless time,

the greatest by thyself, the rest by other gods,

all with perfection, to the uttermost degree;

be kind, protect us, lead us, as in everything,

by thine illustrious children. You entrust them with

our destinies, fulfilled as just they ought to be.

[2]   *Hymn 2: Second Perennial Hymn, to the Gods*

O noble children of All-Father, Being, Zên,

you govern us with justice under his command;

so let us never fail to have you as our guides,

obeying laws that are both right and dear to you,

as best we can, the only laws to rule us well.

And you, O gods, direct us, straightening our minds,

which you have made with nature similar to yours.

Moreover, grant to us good order in our lives,

but most of all, with you to celebrate great Zeus.

[3] ***Hymn 3: First Monthly Hymn, to Zeus***

Great Zeus, Self-Father, Ianos, the Progenitor

of all receiving being and receiving birth,

in truth performed not one of these things thoughtlessly;

but just as he exists, so do the other gods,

whom, never idle, he made sim'lar to himself;

and never less than is his pow'r, he does it well

and properly, because his nature is the Good.

O Zeus, we hail thee, guarding all and reigning; hail,

most blessed; hail thee, gracious giver of all goods.

[4] ***Hymn 4: Second Monthly Hymn, to Poseidon***

O Lord Poseidon, thou art firstborn son of Zeus,

in splendor and in strength surpassing everything,

for everything received its origin from Zeus.

With might you make and master, second to your sire,

preeminent, as great as is infinity,

because of all that is, alone is he unborn,

and by thy sire's command was granted thee to make

the widespread heavens where we have been placed by thee.

O Father, always kind and gentle be to us.

[5] ***Hymn 5: Third Monthly Hymn, to Hera***

August One, goddess Hera, daughter of great Zeus,

O thou whose husband is Poseidon, thou who art

most fair, the mother of the gods within the sky,

the cause of matter, and the seat here for the forms,

dispenser of all powers, and among the rest

what leads us into excellence and all that's fair;

you bring together laws for everything from which

the multitude eternally comes forth; you grant

us to live well; to virtue bring us graciously.

[6]   *Hymn 6: Fourth Monthly Hymn, to the Gods of Olympus*

Poseidon, King, the best and greatest child of Zeus,

who also governs all things from thy father born,

and Hera, holy wife of him and noble queen,

Apollo, Artemis, Hephaistos, Bacchus, and

Athena too, you seven gods are mightier

than all the rest save him, the mightiest on high.

You other gods who dwell upon Olympus peak,

ancestors[576] of immortal souls, including us,

be ye propitious and be gracious unto us.

[7]   *Hymn 7: Fifth Monthly Hymn, to Apollo*

O Lord Apollo, chief and leader of each kind's

identity, who guides all things to unity,

who doth subject the One itself, a multitude

and a polyphony, beneath one harmony,

from concord you impart both prudence to our souls,

and justice, qualities most beautiful to have,

combined with beauty in our bodies, joined with health.

---

576. The word πατέρας, literally "fathers," can also mean ancestors or even creators, as appropriate here
for goddesses as well as gods.

Moreover always give our souls, O Lord, desire

for things divine and beautiful. O hail, Paián!

[8]   *Hymn 8: Sixth Monthly Hymn, to Artemis*

O Lady Artemis, who rules and who protects

the form of difference, you receive as one the Whole,

and then up to the limit you divide each form

in many forms, from forms to individuals,

and from the whole to limbs and joints, and separate

our souls from what is worse in us, and give them strength

and self-control, and to our bodies might and health.

But grant to us, O Queen, to flee from shameful things

and straighten up our lives in every circumstance.

[9]   *Hymn 9: Seventh Monthly Hymn, to the Gods of Heaven*

O lord of heaven, Helios, be kind to us,

and you, Seléne, holy mistress, be thou kind,

and Phôsphoros [Venus] and Stílbôn [Mercury], of the shining Sun

attendants always, Phaínôn [Saturn] and Phaéthôn [Jupiter] too,

and you Pyróeis [Mars]; all are subject to the Sun,

your lord, whom you assist in his concern for us

that we not suffer need, and so we sing to you

this hymn, to you who are our splendid guardians,

and to the stars sent forth by providence divine.

[10] *Hymn 10: Eighth Monthly Hymn, to Athena*

Athena, Lady, you who rule and govern form,

the form that is to matter always bound, and you

who are creator after the wide-ruling one,

Poseidon, who before you holds all form, and you

who are the source of ev'ry motion caused by force,

when anything superfluous becomes attached,

you drive off each and ev'ry one. Whenever we

act foolishly in error, then draw near to us,

O goddess, rouse our hearts to duty with good sense.

[11] ***Hymn 11: Ninth Monthly Hymn, to Dionysos***

O Bacchus, Father, maker of all rational souls,

of the celestials, and of daimons, and of us,

who after great Poseidon art the next in this,

you cause the motion drawing us by love to good,

ascending thereby to a more desired state.

Grant thou whenever we depart each time the good,

from action that is holier, through mindless thought,

to lead us quickly, wisely to the good again,

nor let us be so mindless of the good too long.

[12] ***Hymn 12: Tenth Monthly Hymn, to the Titans***

Come, let us sing to mortal nature's demiurge,

to Kronos, Lord, the son of Zeus, and eldest one

of Zeus's children who are illegitimate,

Tartarean Titans, whom along with him we sing,

who are in all ways good, from evil far apart,

although creating what is mortal and short-lived.

We sing of Aphrodite, Kronos's sacred wife,

and Pan the lord of beasts, Deméter of the plants,

and Kore of our mortal nature, and the rest.

[13] ***Hymn 13: Eleventh Monthly Hymn, to Hephaistos***

> Hephaistos, Lord, you rule the supercelestial gods,
>
> together the Olympians and Tartareans;
>
> you govern with Poseidon, the wide-ruling one,
>
> and also give to each their station and their seat;
>
> and you're the cause of rest in this and everything,
>
> and also you provide them everlastingness,
>
> yourself, or with Poseidon, by his father's will.
>
> Watch over us, and grant especially to us,
>
> who're born, to firmly stand in noble deeds each time.

[14] ***Hymn 14: Twelfth Monthly Hymn, to the Daimons***

> We sing to holy daimons, who are near to us,
>
> to them and also to the other deathless ones,
>
> for they, who serve quite well the gods who're more divine,
>
> bestow the many benefits on our behalf,
>
> disperse them all, which they receive from Zeus himself,
>
> and which descend to us through all the other gods.
>
> And thus they save us, with some purifying us,
>
> and others elevating or protecting us,
>
> and easily straightening our minds. And so, be kind.

[15] ***Hymn 15: Thirteenth Monthly Hymn, to All the Gods***

> O Zeus, supreme, who art the greatest of all gods,
>
> the eldest Demiurge, and the All-Father too,
>
> and all you other gods, who are Olympians,
>
> or are Tartareans, or Celestials, or of Earth;

if we commit some bad mistake or reckless deed,

allow us, purified, to near your blameless state,

and let our lives be blessed; especially you, O Zeus,

thou art, above all, the most powerful of all,

thou art together both the first and final Good.

[16] ***Hymn 16: First Sacred Hymn, to Zeus***

King Zeus, entirely unborn and Being-Itself,

All-Father, All-Preserver, who all things conceals

within himself, in unity and not apart,

distributes each of them, completely one and whole,

accomplishing the task as fully beautiful

as can be, all in one, from envy wholly free.

But you, O Zeus, and your illustrious children, lead

us with the Whole, as you have judged, aligning all,

and grant that starts are well begun and tasks are done.

[17] ***Hymn 17: Second Sacred Hymn, to the Gods of Olympus***

Oh come and let us celebrate Poseidon, Lord,

who is the eldest of all children born of Zeus,

the strongest, who is second from the father, chief

of all the progeny, of all that's near to us

the demiurge; with him is also Hera, Queen,

who is the eldest goddess born of Father Zeus;

but also let us celebrate the other gods,

who're in Olympus, and all cocreators and

protectors of immortal things. Be kind to us.

[18] *Hymn 18: Third Sacred Hymn, to All the Gods*

O gods who're after Zên, who is supremely good,

you're all completely blameless and exempt from death;

Poseidon is your chief and leader after Zeus,

O ye above the heavens or within the sky;

illustrious are ye all, and you we celebrate,

because we have a nature that's akin to yours.

O blessed ones, hail to you, the givers of all goods;

but give to us, with lives not always free of care,

whatever is both fair and good, and set us straight.

[19] *Hymn 19: Fourth Sacred Hymn, to All Gods Inferior to Those of Olympus*

O Kronos, of the supercelestial Titans Lord,

who governs them, and you who all the heavens rule,

O Helios, and the other Planets following you;

by you two the whole race of mortals is produced,

from both of you, from Kronos and from Helios.

Ye Titans and ye Planets, subject to these two,

are one way or another helpers; hence to you

sing we who have these many benefits from you,

and with you to the holy Daimons and Fixed Stars.

[20] *Hymn 20: Fifth Sacred Hymn, to Pluto*

Lord Pluto, thou who art of human nature chief

and guardian, allotted thee by Zeus himself,

and holding everything as one that separately

occurs for us and happens; you protect us well

in all things here, and after when to thee we're raised;

with thee are Heroes, of a kind surpassing ours,

and also others dear to us, both fair and good,

and Kore, thy good wife and god of Tartarus,

who binds us, as required, to mortal life. Be kind.

[21] **Hymn 21: Sixth Sacred Hymn, to Zeus**

Zeus, Father, powerful, strong acting, cause of good,

All-Parent, and by thine own mind transcendent good,

we too are born with shares of goodness from the gods.

By force of our mortality we're fallible

but ever subject to correction once again.

Bestow on us release from misery of mistakes

by means of thine own children to whom it's assigned,

approaching near the guiltless having a right mind,

so we may follow thee, who art both gentle, kind.

[22] **Hymn 22: First Daily Hymn, Sung on the Second Day**

Let me not cease from thanking you, O blessed gods,

for all the benefits I have because of you

or ever will; the highest source of them is Zeus.

And may I not neglect the welfare of my kind,

whatever's in my power, working willingly

for common good, and know it greatly aids me too.

May I not be the cause of evils such as come

to people, but so far as I am able, good,

so that, becoming more like you, I may be blessed.

[23] *Hymn 23: Second Daily Hymn, Sung on the Third Day*

O gods, don't let me savor pleasures to excess,

but put a limit onto them, in case there comes

from them some evil to my body or my soul.

Don't let me be insatiable for resources,

but measured, and in those things that the body needs

be moderate, so independence I enjoy.

Don't let me be enslaved to false and empty words,

but let me judge as useful only those of them

that bring to me divine and genuine excellence.

[24] *Hymn 24: Third Daily Hymn, Sung on the Fourth Day*

O gods, don't let these accidents that sometimes strike

my mortal part destroy me, knowing that my soul's

immortal, separate from the mortal, and divine.

And do not let the troubles that to people come

disturb me while I exercise my liberty,

nor for some evil notion be in thrall to need.

And when it comes to me to bring about some good,

don't let me spare my mortal part, but let me care

for my immortal soul to always be the best.

[25] *Hymn 25: Fourth Daily Hymn, Sung on the Fifth Day*

Blest they who always care for their immortal soul

so that it be the best, and for their mortal part

are not concerned, not sparing it if there be need.

Blest they who when some mortals, acting thoughtlessly,

attack, will never be enslaved to them, but hold

their soul with firmness, rising o'er that wickedness.

Blest they who do not grieve with bitter heart the luck

that's heaven-sent, but bear it easily and mark

alone as good what lies in their immortal part.

[26] *Hymn 26: Fifth Daily Hymn, Sung on the Sixth Day*

Blest they who don't unwisely cling to speakers' vain

opinions, but by thinking for themselves pursue

with straight intelligence the virtue that's ordained.

Blest they who do not to an infinite degree

pursue possessions foolishly, but do define

a measure by the body's well-determined needs.

Blest they who keep a godly bound to pleasure that

does not invite some evil for the soul or for

the body, but accords with virtue that's ordained.

[27] *Hymn 27: Sixth Daily Hymn, Sung on the Seventh Day*

Blest they who are not greedy for themselves, nor by

a fearful folly cause for people evil things,

but always good things, like the blessed gods themselves.

Blest they who do not slight the race's common good,

especially knowing that the common is the gods'

concern, and therefore they do not abandon it.

Blest they who give the gods their thanks for benefits,

whatever they might have, before all Zên himself,

from whom came first the fair and good in everything.

[28] These hymns in honor of the gods are twenty-seven in all, each of nine verses. They are sung on the meter of the heroic hexameter, which is the most beautiful of all rhythms.[577] For the syllables are either long or short: the short always of one beat, and the long most commonly of two beats, but sometimes of a greater number when sung with words. But the heroic verse uses only two feet, the dactyl and spondee. The dactyl is formed with a long syllable for the downbeat, followed by two short ones for the upbeat; the spondee is formed of a long one for the downbeat and a long one for the upbeat. Thus, the equality of these two feet, both beginning with a long syllable and ending on the upbeat, give to this rhythm a majestic character that no other approaches.

Chapter 36: Instruction for the use of addresses and hymns

[1] Now that we have made the addresses and hymns known, we must explain how to use them and first the timing of each address. The Morning Address must be done between bed and breakfast, for those who breakfast, of course, and for others before engaging in their business. The Afternoon Address should be made between the middle of the day and supper time. Last, the evening one between the meal and bedtime, except on days of fasting; on these days it will be done after sunset and always before the meal. These are the times marked for each address. The places are temples and [locations] that are pure of all human excrement, of all mortal human remains, and of anything that could contain them.

[2] Here is how to proceed with each [ritual]. First of all, for each of them a proclamation is made by the sacred herald, if there is one regularly instituted by a priest to fulfill this function; otherwise, one will be designated for the occasion, either by the priest, if there is one, or by whoever

---

577. The following remarks on meter refer, of course, to the original Greek, not to the preceding English translations, which are iambic hexameters.

present who is the most respectable by age or otherwise. The proclamation is as follows: "Hear ye, worshipers of the gods, now is the time for our morning (or afternoon, or evening) address to the gods. With all our reason, with all our judgment, with all our soul, let us invoke all the gods and especially Zeus who reigns over them."

[3] This proclamation is made on unconsecrated days only once, twice on holy days, and three times on New Moon.

[4] Immediately, everyone must look up, kneel on both knees, raise their hands by throwing them back, and then intone: "O gods, be propitious." At the same time that this invocation is made, we must adore the gods, first those of Olympus, by placing the right hand on the ground and raising at the same time on one of the two knees. The invocation being thus made once and the adoration once, it is then necessary to worship in the same way, but with the left hand, all the other gods by intoning the same formula. In the third place, it is necessary to address Zeus the king while intoning, "Zeus, King, be propitious," and this time prostrating on both knees and both hands and touching the head to the ground. This proclamation must be sung three times, and three times followed by the prostration, but all together counts for one prostration only. Every day this [rite] must be used once for each address, but on the holy days it is necessary to repeat the whole thing three times.

[5] Prostration must be led by a priest or by the most distinguished of those present. Moreover, the proclamation to the gods must be in the Hypophrygian mode in the prostration on the right hand, in the Phrygian mode in the prostration on the left hand, and in the Hypodorian mode in that which we make to Zeus.

[6] Then the sacred herald will make a new proclamation: "Let us listen to the address," either the Morning [Address] to the Gods; or the First or Second [Afternoon Address], or the Third [Afternoon Address] to King Zeus; or the Evening [Address] to the Gods, or the Evening [Address after the Fast] to Zeus. Everybody reclines on both knees, and the one

who has been appointed by the most important person in the assembly reads for all those present the proper address for the occasion.

[7]   The speech or the speeches being finished, the sacred herald makes this new proclamation: "Let us listen to the hymns to the gods," and we immediately sing the hymns, on secular days ordinarily without accompaniment, but on holy days usually with musical accompaniment. On secular days one always begins with the monthly hymn, then comes the daily hymn that is appropriate for the ceremony, and thirdly the first perennial hymn to Zeus; each of them must be sung once. But on holy days one begins with the sacred hymn which is appropriate for the ceremony and continues with the monthly hymn, except the first [of the monthly hymns], which must precede all the sacred hymns. Each of the two hymns will be sung twice on the holy days, and thereafter the perennial hymn in honor of Zeus three times. The second perennial hymn, addressed to the gods, is to be sung between the afternoon addresses twice, between the first and the second and between the second and the third, and each time entirely on holy days, but on secular days more than half[578] is sung in the first interval, and the rest in the second.

[8]   When the hymns are sung to music, the two perennial hymns, the first and thirteenth of the monthly, and the first, third, and sixth of the sacred hymns are sung in the Hypodorian [mode], for we assign this mode to Zeus the King and all gods collectively, because of its grandeur and because none is better suited to the expression of proud and heroic feelings. The second, third, fourth, fifth, sixth, eighth, ninth, and eleventh of the monthly hymns, and in addition the second of the sacred hymns, are sung in the Hypophrygian [mode], because we attribute to the gods of Olympus the mode that holds the second rank for grandeur and that is apt to express the admiration of beautiful things. The seventh, tenth, and twelfth of the monthly hymns, as well as the fourth of the sacred

---

578. Looking at the hymn, I believe this must be the first *five* verses (cf. Pellissier translation at Alexandre, *Pléthon*, 235).

hymns, are sung in the Phrygian [mode], since we attribute to the gods of a class inferior to the Olympians the mode that for greatness occupies an intermediate rank and is suitable for the expression of gentle and peaceful feelings. Finally, the fifth of the sacred hymns, and all the daily hymns when they are sung to music, receive the Dorian, the mode reserved for people and for the gods who preside over human destinies, because of its especially agonistic character and the struggle always inherent in human affairs, due to the missteps and mistakes of our nature.

[9]   There are thirteen monthly hymns, and the months being of the same number when the year admits an intercalary month, we sing these hymns according to their order, each during the month corresponding to it, beginning the evening preceding the New Moon and ending on the afternoon of Old-and-New. However, when the year is only twelve months long, the twelfth [monthly] hymn is sung with the evening address during Twelfth Month,[579] and the thirteenth [monthly] hymn with the morning and afternoon addresses.

[10]   As for the sacred hymns, as they are six in number, and as the full months have just as many holy days, with the exception only of First and Last Month which have more, we sing the first of these hymns on New Moon, the second on Eighth Waxing, the third on Midmonth, the fourth on Eighth Waning, the fifth on the day of the Old Moon and the sixth on the day Old-and-New, observing that for the singing of the hymns each day is supposed to begin the evening preceding the corresponding holy day and to finish in the afternoon of the same day. But when the month is not full, as then the day of Old Moon is missing, the fifth [sacred] hymn is sung the evening before Old-and-New, and the sixth in the morning and afternoon of Old-and-New.

[11]   The Second and Third Waxing days of First Month are holy days; on the evening preceding each of these days the hymn of the day is added to

---

579. As explained in *Laws* III.36.20–21, Plethon names the months by their ordinal position, and so I have capitalized them. Similarly, I have capitalized the days, also named after ordinal position.

the monthly hymn—namely, the first [daily] hymn [i.e., for day 2] on the eve of the second day, and the second [daily] hymn [for day 3] on the eve of the third day, each of them sung twice with music, since each evening belongs to the following holy day. In the morning and afternoon of the second and third day, the same hymns are sung and in the same way as on New Moon. During the rest of this first week of First Month, the daily hymn is sung every day with the monthly hymn, only once but with music, although music is not usually used on secular days, but only on the holy days, where it is always used unless one lacks musicians.

[12] The hymns are sung in the same way, once and with music, during the last part of Last Month, from Seventh to Fourth Departing, and also the day before and the day after three special holy days placed in the body of the year, namely, Eighth Waxing of Fourth Month, Midmonth of Seventh Month, and Eighth Waning of Tenth Month. On these days, though they are not consecrated, we sing the daily hymn of the day once with music.

[13] On the Fourth Departing day of Last Month—that is to say, the evening before the holy days that finish it—it is necessary to sing with the monthly hymn the second of the daily hymns [i.e., for day 3], each twice with music. In the morning and afternoon of the Third [Departing] day, the fifth of the sacred hymns is sung before the monthly hymn. The evening preceding the Second [Departing] day, the first of the daily hymns [for day 2] is joined to the monthly hymn, and both are sung twice and with music; in the morning and the afternoon of this Second [Departing] day the same hymns are sung and in the same way as on Old-and-New Moon. The next day, which is that of the Old Moon if the month is full, in the morning and the afternoon the same hymns are sung again, and in the evening the fifth of the sacred hymns, then the monthly hymn.[580]

---

580. This is the text in both Alexandre (*Pléthon*, 240.4–7) and MS Add. 5424, fol. 131v.22–24. However, it would seem to be more consistent to use the fifth sacred hymn (which is for Old Moon) in the morning and afternoon and the sixth sacred hymn (for Old-and-New) in the evening.

If the month is hollow and instead of the Old Moon, which is missing, we celebrate the fast on the Fourth Departing day, the evening before we will sing the third of the daily hymns [for day 4], and on the fourth day will sing the same hymns and in the same way as on Old-and-New Moon.[581]

[14] It is obvious that the perennial hymn to Zeus must be sung third and last[582] after the others, whenever any hymns are sung. [On secular days], the other hymns are sung once and this one [for Zeus] once, but [on holy days], the others twice but this one [for Zeus] three times; and this is the manner of the prostrations, the addresses, and the hymns.

[15] If some laziness afflicts them, more serious people might leave out the addresses entirely and, especially on secular days, use just the hymns after the prostrations. Those indeed who are lazier or wholly illiterate might also omit the hymns and address the gods with prostrations alone. If some human infirmity afflicts someone so they cannot prostrate easily, then singing the plain (or "without music") salutations of the prostrations will suffice for anyone in this situation. Indeed someone may leave out all of this, such as perhaps someone obliged by very scornful people to live piously among those who are very indifferent, and do so as rightly as possible; each one addresses the gods however they want and are able and kisses their upturned right hand when they are done. Alternately, this book of laws might lie open in the temple or some other place; after touching it at the close [of the ceremony], they kiss their hand in this way. These things are for those afflicted with inability or laziness; it is for the healthy people to take upon themselves to make these addresses to the gods and after the hymns to herald the proclamation:

---

581. This is the text in both Alexandre (*Pléthon*, 240.10) and MS Add. 5424, fol. 132.3. However, since Fourth Departing is substituting for Old Moon, it would seem more consistent to sing the hymns from that day (fifth sacred) rather than those of Old-and-New.

582. The following text, up to the next section, "The Order of the Months and Years," was omitted from Alexandre, *Pléthon*, but is found in British Library Manuscript Add. 5424, fol. 132.5–133.4 (Hladký, *Plethon*, 318–19).

Because we have addressed the gods and performed the sacred rites according to law, we are indeed liberated, each of us having become better by our association with them. In everything we do, let us be mindful of Zeus and the gods, so far as our nature may follow. Let us strive, so far as we are able, first for freedom from the worst part of ourselves and from suffering, and thereafter for power over ourselves, for independence, and for decency according to nature. Let us take care for the preservation of the natural qualities of each of us by the restitution of what has been established, especially so that we might be perfected (or "completed"). In all these things and in every way, insofar as we are such, let us follow the gods, and thereby in this way alone let us prepare, as is the ability of each of us, for blessedness to come. But also, because we have reclined on both knees and offered this final prayer, let us be liberated.

[16] On secular days, however, remove most of this and proclaim, "Since we have addressed the gods and have been our best according to law, and since we have reclined on both knees and offered this final prayer, let us be liberated."

[17] Then, if perhaps a priest is present, he turns to the laity and three times raises his upturned hands and adds this prayer, "May King Zeus and all the gods, who as overseers under Zeus have settled our matters, be kind to all of you."

[18] After which the laity answer, singing in the Dorian mode, "Be it so! Be it so! Be it so also for you, divine man!" But if no priest is present, the individual who began the adoration also adds the prayer, but without raising their hands, in addition saying "us" instead of "you"; and the rest, after answering "Be it so! Be it so! Be it so!" are thereby released.

The Order of the Months and Years[583]

[19] We will follow the order indicated by nature for the months and years; that is to say, we will use lunar months and solar years, by adjusting the latter on the solstices and taking as a starting point the winter solstice, when Helios, having arrived at his furthest point, begins to approach us. The day called Old-and-New is the day when Selene is in conjunction with Helios according to the calculation of the most experienced people in astronomy. The next day, from midnight following the conjunction of these two deities, will be New Moon or the first of the month, from which we count all the other days of the month to the number of 30 for the full months, or to 29 for the hollow months, so that the evening of each night always belongs to the day before, and the morning to the present day, midnight being the boundary of the two days.

[20] Here is the way of counting the days of each month: after New Moon we shall have Second Waxing, then the Third, the Fourth, and so on until the Eighth [Waxing]; after the Eighth, will come the Seventh Middle of the month, then the Sixth, and thus descending to the Second [Middle], which will precede Midmonth. We will then continue with the Second Waning, the Third, and so on until the Eighth [Waning], after which will come the Seventh Departing, the Sixth, and so on, down, until the Second [Departing], which will be followed, in the full months by the Old Moon first and then Old-and-New Moon, or if the month is hollow, immediately by Old-and-New Moon. As for the months, the month following the winter solstice will be the First Month of the year, and the others will be designated only by their rank up to the Twelfth in some years, up to the Thirteenth in others, when Twelfth Month will not reach the winter solstice. For the determination of the solstice, we will use sundials employed with the greatest possible precision.[584]

---

583. The section title is from British Library Manuscript Add. 5424, fol. 133.4–5 (Hladký, *Plethon*, 319).

584. A *heliotropion* is a sundial or similar instrument for determining solstices and equinoxes.

[21] We celebrate these and only these holy days: The first and most sacred holy day of each month, New Moon, is for Zeus the King. Second, Eighth Waxing is for Poseidon and the Olympian gods. Third, Midmonth is for all the gods below Zeus, and it is second in dignity after New Moon. Fourth, Eighth Waning is for Helios, Kronos, and all the gods below the Olympians. Fifth, Old Moon, is for Pluto alone of the gods, for the heroes altogether, for our friends, and for kinfolk escaping memory. Sixth, Old-and-New, is for inspection of ourselves and our mistakes, deficiencies, and wrongs, and then especially for correcting ourselves. If the month is hollow and Old Moon is missing, celebrate both: for Pluto and memory of the departed, and for inspecting ourselves; its worth I judge to be not less than Midmonth. In First Month, celebrate holy days also on Second and Third Waxing. The Second is for Hera and the Third for Poseidon. And for Last Month, either Twelfth or intercalated [Thirteenth], if it is full then [we celebrate] on Third and Second Waning, but if hollow then on Fourth, Third, and Second [Waning]; on Third [Waning] instead of Old Moon celebrate Pluto and the memory of those departed, and also on either Second and Old Moon or on Fourth and Second, after which Old-and-New is for inspecting and correcting ourselves.[585]

Chapter 43: Epinomis or conclusion

[1] What we had proposed at the beginning of this work was accomplished with the help of those among the gods who preside over this kind of work; to them, as well as to Poseidon their leader, we pay homage in this work. It is completed to the extent necessary, for we have shown what is the principle of all things, and among all things what are the natures of the first order immediately attached to the supreme principle, what are those

---

585. This paragraph, which is absent from Alexandre, *Pléthon*, is found in British Library Manuscript Add. 5424, fol. 133v.7–134.4 (Hladký, *Plethon*, 319–20). It replaces four redundant paragraphs from Theodore of Gaza's *On the Months* included in Alexandre, *Pléthon*, 60–62.

of the second and those of the third and last order, what place humans occupy among them, of what elements they are composed, and according to their nature what kind of life suits living happily. This [happiness] is the supreme and common goal that all people pursue, but not all seek it in the same kind of life. Where it is to be sought and by what actions is what we have shown in detail by considerations and axioms that are neither weak nor questionable, but which are based on three fundamental ones. The first is that the principle of all things, that supreme god who, in the language of our fathers, is called Zeus, is supremely good, lacking no perfection, and the best possible; the second, that there must be a reciprocal relationship between essences and their mode of generation; the third, that the actions of different beings must have a certain relation with their essences, and their essences with their actions.

[2] Once these principles are firmly established, the first reveals to us, among other important truths, that the All coexists perpetually with Zeus, and that this marvelous [All] will remain immutable in its state through all eternity, constant in the form that was originally given to it. It would not be possible, indeed, that a god who is the very best would not produce his work and do no good (for what is best must necessarily involve other beings in this goodness as much as possible); and if he creates and produces well, he cannot create with limited power, nor produce work that is inferior to his power or that can ever be or become less perfect than the best possible. For it is evident that if Zeus changed anything in the established order, he would make the All worse, either now or later. Indeed, if the smallest piece of it is changed, either because it does not usually change or because it changes differently than usual, then it is impossible that the whole configuration not change with this piece. For the same configuration cannot be preserved unless all the parts remain the same.

[3] The second axiom enlightens us on the constitution of divine beings. For the essence of all things is divided [into three orders]: (1)[586] into

---

586. Parenthesized numbers added for clarity.

what is always the same and immutable in all respects; (2) then into what changes in time but is everlasting; (3) third, into mortal nature. Because it is necessary for each essence to have a generation proper and in conformity with its nature, we attribute (1) the first creation to the principle of all things, Zeus; (2) the second to Poseidon, the leader in the first order of essence, who is helped in different ways by each of his legitimate siblings; (3) the third to the eldest of Zeus's illegitimate children, Kronos, and to Helios, the most powerful of the legitimate sons of Poseidon, both being assisted in this work, Kronos by all his illegitimate siblings, Helios by all his legitimate siblings, called planets because of the irregularity of their movement.

[4]   The third axiom reveals to us the nature of humans: namely, that they are a compound of two natures, one animal and mortal, the other immortal and akin to the gods. For, of course, since humans sometimes perform acts worthy of the beast, and sometimes similar to those of the gods, it is necessary to assign to these two kinds of actions an essence of their own and connected with them. Some human actions are similar to those of the gods, and these are obviously the most important. Indeed, we cannot say that for the gods there is a more important action than the contemplation of beings, the chief of which is the conception of Zeus. But humans obviously have in common with them the contemplation of beings, and they even participate in the conception of Zeus, the last limit to which the gods themselves can reach. Humans, therefore, need an essence like that of the gods, which can produce actions like theirs, and that is moreover immortal, since the essence of the gods is immortal, for there cannot be the least resemblance between a mortal nature and an immortal nature, or a comparison between what has only an imperfect and limited capacity to what has an infinite and limitless one. So it is in the actions suitable to their kinship with the gods that we come, after many other capable teachers, to show people their happiness, the aim of our book being to make those who listen to our lessons as happy as a human is allowed to be.

[5]   That the human being is a compound of two natures is a truth we dem-
onstrate by another equally incontestable axiom: that there is not a single
being that goes of its own accord to its destruction; all, on the contrary,
make their efforts to support and preserve their existence, as much as it
depends on them. Once this principle is established, when we see certain
people killing themselves, we understand very clearly that it is not the
mortal part of our being that kills itself, but that it is the act of a different part, and the best, which cannot perish with the body and which is
not subordinate to it, as are all mortal species subject to the bodies to
which they are attached and incapable of surviving them when they perish. Because if this part of our being depended on the body, it wouldn't
act against it either to such a degree or in the slightest thing. But having
its own essence that subsists by itself, as soon as it has judged that living together with the mortal element would no longer be useful to it
(whether it has judged rightly or wrongly, it matters not), it kills that
body as being foreign to it and thus frees itself from a companion that
seems annoying and inconvenient to it.

[6]   We judge this mixture in us of two natures, one mortal and the other
immortal, to be made by the gods creating us according to the orders
of Zeus, with a view to the harmony of the All. They wanted these two
elements of the world, the mortal and the immortal, to unite in human
nature, which is placed in the middle of them. Indeed, to be complete
and whole, the All had to contain, brought together and welded together,
these two elements, the mortal and the immortal; thus, instead of being
divided and torn apart, it forms one system in reality. For just as these
many different things can unite thanks to their common boundaries, so
mortal was bound to immortal in the human, which serves them both
as boundary. If in humans the mortal always remained united with the
immortal, the first would itself be immortalized, made such indeed by
this constant union with the immortal, and humans would no longer
be the boundary between the two natures, as they should be, but would
be arrayed entirely among the immortals. If, on the other hand, the

immortal united just once with the mortal and abandoned it the rest of the time, being only a fleeting boundary between immortal and mortal, it would not be an everlasting boundary, nor permanently unite the mortal with the immortal, but connected once and then released from the mortal, the harmony would be dissolved. It therefore remains to say that the immortal [part] is connected partly with the mortal, and it exists partly by itself each time it is released from [the mortal part], which is repeated indefinitely throughout eternity.

[7]   These are reputed to be the doctrines of the wise disciples of Pythagoras, especially, and of Plato. They are from the exegetes among other peoples, and also indeed from those of our ancestors who received well the sound religious service of the Kouretes. They are from Zoroaster and his disciples. It is to him, the most ancient of those in our memory, to whom we attribute them, not supposing, however, that he discovered them, for these true doctrines are co-eternal with the whole heaven, and indeed among people. If they gather sometimes more, sometimes fewer by their strength, at least they always have those of us who behave according to the common ideas that the gods have put in our souls. But the fact is that of all those who are remembered, [Zoroaster] is the oldest exegete of these correct doctrines; he is said to be more than five thousand years prior to the return of the Heracleidae.

[8]   As for Mênês, the lawgiver of the Egyptians, who is claimed to be earlier by more than three thousand years, he cannot be considered as a wise lawgiver and worthy of esteem. He would never have established a religion so charged with useless and bad rites for the gods, if he had not held to vicious doctrines. If the priests who followed him had doctrines similar to those of Zoroaster, we must not believe that they received them from Mênês, but found them later in their search for wisdom. Yet they could not bring any reform to the rites, because Mênês had imposed a law on them, doubtless useful and beneficial to people who have good legislation, but not to those with bad laws: he had forbidden them from

making the slightest change in the laws of the country; thus, while they themselves recognized the true doctrines, they left the multitude to their bad rites.

[9] In addition, some other legislations may have had their good sides—several even were not unrelated to the doctrines of Zoroaster—but they remained far from accurate. Such are the laws of the Indians and the Western Iberians, which date almost from the same period as those of Zoroaster. The name of the lawgiver of the Iberians has not come down to us, and nothing has been preserved from their laws. As for the Indians, part of their legislation still exists, and their lawgiver was called Dionysos. Coming from without, he conquered the Indians, established his empire there, and by the wisdom of his institutions civilized, it is said, the inhabitants. Another Dionysos, the son of Semele, was born much later, but must have been identical to the first in his soul or at least imitating his life; both, in any case, were very unwarlike. We can almost believe the same thing of the two Heracles, one the son of Amphytrion and Alcmene, the other born earlier in Tyre, who both on the contrary were very warlike. Indeed, the cycles of time bring and will always bring similar lives and actions, so that nothing exactly new has happened, nor happens now that has not already happened in form and will happen again one day.

[10] Although no people are atheists, people have very different opinions on divinity. It is therefore necessary that there be one that is always the same, which is the best, with the others being worse, some closer to or farther from the truth, and some necessarily more remote than all the others. For us, we remain attached to the doctrine that we know best, that of Zoroaster, professed also by Pythagoras and Plato; it exceeds all other doctrines in accuracy, and moreover it is our heritage. We think in this [philosophy] alone is the purest happiness possible to us. As for the other doctrines, the further they depart from ours, the more those who attach themselves to them stray from happiness and get closer to misery, and

those who profess the most different opinions from ours are those who fall in the last degree of misery, since they are wallowing in frightful darkness by their ignorance of the most important things.

[11] But, it may be said, some sophists,[587] admired by the crowd, promise to their followers goods greater than those we announce to humankind; they promise an unalloyed immortality not defiled by any mortal mixture, whereas, according to our doctrine, our souls will not cease, whenever their turn has come, to have again some share of mortality. But first of all, it is wise in general not to prefer those who promise the most, but rather those who deserve the most confidence, and likewise, one should not prefer the doctrines that spread overly great hopes to those more worthy of trust. There is no profit in persisting in hopes about the most important things that are overly great but vain and ineffectual and in thus being charmed by falsehoods and unhealthy opinions. It is the height of misfortune to be deceived about the gods and the beliefs most important to people, and to have other opinions [contrary to the truth].

[12] But besides, it would not be astonishing if the destinies we announce to the human race appear to good judges still preferable to the promises of these sophists. In the first place, they recognize an absolute and complete eternity neither in the whole heaven nor in the human soul, granting beings eternity not in both directions, but in one, that of the future. They argue that heaven had a beginning in time, and that it will be subject to the same change as human circumstances. In order that these things appear more persuasive to their hearers, on the one hand they maintain that human circumstances will not change alone but with the Whole, and on the other hand, they announce that there will be evils for a short time, and that afterward and ever after God will restore matters to be good. And indeed it would be more persuasive if they said there are evils for an infinite time, after which he restores the good. We, however, by recognizing the human soul is eternally complete, not amputated and

---

587. He is apparently talking about Christian theologians.

lame, thereby treat it better. For it is clear, indeed, that this two-way eternity is better and more beautiful than that truncated one, and thus that in this way its eternity is more perfect and beautiful.

[13] But perhaps someone will object that what is past is no more and that one will not have to experience it again, while the future, although not yet, must one day be, and therefore has more existence than what is not, and that the future is in this sense preferable. It is thus, it will be said, that desire neglects the past to turn toward the future as having more existence. Consequently, this two-way eternity is not surpassed by that which embraces the future only through non-being, which is in reality neither greater nor better. But we ...

The rest is to seek and never to find, for it was destroyed, they say, by Scholarios.[588]

---

588. Alexandre, *Pléthon*, 261, n. 11. A sad copiest added this line to a Florentine manuscript of Plethon's fragmentary *Book of Laws*.

APPENDIX C

Plethon's Commentary on the Magical Oracles of the Magi of Zoroaster

Translated by Thomas Stanley (1661), modernized by John Opsopaus[589]

---

*(1) Seek thou the soul's way, whence or in what rank
to serve the body; to that rank from which thou flowed,
thou mayst rise up again; join act with sacred speech.*[590]

---

589. Plethon's commentary is titled *The Magical Oracles of Zoroaster's Magi* (Μαγικὰ λόγια τῶν ἀπὸ Ζωροάστρου μάγων). Of course, these oracles do not come from the Magi (as Plethon believed), and they are more widely known as the "Chaldean Oracles," which is equally a misnomer. The translations of the oracles are my own; the commentary by Plethon is from Opsopoeus, *Oracula Magica Zoroastris*, translated in Thomas Stanley, *Chaldaick Oracles*, which I have modernized and checked against the Greek text in Tambrun-Krasker, Μαγικὰ λόγια. The oracles are numbered as they are in the manuscripts (if they are numbered at all). In a footnote, the number after "P" is the oracle's number in the most recent edition of Plethon's commentary, Tambrun-Krasker, Μαγικὰ λόγια; the number after "CO" is its number in more comprehensive collections of the Chaldean Oracles such as des Places, *Oracula Chaldaica*, and Majercik, *Chaldean Oracles*. Plethon got his text for the oracles from Michael Psellos's exposition, Migne, *Patrologiae Graeca*, 122:1123–54, but modified it in a few cases.

590. P 1, CO 110. Plethon has conjectured corrections to Psellos's text, and so his text for this oracle differs in a few respects from that in modern editions.

The *Magi*, who are followers of *Zoroaster*, as also many others, hold that the human soul is immortal and descended from above to serve the mortal body—that is, to operate therein for a certain time, and to animate and adorn it to her power, and then to return to the place from which she came. And whereas there are many lands there for the soul, one *radiant*, another *wrapped in darkness*, others betwixt both, *partly bright, partly dark,* the soul, being descended from that which is wholly bright into the body, if she perform her office well, runs back into the same land; but if not well, she retires into worse lands, according to the things which she has done in life.

The oracle therefore says, *Seek thou the soul's way*, or the stream by which the soul flowed into you; or by what course (of life), having performed your charge toward the body, you may mount up to the same place from which you flowed down, namely, the same track of the soul, *joining act to sacred speech*. By *sacred speech*, it means that which concerns divine worship; by *act*, divine rites. The oracle therefore says that to this exaltation of the soul, both speech concerning divine worship (prayers) and religious rites (sacrifices) are requisite.

> *(2) Incline not down. Beneath the Earth there lies a cliff,*
> *which draws one down the seven steps...*
> *beneath her is the throne of dire Necessity.*[591]

It calls the descent into wickedness and misery a *cliff*; the terrestrial and mortal body, the *Earth*, for by the Earth, it means mortal nature, as by the fire frequently the divine; by the place with *seven steps*, it means Fate dependent on the planets, beneath which there is seated a certain dire and unalterable *Necessity*. The oracle therefore advises that you not stoop down toward the mortal body, which being subject only to the Fate that proceeds from the planets, may be reckoned among those things that are not up to us, for you will be unhappy if you stoop down wholly to the body, and unfortunate and continually failing of your desires, in regard to the necessity that is attached to the body.

---

591. P 2, CO 164+. This oracle is incomplete in Psellos, and Plethon has different conjectures for the missing words from modern editors. Also, modern editors do not consider the third line, which is not in verse, to be part of the oracle.

(3) Thy vessel earthly beasts shall occupy.[592]

The *vessel* of your soul—that is, this mortal body—shall be *inhabited* by worms and other vile creatures.

(4) Enlarge not thou thy Destiny.[593]

Endeavor not to increase your Fate, or to do more than is given to you in charge, for you will not be able.

(5) Naught incomplete rolls from Paternal Principle.[594]

For from the *Paternal Principle*, which is that of the Supreme God, nothing incomplete proceeds, so that you yourself might complete it; for all things proceeding from thence are perfect, as appears, in that they tend to the perfection of the Universe.

(6) But the Paternal Mind accepteth not her will,
until she flee oblivion, and pronounce a word,
inserting memory of the pure paternal sign.[595]

The *Paternal Mind* (the Second God and diligent maker of the soul) admits not her *will* or desire until she come out of the *oblivion* that she contracted by connection with the body; and until she speaks a certain *word*, or conceives in her thoughts a certain speech, calling to remembrance the paternal divine *symbol* or watchword, which is the pursuit of the good, and the soul recalling this hereby becomes most acceptable to her maker.

---

592. P 3, CO 157.

593. P 4, CO 103.

594. P 5, CO 13.

595. P 6, CO 109.

> *(7) You must make haste to light, and to the Father's beams,*
> *from whence was sent to thee a soul full-clothed with mind.*[596]

The light and splendor of the Father is that land of the soul that is radiant, from whence the soul arrayed with mind [*nous*] was sent hither, wherefore we must hasten to return to the same light.

> *(8) Alas! The Earth bewails them, even to their children.*[597]

Those who don't hasten to the light, from which their soul was sent to them, the Earth or mortal Nature bewails, for they, being sent hither to adorn her, not only don't adorn her, but also blemish themselves by living wickedly. Moreover the wickedness of the parents is transmitted to the children, corrupted by them through ill education.

> *(9) The soul's expellers with the breath are easily released.*[598]

The reasons (*logoi*), which expel the soul from wickedness and give her breath, are easily released, and the oblivion that keeps them in is easily put off.

> *(10) Within the left side of the bed is virtue's fount,*
> *remaining all inside, nor losing chastity.*[599]

In the left side of your bed, there is the power or fount of virtue, residing wholly within, and never casting off her chastity or nature void of passion, for there is always in us the power of virtue without passion that cannot be put off, although her energy or activity may be interrupted. It says the *power* of virtue is placed on the left side because her *activity* is seated on the right; by the *bed* is meant the seat of the soul, subject to her several habits.

---

596. P 7, CO 115.

597. P 8, CO 162.

598. P 9, CO 124.

599. P 10, CO 52. Plethon's text has κοίτης (bed, couch) where Psellos and modern editions have Ἑκάτης (Hekate), in which case the first line can be translated "Within Hekate's left flank virtue's fount exists."

> *(11) The human soul will somehow clasp God to herself,*
> *and having nothing mortal, she is wholly drunk with God,*
> *for she boasts harmony, where mortal bodies stand.*[600]

The human soul will somehow clasp God, and join him strictly *to herself* (who is her continual defense) by resembling him as much as she possibly can; *having nothing mortal* within her, *she is wholly drunk with God*, or replenished with divine goods, for though she is fettered to this mortal body, yet she *glories in the harmony* or union *in which the mortal body exists.* That is, she is not ashamed of it, but thinks well of herself for it, for she is a cause and affords to the All that, as mortals are united with immortals in humanity, the All is adorned with one harmony.

> *(12) Since Psychê, by the Father's Power a radiant fire,*
> *remains immortal, she is Mistress of all Life,*
> *and holds full measures of the Cosmos' many clefts.*[601]

The Second God, who first before all other things proceeded from the Father and supreme god, these oracles call all along *the Father's Power*, his *Intellectual Power*, and the *Paternal Mind*. It says, therefore, that *Psychê* (*the soul*), *procreated by this Power of the Father, is a radiant fire*—that is, a divine and intellectual essence—and *persists immortal* through the divinity of its essence, *and is Mistress of Life*, namely of herself, possessing life that cannot be taken away from her. For how can we be said to be masters of such things as may be taken from us, seeing that use of them is only allowed us? But of those things which cannot be taken from us, we are absolute masters. The soul, due to her own perpetuity, *holds full-measures in the clefts* of the *cosmos*, or her diverse places in the world, which are allotted each time according to how she has led her life past.

> *(13) Seek Paradise.*[602]

The radiant land of the soul.

---

600. P 11, CO 97.

601. P 12, CO 96.

602. P 13, CO 165. *Paradeisos* is a Persian word for "park."

(14) Neither spirit do you stain, nor deepen down the plane...[603]

The followers of *Pythagoras* and *Plato* conceive the soul to be a substance not wholly separate from all body, nor wholly inseparable; but partly separable, partly inseparable; separable potentially, but ever inseparable actually. For they assert three kinds of Forms: [1] One wholly separate from matter, the Supercelestial Intelligences (*Noes*). [2] Another wholly inseparable from matter, having a substance not subsistent by itself but dependent on matter; together with which matter, which is sometimes dissolved by reason of its nature subject to mutation, this kind of soul is dissolved also and perishes; this kind they hold to be wholly irrational.

[3] Between these they place a middle kind, the rational soul, differing from the Supercelestial Intelligences, in that it always co-exists with matter, and from the irrational kind, in that it is not dependent on matter, but, on the contrary, matter is dependent on it, and it has a proper substance potentially subsistent by itself. It is also indivisible like the Supercelestial Intelligences, and performs some works in some manner allied to theirs, being itself also busied in the knowledge and contemplation of beings even unto the Supreme God, and for this reason is indestructible.

This kind of soul is always co-existent with an aethereal body as its *vehicle*, which she by continual connection makes also immortal; neither is her vehicle inanimate in itself, but is itself animated with the other species of the soul: the irrational (which the wise call the image of the rational soul) adorned with imagination and sensation that sees and hears altogether as a whole, and is furnished with all the senses and with all the rest of the irrational faculties of the soul.

Thus, by the principal faculty of this body, imagination, the rational soul is continually joined to such a body and by such a body sometimes the human soul is joined with a mortal body by a certain affinity of nature, the whole being enfolded in the whole vital spirit of the embryo, this vehicle itself being of the nature of a spirit.

The daimons' souls differ not much from the human, only they are more noble and use more noble vehicles; moreover, they cannot be mingled with corruptible nature. Likewise, the souls of the stars are much better than the daimons' and use better vehicles, which are bright bodies by reason of the greatness of their active potentiality.

---

603. P 14, CO 104.

These doctrines concerning the soul the Magi, followers of Zoroaster, seem to have held long ago. *Stain not* this kind of spirit of the soul, says the oracle, nor *deepen down the plane*. He calls it planar, not as if it lacked a third dimension, for it is a body, but to signify its extraordinary rarity; nor make it become gross by accession of more matter to its bulk, for this spirit of the soul becomes gross if it declines too much toward the mortal body.

(15) And of the radiant place, the image has a piece.[604]

It calls the *image* of the soul that irrational part that is joined to the rational part and depends upon the vehicle thereof. Now it says that this kind of image has a piece of the radiant land, for the soul never lays down the vehicle adherent to her.

(16) Leave not the dross of matter on a precipice.[605]

It calls the mortal body *the dross of matter*, and exhorts us not to neglect it through misfortune, but take care of it while in this life, to preserve it in health as much as possible, so that it may be pure and in all other respects correspond with the soul.

(17) Do not release, lest holding something she goes forth.[606]

Do not release, meaning the soul, out of the mortal body *lest by going forth* she incur some danger, implying as much as to carry her forth beyond the laws of Nature.

---

604. P 15a, CO 158.2. Plethon's oracles 15 and 16 are quoted by Synesius as one oracle (but in the order 16, 15), and so recent editions of Plethon's commentary label them 15a and 15b (the "P" numbers here). Psellos, like Plethon, gives them as separate oracles in this order of 15, 16. See Majercik, *Chaldean Oracles*, 108.

605. P 15b, CO 158.1.

606. P 16, CO 166.

> *(18) If thou extend the fiery mind to piety's work,*
> *the flowing body thou shalt save.*[607]

Extending your divine mind up to the exercise of piety or to religious rites, you will preserve the mortal body, making it more sound by performing these rites.

> *(19) From the cavities within the Earth*
> *spring earthly dogs who never show*
> *a sign that's true to mortals . . .*[608]

Sometimes to many initiates there appear, during rites, some apparitions in the shape of *dogs* and several other figures. Now the oracle says that these *issue out of the receptacles of the Earth*—that is, out of the terrestrial and mortal body and the irrational passions planted in it that are not yet sufficiently adorned with reason. These are apparitions of the passions of the soul in performing divine rites, mere appearances having no substance, and therefore *not signifying anything true.*

> *(20) And Nature prompts belief that daimons all are pure,*
> *and evil matter's offspring are both kind and good.*[609]

Nature or natural reason *prompts belief that daimons are all pure* and that all things proceeding from God, who is in himself good, *are beneficial*; and *the very offspring of evil matter*, or the forms dependent upon matter, are such. Also it calls matter *evil*, not as to its essence—for how can the essence be bad, the offspring of which are beneficial and good?—but because it is ranked last among the essences and is the least participant of good, this littleness of good is here expressed by the word "evil." Now the oracle means that if the offspring of "evil matter," namely of the last of essences, are good, then much more so are the daimons such, who are in an excellent rank as partaking of rational nature and being unmixed with mortal nature.

---

607. P 17, CO 128.

608. P 18, CO 90.

609. P 19, CO 88.

(21) Avengers, the restraints of people. [610]

The avengers or the vindictive daimons clasp people close or restrain and drive them from vice and excite them to virtue.

(22) Let lead the soul's immortal depth;
and all thine eyes extend quite upward. [611]

Let the *divine depth of your soul* govern and lift *all thine eyes* or all your knowing faculties *upward.*

(23) O human, thou machine of boldest Nature! [612]

It calls the *human* the *machine of boldest Nature,* because people attempt great things.

(24) If thou speak'st often to me, thou shalt see what's said, [613]
for neither then appears the heavens' concave bulk,
nor shine the stars; the brilliance of the Moon is hid;
the Earth stands not; all things appear as thunderbolts. [614]

The oracle speaks as from God to an initiate: *If thou speak'st often to me* or invoke me, *thou shalt see everywhere that of which you speak,* namely me whom you invoke, for then you will perceive nothing but *thunderbolts* all about, fire darting up and down all over the world.

---

610. P 20, CO 161.

611. P 21, CO 112. Plethon had a slightly different text for this oracle from Psellos and modern editions. Plethon and Psellos both had ἡγείσθω for the first word, but with the correct οἰγνύσθω the translation would be "Unclose the soul's immortal depth." His interpretation still holds.

612. P 22, CO 106.

613. Plethon read λέκτον, whereas Psellos and recent editions have λέοντα, in which case the first line is "If thou speak'st often to me, thou shalt see a lion."

614. P 23, CO 147. Contemporary editions have a slightly different text: "all things appear *by* thunderbolts."

(25) Call not on Nature's self-revealing image.[615]

Seek not to behold the self-revealing *Image of Nature*—that is, the Nature of God—which is not visible to our eyes. For those things that appear to initiates, such as thunder, lightning, and all else whatsoever, are only symbols, not the Nature of God.

(26) From all sides to the pristine soul stretch reins of fire.[616]

Draw unto yourself from all sides the *reins of fire* that appear to you during the rite with a sincere soul, one that is simple and unsoiled with knavery.

> *(27) But when you see the very holy shapeless fire,*
> *which shines by leaps and bounds throughout the whole world's depths,*
> *attend the fire's voice...* [617]

When you behold the divine fire devoid of shape *brightly gliding up and down the world* with grace and benevolence, listen to this voice, which brings a most truthful foreknowledge.

(28) Paternal Mind implanted symbols into souls.[618]

The Paternal Mind (Nous), namely, the attentive Demiurge of the substance of the soul, has *implanted symbols* or the images of intelligibles *into souls,* by which every soul possesses in herself the reasons of beings.

---

615. P 24, CO 101.

616. P 25, CO 127.

617. P 26, CO 148.

618. P 27, CO 108. Plethon's text differs slightly from Psellos's. Instead of Plethon's ταῖς ψυχαῖς, the modern edition has κατὰ κόσμον, which would be translated "Paternal Nous implanted symbols in the world."

(29) Learn the noetic, which exists beyond thy mind. [619]

Learn the noetic (intelligible), *because it exists beyond thy mind* (nous), that is, in actuality. For though the images of intellectual things are planted in you by the Demiurge, yet they are in your soul only potentially, but it behooves you to have knowledge of the intelligible in actuality.

(30) There is a notion known by just the flower of mind. [620]

The Supreme God, who is perfectly one, is not conceived after the same manner as other things, but *by the flower of the mind*—that is, the supreme and singular part of your understanding. (The verbal resonances of the oracle cannot be preserved in the translation: "There is a notion [*noêton*] known [*noein*] by just the flower of nous [*noou*].")

(31) ... all things were born of the One Fire. [621]

All things were generated from *One Fire*, that is, God.

(32) The Father finished [622] *everything and handed them
to Second Nous, whom you, the human tribe, call First.* [623]

The Father finished everything, namely the intelligible species (for they are absolute and perfect), *and delivered them over to the Second God* next after him to rule and guide them. Therefore, if anything be brought forth by this God, and formed after the likeness of him and the remaining intelligible substance, it proceeds from the

---

619. P 28a, CO 1.13. Oracles 29 and 30 in Plethon's list (numbered 28a and 28b in recent editions) are single verses from a longer oracle (CO 1). Plethon's text differs slightly from Psellos's but has the same meaning.

620. P 28b, CO 1.1.

621. P 29, CO 10. Stanley did not translate this oracle or Plethon's commentary on it.

622. "Finished" (ἐξετέλεσσε) means to perfect or bring to a perfect end; that is, the Father thinks the model perfectly and passes it on to the Demiurge (Majercik, *Chaldean Oracles*, 144). The Demiurge is often mistaken for the First God, because his work is more manifest to us.

623. P 30, CO 7.

Supreme Father. This other God *the human tribe call First;* that is, they think him the Demiurge of the Cosmos, to whom there is none superior.

> *(33) The Iynges, thought by Father, also think themselves,*
> *by his unutterable counsels moved to understand.* [624]

It calls *Iynges* the intellectual species that are *conceived by the Father, they themselves also conceiving,* and exciting conceptions or notions, *by unutterable* or unspeakable *counsels.* By *motion* here is understood intellection not displacement, but simply a relation to notions, and so *unspeakable* counsels also means unmoved, for speaking consists in motion. The meaning is this, that these forms have an unchangeable relation to notions, not a transient one like the soul's.

> *(34) Oh, how the world hath rigid intellectual guides!* [625]

The most excellent of the intelligible (noetic) Ideas, and of those which are brought down by the immortals into this heaven, it calls *the intellectual (noeric) guides of the world,* the chorus leader of whom it conceives to be a god, who is the second from the Father. The oracle saying that *the world hath rigid guides* means that it is incorruptible.

> *(35) ... the Father snatched himself away,*
> *and didn't close his fire in Noeric Power.* [626]

The Father has kept himself apart from all others, not including himself either *in his own Intellectual (Noeric) Power,* i.e., in the Second God who is next after him, or limiting *his own fire,* i.e., his own divinity. For he is absolutely uncreated and himself existing by himself, so that his divinity is separate from all others, as it is incommunicable to any other, although it be loved by all. That he doesn't communicate himself is not out of envy, but only by reason of its impossibility.

---

624. P 31, CO 77.

625. P 32, CO 79. Plethon has corrected Psellos's text to be consistent with his philosophy. Current editions have a somewhat different text, but with a similar meaning, "The world entire hath rigid intellectual guides."

626. P 33, CO 3.

(36) The Father makes not fear, but pours persuasion on.[627]

The Father makes no impression of fear, but pours on persuasion or love; for he, being extremely good, is not the cause of harm and therefore frightening, but he is the cause of all good to all; whence, he is loved by all.

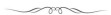

[Epilogue] These Oracles of *Zoroaster* many eminent persons have confirmed by following the like opinions, especially the *Pythagoreans* and *Platonists*,[628] since these oracles of the disciples of Zoroaster, to whom Plutarch refers when speaking of Zoroaster, also seem to be in complete agreement with Plato's writings. Plutarch says Zoroaster would divide beings into three.[629] Over the first part of these beings presides Hôromazês [Ahura Mazda], who is called *Father* by the Oracles; over the last is Ahriman; Mithra is over the middle, and he is the one called *Second Intellect* (*Nous*) by the Oracles. Hôromazês, on one hand, has removed himself three times as much from the sun, which in Persian is also called "Cyrus" (*Kyros*),[630] but Mithra, the one who comes after Hôromazês, by twice as much. Now, this is also very much in agreement with these words of Plato: "Related to the King of All are all things, and for his sake they are, and of all things fair he is the cause. And related to the Second are the second things and related to the Third the third."[631]

As for the three parts into which Zoroaster and Plato have divided beings, the first is the one that is eternal; the second is the one that is temporal, but which is everlasting; the third is the mortal part. Zoroaster, says Plutarch, is someone so ancient that it is said that he lived five thousand years before the Trojan War.[632]

---

627. P 34, CO 14.

628. Stanley did not translate the remainder of this last part of Plethon's commentary, which I have translated.

629. Plutarch, *Isis and Osiris* 46.369E–47.370A, in Plutarch, *Moralia V*, 110–15.

630. Plutarch, *Artaxerxes* 1.1012a, in Plutarch, *Lives XI*, 128–29. However, Old Persian *Kūrush* (Cyrus) is not the word for "sun," which is *khorshid* (Woodhouse, *Plethon*, 25).

631. Plato, *Epistle II*, 312 d10–e4, trans. Bury, in *Plato in Twelve Volumes*, Vol. 9, 410–11.

632. Plutarch, *Isis and Osiris* 46.369E, in Plutarch, *Moralia V*, 110–13.

Further Reading

I hope you have found this book to be an interesting and thorough introduction to Plethon's philosophy and to the practice of his Neopagan Hellenism. Although this is the only book teaching this practice, and I have tried to make it sufficiently complete, you may want to delve more deeply into his ideas. The best current presentation in English of Plethon's philosophy is *The Philosophy of Gemistos Plethon: Platonism in Late Byzantium, between Hellenism and Orthodoxy* (Farnham, UK: Ashgate, 2014) by Vojtěch Hladký. I have found it to be very informative and, although he is reluctant to accept Plethon's rather blatant Paganism, you can't do much better if you want to understand Plethon's philosophy in detail. It is an academic book and quite expensive, but you might be able to find a copy in a university library. The second most important source is an old classic, *George Gemistos Plethon: The Last of the Hellenes* (Oxford: Oxford University Press, 1986) by C. M. Woodhouse, which first interested me in Plethon's Neopaganism. He does not go as deeply into the philosophy as does Hladký, but he provides more information on Gemistos Plethon's life and times. I believe it is out of print, so you may have to find it in a library. For Plethon's calendar and some aspects of his rituals and their sources, the principal source is "Pletho's Calendar and Liturgy" (*Dumbarton Oaks Papers* 4 (1948): 183–305) by Milton V. Anastos, but it is fairly technical and out of date in some respects. The standard Greek text of Plethon's *Book of Laws*, with a French translation, is in *Pléthon: Traité des Lois* (translated by A. Pellissier, Paris: Firmin Didot frères, 1858) edited by C. Alexandre, which is available online, but this text is incomplete and not entirely reliable. A new generation of scholars is studying George Gemistos Plethon, and new texts and translations are in progress. None of these sources, so far, provide all the details of Plethon's religion or explain it for practitioners, which is why I have written this book!

Bibliography

Addey, Crystal. "The Daimonion of Socrates: Daimones and Divination in Neoplatonism." In *The Neoplatonic Socrates*, edited by D. A. Layne & H. Tarrant, chapter 3. Philadelphia: University of Pennsylvania Press, 2014.

———. *Divination and Theurgy in Neoplatonism: Oracles of the Gods*. Burlington, VT: Ashgate, 2014.

Addey, Tim. *The Unfolding Wings*: *The Way of Perfection in the Platonic Tradition*. Somerset, UK: Prometheus Trust, 2003.

Alexandre, Charles, ed. *Pléthon: Traité des Lois*. Translated by Augustin Pellissier. Paris: Firmin Didot frères, 1858.

Anastos, Milton V. "Plethon's Calendar and Liturgy." *Dunbarton Oaks Papers* 4 (1948): 183–303.

Apollodorus. *The Library*. Translated by James George Frazer. Vol. 1. Loeb Classical Library 121. Cambridge: Harvard University Press, 1921.

Apuleius. *The Works of Apuleius*. Anonymous translation. London: Bell, 1911.

Aristotle. *On the Soul. Parva Naturalia. On Breath*. Translated by Walter Stanley Hett. Loeb Classical Library 288. Cambridge: Harvard University Press, 1957.

Aristotle, *Politics*. Translated by H. Rackham. Loeb Classical Library 264. Cambridge: Harvard University Press, 1932.

Bell, John. *Bell's New Pantheon*. London: Bell, 1790.

Blockley, R. C. *The Fragmentary Classicising Historians of the Later Roman Empire.* Vol. 2. Liverpool, UK: Francis Cairns, 1983

Brennan, Chris. *Hellenistic Astrology: The Study of Fate and Fortune.* Denver, CO: Amor Fati, 2017.

Calcidius. *On Demons (Commentarius Ch. 127–136).* Translated by J. den Boeft. Leiden, Netherlands: E. J. Brill, 1977.

Cicero. *Librorum de re publica sex.* Edited by C. F. W. Mueller. Leipzig: Teubner, 1889.

De Biasi, Jean-Louis, and Patricia Bourin. *The Ultimate Pagan Almanac 2021: Northern Hemisphere.* Las Vegas: Theurgia Publications, 2020.

Delatte, A. "Les doctrines pythagoriciennes des livres de Numa." *Académie royale de Belgique, Bulletin de la classe des lettres et des sciences morales et politiques* 22 (1936): 19–40.

Des Places, É. *Oracula Chaldaica* [*Oracles chaldaïques*]. Introduction, edition, translation, and commentary by É. des Places. Paris: Les Belles Lettres, 1971.

Dillon, John, and Lloyd P. Gerson, eds. *Neoplatonic Philosophy: Introductory Readings.* Indianapolis, IN: Hackett, 2004.

Diogenes Laertius. *Lives of Eminent Philosophers.* Translated by Robert Drew Hicks. Vol. 1. Loeb Classical Library 184. Cambridge: Harvard University Press, 1938.

Euripides. *Euripides II: Electra, Orestes, Iphigeneia in Taurica, Andromache, Cyclops.* Translated by Arthur Sanders Way. Loeb Classical Library 10. New York: G. P. Putnam's Sons, 1930.

Evelyn-White, H. G., trans. *Hesiod, the Homeric Hymns, and Homerica.* London: Heinemann, 1914.

Ficino, Marsilio. *Marsilii Ficini Florentini, insignis philosophi platonici, medici atque theologi clarissimi opera* […]. 2 vols. Basle: 1576.

———. *Three Books on Life: A Critical Edition and Translation with Introduction and Notes.* Edited and translated by Carol V. Kaske and John R. Clark. Tempe, AZ: Renaissance Society of America, 1989.

Gaisford, Thomas, ed. *Poetae minores Graeci: praecipua lectionis varietate et indicibus locupletissimis instruxit.* Vol. 2. Leipzig, Germany: Kuehn, 1823.

Gantz, Timothy. *Early Greek Myth*: *A Guide to Literary and Artistic Sources.* Baltimore, MD: Johns Hopkins University Press, 1993.

Guthrie, Kenneth Sylvan, trans. *The Pagan Bible, or Angels Ancient & Modern.* Teocalli, NY: Platonist Press, 1925.

Harrison, Jane Ellen. *Epilegomena to the Study of Greek Religions and Themis: A Study of the Social Origins of Greek Religion.* New Hyde Park: University Books, 1962. This edition combines *Epilegomena* (1921) and *Themis* (1927).

Hercher, Rudolf, ed. *Epistolographi graeci.* Amsterdam: A. M. Hakkert, 1965.

Herodotus. *The Persian Wars.* Translated by A. D. Godley. Loeb Classical Library 117–20. 4 vols. Cambridge, MA: Harvard University Press, 1920–24.

Hesiod. *Hesiod*: *Vol. I, Theogony. Works and Days. Testimonia.* Translated by Glenn W. Most. Loeb Classical Library 57N. Cambridge: Harvard University Press, 2007.

Hladký, Vojtěch. *The Philosophy of Gemistos Plethon*: *Platonism in Late Byzantium, between Hellenism and Orthodoxy.* Farnham, UK: Ashgate, 2014.

Homer. *The Iliad.* Vol. 1. Translated by A. T. Murray. Loeb Classical Library 170. Cambridge: Harvard University Press. 1924.

Hornblower, Simon, Antony Spawforth, and Esther Eidinow, eds. *Oxford Classical Dictionary.* 4th ed. Oxford, UK: Oxford University Press, 2012.

Hyginus. *Hygini Fabulae.* Edited by Moritz Schmidt. Jenae: Hermannum Dufft, 1872.

Iamblichus. *On the Pythagorean Way of Life.* Translated by John Dillon and Jackson Hershbell. Atlanta, GA: Scholars Press, 1991.

———. *On the Mysteries: Translated with Introduction and Notes.* Translated by Emma C. Clarke, John. M. Dillon, and Jackson. P. Hershbell. Vol. 4 of *Writings of the Greco-Roman World.* Atlanta, GA: Society of Biblical Literature, 2003.

————. *The Theology of Arithmetic.* Translated by Robin Waterfield. Grand Rapids, MI: Phanes Press, 1988.

Julian. *The Works of the Emperor Julian.* Translated by Wilmer. C. Wright. 3 vols. Loeb Classical Library 13, 29, 157. Cambridge, MA: Harvard University Press, 1913–23.

Kerényi, Carl. *The Gods of the Greeks.* Translated by Norman Cameron. London: Thames & Hudson, 1979.

Laks, André, and Glenn W. Most, trans. *Early Greek Philosophy III*: *Early Ionian Thinkers, Part 2.* Loeb Classical Library 526. Cambridge, MA: Harvard University Press, 2016.

————. *Early Greek Philosophy V: Western Greek Thinkers, Part 2.* Loeb Classical Library 528. Cambridge, MA: Harvard University Press, 2016.

Livy. *History of Rome*: *Books 1–2.* Translated by B. O. Foster. Loeb Classical Library 114. Cambridge, MA: Harvard University Press, 1919.

Lucretius, *On the Nature of Things.* Translated by W. H. D. Rouse. Revised by Martin F. Smith. Loeb Classical Library 181. Cambridge, MA: Harvard University Press, 1924.

MacLennan, Bruce. *The Wisdom of Hypatia: Ancient Spiritual Practices for a More Meaningful Life.* Woodbury, MN: Llewellyn Publications, 2013.

Macrobius. *Commentary on the Dream of Scipio.* Translated by William Harris Stahl. New York: Columbia University Press, 1990.

Majercik, Ruth, trans. *The Chaldean Oracles: Text, Translation, and Commentary.* Leiden, Netherlands: Brill, 1989.

Marcus Aurelius. *The Communings with Himself of Marcus Aurelius Antoninus, Emperor of Rome, Together with his Speeches and Sayings.* Translated by C. R. Haines. Loeb Classical Library 58. London: W. Heinemann, 1916.

Marinos of Neapolis. *The Extant Works or the Life of Proklos and the Commentary on the Dedomena of Euclid*. Translated by A. N. Oikonomides. Chicago: Ares Publishers, 1977.

Masai, François. *Pléthon et le Platonisme de Mistra*. Paris: Société d' Édition "Les Belles Lettres," 1956. Reprint, Forlì, Italy: Victrix Edizioni, 2010.

Migne, J.-P., ed. *Patrologiae Cursus Completus, Series Graeca*. 161 vols. Paris: Migne, 1857–66.

Moore, Thomas. *The Planets Within: The Astrological Psychology of Marsilio Ficino*. Hudson, NY: Lindisfarne, 1989.

O'Neill, W., trans. *Proclus: Alcibiades I*. 2nd ed. The Hague: Springer, 1971.

Opsopoeus, Johannes, ed. *Oracula magica Zoroastris cum scholiis Plethonis et Pselli*. Paris: 1589.

Parker, Robert. *Miasma: Pollution and Purification in Early Greek Religion*. Oxford, UK: Clarendon, 1996.

Plato. *Dialogues of Plato*. Translated by Benjamin Jowett. Vol. 3. Oxford, UK: Clarendon Press, 1892.

———. *Phaedrus*. Edited by Harvey Yunis. Cambridge, UK: Cambridge University Press, 2011.

———. *Plato in Twelve Volumes*. Translated by Harold North Fowler, W. R. M. Lamb, Robert Gregg Bury, and Paul Shorey. 12 vols. Cambridge, MA: Harvard University Press, 1966.

Plethon, George Gemistos. *Contra Scholarii pro Aristotele obiectiones*. In Migne, J.-P. *Patrologiae Cursus Completus, Series Graeca*. Vol. 160. Paris: Migne, 1857–66.

———. Μαγικὰ λόγια τῶν ἀπὸ Ζωροάστρου μάγων—Ἐξήγησις εἰς τὰ αὐτὰ λόγια [The Magical Oracles of the Magi of Zoroaster—Commentary on these Oracles]. Edited and translated by B. Tambrun-Krasker and M. Tardieu. Athens: Academy of Athens, 1995.

————. Additional Manuscript 5424, folios 100r–145v. British Library. Accessed May 11, 2021. http://www.bl.uk/manuscripts/Viewer.aspx?ref=add _ms_5424_f100r.

————. Περὶ ἀρετῶν [On Virtues]. Edited and translated by B. Tambrun-Krasker. Leiden, Netherlands: Brill, 1987.

Pliny. *Natural History*. Translated by H. Rackham, W. H. S. Jones, and D. E. Eichholz. 10 vols. London: Heinemann, 1949–54.

Plotinus, Porphyry, and Marsilio Ficino. *Plotini* […] *Operum philosophicorum omnium libri LIV. in sex enneades distributi*. Basel: Perneam Lecythum, 1580.

Plutarch. *Lives*: Vol. I, *Theseus and Romulus. Lycurgus and Numa. Solon and Publicola*. Translated by Bernadotte Perrin. Loeb Classical Library 46. Cambridge, MA: Harvard University Press, 1914.

————. *Lives*: Vol. XI, *Aratus. Artaxerxes. Galba. Otho. General Index*. Translated by Bernadotte Perrin. Loeb Classical Library 103. Cambridge, MA: Harvard University Press, 1926.

————. *Moralia*: Vol. V, *Isis and Osiris. The E at Delphi. The Oracles at Delphi No Longer Given in Verse. The Obsolescence of Oracles*. Translated by Frank Cole Babbitt. Loeb Classical Library 306. Cambridge, MA: Harvard University Press, 1936.

————. *Moralia*: Vol. VII, *On Love of Wealth. On Compliancy. On Envy and Hate. On Praising Oneself Inoffensively. On the Delays of the Divine Vengeance. On Fate. On the Sign of Socrates. On Exile. Consolation to His Wife*. Translated by Phillip. H. De Lacy and Benedict Einarson. Loeb Classical Library 405. Cambridge, MA: Harvard University Press, 1959.

————. *Moralia*: Vol. X. Translated by Harold North Fowler. Loeb Classical Library 321. Cambridge, MA: Harvard University Press, 1936.

Porphyry. *On Abstinence from Killing Animals*. Translated by Gillian Clark. London: Bloomsbury, 2000.

Psellus, Michael. *Fourteen Byzantine Rulers: The Chronographia*. 3rd ed. Translated by E. R. A. Sewter. Baltimore, MD: Penguin Books, 1979.

Ptolemy. *Tetrabiblos*. Translated by F. E. Robbins. Cambridge, MA: Harvard University Press, 1940.

Sallustius. *Concerning the Gods and the Universe*. Edited and translated by Arthur Darby Nock. Cambridge, MA: Cambridge University Press, 1926.

Schibli, Hermann S., trans. *Hierocles of Alexandria*. Oxford, UK: Oxford University Press, 2002.

Scholarios, Georgios. *Œuvres complètes de Gennade Scholarios*. Edited by Louis Petit, Xénophon A. Sidéridès, and Martin Jugie. 8 vols. Paris: Maison de la bonne presse, 1928–36.

Schultze, Fritz. *Geschichte der Philosophie der Renaissance, Erste Band: Georgios Gemistos Plethon and seine reformatorischen Bestrebungen*. Jena, Germany: Mauke's Verlag, 1874.

Shaw, Gregory. *Theurgy and the Soul: The Neoplatonism of Iamblichus*. University Park: Pennsylvania State University Press, 1995.

Siniossoglou, Niketas. *Radical Platonism in Byzantium: Illumination and Utopia in Gemistos Plethon*. Cambridge, UK: Cambridge University Press, 2011.

Sophocles, Evangelinos Apostolides A. *Greek Lexicon of the Roman and Byzantine Periods*. New York: Scribner's, 1900.

Sorabji, Richard, ed. *The Philosophy of the Commentators 200–600 AD: A Sourcebook*. Vol. 1, *Psychology (with Ethics and Religion)*. Ithaca, NY: Cornell University Press, 2005.

Stanley, Thomas, ed. and trans. *The Chaldaick Oracles of Zoroaster and His Followers with the Expositions of Pletho and Psellus*. London: Thomas Dring, 1661.

Tambrun-Krasker, B. "Philosophie, poésie et musique chez Pléthon." In *Para-Textuelle Verhandlungen zwischen Dichtung und Philosophie in der Frühen Neuzeit* (Actes Du colloque international de Munich, March 4–6, 2010), coll.

"Pluralisierung und Autorität" 26, edited by B. Huss, P. Marzillo, and Th. Ricklin, 248–78. Berlin: De Gruyter, 2011.

Tihon, Anne. "The Astronomy of George Gemistos Plethon." *Journal for the History of Astronomy* 29 (1998): 109–16.

Tihon, Anne, and Raymond Mercier. *George Gemistus Plethon: Manuel d'astronomie.* Louvain-la-Neuve, Belgium: Academia-Bruylant, 1998.

Van den Berg, R. M., trans. *Proclus' Hymns: Essays, Translations, Commentary.* Leiden, Netherlands: Brill, 2001.

Valens, Vettius. *Anthologiarum Libri.* Edited by W. Kroll. Berlin: Weidmann, 1908.

Wallis, R. T. *Neoplatonism.* 2nd ed. Indianapolis, IN: Hackett, 1995.

West, M. L. *Ancient Greek Music.* Oxford, UK: Clarendon Press, 1992.

Westerink, L. G., trans. *Damascius: Commentary on Plato's* Phaedo. 2nd ed. Dilton Marsh, UK: Prometheus Trust, 2009.

Woodhouse, C. M. *George Gemistos Plethon: The Last of the Hellenes.* Oxford, UK: Oxford University Press, 1986.

Index

H

I

L

M

N

T

W

Z